Communication, Mind & Language
Volume 1

Language in Flux
Dialogue Coordination, Language Variation, Change and Evolution

Volume 1
Language in Flux. Dialogue Coordination, Language Variation, Change and Evolution
Robin Cooper and Ruth Kempson, editors.

Communication, Mind & Language Series editors
Robin Cooper   cooper@ling.gu.se
Ruth Kempson   ruth.kempson@kcl.ac.uk

Language in Flux

Dialogue Coordination,
Language Variation,
Change and Evolution

Edited by
Robin Cooper
and
Ruth Kempson

© Individual author and College Publications 2008. All rights reserved.

ISBN 978-1-904987-96-3

College Publications
Scientific Director: Dov Gabbay
Managing Director: Jane Spurr
Department of Computer Science
King's College London, Strand, London WC2R 2LS, UK

http://www.collegepublications.co.uk

Original cover design by orchid creative   www.orchidcreative.co.uk
Printed by Lightning Source, Milton Keynes, UK

All rights reserved. No part of this publication may be reproduced, stored in a retrieval system or transmitted in any form, or by any means, electronic, mechanical, photocopying, recording or otherwise without prior permission, in writing, from the publisher.

CONTENTS

ROBIN COOPER AND RUTH KEMPSON
Introduction   1

PATRICK G. T. HEALEY
Interactive Misalignment: The Role of Repair in the Development of Group Sub-languages   13

ZORAN MACURA & JONATHAN GINZBURG
Dynamics and Adaptiveness of Metacommunicative Interaction in a Foraging Environment   41

GERHARD JÄGER
Language evolution and George Price's "General Theory of Selection"   53

SIMON KIRBY, KENNY SMITH AND HANNAH CORNISH
Language, Learning and Cultural Evolution: How linguistic transmission leads to cumulative adaptation   81

ROBIN COOPER AND AARNE RANTA
Natural Languages as Collections of Resources   109

STAFFAN LARSSON
Formalizing the Dynamics of Semantic Systems in Dialogue   121

ELIZABETH CLOSS TRAUGOTT
'All that he endeavoured to prove was': On the emergence of grammatical constructions in dialogual and dialogic contexts   143

RONNIE CANN & RUTH KEMPSON
Production Pressures, Syntactic Change and the Emergence of Clitic Pronouns   179

MIRIAM BOUZOUITA
At the Syntax-Pragmatics Interface: Clitics in the History of Spanish   221

DEVYANI SHARMA, JOAN BRESNAN, ASHWINI DEO
Variation and change in the individual: Evidence from the Survey of English Dialects   265

INDEX   323

Preface

The papers in this collection present a view of language as an evolving system within which flexibility is systemic, and subject to progressive change driven by pressures of every-day coordinative action, as in conversational dialogue. As these papers demonstrate, these pressures provide a force for variation, hence for adaptation, and change. Themes of the individual papers include formal and game-theoretical models of evolution, diachronic studies of change (semantic, syntactic, lexical) and the role of dialogue factors in promoting such change, psycholinguistic experimental methods probing the nature of coordination in both language and non-language based interaction, formal modelling of dialogue, and probabilistic studies of language variation. Together these papers present a striking cross-disciplinary synergy reflecting the view that human linguistic behaviour is essentially coordinative, and that language is a system of intrinsic flexibility, hence perpetually in a state of flux. This view involves a radical shift in assumptions away from the traditional view that language competence is a static system relative to which the dynamics of language performance has to be defined; and each paper, in its own way, explores what is involved in modifying such a clear-cut division.

Introduction
ROBIN COOPER AND RUTH KEMPSON

A significant increase in our understanding of language came in the early days of generative grammar when it was perceived that one of the main factors in language change had to do with the acquisition of language by children as presented in the early work of Chomsky (for example in [Chomsky, 1965]). One early example of the discussion relating historical linguistics and generative grammar is [King, 1969]. The important idea was that children were not merely imitating what they heard but creating a linguistic system on the basis of data they were exposed to. The linguistic system which children acquire seems to be underdetermined by the actual data to which they are exposed and therefore it is not surprising that the resulting system is not exactly the same as that of the previous generation. In fact it is perfectly consistent with this view to suppose that no two speakers of a language have internalized exactly the same grammar. The idea that language change was related to language acquisition was not new with generative grammar. It is, for example, present in [Paul, 1880], §18, and, as Lightfoot [1999] points out, Paul laid great emphasis on the idea that no two individuals need have the same grammar.

In recent work on language change and evolution there is growing emphasis of two other aspects of language change. Firstly, as we have really known all along, it is not only language learners who are the agents of change but fully competent adult speakers of a language will continue to change their language apparently throughout life. (Again, Paul makes this point clear, as does King.) Secondly, and this is new in recent research, there is a growing perception that the mechanisms of change lie in communication in general and dialogue in particular and that dialogue research has now got to a stage of maturity where it may have something interesting to say about language change and evolution. This volume is devoted to several strands of work that illustrate this development. The contributions represent an inspiring mix of work on historical linguistics, formal grammar, language technology, evolutionary modelling and experimental psychology.

On the kind of view that is being proposed here there are two main questions that need to be answered:

- What are the micromechanisms of change, that is, what features of the everyday use of language create the seeds of linguistic change?

- How does change emerge by propagation through communities?

In the remainder of this introduction we will give an overview of what appear to be the main issues associated with these two questions judging from the papers in the collection and the discussion at the workshop from which it originated. One of the most important micromechanisms is innovation and we will treat that separately in its own section after giving an overview of micromechanisms in general.

1 The micromechanisms of change

We distinguish four kinds of micromechanisms: innovation, coordination, meta-communicative interaction and memory. We will say a few words about each of these in turn.

Innovation. During the course of a dialogue speakers use language in novel ways or even create new language. This may be as a result of the demands of the dialogue, e.g. making oneself adequately understood, or as a result of systemic pressure, i.e. the speaker's language system in unstable and leads her to be innovative. Linguistic innovation can also be non-interactional in that one can dream up new language or new uses of language even when one is not engaged in dialogue.

Coordination. Speakers involved in a dialogue coordinate so that the language of the dialogue participants becomes more similar. The reason for this is that it appears to facilitate understanding. The terms *alignment* and *accommodation* have been used for particular aspects of coordination. Alignment emphasizes that speakers coordinate different levels of representation (phonetic, syntactic, semantic and so on). Accommodation has to do with the fact that one speaker may presuppose something another speaker was not aware of thereby requiring the other speaker to adjust in order to be able to process the dialogue. Accommodation has not only to do with facts that may be presupposed but also with dialogue issues such as what questions are under discussion and grammatical issues such as novel word meanings or syntactic constructions. Coordination is closely related to the notion of *priming*. This is the psychological effect of particular observations of behaviour by an agent giving rise to an increased likelihood of that agent behaving in a similar or related way or being facilitated in the perception of a related behaviour. If I say *doctor* you will recognize *nurse* more quickly than if I had not said anything. Similarly if I say *doctor* in some dialogue you are more likely to say *doctor* than *physician* in that dialogue (unless you are wanting to make a distinction between doctors and physicians).

Coordination is important for the propagation of innovation. If one speaker says something innovative in a dialogue then there appears to be a high likelihood that another dialogue participant will make use of that innovation.

Metacommunicative interaction. Sometimes dealing with innovation in a dialogue is not straightforward. Dialogue participants may not immediately understand an innovative utterance and may ask for clarification. They may be unsure whether they have understood and check whether their understanding is correct. The speaker of a novel utterance may be unsure whether the message has been successfully communicated and will rely on feedback from other dialogue participants in order to be able to judge how well things are going. In general metacommunicative interaction may have an effect on the propagation of innovations. One can imagine that speakers may stop using expressions which always seem to cause communicative difficulties, especially in cases where there is a clear alternative. One can also imagine that there might be cases where the effort involved in establishing a particular novel usage might encourage its future use, especially in cases where there is not a clear alternative. Innovative technical terminology may present examples of this.

Memory. It seems clear that our knowledge of language is related in some way to the previous linguistic situations we have been involved in. We have memories, for example, of how words are pronounced and what kinds of things they can mean in connection with different domains and situations. We clearly do not remember every use of a particular word or phrase that we have encountered. But it could nevertheless be the case that each linguistic event to which we are exposed counts as input to some learning algorithm that adjusts the kind of meanings that can be associated with expressions or the way in which we express concepts. There seems to be a role for statistical notions like weighting and psychological notions like habituation in this, alongside notions associated with grammar like generalization and creativity.

2 Innovation

Given the occurrence of an innovation in a dialogue there are three main questions we can ask:

- For which dialogue participants is it an innovation?
- What is the formal nature of the innovation?
- What gave rise to the innovation?

We will take each of these questions in turn.

New for whom? The innovation may be new for the speaker (or writer). This is the kind of innovation that can take place outside of a dialogue situation. The innovation may be new for a hearer but not for the speaker. It may be new for both the speaker and a hearer. Dialogue participants may collaborate on creating new language.

Formal nature. There are, of course, many kinds of language change that have been documented including phonological, syntactic and semantic. An innovation may be a formal simplification of an old expression for an old concept such as a reduction of two words to one word, a phonological reduction or a simplification due to systemic pressure (e.g. conforming to an emerging generalization in the system). Simplification has parallels in psychological work studying the use of graphical representations where subjects move from figurative to abstract or iconic to symbolic representations on repeated uses. While simplification is commonplace, the complication of an old expression for an old concept seems rarely to occur, if ever. This may seem natural enough given that it involves economy of effort and cognitive load. However, it is interesting to compare this with musical systems where repetition often involves complication (as in baroque ornamentation, classical variations or jazz improvisation). Old expressions often get reused for new concepts. Confronted with a concept for which we do not have an expression we tend to use old expressions which have previously been associated with similar concepts. Note that this requires us to have some kind of similarity measure on concepts or meanings. Less frequent perhaps is the use of a new expression for an old concept (unless speakers are adapting to the usage of other speakers).

Causes of innovation. We have already mentioned that systemic pressure may be one cause of innovation. A particular case of this can be that a hearer may reanalyze a speaker's utterance due to differences between the speaker's and hearer's grammars. Grammaticalization and calcification can involve the creation of more constrained syntax on the basis of the reanalysis of expressions which were originally available as alternatives to express a particular focus or emphasis (as in the emergence of pronominal clitic systems in romance languages). Misunderstanding, that is, differences between what the speaker intended and what the hearer understands, can play an important role in these and other cases of innovation and a good theory of language change and evolution should support an explanatory theory of misunderstanding. We have seen that simplification is one driving force behind innovation. But language can become more complicated when we are confronted with a new domain or ontology which we have to talk about. This puts us into the situation of creating new language or recycling old language with new meaning. One way of doing this is importing or modifying language usage from another related domain.

An interesting research issue is to what extent there may be correlation between the answers to these questions. For example, do innovations resulting from misunderstanding tend to have certain formal properties distinct from those for innovations arising from the need to talk about a new domain or ontology? Do innovations which represent collaborations between dialogue partners tend to have certain forms?

3 The emergence of language in communities

It seems useful to think of speakers as creating languages (or *micro*-languages) for different situations or activities. Even within a given dialogue or activity we may not be using a single monolithic lexicon and set of linguistic principles. Some linguists have talked of *registers* since the fifties. More recently various notions of *resource grammar* have been introduced. One way of expressing the changing view in formal linguistics is to say that Montague's view of "English as a formal language" is giving way to "English as a toolbox for creating formal languages". That is, speakers of English have resources available (and there is no assumption here that English speakers share exactly the same resources) which allow them to create small micro-languages to talk about given domains and situations. This makes a mature speaker of a language much more similar to the generative view of the child acquiring language in that any use of language will involve the creation of a language tailored to the purposes at hand. On such a view it is not surprising that a great deal of innovation may be involved in everyday use of language. Much of this innovation may be local and just associated with one particular conversation with another speaker. However, such exemplars of usage will result in memory traces in agents which can become relevant in other conversations with other speakers. A sufficient amount of exposure to a given usage pattern with a sufficient number of different speakers may result in a given speaker adapting their general language resource to allow such a pattern. A sufficient number of speakers adopting the pattern results in what we perceive as a linguistic change which has spread through the community. Note that this view gives us an inherent variability in the linguistic phenomena without necessarily requiring that the linguistic resources themselves are defined in probabilistic terms. For example, a British speaker in the US may acquire a rule which flaps intervocalic /t/. The speaker may vary between producing flapped and non-flapped /t/'s, perhaps producing increasingly many flapped variants the longer they are exposed to American speech and possibly doing it less often when talking with British speakers. Such variability can be expressed in terms of how much the speaker makes use of this particular resource, rather than saying that the phonology that the speaker has acquired is probabilistic and context dependent.

Why do certain innovations spread in linguistic communities and others not? Feedback must play some role in this. If speakers notice that certain usage patterns consistently result in misunderstandings or clarification questions perhaps they will tend to avoid this usage. There may also be systemic reasons for avoiding certain usages since they violate a certain generalization that is otherwise present in the system.

Why do languages continue to change? The kind of view that we are presenting here might at first suggest that language would achieve a kind of equilibrium and stabilize after a while. If the language system existed in some kind of vacuum it might be the case that it would achieve an optimal equilibrium. But the fact of the matter is that we use language to talk about a changing world and we are constantly challenged to create new language. In addition we have noted that coordination or alignment (i.e. the adaptation of our language to that our of interlocutors) is a source of innovation. As long as we talk about new things to new people, it seems that our language will continue to change.

4 The Contributions

All the papers of this volume contribute to answering these questions from within the individual sub-disciplines of cognitive science: psychology, language evolution, sociolinguistics, and historical linguistics (semantic, syntactic and morphosyntactic change). The result is an inspiring synergy of research interests and methodologies from across the broad span of linguistic study, a coming together of cross-disciplinary evidence which not only suggests new ways of understanding language use and the way language is interpreted in dialogue contexts, but also promises to transform our understanding of the phenomenon of language itself. The shift in perspective, as all these papers severally display, is to take study of dialogue and the creative tension between innovation and coordination which conversational dialogue displays, as central to the study of language in flux. The innovation, explicitly advocated by several papers in this volume, is to see language as a set of procedures for constructing possibly novel interpretations in context.

The papers can be divided following traditional compartmentalization into papers on psycholinguistics [Healey], language evolution [Kirby et al., Jäger, Macura and Ginzburg], grammar development [Cooper and Ranta], semantic change [Traugott, Larsson], syntactic and morphosyntactic change [Cann and Kempson, Bouzouita], and language variation [Sharma et al.]. But more striking than the differences implicit in these divisions is the multifarious links between the individual papers.

Healey sets the scene with a paper on a set of experimental studies involving collaborative tasks in communication involving both linguistic and graphic forms of communication. He goes on to use the results of these studies to develop arguments that interaction provides a key source of constraints on language change, with local processes involved in detection and resolution of interpretive misalignments directly constraining the kinds of sublanguage that people can develop.

The relevance of apparent miscommunication and its resolution is picked up in the paper of Macura and Ginzburg, who describe an artificial life model that is used to provide an evolutionary grounding for metacommunicative interaction, demonstrating via artificial life experiments how the ability of agents to ask for clarification or to acknowledge understanding transforms the speed of evolution of the language system through the guarantee of coordination that clarificatory exchanges provide.

Kirby *et al.* also contribute to the argument that biological evolution by natural selection is not the only explanation for adaptive structure in language, by arguing that to explain the universal structural properties of language we need to look at language as a complex adaptive system - one in which biologically evolved innate biases on individual learning can be seen as challenges to which a culturally evolving language must adapt. Computational, mathematical and experimental models are set out in order to demonstrate that the process of linguistic evolution on a cultural time-scale is one that has significant explanatory power. In particular, they look in some detail at the way in which languages may adapt to be better passed on faithfully in the presence of a "learning bottleneck" either through the emergence of recursive compositionality in the encoding of meanings or through underspecification of meaning at the lexical level.

Jäger contributes to the discussion of language evolution with a demonstration that tools of mathematical description of evolutionary processes are well-suited to modelling aspects of the cultural evolution of language; and he provides a formal model of language evolution in these terms. As illustration of the application of the defined model, he provides two case studies, one involving language acquisition, the second involving exemplar theory. Both processes involve nonfaithful replication, such replications depending in part on the storing in highly detailed fashion of instances of linguistic events (both parsing and production), hence also relating to coordination effects in dialogue (as suggested in Healey).

These themes of underspecification and the reflex of coordination effects of dialogue in the language system are picked up by other papers in this volume. Four papers argue for a radical new perspective on language in which language is seen as an intrinsically dynamic and evolving system. Cooper and Ranta set out a new grammar framework, arguing for a shift in perspective from the view of natural languages as formal languages to viewing natural languages as a collection of resources for constructing local formal languages for use in particular situations. This shift points to a research programme investigating how such resources play a role in linguistic innovation by agents constructing situation-specific local languages and how these can be made dynamic, modified by the agent's exposure to innovative linguistic data. In directly the same spirit as Cooper and Ranta, Larsson shows how semantic (conceptual) change can be shown to happen both in the very short term in a single dialogue as an effect of coordination for individual speakers in the dialogue, and, equally, in the long term across a community. Larsson provides a basic framework for formalizing updates to semantic systems in dialogue, relating this framework to interactional pragmatic processes of semantic coordination in dialogue, such as feedback, negotiation and accommodation, in this linking also to both the Healey and Macura and Ginzburg papers.

A resource-oriented view is also at the heart of the Dynamic Syntax framework in which language is taken to be a set of procedures for building up information as made available in context, with underspecification and its resolution during the construction process as a central structure-building mechanism. Within this framework, the papers by Cann and Kempson, and Bouzouita, develop a view of syntactic change which is very closely related to the account of semantic change of Larsson. Both Cann and Kempson, and Bouzouita, argue that the constant pressure imposed by cognitive constraints on this interpretation process can not merely initiate systemic change in a language but also be reflected in the particular syntactic change that takes place. There is always ongoing interaction between parsing and production tasks [Pickering and Garrod, 2004], and as argued by Larsson for semantic change, such coordinated activity may get consolidated as a routine and subsequently lead to new lexical encodings. Cann and Kempson's case study is clitic clustering in Medieval Spanish: they argue that such clustering is a calcified reflex of production choices made in so-called scrambling environments in the earlier system of Latin, an account bolstered by the explanation it provides for the otherwise mysterious morphological gaps in clitic paradigms (The Person Case Constraint). Bouzouita provides a detailed specification of the diachronic changes in clitic placement with respect to the finite verb in the history of Spanish (13th-20th c.). This involves a shift from the Medieval Spanish system, in which syntactic variation is observed as clitics could occur both in preverbal and postverbal positions, to the Modern Spanish verb-centered system, in which clitics are invariably immediately preverbal. The synchronic variation in Medieval Spanish is shown to be directly correlated to the availability of various processing strategies for the one and the same string. The diachronic changes are the result of routinization processes and a production/parsing mismatch, leading to re-analysis.

In similar style, though in a different framework, Traugott provides an in depth study of how English pseudo-cleft structures have developed, arguing against other current analyses that dialogic argumentation has played a central role in motivating the long-term development of two types of pseudo-clefts. She also takes up methodological issues concerning interpretation of motivations from historical texts that arise in seeking to establish the link between historical change and conversational dialogue pressures.

Like the Traugott and Bouzouita papers, Sharma *et al.* provide a detailed characterization of language variation, this time in the synchronic perspective by providing a unified account of categorical and variable grammars for person, number and negation patterns in English dialects. The methodology of Sharma *et al.* is that of frequency in correlation across speakers in a community rather than either experimental psycholinguistic testing or diachronic textual study: nevertheless their conclusions are notably similar in effect to the analogous cognitive psychological claims. For, as a result of the correlations they establish through detailed corpus study, they conclude that speakers are sensitively tuned to frequencies in the linguistic environment, and this is arguably simply an alternative perspective on data that could equally be described in cognitive psychological terms as routinized strategies. The one is a community-wide form of generalization, the alternative its individualistic counterpart. Thus there is a clear link between the Sharma *et al.* paper to the various papers invoking alignment properties, despite its very different optimality-theoretic methodology.

The overall picture provided by these papers is a rich web of emergent research in which study of dialogue takes centre-stage as the most common of all types of language data, following the broad directive for language-related research urged by Pickering and Garrod [2004]. Far from being the peripheral and side-lined epiphenomenon of language performance, with language evolution and acquisition only able to be passed on through genetic-style cross-generation transfer, dialogue is seen as the window through which we can glean a radical new set of hypotheses about the nature of language. Dialogue data can provide us with direct evidence for language as an emergent internalized cognitive system of procedures for language use, for what it means for the linguistic capacity for an individual speaker to develop, and for the shifting nature of language across whole communities and across spans of time. Furthermore the new perspective that this shift provides has the striking advantage that the methodologies involved in such study allow for direct empirical evaluation of all hypotheses made, for study of linguistic competence is no longer carried out in isolation from hypotheses about use of language in context. With its radical new perspective on language, in effect a re-formulation of functionalist approaches to language but allowing for the formulation of explicit formal theories, this volume will attract readers across a broad swathe of cross-disciplinary interests.

The research reported here was brought together under the aegis of the Leverhulme Trust Research Network, *Dialogue Matters: Foundations for Technological Development*. The group of individuals funded as part of this network span a range of disciplines within the broad linguistic umbrella, and we have enjoyed regular fruitful research visits and workshops that have created a synergy well beyond even our most optimistic expectations. We are extremely grateful to the Leverhulme Trust for the impetus it has provided to this research, and for making the production of this volume possible. Thanks are due to Jane Spurr, without whom the volume would never have got off the ground, and whose enthusiasm for setting up a new series, making this first volume, and negotiation with the printers have been very much appreciated. Finally, for all the stalwart work that goes into the preparation of the manuscript itself, we have to thank Chris Howes for her single-handed preparation of the final version of the manuscript of the volume and its index.

BIBLIOGRAPHY

[Bouzouita, this volume] Miriam Bouzouita. At the Syntax-Pragmatics Interface: Clitics in the History of Spanish. In R. Cooper and R. Kempson, editors, *Language in Flux*. Kings College Press, London.

[Cann and Kempson, this volume] Ronnie Cann and Ruth Kempson. Production Pressures, Syntactic Change and the Emergence of Clitic Pronouns. In R. Cooper and R. Kempson, editors, *Language in Flux*. Kings College Press, London.

[Chomsky, 1965] Noam Chomsky. *Aspects of the Theory of Syntax*. MIT Press, 1965.

[Cooper and Ranta, this volume] Robin Cooper and Aarne Ranta. Natural Languages as Collections of Resources In R. Cooper and R. Kempson, editors, *Language in Flux*. Kings College Press, London.

[Healey, this volume] Patrick G. T. Healey. Interactive Misalignment: The Role of Repair in the Development of Group Sub-languages. In R. Cooper and R. Kempson, editors, *Language in Flux*. Kings College Press, London.

[Jäger, this volume] Gerhard Jäger. Language evolution and George Price's "General Theory of Selection". In R. Cooper and R. Kempson, editors, *Language in Flux*. Kings College Press, London.

[King, 1969] Robert D. King. *Historical Linguistics and Generative Grammar*. Prentice Hall, 1969.

[Kirby et al., this volume] Simon Kirby, Kenny Smith, and Hannah Cornish. Learning, language and cultural evolution: How linguistic transmission leads to cultural adaptation. In R. Kempson and Cooper R., editors, *Language in Flux*. Kings College Press, London.

[Larsson, this volume] Staffan Larsson. Formalizing the Dynamics of Semantic Systems in Dialogue. In R. Cooper and R. Kempson, editors, *Language in Flux*. Kings College Press, London.

[Lightfoot, 1999] David Lightfoot. *The Development of Language: Acquisition, Change, and Evolution*. Blackwell, 1999.

[Macura and Ginzburg, this volume] Zoran Macura and Jonathan Ginzburg Dynamics and Adaptiveness of Meta-communicative Interaction in a Foraging Environment. In R. Cooper and R. Kempson, editors, *Language in Flux*. Kings College Press, London.

[Paul, 1880] Hermann Paul. *Prinzipien der Sprachgeschichte*, volume 6 of *Konzepte der Sprach- und Literaturwissenschaft*. Niemeyer, Tübingen, 1880. 10., unveränderte Auflage, 1995.

[Pickering and Garrod, 2004] M.J. Pickering and S. Garrod. Toward a mechanistic psychology of dialogue. *Behavioral and Brain Sciences*, 27(02):169–190, 2004.

[Sharma et al., this volume] Devyani Sharma, Joan Bresnan and Ashwini Deo. Variation and change in the individual: Evidence from the Survey of English Dialects. In R. Cooper and R. Kempson, editors, *Language in Flux*. Kings College Press, London.

[Traugott, this volume] Elizabeth C. Traugott. 'All that he endeavoured to prove was': On the emergence of grammatical constructions in dialogual and dialogic contexts In R. Cooper and R. Kempson, editors, *Language in Flux*. Kings College Press, London.

Robin Cooper
Department of Linguistics, University of Gothenburg, Göteborg, Sweden
cooper@ling.gu.se

Ruth Kempson
Department of Philosophy, King's College London, London, England
kempson@dcs.kcl.ac.uk

July 2008

Interactive Misalignment: The Role of Repair in the Development of Group Sub-languages

PATRICK G. T. HEALEY

1 Introduction

Interaction provides a toolkit for creating and maintaining shared languages. Here we argue that it is the tools for dealing with misalignments that primarily control the kinds of sub-language that people can develop. The evidence for this claim is drawn from parallel sets of experimental studies involving two collaborative tasks. In one task communication is verbally mediated in the other it is graphically mediated. The first set of experiments focus on the emergence of group sub-languages in these tasks and show that direct interaction – independently of task exposure or experience – plays a critical role in group sub-language convergence. The second set of experiments selectively interfere with different mechanisms of interaction associated with misalignments. This provides evidence that it is people's ability to juxtapose and contrast elements of one another's turns that is critical to their ability to converge on more tightly coordinated sub-languages.

Psychological models of language change typically focus on identifying cognitive and social processes that can be linked to changes in language structure. As early as the 1920's Bartlett was formulating, and beginning to test experimentally, many of the hypotheses that are still live concerns in contemporary work [Bartlett, 1932]. For example: demonstrating the role of cognitive schemata in processes of simplification and abstraction of symbol systems [Karmiloff-Smith, 1979; Tversky et al., 1991; Tversky, 1995]; the influence of ease of copying and perceptual simplicity on symbol form [Fay et al., 2003; Galantucci, 2005]; the systematic changes caused by repeated production and transmission of graphical and linguistic representations [Tversky, 1995; Healey et al., 2004; Pickering and Garrod, 2004; Galantucci, 2005]. Bartlett also anticipated the potential contribution that cultural and biological models could make to explaining group norms and conventions [Kirby et al., this volume; Pinker and Bloom, 1990; Steels and Belpaeme, 2005].

In Bartlett's original work the process of interaction itself was not seen as introducing important constraints on language change. Communication was treated, in effect, as unanalyzed events of transmission. It provided the points of contact at which people are exposed to particular forms of expression which they then subsequently adopted or rejected.

Contemporary studies, both empirical and computational, have often continued with this idealization. The primary research interest has been in exploring the effects of patterns of exposure in promoting use of one representational form over another and the kinds of learning and inference mechanisms that might explain these effects [Garrod and Doherty, 1994; Steels and McIntyre, 1997; Pickering and Garrod, 2004].

Human interactions are, of course, more structured than a 'point of contact' model implies. Contributions are constructed incrementally, usually by more than one person and are highly context dependent [Sacks, 1995; Clark, 1996b]. The argument developed in this chapter is that these interactive processes constitute the toolkit with which shared languages are constructed. More specifically that the local processes involved in the detection and resolution of interpretive misalignments directly constrain the kinds of sub-language that people can develop.[1]

This emphasis on misalignment may seem counterintuitive. It contrasts with what many people ordinarily regard as the goal of successful communication. It also contrasts with the focus on communicative success that is characteristic of contemporary psycholinguistic models of dialogue. Although some models provide accounts of what happens when communication fails, these are treated as secondary or auxiliary processes [Pickering and Garrod, 2004; Clark, 1996b]. We argue instead that this priority should be reversed with misalignment treated as the primary focus for explanations of how sub-language coordination emerges and is sustained.

The main evidence that will be presented for this claim comes from two parallel sets of communication experiments. One series involves verbally mediated dialogues, the other involves graphically mediated dialogues where people communicate solely by drawing. Despite the difference in modality and task domain there are key parallels in the processes of sub-language formation –graphical or linguistic– observed in each case. In particular, that there are patterns of convergence and divergence that can only be accounted for by reference to the specific interaction mechanisms people use to deal with misalignments of interpretation.

Before developing this argument in detail we first try to strengthen the motivation for this approach by arguing that misalignment is a ubiquitous and highly structured feature of human interaction.

---

[1] What we mean by kinds of sub-language will be clarified below

1.1 The Importance of Interactive Misalignment

A characteristic feature of ordinary conversation is the continuous work people do to detect and deal with problems with mutual intelligibility. As Fodor and Lepore observe, it is a "patent truth that no two speakers of the same language ever speak exactly the same dialect of that language" [Fodor and Lepore, 1992, p10].

Place of residence, education, religion, occupation, hobby, age group, and sub-culture can all feed into differences in meaning [Clark, 1998, 1996a; Krauss and Fussell, 1990]. Families, friends, colleagues, and other small groups develop specialized forms of expression that are not readily understood by people outside those communities. This is documented, for example, in ethnographic studies of communication between different social groups [Gumperz, 1976, 1982, 1996] and in studies of linguistic sub-communities in different institutional contexts [Robinson and Bannon, 1991; Schmidt and Bannon, 1992; Shaw and Gaines, 1988; Bergmann and Luckmann, 1994].

There are specialized conversational mechanisms that help people to cope with this background of sub-language differences. Conversation analysts have provided a detailed structural characterization of these repair procedures [Sacks et al., 1974; Jefferson, 1983; Schegloff, 1987, 1992]. The structure of repairs depends, amongst other things, on whether it is the speaker ('self') or the recipient ('other') who signals a problem, who executes the repair and where the repair initiation and the repair itself occur; in the same turn as the problem, in the turn after the problem turn or in some subsequent turn.[2]

Repair is one of the most commonly observed conversation analytic structures and can occur in any dialogue context [Schegloff, 1992]. Healey et al. [2005] constructed a coding protocol based on the conversation analytic distinctions to obtain quantitative estimates of repair frequencies. Applied to the HCRC Map task corpus of task-oriented dialogues [Anderson et al., 1991] this gives an overall estimate of one repair event every 20 words (average turn length in this corpus is just over 8 words).[3] This is broadly consistent with the estimated frequency of repairs reported in Brennan and Schober [2001].

In addition to these explicit or 'exposed' repairs there are also a range of more indirect ways in which problems with coordination can be addressed during interaction. For example, Jefferson [1983] discusses the use of embedded correction in which people repeat part of a turn with a word or phrase substituted. This is illustrated for the Maze Task (described in more detail below) in Excerpt 1. Here B produces a description of a location which A repeats back

---

[2] Strictly, this should be formulated in terms of 'positions' rather than turns but for the sake of simplicity we suppress this distinction.

[3] This is likely to be a conservative estimate since the map task transcripts are less detailed than those typically used in conversation analysis.

but substitutes "second from top" for "second row". These changes are significant in the context of this task and are introduced without being coded as an explicit signal of change in the way that, say, a clarification question "You mean second from top?" would be. Instead they are presented and treated as a 'read-back' of the original description.

B:	right this is the **second row** and it's the third square so
A:	okay **second from top**
B:	yeah
A:	and third from the left
B:	third from the left yeah,

Excerpt 1: Example Embedded Repair form the Maze Task Corpus (substituted elements in bold)

Saxton [1997] has shown experimentally that sequences of this kind are important in child language acquisition. In part because they exploit the information provided by the unchanged elements as a frame in which to make relatively precise adjustments to other constituents [Chouinard and Clark, 2003; Saxton et al., 2005].

Embedded repairs and other indirect ways of dealing with coordination problems are inherently difficult to quantify but they extend the range of interactional mechanisms available for dealing with misalignments. Combined with more explicit repairs, the mechanisms for detecting and dealing with misalignments constitute a substantial part of the machinery of conversation.

The final point to make is that there is evidence that repair processes can have a positive effect on measures of interactional outcome. While this seems obvious for phenomena such as clarification requests it also applies to phenomena that are sometimes treated as noise in the signal or 'disfluencies'. For example, in the map task corpus there is a reliable positive correlation between the number of times the person describing landmarks on the map attempts to reformulate their descriptions – position one 'formulation' repairs – and the task outcome measure of route accuracy (Pearson correlation = 0.191, $p < 0.05$, n =128). Brennan and Schober [2001] report a parallel finding for an object selection task in which people respond more quickly, and just as accurately, to turns containing repairs than to equivalent fluent turns.

There is thus a *prima facie* case that misalignment is frequent, highly structured and that, even for 'disfluencies', it is critical to dialogue coordination. It follows that models of dialogue coordination should address these phenomena. This is not only an issue for empirical models. As Ginzburg [forthcoming] argues, a plausible adequacy criterion for contemporary semantic theory is that it should be able to characterize the range of possible responses to misalignments in dialogue, especially possible answers to clarification questions.

Here we argue that the processes associated with detecting and resolving misalignments are not just a matter of dealing with error or putting a dialogue 'back on course'. Rather, they directly constrain the kinds of sub-language that can emerge within a group. The argument has three steps. First we show that particular histories of interaction – independently of task exposure or experience – play a critical role in group sub-language convergence. Second we provide evidence that these effects depend on specific interactional mechanisms; people's ability to juxtapose and contrast elements of one another's turns. Finally we argue that the primary function of these mechanisms is to detect and resolve misalignments.

The experimental evidence comes from two communication tasks, one graphical and one verbal, which can be solved using different kinds of 'sub-language'. We first describe the basic characteristics of the two tasks and introduce a distinction between two generic types of sub-language that participants develop for them.

2 The Experimental Tasks

The experiments described below come from two parallel strands of research one on verbally mediated dialogues involving the Maze Task [Healey, 1997; Healey and Mills, 2006; Mills and Healey, 2006] and one on graphically mediated dialogues involving the Music Drawing task [Healey et al., 2007; Healey et al., 2002a; Healey et al., 2002c].

2.1 The Maze Task

The Maze Task was originally devised by Garrod and Anderson [1987] as an interactive game in which pairs of people collaborate to navigate through a maze to reach a goal point. The task is designed so that participants need to know each other's location but cannot see each other's cursors in the maze. As a result they are faced with a recurrent need to describe locations in the maze to one another.

In the experiment reported below a simplified, paper-based, version of this task is used. A number of different pairs of maze configurations are constructed as illustrated in Figure 1. One maze has a target location, indicated by a cross, on it and the other has the same configuration but no cross. The task is for the person with the target location to describe it so that their partner can mark its location on their copy of the maze. This is repeated for a number of trials with different maze configurations and target locations on each trial. In addition, the target location alternates between participants on each trial. As a result both participants repeatedly produce and interpret location descriptions.

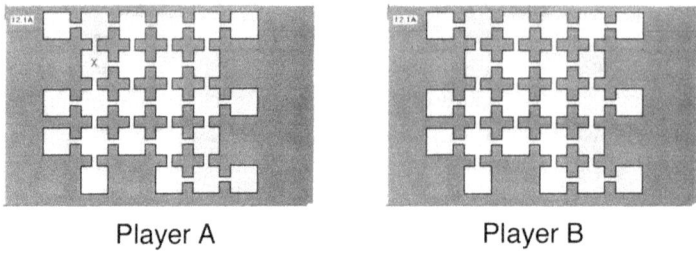

Player A   Player B

Figure 1. Example Pair of Maze Configurations

2.2 The Music Drawing Task

The Music Drawing Task was devised by Healey *et al.* [2002c]. It is designed to involve communication solely by drawing – i.e. concurrent verbal and gestural exchanges are prevented – and to promote the development of novel graphical conventions.

In essence it is like a musical version of the game 'Pictionary'; people try to communicate about pieces of music by drawing them. In the typical set up two people are seated in different rooms with a specially designed shared electronic whiteboard, on a PC, as the only connection between them [Healey *et al.*, 2002b]. This set-up is illustrated in Figure 2.

Each participant has a 20 second piece of target music. Playback is self-paced and controlled by buttons at the top of the whiteboard. The task is for the pair to decide, by drawing alone, if they have the same or different pieces of music. On half of the trials the pieces are, in fact, the same and on half different. Participants are free to draw anything they like subject to the constraint that they do not use letters or numbers. Once they have decided they press one of two buttons at the top of the whiteboard to indicate their choice 'SAME' or 'DIFFERENT'.

The target pieces of music are assigned randomly but with the constraint that they match on 50% of trials. They include classical and jazz pieces in a range of tempos and keys. All are piano solos – to ensure that drawing the instruments provides no cues – and all are unfamiliar pieces so that participants cannot do the task just by drawing their titles.

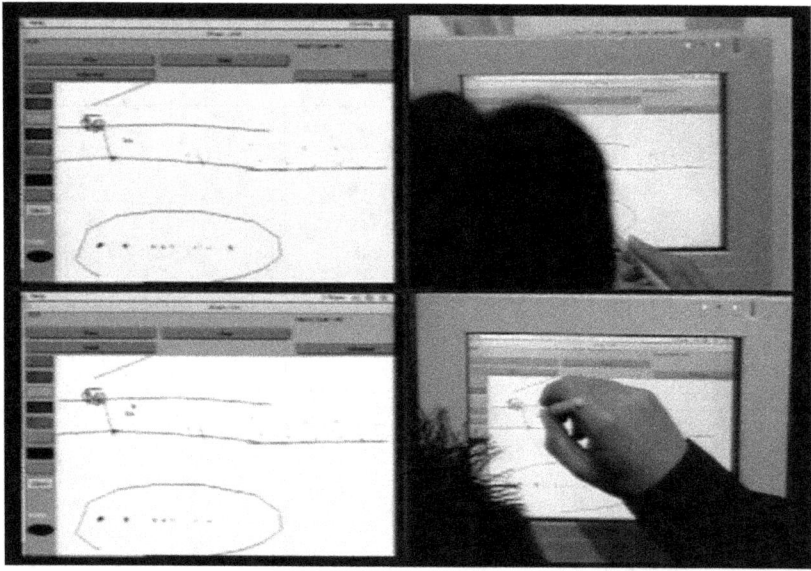

Figure 2. Music Task (Screen Capture from Split-screen Video)

3 Task Sub-Languages

A feature of both the tasks is that participants develop local sub-languages that can be reliably classified into two broad categories that we will term Type 1 and Type 2. This contrast has two important roles in what follows. First, we argue that in both tasks we find the same basic difference in the type of semantic coordination participants achieve. Specifically, that Type 1 sub-languages reflect a relatively concrete and instance specific form of coordination whereas Type 2 sub-languages reflect a more systematic and generalizable form of coordination. Second, that the observed patterns of use of these two categories of sub-language is, in important respects, the same in the two different tasks.

3.1 Sub-language Types in The Music Task

The drawings produced in the music task can be reliably classified by independent judges into two basic categories: Figurative or Abstract. A third category, Composite, consists of mixtures of the two (Kappa = 0.9, N = 287, k= 2: [Healey et al., 2001]). The judges make this categorization on the basis of superficial form alone, i.e. by inspecting the final drawing only and without hearing the music that was being drawn.

Figure 3. Sequence of Six 'Figurative' Trials from One Pair

The Type 1 sub-language in this task is constituted by the Figurative drawings, illustrated in Figure 3 (note that in the originals participants used colour). They are based on ad-hoc associations for each target piece. They make use of recognizable objects, figures or scenes and represent the piece as a whole in terms of its mood or salient associations. For example a cityscape and a saxophone for a jazz piece or a rainy day for a sombre piece.

The Type 2 sub-language for this task is constituted by the Abstract drawings. These consist of graph-like representations of aspects of the internal musical structure of a piece such as pitch, tempo, melody, stress, rhythm or intensity together with a time-based axis. A sequence of six trials from one pair is shown in Figure 4 (again, in the originals participants used colour).

Further details on this distinction and how it relates to aspects of drawing behaviour and task performance are provided in [Healey et al., 2007].

Figure 4. Sequence of Six 'Abstract' Trials from One Pair

3.2 Sub-Language Types in the Maze Task

Location descriptions in the Maze Task can also be classified into basic sub-types. In the original work: Figural, Path, and Line and Matrix [Garrod and Anderson, 1987].

The Type 1 sub-language for this task consists of the Figural (Excerpt 2) and Path (Excerpt 3) descriptions. These depend on the particular configuration of boxes and links in the maze in each case. Figural descriptions invoke salient landmarks or shapes in the maze. Path descriptions identify a particular route that can be followed given the available boxes and links.[4]

The Type 2 sub-language for the Maze Task is constituted by the Line and

---

[4]The examples are taken from the corpus reported in [Healey, 1997]. Notational conventions: "[n]" indicates the point at which item n was completed in a trial. "[utterance]" in adjacent turns indicates overlapping talk, "," indicates a short pause, "..." indicates a long pause.

A:	right on the right hand side there are four boxes,
B:	mmhum
A:	then there are two shapes and then there's another four linked boxes,
B:	yes
A:	right it's the second from the bottom
B:	mmhum
A:	of those four linked boxes in the middle,
B:	ok, right ...[7]

Excerpt 2: Example Figural Description

B:	mmm, ummm, take the bottom left hand corner,
A:	yes
B:	up one box
A:	yes
B:	right one box
A:	yes
B:	up one box
A:	yes
B:	in the centre ...[8]

Excerpt 3: Example Path Description

Matrix description types. Although each instance of the maze has a different configuration of boxes, the Type 2 descriptions treat them as variations on the same underlying 'grid' model that generalizes across instances. In the case of Line descriptions (Excerpt 4) this is organized in terms of rows or columns. In the case of Matrix descriptions (Excerpt 5) locations are specified as coordinates.

More extensive discussion of the coding criteria and the differences between the basic description types can be found in Anderson and Garrod [1987] and Garrod and Anderson [1987].

3.3 Type 1 vs. Type 2 Sub-languages

There is considerable variation within the categories of task sub-language described above. Nonetheless there are important commonalities across the two tasks.

The Type 1 sub-languages use relatively simple, instance-specific forms of

A:	ummm, fourth row down and the second from the right, [12]
B:	okay it's the second row down and second in from the left, [13]
A:	ummm third row down first box from the left, [14]
B:	okay it's the third row down and it's the first box on the right, [15]

Excerpt 4: Example Line Descriptions

B:	er: two two, [3]
A:	six: six three, [4]
B:	four three, [5]

Excerpt 5: Example Matrix Descriptions

representation. They focus on salient features of the current item (maze or target piece) and exploit a range of *ad hoc* associations and conventions that people could reasonably expect to share prior to engaging in the task. For example, in the Music Drawing Task people use emblematic sketches of landscapes, figures or scenes and in the Maze Task they cite recognizable shapes (e.g. "triangle", "arm", "block").

The Type 2 sub-languages, by contrast, employ more specialized semantic models that capture task-related generalizations. In the case of the Maze Task these models consist of an array of possible locations, sometimes organized into higher order structures such as rows, that provide a relatively efficient semantic model for systematically capturing variations in the maze configurations. In the Music Drawing Task these models consist of parameters of musical structure combined with a time based axis that provide a relatively efficient way of systematically capturing variations in the structure of the target pieces.

One corollary of this contrast is a difference in how effective the two sub-language types are for making comparisons between items.[5] For example, it is harder to get a sense of the degree of musical similarity between target pieces on different trials in Figure 3 than in Figure 4. Similarly, the spatial relationship between locations on two different trials in the Maze is relatively obscure when Figural or Path descriptions are used but clear if, say, the locations are both given as co-ordinates in the same grid.

The distinction between Type 1 and Type 2 languages is also made on empirical grounds. For example, the use of Type 1 sub-languages declines across trials whereas the use of Type 2 sub-languages increases (Maze Task:

---

[5]Healey *et al.* [2007] refer to this property as systematicity.

[Garrod and Anderson, 1987]; Music Drawing Task: [Healey *et al.*, 2002c]). Type 2 sub-languages are also preferred, for example, for versions of the Music Drawing Task which require more comparison of pieces [Healey *et al.*, 2002c]. However, the strongest empirical evidence for this distinction comes from the experiments to be described below.

4 Experimental Evidence

The experimental evidence is grouped into two sets of experiments. The first are concerned with exploring the development of group sub-languages, the second with the contribution of particular mechanisms of interaction to these sub-languages.

4.1 Group Sub-language Experiments

The first experiments described here focus on the role of direct interaction in the emergence of group-specific sub-languages. The data for the Music Task comes from Healey *et al.* [2007]. The data for the Maze task comes from a replication of Healey [1997] and is reported here in full for the first time. Both experiments follow the same basic design and are therefore presented together.

The conclusions we draw for both tasks are that the Type 2 sub-languages emerge from the group interactions, not individual experience. Moreover, in both tasks people deal with communicative misalignment by reverting to Type 1 sub-languages.

Hypotheses

One 'Experience' based hypothesis about coordination on Type 2 sub-languages is that it develops as a consequence of task expertise. As participants develop an understanding of the range of target items they need to represent (i.e. maze locations or pieces of music) they begin to identify more efficient and effective schemes for dealing with them.

An alternative 'Language game' hypothesis is that Type 2 sub-languages emerge as local 'language games' i.e. not as a matter of individual experience *per se* but as an emergent product of particular histories of interaction between particular participants. [Wilkes-Gibbs and Clark, 1992; Brennan and Clark, 1996].

Experimental Design

To distinguish these accounts experimentally we need to separate the contribution of individual experience from the contribution of interaction. The basic strategy is to foster the development of a number of linguistic sub-communities that, over time, converge on a sub-language. We then create two new groups: people communicating within a sub-community and people communicating between sub-communities. If task experience and exposure are appropriately controlled, the 'Experience' hypothesis predicts that communication within and between sub-communities should be equally effective. By contrast, the 'Language Game' hypothesis predicts that members of different sub-communities should find interaction more problematic when they try to communicate across sub-community boundaries.

This design is illustrated schematically in Figure 5. On each round, participants are paired into dyads who repeat the task for a number of trials.

The sub-community manipulation takes place in two phases. In the convergence phase participants are first divided into sub-communities and pairs are always composed of individuals drawn from within a sub-community. This ensures that each sub-community progressively accumulates a common interaction history; pairs are increasingly composed of individuals who have already encountered the same person in preceding trials (or a person who has encountered a person they have encountered and so on). In effect creating multiple instances of the single community group used in Garrod and Doherty [1994].

In the second, experimental, phase half the dyads are composed, as before, of individuals from the same sub-community and half are composed of individuals drawn from different sub-communities.

Participants switch partners on every round, they all perform the task in the same room at the same time and they are given no cues about the manipulation of dyads and sub-groups. As a result task experience is equivalent across dyads and sub-groups and participants have no explicit knowledge of sub-group membership.

Participants

Maze Task: 24 participants (13 male, 11 female) were recruited from amongst staff and students at the University of Edinburgh (average age: 25 years). Each was paid £3 for participating.

Music Drawing Task: 66 participants (50 male and 16 female, average age 21.5) were recruited from undergraduate and masters students from at Queen Mary, University of London. Each was paid £10 for participation.

Materials

Maze Task: 120 different maze configurations (see Figure 1) were produced and divided up into sets of 20 items, each forming a pair of booklets with each pair of pages showing the same maze configuration but only one with a target location marked.

Music Drawing Task: The MAGIC whiteboard [Healey et al., 2002b] was used to assign target pieces of music on each trial and to log all drawing activity. Target pieces consisted of 112, thirty second, piano solos balanced for genre, mode, and tempo. Stereo headsets were used for playback. Drawing input was via a standard mouse.

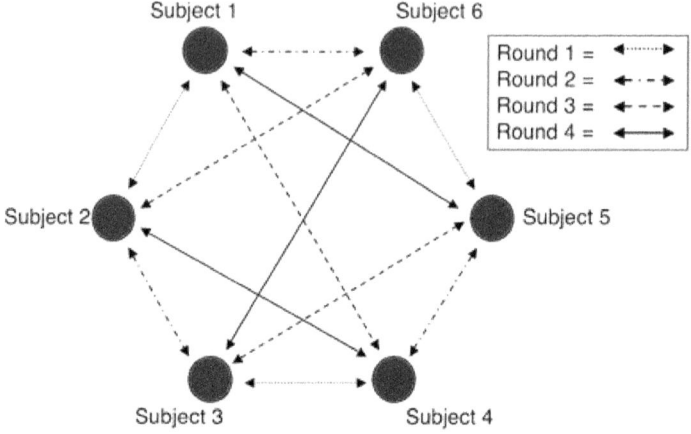

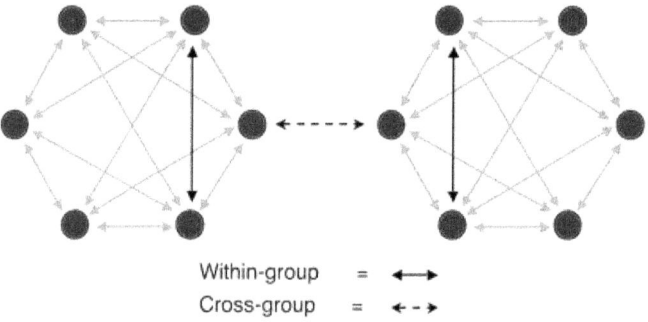

Figure 5. Schematic Representation of the Manipulation of Dyad and Community Composition

Procedure

Participants received instructions as a group and all carried out the task in the same room. The initial assignment to sub-groups was made randomly and dyads were subsequently paired according to the patterns shown in Figure 5.

In the Music Drawing Task there were ten subgroups of six participants and a total of five rounds. In the Maze Task there were three sub-groups of eight participants and a total of 6 rounds.

In the Maze Task participants had three minutes to complete as many items as possible up to a total of 20. Participants were separated by a partition and could not see each other's booklets. There were no restrictions on what they could say. As soon as they were satisfied they had agreed on the target location and it had been marked on the 'blank' maze they moved onto the next item. All dialogues were recorded on audio tape for transcription.

In the Music Drawing Task participants had two minutes to complete each trial i.e. each pair of target pieces, after which the whiteboard was frozen and they were prompted for a decision. This was repeated for 12 trials in each round. If both subjects correctly selected SAME or DIFFERENT they received the feedback: "Congratulations! You were both correct". If either of them made an incorrect selection they received the feedback: "Sorry one OR both of you were incorrect". All drawing activity was recorded by the Whiteboard software.

4.2 Results

During phase one there are reliable improvements in task performance in both tasks. In the Maze Task the average number of items attempted by each pair increases from 13.4 in round one to 19.3 in round five (Linear trend; $t_{(66)}=3.50$, p(one-tailed)=0.00) and errors are consistently low (by round: 7%, 8%, 9%, 5%, 4%, 6%). In the Music Drawing Task participants become faster, going from 53 sec in round one to 43 sec in round five ($F_{(4,149)} = 1.676$, Linear Trend p=0.02), and more accurate, rising from 37% correct in round one to 52% in round five ($F_{(4,149)} = 3.61$, p=0.00).[6]

Sub-languages:

The Maze Task produced 71 three minute Maze Task dialogues (one dyad excluded because of equipment failure). These were transcribed producing a corpus of 1,207 descriptions. These were coded as Type 1 (Figural: 9%, Path: 36%) and Type 2 (Line: 26% and Matrix: 29%). A second judge independently coded a random sample of 25% of the dialogues. Inter-coder reliability was acceptable (Kappa: $K = 0.76, N = 445, k = 2$.). Each location description

---

[6]Note that in this task because both participants must make a correct choice between 'same' or 'different' chance is 25%.

was also coded for whether it was subject to clarification.[7]

The Music Drawing Task produced a total of 3,611 drawings. These were classified as Type 1 (Abstract : 60%) and Type 2 (Figurative: 15%) and mixed Type 1 / Type 2 (Composite: 19%). The remaining 6% of the drawings were classified as 'None' in cases where there was no picture at the end of the trial (this occurred where subjects had either erased their drawings or produced only a tick or cross to signal agreement).

Within Group vs Cross Group Comparisons

The key concern here is the contrast between the within-group and cross-group pairs. In both tasks, there is a reliable difference in the frequency of use of the Type 1 and Type 2 sub-languages in the within-group and cross-group pairs (Maze Task: $Chi^2_{(2)} = 22.93$, p = 0.00; Music Drawing Task: $Chi^2_{(2)} = 19.05$, p = 0.00). As Figures 6 and 7 show, in both cases the basic effect of crossing between sub-groups is to decrease the use of Type 2 sub-languages and increase the use of Type 1 sub-languages.

An indication of the degree of change in sub-language use caused by moving between groups is provided by comparing the cross-group pairs with the naïve pairs from the first round of each experiment. In both cases there is no reliable difference between the experienced cross-group pairs and the naïve pairs in their choice of sub-language type (Maze Task: $Chi^2_{(2)} = 3.34$, p = 0.19; Music Drawing Task: $Chi^2_{(2)} = 1.01$, p =0.68). The within-group pairs are however reliably different from naïve pairs (Maze Task: $Chi^2_{(2)} = 46.1$, p = 0.00; Music Drawing Task: $Chi^2_{(2)} = 7.32$, p =0.03).

In both tasks there is also evidence that communication in the cross-group pairs is more problematic than in the within-group pairs. In the Maze task, location descriptions in the cross-group pairs are subject to clarification approximately twice as often as in the within-group pairs (within-group 16%, cross-group, 37%; $Chi^2_{(1)}=6.54$, p=0.01). In addition, the cross-group pairs are not reliably different from naïve pairs on trial 1 in frequency of clarification ($Chi^2_{(1)}=1.14$, p=0.29).

Difficulty of communication in the Music Drawing Task can be approximated by the amount of 'ink' (pixels) used to produce drawings. Overall cross-group pairs draw approximately 20% more than within-group pairs. This addi-

---

[7] Descriptions were treated as clarified if a possible completion was followed by additional turns directed at clarifying, checking or reformulating aspects of the description. Descriptions were encoded as not clarified if a) the participants proceeded directly to the next description b) proceeded after only a simple acknowledgement (e.g. "yeah, or "okay") or c) proceeded after unmodified repetition of the preceding material that provoked no additional turns addressed to the repeated material. Criterion c) was included in order to discriminate simple echoes produced as place-holders while instructions were carried out from those repeats designed to signal a problem.

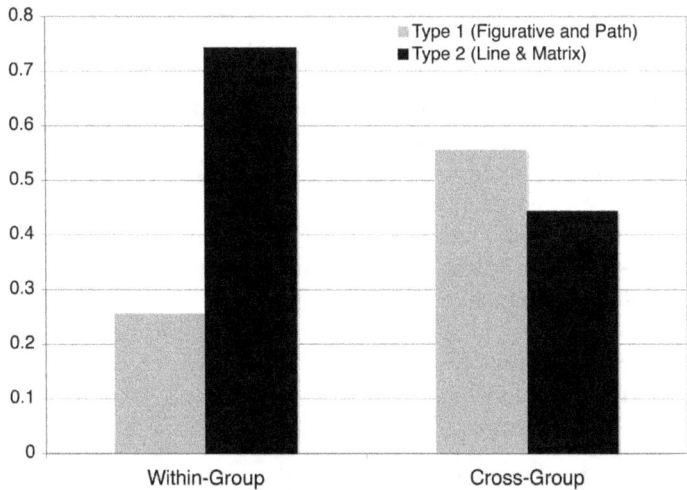

Figure 6. Distribution of Type 1 and Type 2 Sub-languages in the Within and Cross-group Pairs in the Maze Task

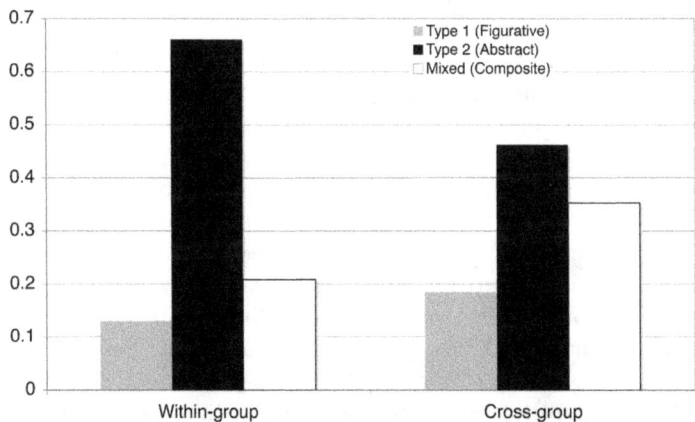

Figure 7. Distribution of Type 1 and Type 2 Sub-languages in the Within and Cross-group Pairs in the Music Drawing Task

tional drawing effort is almost entirely associated with the Type 2 (Abstract) drawings. Analysis of variance with Drawing type (Abstract, Figurative or Composite) × Group Membership (within-group or cross-group) shows a main effect of Drawing Type ($F_{(2,19)} = 6.03$, p = 0.00) and a Group × Drawing Type interaction ($F_{(2,19)} = 4.06$, p = 0.03). Focused comparisons show that more ink is used for the Abstract drawings ($F_{(1,19)} = 4.90$, p = 0.04) but there is no relabiable difference for Figurative ($F_{(1,13)} = 0.27$, p = 0.61) or Composite ($F_{(1,19)} = 0.06$, p = 0.81).

It it worth noting that although the within and cross-group pairs differ on the measures of communicative coordination they do not differ on simple measures of task performance. In the Maze Task within-group pairs complete an average of 19.5 items and cross-group pairs an average of 19.2.[8] In the Music Drawing Task average response time and accuracy scores in the within and cross-group conditions show no reliable difference (Accuracy: $F_{(1,20)} = 0.24$, p = 0.87; Response time: $F_{(1,20)} = 0.09$, p = 0.92).

Discussion: Group-Specific Sub-languages

Previous work has shown that in isolated dyads use of the Type 2 sub-languages normally increases over time (see above). The results reported here show that this is not a straightforward function of task experience or learning. People in the within-group and cross-group pairs have equivalent task experience and yet their patterns of sub-language use are different. People in the cross-group pairs use fewer Type 2 and more Type 1 sub-languages than people in the within-group pairs. They also work 'harder' - i.e. draw more or clarify more, in order to preserve performance.

The fact that communication across community boundaries is more problematic demonstrates that the emerging Type 2 sub-languages are to some degree, group-specific. It is important to note that these effects are not mediated by explicit knowledge of group membership. Participants have no explicit cues to group membership; from each participant's point of view there is simply a succession of different dyadic interactions. Rather they depend on aspects of group membership that are implicitly mediated by interaction.

This provides basic support for the Language Game hypothesis; the specific history of interaction within each group contributes directly to the character of the sub-language that emerges in the group. These sub-languages are de-stabilized in cross-group communication and people tend to revert to the kinds of sub-language they used when engaging in the task for the first time. It is clear that this pattern cannot be explained by patterns of exposure or

---

[8] Because the unit of analysis for number of items completed is the pair there are only six data points in each condition. This precludes statistical analysis but the means do not suggest any trend towards a difference. Healey [1997], using a larger data set and the same experimental design, shows no reliable statistical difference on this measure.

repetition *per se*.

4.3 Interaction Mechanism Experiments

What is interaction contributing to the process of coordination on Type 2 sub-languages? We turn now to consider the evidence that this coordination process depends on particular interactional mechanisms.

Interaction in The Music Drawing Task

Healey *et al.* [2001] compared two versions of the task. In the 'non-interactive' version people worked in dyads but only one participant drew at a time. One person drew a target piece and the other, who was prevented from drawing, watched the whiteboard (in a separate room) and chose between two pieces, the target and a distractor. These roles alternated over a number of trials. This contrasted with an 'interactive' version similar to the one described above; both participants had a target piece and both were able to draw concurrently on the whiteboard. In this case the task was to decide whether they had the same or different pieces.

Although participants make the same number of drawings of the same target pieces in the two experiments, the distribution of drawing types in the interactive and non-interactive conditions is different. As Table 1 shows, Type 1 drawings predominate in the non-interactive condition whereas Type 2 drawings predominate in the interactive condition.

Table 1. Summary of Distribution of Drawing Types (from Healey *et. al* [2001]

Task Version	Drawing Type		
	Type 1	Type 2	Other
Interactive	21%	59%	20%
Non-Interactive	64%	27%	9%

Playback of recordings of these experiments shows that whereas in the non-interative task participants concentrate on representing the target piece in the interactive trials they also use a variety of additional graphical devices for editing and annotation (recall that letters or numbers cannot be used). Some of these are used to localize elements e.g. by circling or underlining parts of a drawing that are problematic in some way. Others, such as arrows and parentheses are used to suggest possible points of alignment or contrast between drawings.

Healey *et al.* [2007] provided a direct test of the hypothesis that these devices aid coordination by selectively interfering with them. Two manipulations of the shared whiteboard were used. One in which participants were selectively prevented from editing or annotating each other's drawings and a second in which participant's ability to signal possible points of alignment and contrast was restricted. As the results in Table 2 demonstrate, restricting the kinds of interaction mechanism available to participants had a direct effect on the kind of sub-language that they use. When interaction is restricted participants rely more on Type 1 sub-languages, when it is unrestricted they rely more on Type 2.

Table 2. Summary of Distribution of Drawing Types (from Healey et al. [2007])

	Drawing Type		
Task Version	Type 1	Type 2	Other
Unrestricted Interaction	18%	63%	19%
Restricted Interaction	59%	26%	15%

In all the experimental conditions drawing was synchronous and the task and target items were the same. The opportunities for seeding new drawing types or being exposed to new drawing types are identical as are the opportunities for signaling agreement or disagreement – typically by using a tick or a cross. Perhaps most importantly people's ability to edit and revise their own contributions is unaffected by these manipulations. It is only the ability to edit and annotate *each other's* drawings that is restricted. It is people's ability to juxtapose and contrast each other's drawings that is critical to the coordinated use of the Type 2 sub-language in this task.

Interaction in The Maze Task

The experimental evidence for the role of direct interaction in the Maze Task is more indirect. It primarily comes from a study which compares the kinds of description type people use when talking to different participants in a multi-party interaction [Healey and Mills, 2006].

In this study participants carried out a standard version of the Maze Task but interacted via a special text-based chat tool developed by [Healey et al., 2003]. This tool enables the insertion of experimental probe questions into an ongoing dialogue without disrupting the interaction or alerting the participants that they are responding to 'spoof' turns. Healey and Mills [2006] used this to insert 'spoof' questions that periodically ask participants to describe various neutral locations in the Maze e.g. "Where is your goal?" or "Where did you start from?".

The experiment focuses on manipulation of the apparent origin of the probe questions. All chat turns are preceded by the name of the sender e.g. "Pat: message". For the spoof location questions this was manipulated so that the turn appeared to originate either from a) the other primary participant or b) from a third peripheral participant (the experimenter). Both experimental participants receive the spoof questions simultaneously, their answer is captured and the chat server produces an acknowledgement after which the dialogue with the other participant resumes. Neither participant sees the other's spoof question or answer.

There are two points about the results from this experiment which are relevant here. First, this procedure makes it possible to show that the same question, in the same dialogue context, receives systematically different answers (in terms of description type) depending on its origin. This provides further evidence that recency, exposure or priming of description types do not reliably predict use (*contra* Pickering and Garrod [2004]).

Second, participants use more Type 2 descriptions when responding to the spoof peripheral participant than the spoof primary participant. Considered alone this might be reflect an 'experimenter' effect in which participants assume the experimenter is an expert. However, the pattern of change is different in the two cases. Whereas the primary participants follow the same pattern of migration for Type 1 to Type 2 sub-languages established in the other studies their responses to the peripheral participant (experimenter) do not change.

If a stable Type 2 sub-language is available from the start of the experiment, then, all things being equal, it should be used for both peripheral and primary participants. What this suggests instead is that the process of interaction leads the primary participants to discover problems in the intelligibility of their descriptions. Like the cross-group pairs described above, they respond to these problems by using more Type 1 descriptions and then gradually build up to coordinated use of Type 2 descriptions over a number of trials.

Although not conclusive, this is consistent with an account in which coordination is built out of the progressive discovery and resolution of problems in interpreting other people's descriptions. More direct tests of the role of particular interaction mechanisms in the Maze Task are currently in progress.

5 General Discussion

Considered together, the experiments summarized above provide evidence that the process of interaction itself places important constraints on the kinds of sub-language that people can develop in these tasks. Interaction provides more than just points of contact for transmission of new representational schemes or exposure to existing schemes. It provides a specialized toolkit for creating and maintaining shared sub-languages. The form and organization of a sub-language depends on which tools people are able to make use of in constructing their shared language.

The interactional tools identified as critical for the Music Drawing Task –

juxtaposition and contrast– have verbal analogues in the repair mechanisms discussed in the introduction. An important feature of conversational repair is the way problems are localized. For example, a simple "uh?" or "what?" provides much less information about what might be wrong than a repeat of a problem word or even a repeat of the preceding word e.g. A: "Can I have some toast please", B: "Some?" [Purver et al., 2003]. Similarly, the forms of embedded repair described in the introduction also exploit the potential for repeating part of the target utterance in order to localize a proposed change. In conversation the sequential organization of turns is used to juxtapose and localize possible contrasts for repair. In the case of drawing the spatial organization of marks on the whiteboard is used to the same effect. Healey et al. [2007] develop this parallel in more detail.

The claim that the key interactional tools for coordination are those that deal with misalignments forms a basic contrast with models such as interactive alignment [Pickering and Garrod, 2004, 2006] and 'point of contact' models. In these models, coordination is primarily treated as a matter of converging on the right reference scheme from a set of pre-existing alternatives (in Lewis' [1969] terms this is the problem of selecting from a set of arbitrary, equivalent coordination equilibria). Which scheme people use matters less than the fact that they select the same scheme. On this view the primary theoretical problem is to account for how people actually do select the same same scheme. For example, for Pickering and Garrod [2004] this is by priming; for Lewis [1969] it is through salience and precedence.

The experimental data present problems for this view. There are systematic differences in the distribution of sub-language types which show that they are not equivalent 'coordination equilibria'. People systematically migrate from Type 1 to Type 2 sub-languages i.e. there is a consistent tendency to depart from currently shared conventions. Moreover, where trouble occurs, this direction of change is reversed. People systematically prefer Type 1 sub-languages where there are difficulties in the interaction i.e. in the cross-group pairs and where interaction is limited. These patterns are not explained by priming, precedence or salience. In the experimental data presented here this non-equivalence is highlighted by the fact that there are no reliable differences in overall alignment between the within and cross-group pairs in either task despite the differences in the forms of coordination they use.[9]

---

[9]Following Garrod and Doherty [1994] alignment in the Maze Task is calculated as the number of description types that match the preceding description type produced by a partner, divided by the total number of exchanges. In the data described above the within-group pairs and the cross-group pairs are not reliably different (average cross-group: 0.54; average within-group: 0.54; Anova Within × Cross: $F_{1,22} = 0.00$, p=0.96). Re-analysis of the Maze Task data reported in Healey [1997] also shows no reliable difference ($F_{(1,22)}=2.34$, p=0.14). In the Music Task each participant produces a drawing on each trial. Entrainment is thus

The idealization that different reference schemes are drawn from a preexisting shared repertoire is also problematic. As argued in the introduction, it is possible that no two people never use the same words in exactly the same way. On close inspection –even in the apparently highly restricted context of the maze task– simple words such as "box" display a wide variety of denotations (e.g. for a single box, for clusters of boxes, for the gaps between the boxes, for the links between boxes etc.). The meaning of words like "box" also depends in more subtle ways on the wider language game, e.g. varieties of path vs. matrix, in which they are embedded. This affects, for example, whether people speak of a "gap" or a "missing box". This point is reinforced empirically by the observed complexity and prevalence of repair in conversation which suggests that misalignment is an important and routine practical problem.

In this context it is more informative from a participant's point of view to identify definite points of contrast, i.e. misalignments, than to focus on a potentially indeterminate variety of possible points of commonality. This is similar to the point that Saxton [1997] makes about cycles of embedded repair. Localized negative evidence provides relatively precise information about what needs to be modified and how the modification may interact with the language system as a whole. The iterative use of interaction to identify and respond to local misalignments thus provides a mechanism that could drive more gradual, global changes. It also explains why the sub-languages that emerge from this process are specific to the sub-groups in which they develop. As interaction history accumulates so does the number of local modifications and adaptations of the group sub-language.

It may be worth noting that this does not involve appeal to explicit negotiation. Empirically, explicit negotiation is rare. In the Maze Task corpus described above only 3.5% of location descriptions involve explicit negotiation. Where it does occur, it appears to be as likely to impede as to promote coordination [Garrod and Anderson, 1987; Garrod and Doherty, 1994]. Moreover, it is much more common in dyads who have already coordinated on an abstract reference scheme, suggesting that coordination of semantic ontology or frame of reference has to precede any explicit negotiation. In the Music Drawing Task there is no meta-language available in which to conduct explicit negotiations.

The use of juxtaposition and contrast to progressively narrow down differences in interpretation through interaction can provide a 'bottom-up' coordination mechanism. It is a process through which Type 2 sub-languages, and the more specialized, task-specific semantic models associated with them, can

---

calculated as the proportion of trials on which participants produce drawings of the same type. Again there is no reliable difference in alignment in the within and cross-group pairs (Average cross-group: 0.39; average within-group: 0.49; Anova Within × Cross: $F_{1,394} = 2.53$, p=0.10).

emerge. Where interaction is restricted, or where the history of interactions they presuppose as part of their context is removed, people revert to the Type 1 sub-languages favoured by naïve participants and then rebuild coordination from the bottom up.

Overall, this amounts to the claim that shared sub-languages are an emergent product of successful interaction, not a pre-requisite for it. People use interaction to continuously adapt and modify semantic models to their current purposes.

6 Conclusions

This chapter has argued that interaction plays a key role in sub-language change that is distinct from individual perceptual-cognitive abilities, distinct from individual learning processes and distinct from 'passive' patterns of contact in a population. The fact that the same patterns are observed for two different tasks and two different modalities strengthens the conclusion that these are generic interaction mechanisms. In addition we have proposed that these effects are specifically associated with the processes used to detect and deal with communicative misalignments.

Interaction in general, and misalignment in particular, have received relatively little attention in experimental studies. More work is required to explore the specific interactional process involved and the ways they impact on coordination. Nonetheless, there is a significant empirical evidence that supports the present proposal. Whatever the outcome of further work it seems clear that misalignment is a ubiquitous, structured and basic feature of human interaction that merits detailed analysis in its own right.

Acknowledgements

This work was supported by the ESRC/EPSRC PACCIT project "MAGIC: Multimodality and Graphics in Interactive Communication" (L328 25 3003) and the EPSRC project "DiET: Dialogue Experiments Toolkit" (EP D0574 26 1). This work would not have been possible without inspiration and help from James King, Greg Mills, Nik Swoboda and Ichiro Umata.

BIBLIOGRAPHY

[Anderson and Garrod, 1987]   A. Anderson and S. Garrod. The dynamics of referential meaning in spontaneous dialogue. In R. G. Reilley, editor, *Communication Failure in Dialogue and Discourse*, pages 161–183. Amsterdam: Elsevier, 1987.

[Anderson et al., 1991]   A. Anderson, M. Bader, E. Bard, E. Boyle, G. M. Doherty, S. Garrod, S. Isard, J. Kowtko, J. McAllister, J. Miller, C. Sotillo, H. S. Thompson, and R Weinert. The hcrc map task corpus. *Language and Speech*, 34:351–366, 1991.

[Bartlett, 1932]   F. C. Bartlett. *Remembering*. Cambridge: Cambridge University Press, 1932.

[Bergmann and Luckmann, 1994]   J. R. Bergmann and T. Luckmann. Reconstructive genres of everyday communication. In U. Quasthoff, editor, *Aspects of Oral Communications*, pages 289–304. Berlin: Mouton de Gruyter, 1994.

[Brennan and Clark, 1996]   Susan E. Brennan and Herbert H. Clark. Conceptual pacts and lexical choice in conversation. *Journal of Experimental Psychology: Learning, Memory and Cognition*, 22:1482–1493, 1996.

[Brennan and Schober, 2001]   Susan E. Brennan and M. Schober. How listeners compensate for disfluencies in spontaneous speech. *Journal of Memory and Language*, 44:274–296, 2001.

[Chouinard and Clark, 2003]   M.M. Chouinard and E.V. Clark. Adult reformulations of child errors as negative evidence. *Journal of Child Language*, 30:637–669, 2003.

[Clark, 1996a]   Herbert H. Clark. Communities, commonalities, and communication. In John J. Gumperz and Stephen C. Levinson, editors, *Rethinking linguistic relativity*, pages 324–355. Cambridge: Cambridge University Press, 1996.

[Clark, 1996b]   Herbert H. Clark. *Using Language*. Cambridge: Cambridge University Press, 1996.

[Clark, 1998]   Herbert H. Clark. Communal lexicons. In K. Malmkjoer and J. Williams, editors, *Context in language learning and language understanding*, pages 63–87. Cambridge: CUP, 3rd edition, 1998.

[Fay et al., 2003]   N. Fay, S. Garrod, J. Lee, and J. Oberlander. Understanding interactive graphical communication. In R. Alterman and D. Kirsh, editors, *Proceedings of the 25th Annual Conference of the Cognitive Science Society*. Mahwah, N.J.: LEA, 2003.

[Fodor and Lepore, 1992]   Jerry Fodor and Ernest Lepore. *Holism: A Shopper's Guide*. Oxford: Basil Blackwell, 1992.

[Galantucci, 2005]   B. Galantucci. An experimental study of the emergence of human communication systems. *Cognitive Science*, 29(5):737–767, 2005.

[Garrod and Anderson, 1987]   Simon C. Garrod and Anthony Anderson. Saying what you mean in dialogue: A study in conceptual and semantic coordination. *Cognition*, 27:181–218, 1987.

[Garrod and Doherty, 1994]   Simon C. Garrod and Gwyneth Doherty. Conversation, coordination and convention: an empirical investigation of how groups establish linguistic conventions. *Cognition*, 53:181–215, 1994.

[Ginzburg, forthcoming]   Jonathan Ginzburg. *Semantics for Conversation*. CSLI Publications, forthcoming.

[Gumperz, 1976]   John J Gumperz. Social network and language shift. In *Papers on Language and Context, Working Paper 46* Language Behaviour Research Laboratory, University of California, Berkeley, 1976.

[Gumperz, 1982]   John J. Gumperz. Conversational code switching. In John J. Gumperz, editor, *Discourse Strategies*, pages 59–99. Cambridge: Cambridge University Press, 1982.

[Gumperz, 1996]   John J. Gumperz. The linguistic and cultural relativity of conversational inference. In John J. Gumperz and Stephen C. Levinson, editors, *Rethinking linguistic relativity*, pages 374–406. Cambridge: Cambridge University Press, 1996.

[Healey and Mills, 2006]   P.G.T. Healey and G. Mills. Participation, precedence and coordination in dialogue. In R. Sun and N. Miyake, editors, *Proceedings of the 28th Annual Conference of the Cognitive Science Society*, pages 1470–1475, 2006.

[Healey et al., 2001] P.G.T. Healey, N. Swoboda, I. Umata, and Y. Katagiri. Representational form and communicative use. In J.D. Moore and K. Stenning, editors, *Proceedings of the 23rd Annual Conference of the Cognitive Science Society*, pages 411–416. Mahwah, N.J.: LEA, 2001.

[Healey et al., 2002a] P.G.T. Healey, S. Garrod, N. Fay, J. Lee, and J. Oberlander. Interactional context in graphical communication. In W.D. Gray and C.D. Schunn, editors, *Proceedings of the 24th Annual Conference of the Cognitive Science Society*, pages 441–446, August 7th-10th 2002.

[Healey et al., 2002b] P.G.T. Healey, N. Swoboda, and J. King. A tool for performing and analysing experiments on graphical communication. In X. Faulkner, J. Finlay, and F. Détienne, editors, *People and Computers XVI: Proceedings of HCI2002: The 16th British HCI Group Annual Conference*, pages 55–68, 2002.

[Healey et al., 2002c] P.G.T. Healey, N. Swoboda, I. Umata, and Y. Katagiri. Graphical representation in graphical dialogue. *International Journal of Human Computer Studies*, 57(4):375–395, 2002. Special issue on Interactive Graphical Communication.

[Healey et al., 2003] P.G.T. Healey, M. Purver, J. King, J. Ginzburg, and G. Mills. Experimenting with clarification in dialogue. In R. Alterman and D. Kirsh, editors, *Proceedings of the 25th Annual Conference of the Cognitive Science Society*, pages 539–544. Mahwah, N.J.: LEA, 2003.

[Healey et al., 2004] P.G.T. Healey, J. King, and N. Swoboda. Coordinating conventions in graphical dialogue: Effects of repetition and interaction. In A. Blackwell, K. Marriott, and A. Shimojima, editors, *Diagrammatic Representation and Inference: Proceedings of the 3rd International Conference, Diagrams 2004*, pages 286–300. Berlin: Springer-Verlag, 2004. LNAI 2980.

[Healey et al., 2005] P.G.T. Healey, M. Colman, and M. Thirlwell. Analysing multi-modal communication: Repair-based measures of human communicative coordination. In J. van Kuppevelt, L. Dybkjaer, and N. Bernsen, editors, *Natural, Intelligent and Effective Interaction in Multimodal Dialogue Systems*. Dordrecht: Kluwer Academic, 2005.

[Healey et al., 2007] P.G.T. Healey, N. Swoboda, I. Umata, and J. King. Graphical language games: Interactional constraints on representational form. *Cognitive Science*, 31(2):285–309, 2007.

[Healey, 1997] P.G.T. Healey. Expertise or expert-*ese*?: The emergence of task-oriented sub-languages. In M.G. Shafto and P. Langley, editors, *Proceedings of the 19th Annual Conference of the Cognitive Science Society*, pages 301–306, 1997.

[Jefferson, 1983] G. Jefferson. On exposed and embedded correction in conversation. *Studium Linguistik*, 14:58–68, 1983.

[Karmiloff-Smith, 1979] Annette Karmiloff-Smith. Micro- and macro developmental changes in language acquisition and other representational systems. *Cognitive Science*, 3:91–118, 1979.

[Kirby et al., this volume] S. Kirby, K. Smith, and H. Cornish. Learning, language and cultural evolution: How linguistic transmission leads to cultural adaptation. In R. Cooper and R. Kempson, editors, *Language in Flux: Dialogue Coordination, Language Variation, Language Change and Evolution*. Kings College Press, this volume.

[Krauss and Fussell, 1990] R.M. Krauss and Susan R. Fussell. Mutual knowledge and communicative effectiveness. In J. Galegher, R. Kraut, and C. Egido, editors, *Intellectual Teamwork: Social and Technological Foundations of Cooperative Work*, pages 111–145. Hillsdale, N.J.: Lawrence Earlbaum Associates, 1990.

[Lewis, 1969] D. Lewis. *Convention: A Philosophical Study*. Oxford: Basil Blackwell, 1969.

[Mills and Healey, 2006] G. Mills and P.G.T. Healey. Clarifying spatial descriptions: Local and global effects on semantic coordination. In D. Schlangen and R. Fernandez, editors, *Proceedings of Brandial06 The 10th Workshop on the Semantics and Pragmatics of Dialogue*, pages 122–129, 2006.

[Pickering and Garrod, 2004] M.J. Pickering and S. Garrod. The interactive alignment model. *Behavioral and Brain Sciences*, 27(2):169–189, 2004.

[Pickering and Garrod, 2006] M.J. Pickering and S. Garrod. Alignment as the basis for successful communication. *Research on Language and Computation*, 4:203–228, 2006.

[Pinker and Bloom, 1990] S. Pinker and P. Bloom. Natural language and natural selection. *Behavioral and Brain Sciences*, 13(4):707–784, 1990.

[Purver et al., 2003] M. Purver, P.G. T. Healey, J. King, J. Ginzburg, and G. J. Mills. Answering clarification questions. In *Proceedings of the 4th SIGdial Workshop on Discourse and Dialogue*, pages 23–33, Sapporo, July 2003. Association for Computational Linguistics.

[Robinson and Bannon, 1991] M. Robinson and Liam Bannon. Questioning representations. In L. Bannon, M. Robinson, and K. Schmidt, editors, *Proceedings of the Second European Conference on CSCW*, pages 219–233. Dordrecht: Kluwer, 1991.

[Sacks et al., 1974] H. Sacks, E.A. Schegloff, and G. Jefferson. A simplest systematics for the organization of turn-taking for conversation. *Language*, 50:696–735, 1974.

[Sacks, 1995] Harvey Sacks. *Lectures on Conversation: Volumes I and II*. Oxford: Blackwell, 1995. Edited by Gail Jefferson.

[Saxton et al., 2005] M. Saxton, C. Houston-Price, and N. Dawson. The prompt hypothesis: Clarification requests as corrective input for grammatical errors. *J. Child Language*, 32:643–672, 2005.

[Saxton, 1997] M. Saxton. The contrast theory of negative input. *J. Child Language*, 24:139–161, 1997.

[Schegloff, 1987] Emanuel A. Schegloff. Some sources of misunderstanding in talk-in-interaction. *Linguistics*, 25:201–218, 1987.

[Schegloff, 1992] Emanuel A. Schegloff. Repair after the next turn: The last structurally provided defense of intersubjectivity in conversation. *American Journal of Sociology*, 97(5):1295–1345, 1992.

[Schmidt and Bannon, 1992] K. Schmidt and L. Bannon. Taking cscw seriously: Supporting articulation work. *Computer Supported Cooperative Work (CSCW)*, 1:7–40, 1992.

[Shaw and Gaines, 1988] Mildred L. G. Shaw and Brian R. Gaines. A methodology for recognising consensus, correspondence, conflict and contrast in a knowledge acquisition system. In *Third Workshop on Knowledge Acquisition for Knowledge-Based Systems*. Banff, 1988.

[Steels and Belpaeme, 2005] L. Steels and T. Belpaeme. Coordinating perceptually grounded categories through language: A case study for colour. *Behavioral and Brain Sciences*, 28(4):469–529, 2005.

[Steels and McIntyre, 1997] L. Steels and A. McIntyre. Spatially distributed naming games. *Advances in Complex Systems*, 1(4):301–323, 1997.

[Tversky et al., 1991] B. Tversky, S. Kugelmass, and A. Winter. Cross-cultural and developmental trends in graphic productions. *Cognitive Psychology*, 23:515–557, 1991.

[Tversky, 1995] B. Tversky. Cognitive origins of graphic conventions. In F.T. Marchese, editor, *Understanding Images*, pages 29–53. New York: Springer-Verlag, 1995.

[Wilkes-Gibbs and Clark, 1992] D. Wilkes-Gibbs and H. H. Clark. Coordinating beliefs in conversation. *Journal of Memory and Language*, 31:183–194, 1992.

Patrick G. T. Healey
Department of Computer Science,
Queen Mary University of London
London
ph@dcs.qmul.ac.uk

Dynamics and Adaptiveness of Metacommunicative Interaction in a Foraging Environment

ZORAN MACURA & JONATHAN GINZBURG

1 Introduction

A key feature of natural language is metacommunicative interaction (MCI)—utterance acts in which conversationalists acknowledge understanding or request clarification. The need to verify that mutual understanding among interlocutors has been achieved with respect to any given utterance—and engage in discussion of a clarification request if this is not the case—is one of the central organizing principles of conversation [Schegloff, 1992; Clark, 1996]. Given this, acknowledgements, clarification requests (CRs) and corrections are a key communicative component for a linguistic community. They serve as devices for allaying worries about miscommunication (acknowledgements) or for reducing mismatches about the linguistic system among agents (CRs and corrections).

Communication is critical to social organization. But it is a fragile process, and people often differ in their interpretation of utterances, resulting in miscommunication. The work conducted by Macura and Ginzburg (M&G) [Macura and Ginzburg, 2006b; Ginzburg and Macura, 2007] has provided some evolutionary grounding for MCI, which had not previously been addressed. M&G investigate the significance of MCI in a linguistic population from an evolutionary perspective, building on a formal semantic model of Ginzburg [forthcoming]. The hypothesis that MCI plays a key role in the maintenance of a linguistic interaction system is tested in M&G's work through the use of multi-agent simulation studies. Specifically, artificial life experiments are run on populations of agents who are able to communicate about entities in a simulated environment. Populations which possess MCI capabilities are quantitatively compared with those that lack them with respect to their lexical dynamics.

M&G investigate the significance of MCI in both mono-generational. and multi-generational population settings. In a mono-generational population, where only horizontal language transmission is modelled, both MCI-realized and MCI-non-realized (introspective) populations converge to a shared lexicon, although MCI-realized populations are faster at achieving this. In a multi-generational population, where both horizontal and vertical language transmissions are modelled, the ability to use MCI leads to lexicon sharing, whereas lacking this ability leads to a rapid divergence. That is, while MCI is a part of a linguistic interaction system, a stable language can be maintained over generations. Whereas, without this MCI capacity a language effectively fails.

In this paper we extend M&G's model in order to investigate whether MCI capacity provides an adaptive advantage to a population of foraging agents.

2 Model of MCI with an Ecologically Functional Language

The main emphasis in M&G's model is on the role of cultural transmission of language rather than on biological evolution. Thus, language in this model has no ecological function, and there is no notion of agents' 'fitness' which can be used as a selective bias. Such cultural transmission models (e.g. [Kirby, 2001]) do not put much emphasis on the role of natural selection in language evolution and thus discount the ecological value of language. That is, the main concern is on the role of cultural transmission and individual learning in language evolution. In human societies language does have an ecological function, where sharing of information can be used to enhance some aspects of behaviour. This might be increasing the likelihood of locating food by indicating the whereabouts of food resources or avoiding dangers (such as predators) by indicating presence.

A small number of models have been developed in which language has an ecological effect, improving the viability of agents. Cangelosi and collaborators [Cangelosi and Parisi, 1998; Cangelosi and Harnad, 2001] developed a model in which the emergence of symbolic communication is studied in an environment containing edible and poisonous mushrooms. In this model functional communication systems have been shown to emerge as a consequence of the evolution of internal representations. Another ecological model was inspired by the vervet monkeys' alarm call system [de Jong, 2000]. This model demonstrated that agents can successfully develop a functional lexicon (to avoid predators) by developing categories that represent the agent's and predator's positions, and the appropriate action to take. In both models language has an ecological function with the emphasis on natural selection. But the language itself is innate (and thus discounting the role of cultural transmission), and only the 'fittest' agents are able to reproduce. This is quite a contrast to cultural transmission models, where generational turnover is random.

In this paper we extend M&G's model into a foraging model with an ecologically functional language that is culturally transmitted, and not innate. Agents in this extended model, as well as being able to communicate about plants, can also consume edible plants, ask about their location, and use deception. By consuming edible plants, agents' level of vitality increases, hence increasing their fitness (i.e. likelihood of reproduction). A more detailed description of the model follows.

2.1 Foraging Environment

The environment is modelled loosely after the Sugarscape environment [Epstein and Axtell, 1996], in that it is a spatial grid containing different plants. This environment is similar to the mushroom environment in [Cangelosi and Parisi, 1998; Cangelosi and Harnad, 2001]. Plants can be perceived and disambiguated by the agents. Agents walk randomly in the environment and when proximate to one another engage in a brief conversational interaction concerning visible plants.[1]

As well as being used as topics for conversation, plants in this extended model are also used as a food resource. Two types of plants exist in the environment: *edible* and *inedible*. Edible plants have an energy value, which indicates the energy an agent can gain by consuming them. When a plant is eaten by an agent its energy becomes 0. A plant grows back at the same location according to its 'growth rate' after being consumed, which is the same for every plant. Inedible plants are used just as topics for conversation.

2.2 The Agent

The agent behaviour is extended from the previous behaviour in M&G model. Agents in this model are endowed with the ability to distinguish edible from inedible plants. At every time step, throughout the simulation, each agent goes through the same process of walking, looking, communicating and in addition potentially feeding.

When an agent feeds depends on two conditions: whether the agent can see an edible plant and whether the agent is hungry. Hunger is defined by the time an agent last ate, and it is the same for every agent. An agent can consume a plant only when standing on it—when both the agent and plant are at the same location (i.e. in the same cell in the grid). Upon feeding, an agent gains the amount of energy of the consumed plant. Each agent has a *vitality* which indicates the energy of an agent—gained by consuming edible plants. The vitality value is exclusively used as a selective bias for reproduction. The higher an agent's vitality value is, the likelier it is that this agent will be able to reproduce. But vitality is not used to determine agents' deaths. That is, agents only die from old age (when reaching their maximum age, which is randomly set at the beginning of the simulation) and thus foraging efficiency

---
[1] An agent's field of vision consists of a grid of fixed size originating from his location. Hence proximate agents have overlapping but not identical fields of vision.

does not affect the survivability of an agent—only reproduction.

2.3 Communication Protocol

The fitness of an agent in this foraging model is dependent on her vitality (i.e. the higher her vitality the likelier that she will 'reproduce') and not on communicative success. But in M&G's model, language has no effect on fitness. Agents communicate about random plants and the outcome of their conversation does not affect their subsequent behaviour. The conversation is only used in order to allow the modeller to compare their lexicon dynamics.

In this extended model, conversational interactions are affected by agents' internal states and they also do affect agents' subsequent behaviours. That is, unlike in M&G's original model where a speaker always talks about a random plant in his field of vision, in this model the speaking agent's state of hunger plays a role in determining the topic of conversation. If the speaker is not hungry then the conversational interaction proceeds as 'normal' where the speaker checks for plants in vision and picks a random plant as the topic. The speaker then chooses a word for the topic—the word with the highest association score in his internal lexicon—which he sends to the hearer. The hearer updates her lexicon in the same way as in M&G's model and the conversational interaction terminates.

Deception

A hungry speaker, on the other hand, chooses an inedible plant or one with the lowest energy value as the topic of conversation (depending on the context—plants in vision). This is because the speaker tries to distract the hearer from the edible plant he sees—giving himself an opportunity to eat the plant while the hearer walks away from it (possibly in the direction of the topic plant). Some motivation for this comes from the deceptive strategies found in primate societies [de Waal, 1998]. In the wild, chimps usually forage on their own. But sometimes when coming across food in presence of other chimps, a chimp tries to deceive the others either by behaving indifferently as if not noticing the food and coming back to it when the other chimps are not looking, or by leading the other chimps in the opposite direction away from the food—eventually returning to consume it afterwards.

The deceptive strategy can be useful to the speaker—but only if the hearer understands the word and walks towards the 'correctly' perceived plant. In this case, the speaker benefits from the deception as the hearer steps away from the edible plant—even though the hearer might see it as well and be hungry herself—potentially giving enough time to the speaker to consume the edible plant himself. But the hearer might associate the word heard with a different plant thus move towards the edible plant giving herself a greater chance to consume it before the speaker. In this scenario the misunderstanding is not beneficial to the speaker but it is to the hearer.

Asking for Food Locations

Apart from this new deceptive capability, agents also have the capability to ask for locations of edible plants. This only happens in conversational interactions when the speaker is hungry and has no plants in his visual field. By asking for food locations, the speaker might receive useful information from the hearer potentially reducing the time in finding a food resource. The hearer's reply to the food location query is of the form [*plantName, location*] where *plantName* is the word for a specific edible plant and *location* is the x and y coordinates of that plant. The hearer can either give the name and location of a plant she last consumed, or of an edible plant that is currently in her field of vision.

Upon getting a reply to his query a speaker might react to this information in different ways depending on his MCI capability. If the speaker understands the word *plantName* and thinks it refers to an edible plant then he starts walking towards the *location* in the next time step—even though he does not know the plant's current energy value. On the other hand, if the speaker does not understand *plantName* or thinks that it is inedible he can either make a clarification request trying to clarify the edibility of *plantName* or ignore the hearer's response and continue with the random walk.

2.4 Summary

In this extended model conversational interactions have an effect on agent behaviour. Depending on the situation, speakers and hearers might benefit from successful and unsuccessful conversations. But because of the complex dynamics involved, it is not clear whether or not agents with MCI capacity will have an adaptive advantage. In the next section we will present results of this foraging model where the adaptiveness of MCI agents is investigated in a mixed multi-generational population consisting of both MCI-realized and introspective communities.

3 Experimental Results

3.1 Initial Setup

Before running the experiments an environment is created containing 120 randomly distributed plants. A scarce environment is modelled, where 10% of the plants are edible—12 plant instances in total. The number of different plant types that are edible depends on the plant diversity (i.e. the meaning space). For example, a meaning space of 10 indicates that there are 10 plant types with 12 instances of each plant type in the environment, making up a total of 120 plants. In this case only one plant type is edible. Increasing the meaning space to 20 does not affect the number of edible plants in the environment. Rather the number of edible plant types increases to two, but each plant type now has six plant instances—maintaining the total number of edible plant instances at 12.

The foraging model is initialized with a population of 40 randomly distributed agents—20% of which are infants—and a meaning space of 40. The population consists of two linguistic communities, each community with a distinctive language. That is, there are no common words in the two initial languages. Results are collected at regular intervals in a simulation run—at every 5,000 time steps—and the simulation is stopped when it reaches 1.5 million time steps. All results presented here are averages of 10 simulation runs.

3.2 Lexicon Dynamics

In this section lexicon dynamics of populations that acquire words solely by introspection and those that can learn using MCI are detailed. Specifically, three population types are compared: homogeneous introspective population, homogeneous MCI-realized population and a mixed population—initially made up of both introspective and MCI agents in a 1:1 ratio. Lexicon dynamics are based upon four different behaviours:

Lexical Accuracy The population average of 'correctly' acquired words, where a word is said to be correctly acquired if it is associated with the same meaning as in either of the two initial community lexicons.

Communicative Success The percentage of successfully completed conversations, where a conversation is deemed as successful when the intended meaning by the speaker matches the perceived meaning by the hearer.

Meaning Coverage The average number of meanings expressible by the population, where there is no requirement that meanings have correct associations with words.

Word Coverage The average number of words expressible by the population, where correctness with an associated meaning is not taken into account.

Figure 1 shows the lexicon dynamics for the three population types being investigated. A sharp initial drop in lexical accuracy can be seen in all different population types (Figure 1(a)). The main reason is that as the simulation starts with two distinctive language communities, the initial sharp drop in lexical accuracy occurs because some of the words from one language become predominant thus pass the generational bottleneck, while the competing words are in turn used less frequently and thus do not make it through the generational bottleneck. The fact that infant agents only learn the words uttered by

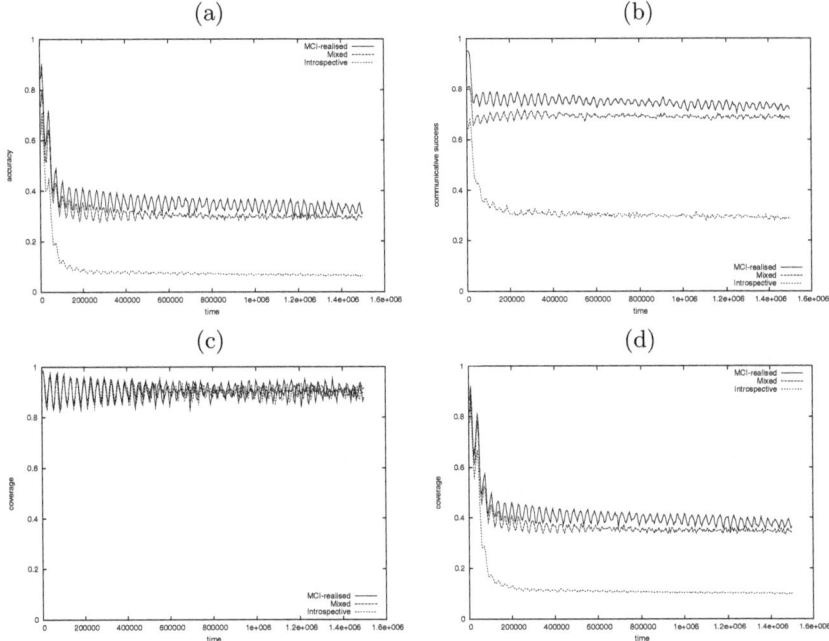

Figure 1. Lexicon dynamics for different populations in which the four behaviours represented are (a) Lexical Accuracy, (b) Communicative Success, (c) Meaning Coverage, and (d) Word Coverage.

their parents makes it very unlikely that the infrequently uttered words will pass to the next generation. After around three generations (100,000 ticks) the lexicon stabilizes for every population, but there is a significant difference in performance between MCI-realized and introspective populations.

The reason for the lexicon stabilization can be explained by looking at the meaning and word coverage results. The meaning coverage for different populations is stable throughout the simulation (all of them are able to express nearly every meaning) as shown in Figure 1(c). The word coverage however drops rapidly along with the lexical accuracy, as seen in Figure 1(d). This is an indication that only the dominant words are surviving. That is, only the dominant words (which are used with the greatest frequency) are acquired by the infants—i.e. pass the generational bottleneck. The less frequently used words are not able to pass through this filter and therefore disappear from the population, which in turn causes the word coverage to decrease. Eventually after a couple of generations the number of words expressible by the MCI-realized populations stabilizes where the number of words is similar to the number of meanings.[2] Thus, every meaning is associated with one (dominant) word. These words can be successfully passed on to the next generation as they are used with greater frequency, causing the lexicon to stabilize.

This is only the case for MCI-realized populations, and not for the introspective population. The lexicon for the introspective population diverges more rapidly, eventually stabilizing at only 10% lexical accuracy. Looking again at Figure 1(d) explains why this happens. The word coverage also drops very sharply, where in the end only 10% of the words are known by the whole population—i.e. four words in total. As the meaning coverage for the introspective population is comparable with other populations (see Figure 1(c)), it can be deduced that these four words are used to express all the 40 meanings. The reason for this is that in an introspective population the words used with the higher frequency are being transmitted to the next generation more effectively, and eventually—as no clarification is ever used—become associated with numerous meanings. This reduces the number of words passed down from generation to generation resulting in a drop in both lexical accuracy and communicative success.

The communicative success is in turn affected by the lexical accuracy, as can be seen in Figure 1(b). The reason is that the higher the lexical accuracy is, the more similar the lexicons are between the agents in the population. Thus the more meaning-word associations the agents share the more successful communications they are likely to have. Note that even though the lexicon is diverging at a fast rate initially, the MCI-realized populations are still able to communicate successfully about different plants. The communicative success in the introspective population, on the other hand, drops very sharply along with the lexical accuracy because of the reasons outlined above.

These results are akin to the non-foraging model previously described in [Macura and Ginzburg, 2006a], where agents are not capable of foraging and the language has no ecological function—agents' communicative abilities do not include deception and asking for food location capabilities.

3.3 Adaptive Advantage of MCI in a Mixed Population

In homogeneous populations all agents are of the same type—have the same MCI capabilities—thus there is no competition for survival between the dif-

---

[2] Note that as there are initially two distinct lexicons the number of words initially in the population is twice as big as the number of meanings—two distinct words per meaning. Once the word coverage drops to around 50%, the number of surviving words still in the population roughly corresponds to the number of meanings.

ferent types of agents (using different MCI strategies). Therefore, the survival/reproduction of a specific type is ensured in such populations, as the offspring at birth will 'inherit' the parent's type (i.e. MCI capability).

In a mixed population, on the other hand, this is not the case. As there are two different communities—one introspective and one MCI-realized—the survival of one type is not ensured. If agents from a specific community have higher vitalities than the agents from the other community they should be more efficient in reproducing. The community with higher natality should have a better chance of survival and become predominant in the population—indicating that it is more adaptive than the other community in this primitive foraging model.

In this section the behaviour of a mixed population in the foraging model is investigated, in order to gain some insight into how the two different communities perform. A mixed population is made up of introspective and MCI-realized agents in a 1:1 ratio (20 agents in each community). The change in the population make-up is monitored over multiple generations in order to determine whether a specific community becomes more predominant in the population—indicating that it has an adaptive advantage.

Results are presented for increasing meaning spaces. Figure 2(a) illustrates the change in the number of MCI and introspective agents when the meaning space is 10. Initially the MCI-realized community increases sharply in numbers reaching a peak of 28 members. The introspective community, on the other hand, reduces in size reaching a total of 12 members. The reason is that MCI agents have higher vitality values and are therefore more likely to have offspring than the introspective agents. After the initial MCI flourishing, the introspective community starts increasing in number and eventually both communities stabilize at 20. Because of their lower vitalities, introspective adults rarely reproduce at first. Therefore, with no infants to feed, the introspective adults accumulate their vitality faster than the MCI parents, thus increasing their likelihood of reproducing later on and eventually recuperating in numbers.

Increasing the meaning space to 20, thus increasing the difficulty of converging to a common language, has a more significant effect on population dynamics as shown by Figure 2(b). The MCI-realized community increases rapidly in number reaching a size of around 30 agents, as was similarly the case for the smaller meaning space of 10. After the initial increase the population stabilizes, where the ratio of MCI to introspective agents is roughly 3:1. The introspective community does not seem to be able to recover from this initial fall, as was observed in Figure 2(a) for a smaller meaning space. Because of the greater difficulty in converging to a common language, introspective agents become less effective in foraging and thus the community is

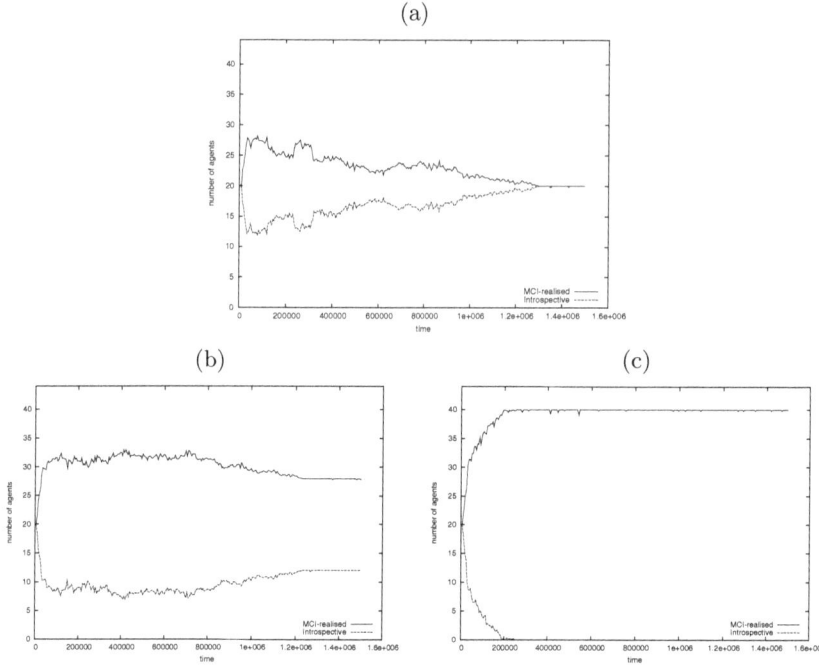

Figure 2. Number of MCI-realized and introspective agents in the population when meaning space equals (a) 10, (b) 20 and (c) 40.

unable to recover in number.

When the meaning space is further increased to 40 the effect on the population dynamics is even more pronounced as shown by Figure 2(c). The MCI-realized community rapidly rises in number and by the 200,000 time steps makes up the whole population. Unlike in the lower meaning spaces experiments, where the introspective community was able to survive to the end of a simulation run, the introspective community was not able to survive when the meaning space was increased to 40.

4 Conclusions

The results demonstrate in a very clear way how adaptive MCI can be in primordial settings of language use. The experiments we ran on foraging populations reveal clear differences in the lexicon dynamics and adaptiveness of populations that acquire words solely by introspection contrasted with populations that learn using MCI. The lexicon diverged at a faster rate for an introspective population, eventually collapsing to a fraction of the initial words which were associated with all meanings. This contrasts sharply with MCI-realized populations in which a lexicon was maintained, where every meaning was associated with a unique word.

With respect to adaptiveness, we have shown that when the meaning space was low—thus an easily learnable language—both communities performed similarly. Even though initially the MCI-realized community had an advantage and increased in number, the introspective community was able to recover and stabilize. Increasing the meaning space made it harder for the introspective community to recover from the initial drop in numbers. No MCI capability meant the agents could not make clarification requests—e.g. after asking for food location—when unsure of the edibility of the plant. Due to a high language divergence, introspective agents had to rely almost exclusively on 'luck' (random walk) in finding food resources, whereas MCI-capable agents could resort to clarification requests when unsure of the edibility of a plant. This increased their competitiveness as they were more successful in finding food resources via communication than the introspective agents. So, in an increasingly complex language MCI is of overwhelming adaptive power and importance. This underscores the importance of integrating MCI into any potentially realistic model of the evolution of language.

BIBLIOGRAPHY

[Cangelosi and Harnad, 2001]   Angelo Cangelosi and Steven Harnad. The adaptive advantage of symbolic theft over sensorimotor toil: Grounding language in perceptual categories. *Evolution of Communication*, 4(1):117–142, 2001.

[Cangelosi and Parisi, 1998]   Angelo Cangelosi and Domenico Parisi. The emergence of a language in an evolving population of neural networks. *Connection Science*, 10(2):83–97, 1998.

[Clark, 1996]   Herbert H. Clark. *Using Language*. Cambridge University Press, Cambridge, 1996.

[de Jong, 2000]   Edwin D. de Jong. *Autonomous Formation of Concepts and Communication*. PhD thesis, Vrije Universiteit Brussel, 2000.

[de Waal, 1998]   Frans de Waal. *Chimpanzee Politics: Power and Sex Among the Apes*. Johns Hopkins University Press, 1998.

[Epstein and Axtell, 1996]   Joshua M. Epstein and Robert Axtell. *Growing Artificial Societies: Social science from the bottom up*. MIT Press, 1996.

[Ginzburg and Macura, 2007]   Jonathan Ginzburg and Zoran Macura. Lexical acquisition with and without metacommunication. In Caroline Lyon, Chrystopher L. Nehaniv, and Angelo Cangelosi, editors, *The Emergence of Communication and Language*, number 4211, pages 287–301, Heidelberg, 2007. Springer Verlag.

[Ginzburg, forthcoming]   Jonathan Ginzburg. *Semantics and Conversation*. Studies in Computational Linguistics. CSLI Publications, Stanford, forthcoming.

[Kirby, 2001]   Simon Kirby. Spontaneous evolution of linguistic structure: an iterated learning model of the emergence of regularity and irregularity. *IEEE Transactions on Evolutionary Computation*, 5(2):102–110, 2001.

[Macura and Ginzburg, 2006a]   Zoran Macura and Jonathan Ginzburg. Acquiring words across generations: introspectively or interactively? In David Schlangen and Raquel Fernandez, editors, *Proceedings of the 10th Workshop on the Semantics and Pragmatics of Dialogue (SemDial-10)*, pages 114–121, 2006.

[Macura and Ginzburg, 2006b]   Zoran Macura and Jonathan Ginzburg. Lexicon convergence in a population with and without metacommunication. In Paul Vogt, editor, *Proceedings of EELC 2006*, number 4211 in Lecture Notes in AI, pages 100–112, Heidelberg, 2006. Springer.

[Schegloff, 1992]   Emanuel A. Schegloff. Repair after next turn: The last structurally provided defense of intersubjectivity in conversation. *American Journal of Sociology*, 97(5):1295–1345, 1992.

Zoran Macura
Department of Computer Science, King's College London, United Kingdom.
zoran.macura@kcl.ac.uk

Jonathan Ginzburg
Department of Computer Science, King's College London, United Kingdom.
jonathan.ginzburg@kcl.ac.uk

Language evolution and George Price's "General Theory of Selection"

GERHARD JÄGER

1 Language evolution

Ever since the development of the evolutionary model in biology in the mid-nineteenth century, people have noted a certain affinity of the evolutionary logic and the development of natural languages. The following well-known citation from Darwin's *The descent of man* perfectly captures this intuition:

> "The formation of different languages and of distinct species, and the proofs that both have been developed through a gradual process, are curiously parallel. ... Max Müller has well remarked: 'A struggle for life is constantly going on amongst the words and grammatical forms in each language. The better, the shorter, the easier forms are constantly gaining the upper hand, and they owe their success to their inherent virtue.' To these important causes of the survival of certain words, mere novelty and fashion may be added; for there is in the mind of man a strong love for slight changes in all things. The survival or preservation of certain favoured words in the struggle for existence is natural selection." [Darwin, 1871, p465f.]

During the twentieth century, the theory of evolution in biology underwent a stunning development. The insights of genetics into the mechanism of heredity clarified the nature of the replication process, leading to the so-called "modern synthesis" of Darwinism with Mendelian genetics (or "Neo-Darwinism", as it is sometimes called). Mathematical frameworks like population genetics or evolutionary game theory led to very exact quantitative models that can be tested empirically with high precision.

In stark contrast to these developments in biology, the evolutionary perspective on natural languages largely remained a metaphor in linguistics during most of the last century. This is undoubtedly due to the fact that the predominant structuralist paradigm focuses on synchronic descriptions of languages rather than on their diachronic development. Also, generative grammar and related frameworks employ mathematical techniques from algebra and formal language theory, which are non-quantitative. As a consequence, languages appear to be discrete objects, while evolution requires a conceptualization of the domain of interest in terms of gradual differences and continuous change.

Nonetheless, the idea of language evolution has attracted a good deal of attention within the last ten years or so. There are at least three independent intellectual developments that led to this renaissance:

- Practical experience has shown that quantitative, statistical models of linguistic phenomena are by far more successful in computational linguistics than the more traditional approaches using discrete mathematics. As a result, quantitative models are taken seriously again in theoretical linguistics. These approaches lend themselves more readily for evolutionary modelling than the traditional algebraic framework (see for instance the work of Kirby [1999] or Wedel [2004]).

- Evolutionary techniques are firmly established by now in neighbouring disciplines like artificial intelligence or artificial life. This serves as a source of inspiration for linguists with a background in computer science (like the work of Luc Steels and his co-workers, see for instance [Steels, 1996]).

- Thanks to the work of popularizers like Richard Dawkins [1976] or Daniel Dennett [1995], the idea of applying the Darwinian logic to cultural phenomena has gained some currency in the humanities in general. Various researchers from historical linguistics have taken up this approach (see for instance [Croft, 2000; Ritt, 2004]).

Partially in parallel, there is also a revived interest in investigating the biological evolution of the human language faculty, as witnessed by publications like [Pinker and Bloom, 1990; Nowak *et al.*, 2002; Hauser *et al.*, 2002].

So while there is a strong interest now in evolutionary approaches to linguistic issues, there is little consensus so far about how exactly language evolution should be conceptualized. The main topic of debate, as far as I can see, is the issue what are the *replicators* in language evolution. The term "replicator" (in the sense of a unit of evolution) was coined by Richard Dawkins in his 1976 book *The Selfish Gene*. According to Dawkins' view, the basic unit of evolution in biology is the gene, the physical carrier of heritable information. Dawkins also argues that any evolutionary process must be based on a population of replicators, i.e. counterparts of genes. He actually invents a new term, "meme", as a unit of replication in cultural evolution.

If this logic is valid, the first step in developing a theory of language evolution is to identify the linguistic units of replication. This proves to be a surprisingly difficult task. There are essentially three modes of replication that play a role in the acquisition and usage of natural language:

a. the biological inheritance of the human language faculty,

b. first language acquisition, which amounts to a vertical replication of language competence from parents (or, more generally, teachers) to infants, and

c. imitation of certain aspects of language performance in language usage (like the repetition of words and constructions, imitation of phonetic idiosyncrasies, priming effects etc.)

It is fairly clear what replicators are for the biological evolution of the language faculty. Since this is just one aspect of biological evolution in general, the carriers of heritable information are of course the genes. For the other two aspects of language evolution, the question is not so easy to answer. What are replicators in iterated language acquisition — entire I-languages? Single Rules? Parameters? Lexical items? The same difficulties arise with respect to replication via language usage. Candidates for the replicator status are phonemes, morphemes, words, constructions etc., or single instances of them (i.e. features of utterances), or mental representations of such instances (so-called "exemplars") etc. A considerable amount of the recent literature on language evolution is actually devoted to foundational questions like this one.

The main point I want to make in this paper is that this issue is actually of little relevance in my view. For one thing, I tend to be sceptical about the usefulness of methodological discussions anyway. The proof of the pudding is in the eating — a certain approach is useful if (and only if) it leads to insightful analyses of linguistic facts. If this is missing, even the most sophisticated discussion of foundational issues will not make up for the lack of it. But quite apart from this general issue, I will try to argue that the programme for analyzing cultural evolution that can be extracted from the work of George Price is perhaps better suited to conceptualize language evolution than Dawkins' memetics or related approaches that assume a very detailed analogy between the cultural and the biological sphere.

2 George Price's "General Theory of Selection"

George Price was certainly one of the more remarkable figures in twentieth century science, even though he has remained relatively obscure even in evolutionary biology, where he made several highly significant contributions. He was a trained chemist, but he dabbled in many intellectual disciplines during his life, including computer science, economics, theology and political science. In 1967, by the age of forty-five, he turned his interest to evolutionary biology. Within the few years until his untimely death in 1975, he made at least three breakthrough discoveries there: he contributed decisively to the advent of evolutionary game theory [Maynard Smith and Price, 1973], he developed the modern interpretation of R.A. Fisher's so-called "Fundamental Theorem of Natural Selection" [Price, 1972b], and he developed the *Price equation*, a very simple and concise mathematical framework to describe evolution via natural selection [Price, 1970, 1972a]. A very recommendable short biography of this remarkable person is given by Schwartz [2000]. Price's contributions to evolutionary biology are described in some detail by Frank [1995].

Around 1971, Price wrote a manuscript titled "The Nature of Selection". It was only published posthumously in 1995 [Price, 1995]. There he sketched a programme for a general theory of evolution (or "selection", as he calls it) which includes biological evolution in the neo-Darwinian sense but encompasses various other kinds of natural and cultural evolution as well. The abstract of the paper starts with:

> "A model that unifies all types of selection (chemical, sociological, genetical, and every other kind of selection) may open the way to develop a general 'Mathematical Theory of Selection' analogous to communication theory." [Price, 1995, p389]

The first paragraph of the paper deserves to be quoted in its entirety:

> "Selection has been studied mainly in genetics, but of course there is much more to selection than just genetical selection. In psychology, for example, trial-and-error learning is simply learning by selection. In chemistry, selection operates in a recrystallization under equilibrium conditions, with impure and irregular crystals dissolving and pure, well-formed crystals growing. In palaeontology and archaeology, selection especially favours stones, pottery, and teeth, and greatly increases the frequency of mandibles among the bones of the hominid skeleton. *In linguistics, selection unceasingly shapes and reshapes phonetics, grammar, and vocabulary*. In history we see political selection in the rise of Macedonia, Rome, and Muscovy. Similarly, economic selection in private enterprise systems causes the rise and fall of firms and products. And science itself is shaped in part by selection, with experimental tests and other criteria selecting among rival hypotheses." [Price, 1995, p389, emphasis added]

Even though Price did not develop a theory of selection in the sense he probably envisioned it, the paper gives good arguments why the Price equation should be the cornerstone of such a theory. In the remainder of this section, I will recapitulate the main argumentation of Price's paper. The interested reader is of course referred to the original article, which is very readable and not overly technical.

First a note on terminology: Price's notion of "selection" is not completely identical to the notion of "evolution" that the present paper deals with. *Selection* can be a one-time process, starting with one state and terminating with a second state. *Evolution (via selection)* (as I use the term) is necessarily an iterated process, spanning several generations. Each generation step is one selection step in the Pricean sense. (Of course there are also notions of "evolution" that do not involve selection at all, which are not further considered here.)

This being said, let us turn to the main points of Price's paper. He distinguishes two senses of the term "selection" (which are both to be covered by a theory of selection). If you go to the marketplace and buy a few apples, you select among all the apples on sale those that you want to buy. This is *subset selection*, because the selected items form a subset of the set on which selection operates. The *Darwinian* notion of selection is different because selection operates on the parent generation while the selected items are the offspring (and these two sets are disjoint). Nevertheless, these two notions can be unified. In either case, we have two points in time, t (before selection takes place) and t' (after selection takes place). Furthermore, there is a set (or a "population") P of entities at t which selection operates on, and a set P' of selected items at t'. In case of subset selection, $P' \subseteq P$. In Darwinian selection, P is the parent generation and P' the offspring. In the example with selection of apples at the marketplace, P is the set of apples that are on sale, and P' is the set of apples that you buy.

Price points out that P and P' need not be finite sets. He also considers an example involving various chemical liquids that are filled from certain containers (time t) into other containers (time t'). Such non-atomic entities like liquids are usually mathematically modelled as infinite (in fact, continuous) sets. The central point for Price's notion of selection is that P and P' are *measurable* quantities. In case of finite sets, the most natural measure is just counting, but continuous measure functions like size, mass or volume, or even more abstract ones like probability, are also applicable. So P and P' are just two measurable quantities. Whatever measure function is applied, the number of items in P is denoted by w, and likewise w' is the number of items in P'. w and w' are non-negative real numbers.

Neither need P and P' be sets of objects of the same nature. Price considers Mussorgsky's creation of "Pictures of an Exhibition" as a case of selection. P is the set of paintings that the composer saw in the exhibition, and P' is the set of musical pieces that were inspired by paintings from P. Another example would be citations: P is a set of journal articles, and P' the set of references (in the sense of lines in the bibliography of some other journal article) to elements of P. Or P could be manuscripts and P' copies of the corresponding books and articles, etc. If P and P' are of a different nature, the measures that are used to obtain w and w' may of course be different. (For evolution via selection, this aspect is of little relevance because the selection process can only be iterated if P' is of the same nature of P.)

The next central ingredient of Price's theory is the idea that P is partitioned into a disjoint portions or *bins*. So technically we have a family of quantities

$p_1, \ldots, p_n$, such that

$$P = \bigcup_{i \leq n} p_i \tag{1}$$

$$p_i \cap p_j = \emptyset \text{ if } i \neq j \tag{2}$$

In the apple example, the obvious partition would be the one where each bin contains exactly one apple. But other partitions are possible as well—like partitioning the apples according to size, or to color, or to price.

To take another example that does not involve subset selection: let P be the set of genes at a certain locus in the parent generation, and P' the corresponding set in the offspring generation. Then P could be partitioned into single molecular copies of the gene in question, i.e. each bin contains one DNA molecule. Alternatively, one might partition P according to alleles. In the latter case, we have few bins, each containing many molecules.

The set P' is partitioned as well, into the same number of bins as P. So we have

$$P' = \bigcup_{i \leq n} p'_i \tag{3}$$

$$p'_i \cap p'_j = \emptyset \text{ if } i \neq j \tag{4}$$

Intuitively, there should be a natural relation between the content of of some bin p'_i and the content of the corresponding bin p_i. Let us again consider subset selection, as illustrated with the apple buying scenario. If I buy the apple in p_i, then $p'_i = p_i$. If, however, I do not buy p_j, then $p'_j = \emptyset$ is just empty. So p'_i is always the set of apples from p_i that I bought.

In the Mussorgsky example, p'_i is the set of musical pieces that were inspired by paintings from p_i. As for citations, p'_i is the set of references to articles in p_i, etc. Needless to say that in the examples with genes, p'_i is the set of DNA molecules that direct copies of some molecule in p_i (at the relevant locus) of some DNA molecule in p_i. Of course p'_i may be empty, or it may contained many more molecules than p_i.

The latter example is instructive because gene copying is mostly but not always *faithful*. Suppose we partitioned P according to alleles. Then all molecules in p_1 will be instances of the same allele — call it r, while all molecules in p_2 are instances of a different allele, say s. DNA copying may involve mutations from s to r and vice versa. Since p'_1 contains exactly the copies of genes in p_1 (including the non-faithful copies), p'_1 may contain s-alleles next to r-alleles. The crucial point here is that the partitioning of P' is induced by the partitioning of P and the copying relation, not by some independent criterion (even if such a criterion was used to partition P). In Price's own words [p392]:

"We will say that a set P' is a *corresponding set* to a set P if there exists a one-to-one correspondence such that, for each member p_i of P there is a corresponding member p'_i of P' which (if not empty) is composed partly or wholly of the same material of p_i, or has been derived directly from p_i, or contains one or more replicas of p_i or some part of p_i, or has some other special close relation to p_i" (emphasis in the original)

(Note that Price does not cleanly distinguish between the set of objects P and the set of bins that jointly constitute P, and—in case p_i is a singleton set—between the set and its only element. No confusion should arise from this though.)

The measure functions that assigned the numbers w and w' to P and P' respectively can also be applied to the various bins of P and P'. So w_i is the amount that is in bin p_i, and w'_i is the amount in p'_i.

The quantity

$$f = \frac{w'}{w}$$

is the growth rate or *fitness* of the entire system. If w and w' are just the number of objects in P and P' respectively, this is the average number of "descendants" that an element of P has in P'. Likewise, we can consider bin-wise fitness

$$f_i = \frac{w'_i}{w_i}$$

which gives the average number of descendants of an object from p_i.

A transition from a set P to a set P' as described so far can only be described as involving *selection* (in a non-technical sense) if the correspondence between elements of P and elements of P' is not random. Rather, whether or not there are many descendants of p_i in p'_i (i.e. whether f_i is high or low) should be correlated with some features of the objects in p_i. Features that lead to high fitness are *selected for*. A smart apple buyer, for instance, will only select high-quality apples (which can be judged from color, surface texture etc.), so only bins containing high quality apples in P will have a non-empty corresponding set in P'. Slightly more technically, high quality apples have a higher fitness than low quality ones. In this case, there is selection for the quality of apples. Analogously, influential papers have a high fitness according to the citation scenario because their corresponding sets contain many citations. An allele has a high fitness if many copies of it are transmitted from generation to generation, etc.

It sounds plausible to say that apples are selected for their quality etc. However, Price's framework is purely quantitative, and therefore selection—in the technical sense—can only operate on quantifiable characters (like size of an apple, or its price, its weight, the percentage of its surface which is red, ...). So let us say that there is is some function μ that measures some quantifiable trait of the objects in P (like total weight, total price etc.). Likewise μ' measures a corresponding trait of objects in P'. Note that μ measures this feature in a cumulative way—$\mu(P)$ is the *total* weight (size, price, ...) of all objects in P taken together. What we are actually interested in though is the *average* value of some objects from P (P') under μ (μ'). Let us call these average values x (before selection) and x' (after selection). They are computed by the formulas:

$$x = \frac{\mu(P)}{w} \tag{5}$$

$$x' = \frac{\mu'(P')}{w'} \tag{6}$$

If P or P' are non-discrete sets, x and x' can be interpreted as something like the average density or concentration of the character μ. The average value of μ can also be calculated for the separate bins:

$$x_i = \frac{\mu(p_i)}{w_i}$$

$$x'_i = \frac{\mu'(p'_i)}{w'_i}$$

(If $w'_i = 0$ for some i, we simply stipulate that $x'_i = 0$ to make sure that this term is always defined.)

Suppose μ is a feature that is usually correlated with high fitness—like a large amount of red skin of an apple. Then objects from P with a high value under μ will have many counterparts in P'. Let us also assume that the degree of μ is passed on with little change from objects in P to their counterparts in P'. In this case, we expect that the average value of μ in P'—x'—will be higher than x. Conversely, if a high value of μ usually goes with low fitness, x' will be smaller than x. The *degree of change* of the average value of μ is notated as Δx. It is defined as

$$\Delta x = x' - x$$

Again this can also be calculated for each bin separately, so we have

$$\Delta x_i = x'_i - x_i$$

Using these definitions, the dynamics of selection can concisely be expressed by the *Price equation*:

$$f\Delta x = \text{Cov}(f_i, x_i) + E(f_i \Delta x_i). \tag{7}$$

We will have to look at each term of this equation separately. The term on the left hand side, $f\Delta x$, is the difference in the average value of μ between t'

(after selection) and t (before selection), multiplied by fitness. So the entire equation is a *difference equation*. (This fact is a bit blurred by the fact that the difference of interest, Δx, is multiplied with f. However, we could as well divide both sides by f to obtain a canonical difference equation.) For the more interesting case that P and P' are sets of the same kind of objects and selection is iterated many times, such an equation can be seen as an update rule that describes the transition from one point in time to the next. More specifically, the equation tells us how the value of x evolves over time. It is important to notice that it is up to the modeller to decide which quantitative character they want to study. x could be the average number of children that a speaker of Esperanto has, but it can also be the probability that a random sentence has OV word order. So essentially the Price equation can be used to study the evolution of any quantitative character, provided the dynamics of the system is well-understood. This, of course, is the difficult part, which is captured by the right hand side of the equation.

The first term, $Cov(f_i, x_i)$, stands for the *covariance* between fitness and the value of x_i, as compared between the different bins. Intuitively, the covariance of two random variables measures how strongly these two variables vary together. If the variables in question are independent of each other, the covariance is 0. If high values of the first variable tend to co-occur with high values of the second variable and vice versa, the covariance, is positive, and if high values of one variable mostly co-occur with low values of the other variable, covariance is negative. This is graphically illustrated in figure 1. Technically the covariance of the two random variables X and Y is defined as

$$Cov(X_i, Y_i) = (\sum_i p_i X_i Y_i) - (\sum_i p_i X_i)(\sum_i p_i Y_i), \tag{8}$$

where the index i gives the number of an event and p_i (which is not to be confused with the i-th bin of P in Price's notation) the probability of this event.

In the Price equation, the events in question are the bins $1, \ldots, n$. If some object is picked out from P at random, the probability that it comes from p_i is $\frac{w_i}{w}$. So spelled out, the first term on the right hand side expands to

$$Cov(f_i, x_i) = (\sum_i \frac{w_i}{w} f_i x_i) - fx. \tag{9}$$

(I made tacit use from the fact that the average fitness is f, and the average value of x_i is x.)

If bins with a high average value of μ, i.e. with a high x_i, tend to have many offspring (meaning: large correspondence sets in P') and vice versa, there is a positive correlation between x_i and f_i. This means that $Cov(f_i, x_i)$

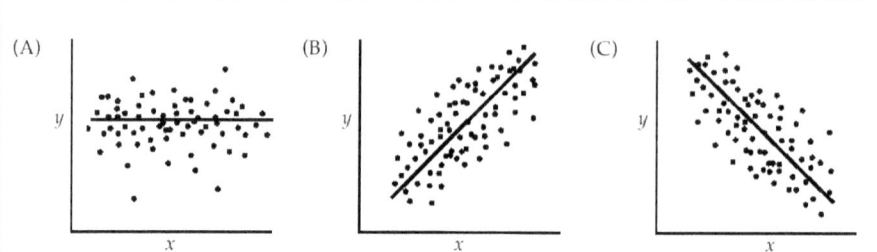

- (A) $Cov(x, y) = 0$: no dependency between x and y
- (B) $Cov(x, y) > 0$: high values of x correspond, on average, to high values of y and vice versa
- (C) $Cov(x, y) < 0$: high values of x correspond, on average, to low values of y and vice versa

Figure 1. The concept of covariance

is positive. Conversely, if high values of x_i are correlated with low fitness, $Cov(f_i, x_i)$ is negative. This is intuitively unsurprising—if a certain character is correlated with high fitness, we expect it to be strongly represented in the next generation, i.e. Δx should be positive. Likewise, if a high value of μ is an indicator of low fitness, the average value of μ will decrease over time. So the first term on the right hand side simply covers the essential intuition of Darwinism: characters that lead to high fitness will spread in the population.

This logic only works if the degree of μ is passed on faithfully from parents to offspring. Price's framework does not require copying fidelity though. Unfaithful reproduction of μ is dealt with by the second term, $E(f_i \Delta x_i)$. $E(X)$ is the expectation value—i.e. the weighted average—of the random variable X. So the second term of the Price equation can be spelled out as

$$E(f_i \Delta x_i) = \sum_i \frac{w_i}{w} f_i \Delta x_i. \tag{10}$$

What is the value of Δx_i? We start with the apple example again. Suppose p_i contains a single apple that is selected. Then $p'_i = p_i$, and $x'_i = x_i$, hence $\Delta x_i = 0$. If, however, the apple in p_i is not selected, both $x'_i = 0$ and $f_i = 0$. Hence $f_i \Delta x_i = 0$ as well. So in this scenario, $E(f_i \Delta x_i) = 0$. Here each "surviving" object in P' is exactly identical to its counterpart in P, hence replication is entirely faithful. Let us consider an example where this is not the case.

Suppose there are two alleles of some gene, s and t. The fitness of s-genes is exactly 2, i.e. each s-gene has exactly two offspring. The fitness of the t-allele is only 0.5—only every second copy has one offspring on average. Also, suppose that there are 300 copies of the gene in question in P, 100 s-alleles and 200 t-alleles. So we have

$$\begin{aligned} w &= 300 \\ w' &= 300 \\ w_s &= 100 \\ w_t &= 200 \\ w'_s &= 200 \\ w'_t &= 100 \\ f &= 1 \\ f_s &= 2 \\ f_t &= \frac{1}{2} \end{aligned}$$

Note that w'_s is not necessarily the number of s-alleles in the offspring generation, but the number of offspring that have an s-parent! In fact, we assume that only t-alleles are entirely faithfully reproduced. An s-allele, however, has a 50% chance to mutate into an t-allele.

Let $\mu = \mu'$ be the function that counts the number of s-alleles in a set. Then we have

$$\begin{aligned}
\mu(P) &= 100 \\
\mu(p_s) &= 100 \\
\mu(p_t) &= 0 \\
x &= \frac{1}{3} \\
x_s &= 1 \\
x_t &= 0 \\
\mu'(p'_s) &= 100 \\
\mu'(p'_t) &= 0 \\
x' &= \frac{1}{3} \\
x'_s &= \frac{1}{2} \\
x'_t &= 0 \\
\Delta x &= 0 \\
\Delta x_s &= -\frac{1}{2} \\
\Delta x_t &= 0
\end{aligned}$$

This means that the first term of the Price equation is positive:

$$Cov(f_i, x_i) = \frac{1}{3}$$

x has a high value—1—within the s-subpopulation, and a low value—0—within the t-subpopulation. Also, s-alleles have a higher fitness than t-alleles. So high values of x go with high fitness and vice versa. Hence the covariance is positive.

The second term is negative though:

$$E(f_i \Delta x_i) = -\frac{1}{3}$$

This is so because the value of x may change from 1 to 0 under mutation, but not vice versa. So the average difference between x' and x under replication is negative. In the example the number are chosen in such a way that P and P' actually have an identical composition and the two terms on the right hand side cancel each other out.

In this example, the covariance term covers the change of x that is due to selection, while the second term takes care of changes that are due to mutation.

Under this interpretation, the Price equation is one way to express the so-called *replication-mutation dynamics* that is well-studied in theoretical biology (but mostly by different analytical means, especially by the so-called *quasi-species* model).

Depending on how the P-population is split into bins, the two terms of the equation may also receive a different interpretation though. Suppose there are two types of individuals in a species, altruistic ones and selfish ones. These are genetically determined traits. Altruistic individuals, by definition, behave in such a way that their interaction partners profit from the interaction, i.e. they receive a higher fitness than without the interaction. The altruists themselves do not profit from the interaction. (We may think of the two strategies of the well-known Prisoner's Dilemma in this context.)

Now suppose the population is structured into groups in such a way that everybody only interacts with partners within the same group. One possible application of the Price equation here is to identify the partition cells p_i with those groups. Then f_i is the fitness, i.e. the average reproduction rate, of an entire group. Let us furthermore assume that there are no mutations whatsoever and reproduction is asexual, so altruistic parents will have altruistic offspring only, and selfish parents selfish offspring.

If a group p_i contains many altruistic individuals, many of its member will benefit from interaction with the altruists and receive a high fitness. So f_i will be high. Conversely, a group consisting mainly of egoists will receive a low average fitness. So if x_i is the relative frequency of altruists within group p_i, high values of x_i go with high fitness and vice versa. So the first term of the equation, $Cov(f_i, x_i)$, is positive. This term measures *selection between groups*. The fact that it is positive means that groups with many altruists have an advantage over groups with many egoists.

The second term, however, measures *selection within groups*. On average a selfish individual will have more offspring than an altruistic one. So the percentage of altruists within one group will decrease from generation to generation. Hence Δx_i (and therefore also $f_i \Delta x_i$) will be negative for all i, which means that $E(f_i \Delta x_i)$ is also negative. So the qualitative interpretation here is that between-group selection favors altruism, while within-group selection favors selfishness. Depending on the relative strength of these two forces, the term on the left hand side will be positive, zero or negative. If between-group selection is strong enough, altruism may actually survive in the long run.

In biology, the Price equation is used mainly to study this kind of competition between group level and individual level selection. However, as the previous example illustrated, the framework is general enough to accommodate very diverse scenarios.

If this framework is used to model population dynamics, we are forced to assume discrete time steps, and one generation is completely replaced by the next generation when going from t to t'. A more realistic model would assume that some small portions of the population reproduce with small time intervals. If the population is large enough, this can legitimately be approximated by a process with continuous time. In [Price, 1972a] it is shown that this continuous time approximation can be described by the following version of the Price equation:

$$\dot{E}(x) = Cov(f_i, x_i) + E(\dot{x}_i) \qquad (11)$$

The expression $\dot{\phi}$ gives the first derivative of some variable ϕ against time. Intuitively this is the rate of change of that variable. If $\dot{\phi} = 0$, the value of ϕ does not change. $\dot{\phi} > 0$ means that the value of ϕ increases and vice versa.

Equation (11) is a *differential equation*—actually one of a particularly well-behaved kind, because it is an ordinary autonomous differential equation. By choosing different quantitative traits for μ/x, we can use (11) to set up a system of such differential equations that describes the dynamics of the domain which is modelled. The theory of this kind of equations is well-understood. In many cases it is even possible to solve them analytically, and even if this is not possible, there are established techniques to predict the qualitative long-run behaviour of the dynamical system in question. Also, there are good numerical algorithms to study the behaviour of such a system.

It is important to appreciate that the Price equation (both the discrete time version and the continuous time version) is a tautology. It follows directly from the assumptions about P and P', their correspondence relation, the partition into bins etc. Even though the derivation of the actual equation is not straightforward (and will not be explained here—the interested reader is referred to literature, for instance to [Frank, 1995]), it does not add any new information. The equations simply makes the implicit assumptions of the model explicit.

The main reason that I find Price's approach appealing for studying language evolution is not that it leads to systems of ordinary differential equations (even though this is certainly an asset). Rather, it imposes a certain intellectual discipline which I think is healthy. At the same time, it gives the modeller all the freedom that is needed to study a certain phenomenon, without enforcing a certain ontology that may be useful in one discipline but misplaced in another one. Let me spell out these two aspects in detail.

To apply Price's model—which means, in the end, to come up with an instance of his equation—the modeller has to be absolutely clear what is being modelled. There has to be absolute clarity about

- what the sets P and P' are,
- how P is partitioned into bins,

- what correspondence relation is assumed and what partition this relation imposes on P', and

- which quantitative character μ (or rather its average x) is being studied.

On the other hand, the approach is extremely flexible and general. P and P' can be any sets you like, as long as P' is, in whatever abstract sense, "later" than P and some well-defined correspondence relation can be established between the sets. P and P' even need not consist of empirical objects. We could imagine a set of empirical objects M and its descendants N; and an abstract sample space Ω (which can for instance be identified with the interval $[0, 1]$). Nothing prevents us from defining P as $M \times \Omega$ and P' as $N \times \Omega$. For instance, this would enable us to split an integral empirical object from M into disjoint fractions and to put them into different bins, which may be useful for a given application.

The only requirement on the correspondence relation is that it uniquely induces a partition of P' from a given partition of P. This is guaranteed if it is a function from P' to P.[1] The correspondence relation is the closest counterpart to the notion of "replication" in other conceptualizations of evolution. However, no specific requirements are made in Price's framework regarding the nature of correspondence. Neither need its domain and range (P' and P) be discrete sets with atomic elements ("replicators"), nor is there any requirement that there is any copying fidelity between correspondents. "Unfaithful" correspondence simply means that the second term (on the right hand side) of the equation is non-negligible. In principle this even covers dynamic systems where the elements are neither created nor destroyed but simply change states according to some transition probabilities (so-called Markov processes). In a Markov process, the fitness of each bin is a constant (namely 1), and the covariance term becomes 0. So the right hand side reduces to the second term.

One might object that such an extreme case cannot be called "evolution" anymore. It is certainly true that the covariance term of the equation pretty much captures the intuitive content of "evolution via replication and selection". However, reality does not care about the conceptual distinction between "evolutionary" and "non-evolutionary" processes, and it therefore strikes me as an advantage that Price's approach is tailored to capture the effects of selection and of non-faithful correspondence within one model.

---

[1] To be perfectly precise, it has to be a measurable function under w/w' and μ/μ'. In the case of finite sets, every function is automatically measurable. For infinite measurable sets, measurability of the function means that the image of a measurable subset of P' is a measurable subset of P.

3 Applications

In this section I will present two applications of the framework described above. My point here is not primarily to propose certain analyses but to give some examples of applications of the Price equation to demonstrate its versatility. The examples are essentially taken from the literature; its formalization in terms of the Price equation is new though.

3.1 Nowak's model of grammar evolution

In a series of publications, Martin Nowak and his co-workers developed a formal model of the evolutionary dynamics that is induced by iterated grammar acquisition (see for instance [Komarova et al., 2001; Nowak et al., 2001]). In the sequel I will use the version from [Nowak, 2006, chapter 13], as basis for discussion.

Grammars are culturally transmitted from the parent generation to infants. This is a form of replication, and thus a candidate for being the base of an evolutionary process. Nowak assumes that there are only finitely many grammars that are compatible with UG, $G_1, \ldots, G_n$.[2] The languages that are generated by these grammars need not be disjoint, but there may be a degree of mutual intelligibility of speakers of different grammars. Let a_{ij} be the probability that a sentence uttered by a speaker of grammar G_i is correctly understood by a speaker of grammar G_j. The chances that speakers of grammars G_i and G_j can communicate with each other (if both assume the roles of speaker and listener with equal probability) is then

$$F(G_i, G_j) = \frac{1}{2}(a_{ij} + a_{ji}) \qquad (12)$$

Now suppose that the population is mixed, and that the number of speakers of grammar G_i is w_i, for all i. The total population size is $w = \sum_i w_i$. If everybody speaks with everybody else with equal probability, the chance of successful communication of a speaker of G_i are then

$$f_i = \sum_j \frac{w_j}{w} F(G_i, G_j) \qquad (13)$$

(This is strictly speaking wrong because it assumes that people talk to themselves with the same probability as with everybody else. If the population is sufficiently large, this effect is negligible though, and the definition above is a licit simplification.)

---

[2]This assumption is not uncontested, and frankly, I consider it wrong because grammars are probabilistic rather than algebraic entities. But it is nevertheless instructive to study the evolutionary consequences of the simplifying assumption of a finite grammar space.

The key assumption of Nowak's model is that communicative success immediately translates into fitness. Briefly put, an eloquent individual is supposed to have, on average, more offspring than a less eloquent one. That this is indeed the case seems plausible, given that eloquence raises social status, which in turn increases reproductive chances. Of course there are many other factors determining fitness, but it is legitimate to construct a simple model where the selective effects of communicative success are studied in isolation.

Nowak's assumption are somewhat stronger even, because the fitness differences induced by differential communicative success have to be quantitatively proportional to the differences in expected communicative success. This is perhaps too strong an assumption, but it is the null hypothesis as long as no more information about the quantitative relation between communicative and replicative success is available.

Ignoring the intricacies of sexual reproduction, the model assumes that each infant acquires its grammar from its parents. Grammars are discrete entities, and effects like bilingualism or language contact are not part of the model. Language acquisition may be imperfect though. There is an error matrix Q with the intended interpretation that a child acquiring its language from a parent using G_i will acquire G_j is Q_{ij}. If language acquisition is fairly accurate, Q_{ii} should be close to 1, but this assumption is not part of the model.

Now all ingredients are in place to apply Price's analytical technique. The population before selection, P, is the set of speakers in the parent generation. P' is the children generation. We assume that every infant acquires its grammar from exactly one adult, so the the natural correspondence relation between a and b is: b acquired its grammar from a. An obvious way to split P into bins is given by the grammars of the speakers: p_i is the set of speakers in the parent generation using grammar G_i. This, together with the correspondence relation, induces a partition of P' as well. p'_i is the set of infants that acquired their grammar from a speaker of G_i. Note that the infants in p'_i need not all be speakers of G_i due to imperfect language acquisition.

Let $\mu^*(M)$ be the number of speakers of grammar G_{i^*} within the set M. We define

$$x_i^* = \frac{\mu^*(p_i)}{w_i} \tag{14}$$

$$x_i'^* = \frac{\mu^*(p'_i)}{f_i w_i} \tag{15}$$

$$f = \sum_i \frac{w_i}{w} f_i \tag{16}$$

$$\Delta x_i^* = x_i'^* - x_i^* \tag{17}$$

Applied to the total population, Δx^* is the change of the relative frequency of

G_{i*} within the population during the transition from the parent generation to the children generation.

The Price equation then says:

$$f\Delta x^* = Cov(f_i, x_i^*) - E(f_i \Delta x_i^*) \tag{18}$$

Let us look at the two terms on the right-hand side in turn.

The covariance term is defined as

$$Cov(f_i, x_i^*) = \sum_i \frac{w_i}{w} f_i x_i^* - f \sum_i \frac{w_i}{w} x_i^* \tag{19}$$

Now note that $x_{i*}^* = 1$ and $x_i^* = 0$ if $i \neq i^*$. So we can simplify to

$$Cov(f_i, x_i^*) = \frac{w_{i*}}{w} f_{i*} - f \frac{w_{i*}}{w} \tag{20}$$

$$= \frac{w_{i*}}{w} (f_{i*} - f) \tag{21}$$

The second term is defined as

$$E(f_i \Delta x_i^*) = \sum_i \frac{w_i}{w} f_i (x_i'^* - x_i^*) \tag{22}$$

Note that $x_i'^* = q_{ii*}$. So we can simplify to

$$E(f_i \Delta x_i^*) = \sum_i \frac{w_i}{w} f_i (q_{ii*} - x_i^*) \tag{23}$$

$$= \frac{w_{i*}}{w} f_{i*} (q_{i*i*} - 1) + \sum_{i \neq i*} \frac{w_i}{w} f_i q_{ii*} \tag{24}$$

$$= \sum_i \frac{w_i}{w} f_i q_{ii*} - \frac{w_{i*}}{w} f_{i*} \tag{25}$$

Putting the two terms together, we get

$$f\Delta x^* = \frac{w_{i*}}{w}(f_{i*} - f) + \sum_i \frac{w_i}{w} f_i q_{ii*} - \frac{w_{i*}}{w} f_{i*} \tag{26}$$

$$= \sum_i \frac{w_i}{w} f_i q_{ii*} - \frac{w_{i*}}{w} f \tag{27}$$

Without going into the details of the continuous time model, I just mention here that the version of the Price equation in this case looks almost identical, namely: Putting the two terms together, we get

$$\dot{x}^* = \sum_i \frac{w_i}{w} f_i q_{ii*} - \frac{w_{i*}}{w} f \tag{28}$$

This is exactly the *replicator-mutator equation* that Nowak uses in his model (even though he derives it in a different way). The bulk of Nowak's work about this model concerns conditions on learning precision that are necessary to guarantee stability of a coherent language in a population. For these investigations, the reader is referred to the original literature. My point in this subsection was to show how the Price framework can be used to model the iterated-learning notion of language evolution in a precise quantitative way, thereby taking the effects of imperfect learning into account.

3.2 Exemplar dynamics and blending inheritance

Exemplar based approaches to cognitive processing and representation, originally deriving from psychology, have gained high interest in several areas of linguistics in recent years (see for instance the articles in [Gahl and Yu, 2006], a special issue of *The Linguistic Review* on exemplar-based models in linguistics). The overarching idea of exemplar theory is that instances of linguistic events (both production and comprehension) are stored in a highly detailed fashion in memory. So even if two utterance tokens belong to the same type—like two utterances of the same word with the same meaning, they are memorized separately and in a detailed fashion. This may include specific information about phonetic parameters (like fundamental and formant frequencies of segments, their length etc.) as well as information about the specific syntactic context (i.e. cooccurrence with other lexical items) and the like. An exemplar is a detailed cognitive representation of an event, alongside with a categorization. So for instance, the exemplar of a vowel consists of a category (like the phoneme /a/) alongside with specific information about its phonetic representation like formant frequencies.

An important aspect of exemplar theories is that they assume a similarity metric over exemplars. Processing of new exemplars is based on analogy with similar exemplars. In the simplest implementation of this idea, exemplars consist of points in an n-dimensional vector space, together with a category label. A new perceptual event is categorized by analogy with the closest exemplars in its neighborhood. Likewise, new exemplars of a given category are located in the neighborhood of previously stored exemplars of the same category.

Since new exemplars are generated in analogy to old ones, the dynamics of the exemplar "population" can be considered an evolutionary process, as has been observed by various authors like Batali [2002] and Wedel [2004]. In this subsection I will analyze a very simple version of exemplar dynamics in detail. It is inspired by Pierrehumbert [2001].

Suppose exemplars are points in some n-dimensional vector space. We can think of them as phonetic events, where the dimensions are parameters like fundamental frequency, formant frequency, length, volume and the like (or rather their articulatory correlates). For simplicity, we only consider exemplars of one category, so the category labels can be ignored. In Pierrehumbert's model it is assumed that each exemplar has an activation level that decays over time. The impact of an old exemplar on new events is correlated with its activation, so that recent exemplars have the strongest impact. For simplicity's sake, I assume that the memory stores m-many exemplars, which all have the same activation level. If a new exemplar is added to the memory, one old item is picked out at random and removed instead.

In each cycle, a new exemplar is generated by picking out k-many exemplars from memory at random (with $k \geq 2$), and forming the average of this random sample. In a vector space, the average of k vectors is simply the arithmetic mean:

$$\text{av}(s_1, \ldots, s_k) = \frac{1}{k} \sum_{i=1}^{k} s_i \qquad (29)$$

Figure 2 gives some snapshots from a computer simulation of this model. Here the vector space has two dimension. The memory always contains $m = 100$ exemplars, and each sample consists of $k = 10$ items. At the beginning of the simulation, the memory is initialized with random exemplars (first picture). The cloud of exemplars constantly gravitates towards the centre, and after about 200 cycles, all items in memory are located in a small area. Pierrehumbert's simulations are somewhat more complex but show the same qualitative behaviour. She points out that this illustrates category formation via entrenchment. Even though the microscopic structure of the exemplar space is continuous (or at least very fine-grained), all exemplars of a category tend to gravitate towards the centre of the extension of this category, which leads to the emergence of categoricity at the macroscopic level.

This model is interesting for the issue of evolutionary modelling because it displays—as pointed out by Wedel [2004]—*blending inheritance*. Each new exemplar is causally connected to the sample of k old exemplars of which it is the arithmetic mean. So in a sense, each new exemplar has k parents. However, the features of the offspring are not faithfully inherited from any of the parents. Rather, they are a blend of the features of all parents. So this dynamics is qualitatively different from the neo-Darwinian conception of biological evolution because there are no discrete units of inheritance that are faithfully passed on. Nonetheless, Price's framework is general enough to cope with this kind of evolution as well.

To fit this version of exemplar dynamics into Price's model, we have to decide what the sets P and P' are, what the correspondence relation is like etc. An obvious starting point is to say that t is a certain point in time when the memory contains a certain population of exemplars, and t' is the point in

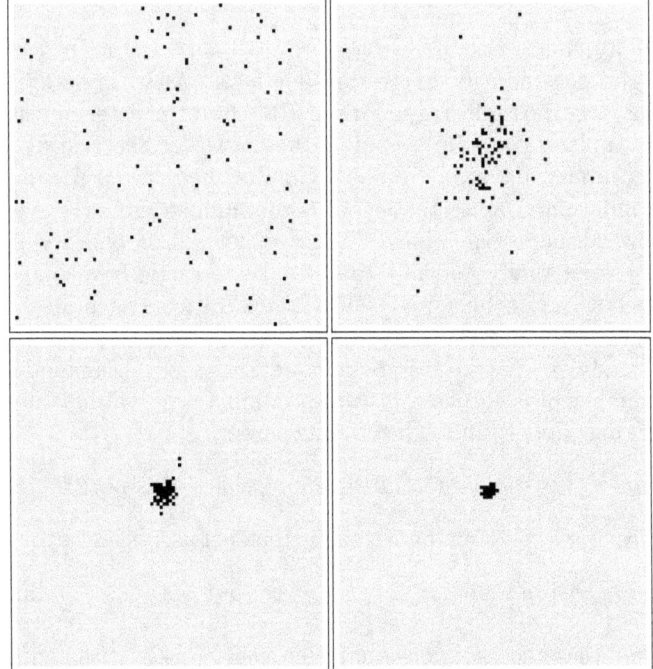

Figure 2. Simulation after 0, 90, 180, and 240 iterations

time when a new exemplar has been added (which replaces an old exemplar). It is not so clear so that the nature of the correspondence relation should be then. All the surviving old exemplars naturally correspond to themselves, but the new exemplar equally corresponds to all of its k "parents". Therefore we have to construct a slightly more abstract model. Let us say that P consists of k isomorphic copies of the memory at time t, and P' accordingly of k copies of the memory at t'. (If this is too abstract, you can also conceptualize this as splitting each exemplars into k equal parts.) Now each copy of the new exemplar corresponds to some copy of one of its parents—and each parent exemplar has a copy that corresponds to one copy of the offspring exemplar. All copies of old exemplars correspond to themselves. In this way each element of P' has exactly one correspondent in P, as desired. For reasons that will become clear immediately, we furthermore assume that P' is not the set of exemplars one time step after t. Instead, we take P' to be the set of exemplars after g-many time-steps, where $g \geq 1$.

Since the dynamics that is investigated here is a random process, it is not possible to give deterministic expressions for f_i etc. All we know are probability distributions over possible trajectories. To obtain a deterministic dynamic system, we apply a common technique here: we let the size of all relevant sets grow to infinity and study the behaviour of the relevant parameters under this model inflation. Due to the law of large numbers, relative average values converge towards expected values. Since we know all probability distributions involved, we can actually calculate those values. So strictly speaking we do not study the behaviour of the actual, finite model, but the asymptotic properties of the model as the model size grows to infinity.

We will study the asymptotic behaviour of the exemplar model described if m, the number of exemplars, grows to infinity. We will also use two more parameters that grow to infinity, but at a slower rate:

- $b = \lceil m^{1/4} \rceil$ is the number of bins into which P is partitioned,[3] and
- $g = \lceil m^{1/2} \rceil$ is the number of time steps between t and t'.

In this way we ensure that $\lim_{m \to \infty} b, g = \infty$, but $\lim_{m \to \infty} \frac{b}{g} = \lim_{m \to \infty} \frac{g}{m} = 0$.

We assume that the n-dimensional vector space is partitioned into b cells. You can imagine this as an ever-finer grid that is laid over the vector space. p_i is the set of copies of exemplars at time t that are within the i-th partition cell. (We can assume, without restriction of generality, that each p_i is non-empty, because empty bins have a 0-weight and therefore have no impact on the expectation values that figure in the Price equation.) p'_i, accordingly, is the set of items that correspond to some item in p_i.

As P and P' are finite sets, the measure function w simply measures the cardinality of sets. So we have

$$f_i = \frac{|p'_i|}{|p_i|}.$$

What is the cardinality of p'_i? The probability that the k copies of some exemplar from p_i do not survive within a single time step is $\frac{w_i}{w}$, so the expected number of items from p_i that do not survive is $\frac{kgw_i}{w}$. The probability that an exemplar from p_i is used to spawn a new exemplar (of which one copy belongs to p'_i) within a single round is $\frac{kw_i}{w}$. So the expected number of new items in p'_i that belong to newly created exemplars is $\frac{kgw_i}{w}$ as well. Hence the expected change in cardinality from p_i to p'_i is 0. Therefore the expected fitness f_i for

---
[3] $\lceil x \rceil$ is the smallest integer $\geq x$.

each i is 1, and, using the notation $\alpha \to \beta$ for "α converges to β if m grows to infinity", we have

$$Cov(f_i, x_i) \to 0, \qquad (30)$$

no matter what parameter x we care to consider—the covariance of a constant with any random variable is always 0. So the entire dynamics is encapsulated in the second term of the Price equation this time.

The parameter x can be anything we like, so we start with studying the arithmetic mean c of all exemplars in memory. If v_j is the j-th exemplar, we have

$$c = \frac{1}{m} \sum_{j=1}^{m} v_j. \qquad (31)$$

In physical terms, this can be interpreted as the centre of gravity of the memory, if each exemplar has the same mass. Let $c(d)$ be the coordinate of c at the d-th dimension.

Let us say that $p_i(d)$ is the arithmetic mean of the d-th dimension of the objects in p_i (which are all n-dimensional vectors). Likewise, $p'_i(d)$ is the average of the d-th coordinates of the copies in p'_i. (If $p'_i = \emptyset$, we stipulate that $p'_i(d) = 0$.) We define

$$x(d) = E(p_i(d)) \qquad (32)$$
$$x'(d) = E(p'_i(d)) \qquad (33)$$
$$\Delta x(d) = x'(d) - x(d). \qquad (34)$$

It follows directly from the definition of c that $x(d)$ is the d-th coordinate of c at time t, and $x'(d)$ is the d-th coordinate of c at time t'.

The discrete-time Price equation now becomes

$$\Delta x(d) = \sum_i \frac{w_i}{w}(p'_i(d) - p_i(d)) \qquad (35)$$
$$= \sum_i \frac{w_i}{w} p'_i(d) - x(d) \qquad (36)$$

Note that $|p'_i| = w_i$ and $p'_i(d) = |p'_i|^{-1} \sum_{v \in p'_i} v(d)$. Also, $|P| = km$. Hence we can simplify to

$$\Delta x(d) = \frac{\sum_{v \in P'} v(d)}{km} - x(d) \qquad (37)$$

Let us consider the term $\frac{\sum_{v \in P'} v(d)}{km}$, which is the centre of gravity of all objects in P'. Each $v \in P'$ is either a survivor from P, or it is a new exemplar, i.e.

the average of some sample of k objects from the previous round. Of the items in P, kg-many do not survive in P'. Each non-surviving exemplar from P is chosen at random, so the expected average of the non-survivors is identical with c, with $x(d)$ as its d-th coordinate. Likewise, each new exemplar is the average of a random sample of exemplars. Hence the expected d-th coordinate of each new exemplar is $x(d)$ as well. There are g-many new exemplars that are added between t and t'. As g converges to infinity as m grows to infinity, the average of the new exemplars converges to their expected value, $x(d)$. Hence the average of the items in P', $\frac{\sum_{v \in P'} v(d)}{km}$, converges to $x(d)$ as well. So we have

$$\Delta x(d) \to x(d) - x(d) \tag{38}$$
$$= 0. \tag{39}$$

In words, the centre of gravity of the population of exemplars remains constant. At least this is the limit behaviour of this dynamics for large population—for smaller populations the centre of gravity undergoes some random drift due to sampling effects.

As a next step, we analyze the evolution of the variance of the population. (Recall that the variance of a random variable X is defined as the expected value of $(X - E(X))^2$.) To this end we can posit another instance of the Price equation. First some notation:

$$Var(P(d)) = \sum_i \frac{w_i}{w}(p_i(d) - x(d))^2 \tag{40}$$

$$Var(P'(d)) = \sum_i \frac{w_i}{w}(p'_i(d) - x(d))^2 \tag{41}$$

$$\Delta Var(d) = Var(P'(d)) - Var(P(d)) \tag{42}$$

Plugging the variance into the Price equation, we get:

$$\Delta Var(d) = E((p'_i(d) - x(d))^2 - (p_i(d) - x(d))^2) \tag{43}$$

What is $p'_i(d)$? It obviously holds that

$$p'_i(d) = \frac{1}{|p'_i|} \sum_{v \in p'_i} v(d) \tag{44}$$

Let D_i be the set of items from p_i that do not survive in p'_i. Also, let N_i be the set of items in p'_i that are copies of new exemplars that have been added between t and t'. Let $N_i(d) = \sum_{v \in N_i} v(d)$, and likewise for $D_i(d)$. We thus have:

$$|p'_i| \rightarrow w_i \tag{45}$$
$$|D_i| \rightarrow \frac{w_i}{w}gk \tag{46}$$
$$|N_i| \rightarrow \frac{w_i}{w}gk \tag{47}$$
$$p'_i = (p_i - D_i) \cup N_i \tag{48}$$
$$p_i \cap N_i = \emptyset \tag{49}$$

We therefore get

$$p'_i(d) = \frac{1}{|p'_i|}(\sum_{v \in p_i} v - \sum_{v \in D_i} v + \sum_{v \in N_i} v) \tag{50}$$
$$= p_i(d) - \frac{1}{|p'_i|}(\sum_{v \in D_i} v + \sum_{v \in N_i} v) \tag{51}$$
$$= p_i(d) - \frac{|D_i|}{|p'_i|}D_i(d) + \frac{|N_i|}{|p'_i|}N_i(d) \tag{52}$$
$$\rightarrow p_i(d) - \frac{gk}{w}D_i(d) + \frac{gk}{w}N_i(d) \tag{53}$$

The elements of D_i are drawn at random from p_i, so

$$D_i(d) \rightarrow p_i(d) \tag{54}$$

Each element of N_i is the average of k random samples from P. So the expected average of N_i is identical to the average of P, and we thus have

$$N_i(d) \rightarrow x(d) \tag{55}$$

Putting all this together, we get

$$p'_i(d) \rightarrow p_i(d) - \frac{gk}{w}p_i(d) + \frac{gk}{w}x(d) \tag{56}$$
$$= (1 - \frac{gk}{w})p_i(d) + \frac{gk}{w}x(d). \tag{57}$$

Therefore

$$p'_i(d) - x(d) \rightarrow (1 - \frac{gk}{w})(p_i(d) - x(d)) \tag{58}$$
$$(p'_i(d) - x(d))^2 \rightarrow (1 - \frac{gk}{w})^2(p_i(d) - x(d))^2 \tag{59}$$
$$(p'_i(d) - x(d))^2 - (p_i(d) - x(d))^2 \rightarrow ((1 - \frac{gk}{w})^2 - 1)(p_i(d) - x(d))^2 \tag{60}$$
$$\tag{61}$$

As abbreviation, we use

$$\alpha = ((1 - \frac{gk}{w})^2 - 1) \qquad (62)$$

Obviously $\alpha < 0$. Equation (43) now reduces to

$$\Delta Var(d) \rightarrow \alpha Var(P(d)) \qquad (63)$$

The continuous time version of the Price equation takes an even simpler form. If we assume that one unit of time corresponds to m update steps, the slope of $Var(d)$ is the limit $\frac{\alpha}{g}$, which converges to 2 as m grows to infinity. Therefore we get

$$\dot{Var}(d) = -2Var(d) \qquad (64)$$

As $\alpha < 0$, both versions of the Price equation predict that the variance of the exemplars decreases at an exponential rate and asymptotically approaches 0. Since the centre of gravity remains constant over time, this means that in the long run, all exemplars are concentrated in an arbitrarily small environment around c. The continuous time version of the Price equation can even be solved analytically; all functions of the form

$$Var(d) = K \exp(-2t) \qquad (65)$$

for some constant K are possible solutions, and each solution converges to 0 as t goes to $+\infty$.

4 Conclusion

The main purpose of this article is to bring the conceptual framework that underlies the Price equation to the attention of linguists that are interested in evolutionary modelling. Price's framework has several attractive features that are briefly recapitulated here:

- Price's framework is very general. It does not over-emphasize certain features of biological evolution that are specific to biology rather than to the notion of evolution via selection—like assuming discrete units of heritable information or the dual ontology of genotype and phenotype. Rather, it focuses on population dynamics as such.

- There are no specific requirements about what the nature of the populations involved or the correspondence relation between them is. It is thus clear that evolution and selection are a perspective under which empirical phenomena can be studied, rather than being objective properties of these phenomena. Identifying a certain set as an evolving population and a certain relation between stages of this set as replication (i.e. correspondence) is a matter of practicality and usefulness, not of truth or falsity.

- In particular, Price's framework does not require anything like copying fidelity of replicators to be applicable. If a certain process does in fact involve faithfully replicating entities, this simplifies the analysis because the second term of the Price equation can be dropped in this case. However, this is a matter of convenience, not of principle.

- While Price's framework admits considerable methodological freedom, it enforces an absolutely rigorous analysis, once the basic modelling decisions are made.

In the second part of the paper, I presented two case studies of applications of the Price framework to language evolution. The examples involved two quite different notions of linguistics replication: first language acquisition in the first case and exemplar imitation in the second case. Both processes involve non-faithful replication; imperfect learning in the first example and blending inheritance in the second one. The main point of the discussion of the examples was to illustrate possible applications of Price's framework in linguistics. In both cases, the Price style model confirmed previous findings: Nowak's different mathematical approach in the first case and Pierrehumbert's computational simulation results in the second case.

BIBLIOGRAPHY

[Batali, 2002] John Batali. The negotiation and acquisition of recursive grammars as a result of competition among exemplars. In Ted Briscoe, editor, *Linguistic evolution through language acquisition: Formal and computational models*, pages 111–172. Cambridge University Press, Cambridge, UK, 2002.

[Croft, 2000] William Croft. *Explaining Language Change*. Longman, New York, 2000.

[Darwin, 1871] Charles Darwin. *The descent of man, and selection in relation to sex*. John Murray, London, 1871.

[Dawkins, 1976] Richard Dawkins. *The Selfish Gene*. Oxford University Press, Oxford, 1976.

[Dennett, 1995] Daniel C. Dennett. *Darwin's Dangerous Idea*. Simon & Schuster, New York, 1995.

[Frank, 1995] Steven A. Frank. George Price's contributions to evolutionary genetics. *Journal of Theoretical Biology*, 175(3):373–388, 1995.

[Gahl and Yu, 2006] Susanne Gahl and Alan C. L. Yu, editors. *Exemplar-Based Models in Linguistics*, volume 23 of *The Linguistic Review*. Walter de Gruyter, Berlin, New York, 2006. Special theme issue.

[Hauser et al., 2002] Marc D. Hauser, Noam Chomsky, and William T. Fitch. The faculty of language: What is it, who has it, and how did it evolve? *Science*, 298(5598):1569, 2002.

[Kirby, 1999] Simon Kirby. *Function, Selection, and Innateness*. Oxford University Press, Oxford, 1999.

[Komarova et al., 2001]   Natalia L. Komarova, Partha Niyogi, and Martin A. Nowak. The evolutionary dynamics of grammar acquisition. *Journal of Theoretical Biology*, 209:43–59, 2001.

[Maynard Smith and Price, 1973]   John Maynard Smith and George R. Price. The logic of animal conflict. *Nature*, 246(5427):15–18, 1973.

[Nowak et al., 2001]   Martin A. Nowak, Natalia L. Komarova, and Partha Niyogi. Evolution of universal grammar. *Science*, 291:114–118, 2001.

[Nowak et al., 2002]   Martin A. Nowak, Natalia L. Komarova, and Partha Niyogi. Computational and evolutionary aspects of language. *Nature*, 417:611–617, 2002.

[Nowak, 2006]   Martin A. Nowak. *Evolutionary Dynamics. Exploring the Equations of Life*. Harvard University Press, Cambridge, Mass. and London, 2006.

[Pierrehumbert, 2001]   Janet Pierrehumbert. Exemplar dynamics: Word frequency, lenition and contrast. *Typological studies in language*, 45:137–158, 2001.

[Pinker and Bloom, 1990]   Steven Pinker and Paul Bloom. Natural language and natural selection. *Behavioral and Brain Sciences*, 13(4):707–784, 1990.

[Price, 1970]   George R. Price. Selection and covariance. *Nature*, 227(5257):520–521, 1970.

[Price, 1972a]   George R. Price. Extension of covariance selection mathematics. *Annals of Human Genetics*, 35(4):485–490, 1972.

[Price, 1972b]   George R. Price. Fisher's 'fundamental theorem' made clear. *Annals of Human Genetics*, 36(2):129–40, 1972.

[Price, 1995]   George R. Price. The nature of selection. *Journal of Theoretical Biology*, 175(3):373–388, 1995.

[Ritt, 2004]   Nikolaus Ritt. *Selfish Sounds and Linguistic Evolution: A Darwinian Approach to Language Change*. Cambridge University Press, 2004.

[Schwartz, 2000]   James Schwartz. Death of an altruist. *Lingua Franca: The Review of Academic Life*, 10:51–61, 2000.

[Steels, 1996]   Luc Steels. Emergent adaptive lexicons. In P. Maes, M. J. Mataric, J. A. Meyer, J. Pollack, and S. W. Wilson, editors, *Fourth International Conference on Simulation of Adaptive Behavior; Cape Cod, Massachusetts*, pages 562–567. MIT, 1996.

[Wedel, 2004]   Andrew Wedel. *Self-Organization and Categorical Behavior in Phonology*. PhD thesis, University of California at Santa Cruz, 2004.

Gerhard Jäger
Department of Linguistics and Literature, University of Bielefeld, Germany.
Gerhard.Jaeger@uni-bielefeld.de

Language, Learning and Cultural Evolution: How linguistic transmission leads to cumulative adaptation

SIMON KIRBY[1], KENNY SMITH AND HANNAH CORNISH

1 Introduction

An explanatory approach to language must, among other things, answer the question why language is structured in the particular way it is and not some other way. In other words, we seek to account for the particular universal properties of linguistic structure. Attempts to tackle this challenge take many forms [Hawkins, 1988], but in this chapter we look at a particular type of explanation, which we can term the *adaptive systems approach*.

This approach to an explanatory account for language focuses on its dynamical aspects, noting that the universal properties of language are actually the result of multiple complex dynamical systems operating on different time-scales each influencing the others. Specifically:

- **Learning/use.** The language produced by an individual is shaped in part by the cognitive mechanisms for learning and processing language. In other words, an individual's language adapts on an ontogenetic time-scale through acquisition and use.

- **Cultural[2] evolution.** The actual language spoken by any individual is also, obviously, a result of the language spoken by other individuals in the community and goes on to affect the language of future generations of speakers. Language universals arise from the interaction of individuals with particular cognitive and usage-based constraints in populations who share language. To put it another way, language is

---

[1]Author to whom correspondence should be addressed.
[2]The use of the term *culture* is potentially problematic. Throughout this chapter we use it in a technical sense to mean any information that is transmitted through a population by means of production of behaviour by an individual and acquisition of similar behaviour by another individual through observation. Language is transmitted culturally in this sense, but this does not mean it is necessarily shaped by other aspects of the "culture" of the individuals that posses it.

transmitted through a repeated cycle of learning and use leading to a process of change and evolution on a cultural time-scale (e.g. [Brighton et al., 2005]).

- **Biological evolution.** Finally, the cognitive machinery that drives the cultural evolution of language is itself the result of biological evolution. This leads to the possibility that the universals that emerge through cultural evolution may alter the fitness landscape of the individuals that learn and use these languages, ultimately leading to the biological evolution of the mechanisms for learning and processing language (e.g. [Briscoe, 2000]).

When we talk about these systems as being *adaptive* we mean that they result in the "appearance of design". That is, there is a fit between the structure that is the result of the dynamical system and some function of that structure. Adaptation is most familiar in the context of biological evolution, where natural selection is often seen as an optimizing process generating phenotypes that are fit for survival and reproduction, but our point is that this is only one example of possible adaptive mechanisms.

At the core of this multiple adaptive systems approach to language is the idea that a) much of language structure is adaptive and b) whilst *appearing* to be designed there is no actual designer involved. This chapter will look mainly at the latter claim with respect to cultural evolution in particular by reference to mathematical, computational and experimental models of the transmission of language. Briefly, we aim to show that the process of transmission of language through repeated acquisition and use leads to cumulative adaptations without the need for biological evolution or any intention to adapt language on the part of those that use it.

2 The orthodox evolutionary view

Faced with explaining the universal properties of linguistic structure, one influential approach has been a direct appeal to biology. In this view, language structure arises from our species-specific biological endowment – we have the types of languages that we do because we have an innately-given language faculty with a particular structure that constrains the possible types of language (e.g. [Hoekstra and Kooij, 1988]). In particular, Chomsky [1975] suggests that it is a set of innate constraints on language acquisition that determines the nature of human language.

For many (e.g. Hurford [1990]) this is an unsatisfying explanation as it stands, since it appears simply to push the need for answers back but not dispel them. It transforms one puzzle "why do we have the particular language universals we do?" into another "why do we have the particular language fac-

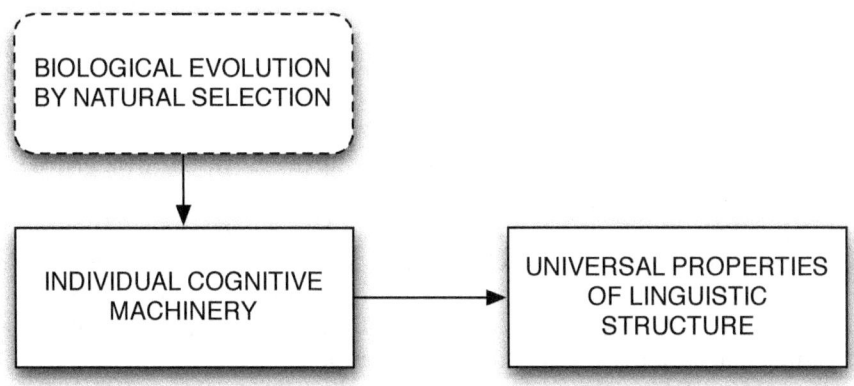

Figure 1. The orthodox evolutionary view. The universal properties of linguistic structure are determined by the nature of our individual cognitive machinery which is the result of biological evolution under natural selection for communication.

ulty we do?". In a landmark paper Pinker and Bloom [1990] set out a strategy for answering this second question in order to support a broadly nativist approach to explanation. This strategy has become what might be called the orthodox evolutionary approach to language (see figure 2).

Pinker and Bloom argue that language structure has all the hallmarks of an adaptation. To them, many of the fundamental features of language appear to be tailored to communicating complex propositions through a serial signalling medium. If Chomsky is right in arguing that these features of language are the way they are because they arise from an innately given faculty for language, then this makes language appear like many other features of our biology. The language faculty, like the heart or the liver, is an organ that appears adapted to a particular survival-relevant function – in this case communication.

If this is correct then the structure of the language faculty, like the structure of other organs, is best explained by appealing to biological evolution by natural selection. As they put it:

> Grammar is a complex mechanism tailored to the transmission of propositional structures through a serial interface... Evolutionary theory offers clear criteria for when a trait should be attributed to natural selection: complex design for some function, and the absence of alternative processes capable of explaining such complexity. Human

language meets this criterion. [Pinker and Bloom, 1990, p707]

This biological/evolutionary approach to linguistic explanation is appealing since it neatly grounds out the explanation of linguistic structure in the well-established mechanism of natural selection.

Despite its appeal, there are reasons to be cautious with this orthodox evolutionary approach as it stands. One problem with the view portrayed in figure 2 is the link between "individual cognitive machinery" and "universal properties of linguistic structure". The Chomskyan approach to explaining language universals rests on a tacit assumption that constraints/biases on language acquisition will directly lead to equivalent constraints/biases on the distribution of possible human languages. But is this assumption justified?

A lesson can be learned from a different way of explaining language universals known as the *functional/typological* approach. Here, universals are explained by appealing not to innate characteristics of our language acquisition machinery, but rather to properties of the uses language is put to. We will not be looking at this literature in any detail here, but one of the criticisms levelled at it is that it fails to solve what has been termed *the problem of linkage*: how exactly does a feature of language use end up being reflected in the cross-linguistic distribution of language types [Kirby, 1999]? The point is not that this problem is insoluble, but rather it is an absolutely crucial part of any explanation. What is the mechanism that links the proposed *explanans* to the *explanandum* in question?

This linkage problem exists just as forcefully for the Chomskyan approach (see [Kirby et al., 2004] for discussion):

Problem of Linkage. Given a set of observed constraints on cross-linguistic variation, and a corresponding pattern of functional preference *or language acquisition biases*, an explanation of this fit will solve the problem: how does the latter give rise to the former? (Italic text added to the original definition from [Kirby, 1999])

What is needed is a way of bridging the gap between an individual-level phenomenon (the structure of a language-learner's cognitive machinery) and a population-level phenomenon (the distribution of possible languages). As Kirby *et al.* [2004] argue, the solution to this problem is to explicitly model the way in which individual behaviour leads to population effects over time. As noted in the introduction, language emerges out of a repeated cycle of language learning and language use, and it is by studying this socio-cultural process directly that we will see how properties of the individual leave their mark on the universal structure of language.

Of course, it may well be that when we examine this linking mechanism we will find that language universals do indeed straightforwardly reflect language learning biases, for example. If this is the case, then the orthodox evolutionary

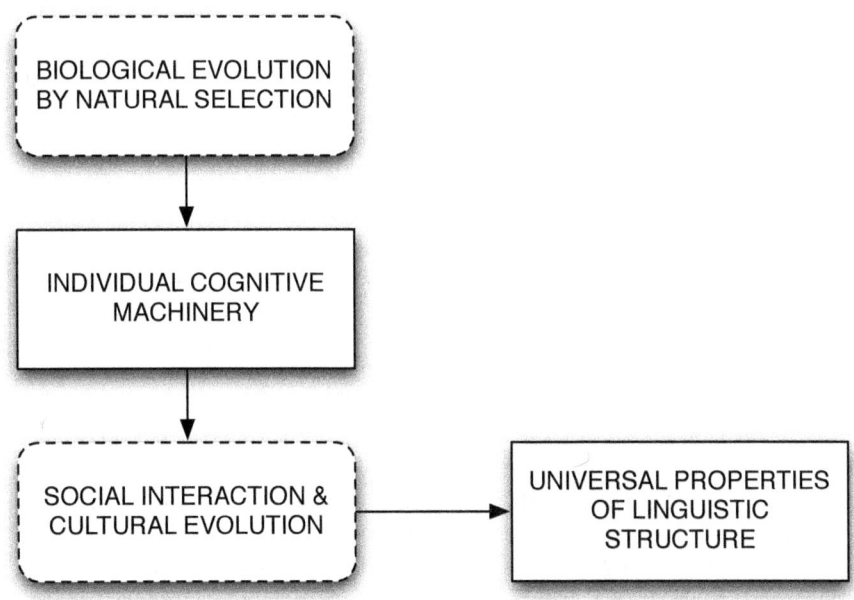

Figure 2. The solution to the Problem of Linkage. The universal properties of language arise from the cultural evolution of language through generations of socially interacting individuals with particular cognitive machinery. Of central importance is the precise contribution of the cultural evolutionary process in determining language structure.

explanation is a reasonable one. However if the extra box in figure 2 does some work for us, then this explanation cannot hold – at least in its present form. Indeed, we may find that the explanatory burden may be lifted to some extent from our innate machinery, and hence from biological adaptation through natural selection.

3 Modelling cultural evolution

So far we have identified the importance of understanding cultural evolution as it applies to language because it represents the solution to the problem of linkage in the orthodox explanation for linguistic structure. The difficulty is that we have a surprisingly poor understanding of exactly how cultural evolution actually works in general (although there is a growing literature, e.g. [Boyd and Richerson, 1985; Mesoudi *et al.*, 2006a]). Compared to our detailed empirical and theoretical understanding of language acquisition, for example, or the process of biological evolution by natural selection, we do not have a strong empirical base for cultural evolution or an accepted set of principles for how individual biases lead to population-level phenomena.

There is, of course, an extensive literature on historical linguistics which appears relevant. It is important to note that our target is subtly different. When linguists study language *change*, they consider how a language at one point in time turns into a different language at a later point. However, we would expect both of these languages to fall within the boundaries described by our theory of language universals. Normally, historical linguists are interested in how languages move around the space of possible languages rather than in the origins of that space in the first place.[3] We will return to this distinction later in a more formal context.

In order to better understand how cultural evolution works in general, and how it operates in shaping language in particular, we have set out to model it in three different ways over the past decade or so (given here in the order they have been explored):

- **Computational models.** Our first approach was to build simulations of populations of individuals with particular language learning machinery and see what types of languages emerge. The goal here was to examine the extent to which the resulting language structure was determined by features of the cultural transmission process rather than being directly encoded in the learning mechanisms (e.g. [Kirby, 1994, 1999; Kirby and Hurford, 2002; Smith, 2002; Smith *et al.*, 2003]).

- **Mathematical models.** Based on our experience of the computational models, we developed an idealized mathematical framework which enabled us to state precisely how much our innate endowment determines the structure of language (e.g. [Kirby *et al.*, 2007]).

- **Experimental models.** Finally, to act as a check on the plausibility of the formal models and to see how closely human subjects behave like their computational idealizations, we developed a novel experimental paradigm for cultural evolution (e.g. [Cornish, 2006]).

All three of these are based on a framework for understanding cultural evolution we have called the *iterated learning model* (see figure 3). Iterated

---

[3]There are some exceptions to this. For example, there have been attempts to apply grammaticalization theory to the origins of language by reconstructing a pre-existing state where language universals would have been different [Heine and Kuteva, 2002].

learning is the fundamental process underlying many forms of cultural evolution, including language. It is the process of the transmission of behaviour where that behaviour is acquired by an individual observing similar behaviour in another who acquired it in the same way. The model, based on Andersen's and Hurford's treats the transmission of language as a repeated transformation between some linguistic representation internal to an individual (or "agent" to use the modeller's parlance) and utterances that are external to that individual and can be observed by another. It is through being repeatedly learned and used by agents in the model that language evolves culturally.

Because our aim here is not a theory of language change, we do not typically start the models off with something that falls within the space of possible human languages. Instead we are interested in how (and whether) such human-like languages emerge in the models when one is not present in the initial conditions (see [Brighton, 2003], for a detailed discussion of the methodological issues this raises). By varying features of the way in which language is transmitted from agent to agent in the models, we can begin to build-up a picture of how cultural evolution might work.

For the remainder of this chapter, we will briefly review the main results so far from the three strands of modelling research listed above and discuss what they tell us about how we should approach linguistic explanation. Of particular interest will be the question: how much of language structure that appears to be designed for communication need not be explained in terms of the intentions of communicating agents at all?

4 Computational models: language transmission is adaptive

Since the early nineties, there have been a variety of attempts by a number of researchers (e.g. [Kirby, 1994, 2002a; Batali, 1998; Teal and Taylor, 1999; Tonkes, 2001; Smith, 2002; Steels et al., 2002; Brighton, 2003; Zuidema, 2003; de Boer, 2001; Vogt, 2005; Smith, 2005; Oudeyer, 2006]) to build simulation models of the cultural evolution of language (see, e.g. [Kirby, 2002b; Steels, 2003] for review and [Brighton et al., 2005] for a detailed account of one particular strand of research). Most of these models adopt a framework similar to the one outlined in figure 3: a population of agents produce language-like behaviour in response to observing similar behaviour in other members of the population. They differ (often radically) in their assumptions about the nature of the population, their model of learning, and exactly what form the agents' language takes. For example, Batali [2002] has a model in which there is a relatively large but static population of agents throughout the simulation, whereas Kirby [2000] implements a model with purely vertical cultural transmission in a chain of "adults" and "children".

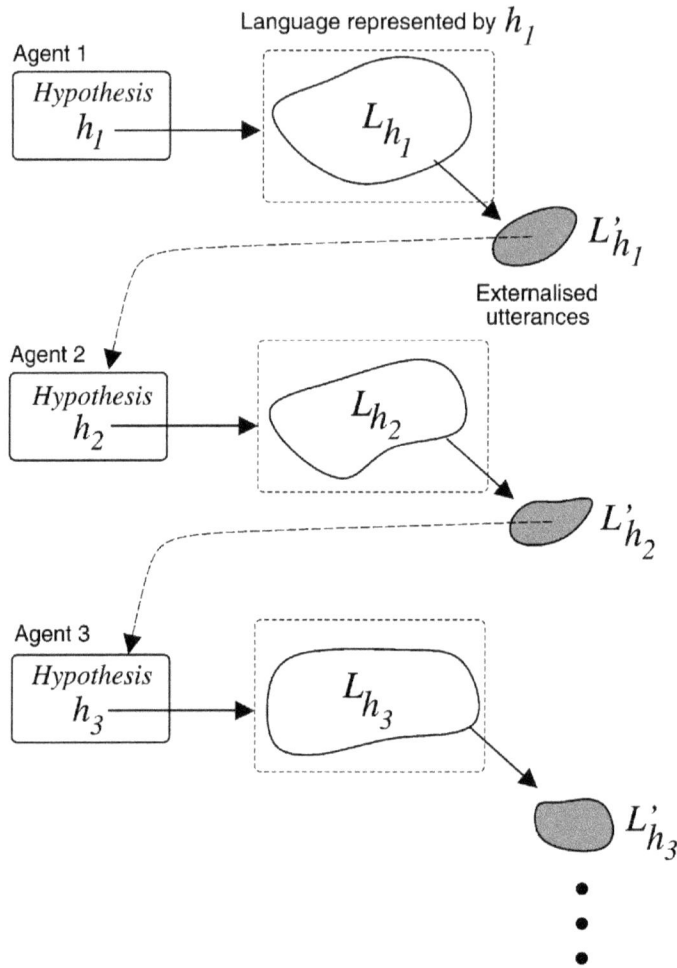

Figure 3. The Iterated Learning Model. The first agent has knowledge of language represented by a hypothesis h_1. *This hypothesis itself represents a language L_{h1}. Some subset of this mapping, L'_{h1}, is externalized as linguistic performance for the next agent to learn from. The process of learning results in a hypothesis h_2. The process is then repeated, generation after generation.*(Taken from [Brighton et al, 2005, p185])

In the former, no-one is born and no-one dies, but in the latter there is strict generational turnover with the children replacing the adults each generation and a new set of children being introduced. In [Batali, 1998] agents are recurrent neural networks being trained using standard connectionist algorithms, whereas Brighton's [2002] agents induce finite state machines using Minimum Description Length learning. In [Kirby, 2002a], agents communicate meanings represented as hierarchical symbolic propositions, whereas Vogt's [2005] agents play communication games grounded in visual stimuli. Despite the large range of different assumptions, methods and motivations across these models one broad conclusion seems warranted (cf. [Christiansen, 1994; Deacon, 1997]):

> **The Principle of Linguistic Adaptation:** if a learner is given imperfect information about the language they are attempting to learn (e.g. if they are subject to noise, processing constraints, or they simply do not hear all the data), then cultural transmission becomes an adaptive system. As a result, languages will emerge that appear to be optimized to the problem of being transmitted from individual to individual.

We can think of the transmission of the knowledge of language from one agent to another as passing through a narrow "bottleneck". A large (or potentially infinite) language must be reconstructed by a learner despite the imperfect information imposed by the bottleneck.[4] The very act of repeatedly squeezing language through this bottleneck causes language to change in such a way that its chance of being transmitted through the bottleneck with high fidelity is maximized.

The literature provides numerous examples of the principle of linguistic adaptation at work in simulations and shows how it can be used to cast light on specific linguistic problems. Here we provide three illustrations from our own work in this area. These summaries are necessarily brief, but nevertheless we hope they will give a flavour of the work in this area.

4.1 Hierarchical universals and competing motivations

Language universals of the sort discussed in the typological literature are often implicational in nature (e.g. [Croft, 1990]). That is, languages are predicted to have property Q if they also have property P, but not necessarily vice versa. In other words: P→Q. In some cases, researchers have uncovered whole chains of implications of the form P→Q & Q→R & R→S etc. These are often rewritten in the form of hierarchies of types: S>R>Q>P. Languages which exhibit a feature at some point in the hierarchy will also exhibit all the features higher in the hierarchy.

---

[4]Note that this way of expressing things suggests an analysis of this sort of cultural evolution along the lines of [Sperber, 1996]. However, it is also possible that the evolution of language in these models could be studied in terms of populations of competing replicators (e.g. [Croft, 2000; Kirby, 1999]).

An influential typological study of relative clause formation provides a prototypical study of hierarchical universals. Keenan and Comrie [1977] present evidence for the following hierarchy of accessibility to relative clause formation:

The Relative Clause Accessibility Hierarchy:
Subject>Direct Object>Indirect Object>Oblique>Genitive>Object of Comparison
If a language can relativize any position on this hierarchy, they can relativize all higher positions in the hierarchy.

How might we explain a universal pattern such as this one? Kirby [1997] examines an explanation due to Hawkins [1994] that appeals to asymmetries in the difficulty in processing different relative clauses. Simplifying somewhat, the idea is that the greater the structural distance between a head noun and the trace (or resumptive pronoun) in a relative clause, the greater the load there is on the working memory of the parser. However, this fails to explain why there should be a link between processing load during parsing and the observed universal – what is the mechanism that links the two?

In order to solve the problem of linkage here, Kirby [1997] sets out to model, in a simple simulation, how this parsing preference actually results in a hierarchical universal.[5] The simulation consists of a population of agents. Each agent has a grammar which either allows or disallows relative clauses for each point on the hierarchy. The population of agents is updated through a process of generational turnover whereby a new population of agents is created; each agent in the previous generation produces example relative clauses according to their grammar; and the new agents acquire their grammars on the basis of the examples produced by the agents from the previous generation. The learning mechanism is set up in such a way that the probability that a learner acquires a particular relative clause type is dependent both on the number of examples the learner hears and the parsing difficulty associated with each clause type. This implements in a straightforward way a parsing-based bottleneck on the cultural transmission of language.

The results of this model immediately demonstrate a problem with the explanation for Keenan and Comrie's [1977] hierarchy as it stands. No matter what the initial distribution of languages is in the population, the only stable end state is one where languages don't allow any relative clauses at all. It is easy to see why this happens: language is simply adapting to the complexity of

---

[5]Although this explanation appeals to parsing preferences that are arguably innately given, it appears to be of a rather different type than the Chomskyan style of explanation from innate language acquisition constraints outlined earlier. Indeed the problem of linkage referred to here is essentially the one that pervades much functional explanation of typological generalizations. Nevertheless, as we shall see, exactly the same linkage problem exists for explanations appealing to acquisition constraints/biases, and the solution to the problem is the same as well.

processing relative clauses. The most adapted languages are those that avoid the problem of relative clause processing by rendering them ungrammatical.

Kirby [1997] shows that this is a general problem with any explanation for hierarchical universals that appeals to an asymmetry in processing difficulty. The solution, verified by the simulation model, is to seek a *competing functional motivation* favouring the structure in question. Interestingly, this competing motivation need not be asymmetrical with respect to the different types on the hierarchy. So, all that is needed to derive the observed distribution of language types in the simulation is a general speaker-driven least-effort principle that *favours* relative clauses of all types equally, for example because they avoid the need for circumlocution. With this pressure acting on speakers (and some assumptions about how the relative strengths of pressures may vary over time) the end result of the simulation is a distribution of languages that obeys the Keenan and Comrie [1977] hierarchy. All the language types at the start of the simulation that do not correspond to those found in the world today disappear.

What these results demonstrate is that languages can adapt to competing needs of speakers and hearers as they influence the bottleneck on linguistic transmission. The hierarchy is not built-in directly as a set of constraints on possible languages – nor do the agents in any way try and optimize the language they have. The universal emerges as a population-level effect from processing pressures acting on individuals influencing the transmission of language through iterated learning.

4.2 Compositionality and morphological regularity

Whereas the early iterated learning models looked at specific language universals of the sort uncovered by typological surveys, with steadily increasing computing power and interest in the evolution of language there has been a desire among many researchers to simulate the emergence of language out of a pre-existing a-lingual state. For example, could some of the fundamental features of syntax be shown to evolve from a largely non-syntactic protolanguage[6] solely through cultural processes?

A particularly fundamental structural feature of language that sets it apart from almost all other communication systems in nature is *compositionality*. It is regular compositionality in the mapping between signals and meanings that, when recursively applied, gives language its completely open-ended expressivity. Drawing on a variety of evidence, Wray [1998] proposes an earlier stage in the evolution of language where signals and meanings are not related compositionally, but rather whole signals correspond to whole meanings. This

---

[6]We use *protolanguage* here in its evolutionary sense (e.g. [Bickerton, 1990; Wray, 1998]) to mean an evolutionarily prior form of language without all the hallmarks of modern human language.

holistic protolanguage is in many ways closer to the communication systems of non-human primates, which are based on a fixed repertoire of expressions lacking generalizable internal structure.

The puzzle is what drives the transition from a holistic stage in language to a more syntactic system of communication. Why and how does compositionality emerge? Can the principle of linguistic adaptation help?

If we think about the difference between holistic and compositional mappings from the point of view of the transmission of language, it becomes obvious that the principle of linguistic adaptation does indeed predict that compositionality will emerge in most cases. Assuming that there is a larger range of meanings that an individual language learner *could* be exposed to in their lifetime than the range of meanings that they actually *are* exposed to, then there is a bottleneck on linguistic transmission because a learner will never see the entire language. This means that a holistic expression for some meaning will only ever be learned if that exact expression is observed by a learner. On the other hand, in a compositional language, a sub-expression (e.g. a word or morpheme) corresponding to a sub-part of a meaning has a much greater opportunity to be learned since evidence for it can be seen by a learner whenever any meaning in which it is involved is expressed. Hence, generalizable linguistic structure is better able to fit through the bottleneck on linguistic transmission. Jim Hurford puts it succinctly in the title to his article: "social transmission favours linguistic generalization" [Hurford, 2000].

Kirby [2001] demonstrates the process at work in a computational simulation. Agents in this model acquire languages from observations of strings of characters being paired with a finite set of very simple structured meanings. Meanings are essentially pairs of features, each of which can take a range of values. The initial expressions in the simulation are random strings of characters paired with whole meanings. In other words, the initial language is holistic because there is no regularity in the mapping between meanings and signals.

Agents are prompted to produce signals for meanings at random and will do so using their internalized language if possible, otherwise they will "invent" a random novel string of characters if necessary. Learners store signal-meaning pairs that they hear in a list, but will also search for any generalizations they can make over the set of pairs that they store. Of course, given a purely holistic language there are no generalizations that can be made, so the language remains holistic.

What happens in such a model? It turns out that it depends critically on how much data learners see in their lifetime. As predicted, this learning bottleneck drives the cultural evolution of language as it is transmitted from generation to generation in the iterated learning model. When learners see large amounts of data, then the language typically is acquired perfectly each generation and therefore does not change. In this case, a completely holistic protolanguage is stable. However, if the number of meaning-signal pairs each learner is exposed to is reduced then the language becomes rather unstable. This is simply because agents will be called upon to produce signals for meanings they have never encountered in their input. Because the language is holistic, their only option is to produce a novel random string. The particular meanings that are subject to this random innovation differ each generation in the simulation (because meanings are picked at random for agents to produce). The upshot of this is that the language can change from generation to generation.

If this were all that happened, it would not be a very interesting model. However, something rather striking occurs when there is a learning bottleneck such as this one: the initially unstable language transforms over time into one that is stable despite, or rather *because of*, the limited input to learners. This new stable language is compositional. Each feature ends up being expressed by some sub-part of the signal. So, for example, a complete meaning might be encoded by using a "morpheme" corresponding to the value of the first feature attached to a "morpheme" corresponding to the value of the second feature. This compositional coding system emerges piecemeal (but surprisingly rapidly) in this simulation as speakers' purely random and holistic innovations are incorrectly over-generalized by learners. The crucial point that arises from the iterated learning model is that these mistaken over-generalizations are then *correctly* picked-up by learners in the next generation. Because generalizations are better able to get through the learning bottleneck, this process snowballs and the inevitable end-result is the emergence of rampant compositionality.

It is important to realize that this result is not simply an artefact of particular features of this one simulation. As noted in the introduction to this section, the same basic behaviour can be seen in simulation models with radically different assumptions and architectures. Furthermore, this type of model can not only provide an explanation for the origins of compositional regularity, but also explain the cases where it does not occur. Whilst most simulation models make the simplifying assumption that all meanings were equally frequent, Kirby [2001] implemented a non-uniform frequency distribution in his model so that some combinations of feature-values were more likely to be expressed by speakers than others.

In this case, only infrequent meanings end up being expressed compositionally. Highly frequent meanings tended to remain with irregular holistic forms (see table 4). This makes sense from the point of view of the principle of linguistic adaptation. If a meaning crops up with high frequency, then information about how that meaning is expressed is reliably provided to the learners. There is no pressure in this case for it to be regularized and become compositional.

	a_0	a_1	a_2	a_3	a_4
b_0	g	s	kf	jf	uhlf
b_1	y	jgi	ki	ji	uhli
b_2	yq	jgq	kq	jq	uhlq
b_3	ybq	jgbq	kbq	jbq	uhlbq
b_4	yuqeg	jguqeg	kuqeg	jugeg	uhluqeg

Figure 4. Simulation result showing a partially regular paradigm. Meanings involve two components, "a" and "b". Frequency of these combinations increases to the upper left of the table. The signals are combinations of letters and exhibit regular compositional structure except for the most frequent meanings. (Taken from [Kirby, 2001])

This result is suggestive in the light of the well-known relationship between frequency and regularity in the morphology of real languages. For example, the top ten verbs in English by frequency all have irregular past-tenses [Francis et al., 1982].

4.3 The adaptation of meanings through iterated learning

Both of the previous examples show how the *form* of language may adapt through a process of cultural evolution. In the second example, the structure of strings in the language end up largely mirroring the pre-existing structure of the meanings in the model. In these simulations, the meaning structure is defined and fixed by the experimenter, leading some researchers to wonder if more flexible meanings can be modelled in simulation (e.g, [Steels et al., 2002; Smith, 2005; Vogt, 2005]).

Indeed, in a simple idealized computational model, Kirby [2007] suggests that semantics as well as syntax might adapt through a process of cultural evolution under pressure from a bottleneck on transmission. To model this, a distinction is made between the meanings that the agents associate with signals on the one hand, and their actual communicative goals on the other. So, for example, I as a speaker may wish to draw the attention of a hearer to a particular person in a room. I might choose to do this in a number of ways: from describing them in every detail, through simply noting their distinctive features, to referring to them by name. In the computational model, each of these correspond to different "meanings" associated with the object of reference. In some sense, it is up to the speaker to choose which meaning they wish to convey, which in turn will affect the actual signal produced. Note that, at one extreme this corresponds to a holistic system of communication – in their simplest form, proper names are holistic. At the other extreme, we might imagine a deeply compositional (but highly inefficient!) form of communication where every discernible aspect of the object of reference is explicitly expressed.

For brevity, we will omit the details of the model here, but the key is that although agents are able to conceptualize every communicative goal in a large number of different ways, corresponding to different meanings, they are only able to express those meanings if they have previously encountered similar expressions in their training data. More precisely, they are able to express a target meaning if they have previously heard a set of meanings within which all aspects of the target meaning appear at least once. To put it another way, just as in the previous model, compositionality allows the learners to recombine sub-parts of other expressions to form novel ones as long as there is sufficient evidence in the input.

Agents are randomly given a particular communicative goal and a "context" of a number of other randomly chosen irrelevant goals. They then try and find a meaning corresponding to their communicative goal for which a suitable expression can be generated. If more than one meaning is possible, then agents pick one which best discriminates the target of communication from the context. If no meanings are possible, then as in the previous model, agents invent a new expression.

The result of these modifications to the previous iterated learning models is that the kinds of meanings that agents use evolves culturally, rather than simply the signals that they associate with meanings. So far the analysis of the model is far from complete, but what is clear is that the language once again shows evidence of adaptation. Where there is pressure from the learning bottleneck, meanings are preferred which allow for the most generalizable forms of compositional language.

There are a number of flaws in this model, unfortunately. For example, although the use of meanings can change over time the set of all possible meanings must still be provided somehow by the experimenter. Work by robotics and artificial life researchers looking at the origins of communication may eventually provide the best way out of this issue by grounding communication in the real world (e.g. [Steels, 2003]) or some model of ecological relevance (e.g. [Cangelosi et al., 2002]). However, the important point here is to show that the principle of linguistic adaptation may potentially have a very wide remit in helping explain many aspects of linguistic structure.[7]

---

[7] The brief overview given here is far from exhaustive in this regard too. For example, work by Oudeyer [2006] demonstrates how similar ideas can explain the origins of the phonemic code.

5 A mathematical model: from weak innateness to strong universals

The computational models reviewed briefly in the previous section lend credence to the notion that language is an adaptive system in its own right. Features of the bottleneck on linguistic transmission end up influencing the structure of language as it adapts through a process of cultural evolution to the challenge of being repeatedly learned by generations of agents.

It is worth reviewing at this point the relevance of linguistic adaptation to the nativist argument outlined in section 2. We highlighted the importance of tackling the problem of linkage when considering nativist explanations. We proposed that cultural evolution is the mechanism that links properties of an individual's language learning machinery with universal features of linguistic structure. If the result of cultural evolution is a straightforward expression of innate biases in cross-linguistic distribution (i.e. if Universal Grammar gets expressed directly as language universals), then there is no particular problem with the orthodox evolutionary view. However, another possibility is that the contribution of cultural evolution is more significant – that it distorts or transforms the innate biases in such a way that their explanatory significance is reduced.

It certainly seems likely that the latter is true given the results of the computational models. For example, it is clear that features such as the amount of training data and the frequency of meanings have significant (and even determining) influence on fundamental features of the structure of the languages that emerge. That said, there are problems with the simulation models as they stand.

Most crucially, it is very difficult to say for any given computational model exactly what the contribution of innate biases actually is, or even what those biases are in the model. The fact that similar results are achieved with hugely different architectures suggest that whatever prior biases the models have (and they surely have some since bias-free learning is impossible) their details might not have a strong bearing on the outcome. It would nevertheless be nice if we could know exactly what the relationship between innateness and universals is in general and it is hard to see how this kind of simulation model is going to be able to do that.

To tackle this question, we can use a general model of learning which makes prior bias explicit and embed this in a mathematical idealization of the iterated learning model ([Kirby *et al.*, 2007], building on [Griffiths and Kalish, 2005]). This model treats learning as a process of selecting the best hypothesis (i.e. grammar) given a set of data (i.e. utterances) and a prior bias towards some hypotheses over others (i.e. a model of innateness). Bayes' law provides us with a neat mathematical characterization of how these interact. We can use it to calculate the probability of a hypothesis given some data (which is what a learner would ideally like to know) from the probability of the data given that hypothesis (which can be estimated if we know how utterances are produced) and the prior probability of that hypothesis independent of any data seen (which is the innate contribution of the learner's machinery):

$$p(h|d) \quad \propto \quad p(d|h) \quad p(h)$$

where h is the hypothesis under question and d is the set of data heard by the learner.

If we assume that learners pick the best hypothesis they can – the one that maximizes $p(h|d)$ – then we can in principle construct a complete view of the dynamics of iterated learning for any model of hypothesis space, innate contribution and production model. We simply calculate for any pair of hypotheses (i.e. languages), h_i and h_j, the probability that a speaker with hypothesis h_i will produce data that a learner will infer has actually been produced by h_j.

This set of probabilities defines a transition matrix over languages (c.f. the Q-matrix of [Nowak et al., 2002]) showing how languages will change over time as they are repeatedly used and acquired. It turns out that there are straightforward mathematical techniques for transforming such a matrix into a probability distribution over languages corresponding to the predicted cross-linguistic distribution as an outcome of iterated learning.[8]

What this set of mathematical tools gives us is a way of plugging-in different assumptions about innateness and seeing exactly how they result in language universals. Kirby et al. [2007] use this to test whether the *strength* of innate biases is reflected in the resulting language universals. For example, are strong innate constraints required to explain big asymmetries in the distribution of language types? Equally, can the nature of innate biases be inferred straightforwardly from observed language universals?

Firstly, the mathematical results back-up the computational models in showing that languages adapt to the nature of the transmission bottleneck. Frequency of meanings and the number of examples learners are exposed to fundamentally shape the language universals that emerge. This in itself acts to

---

[8]This distribution is called the *stationary distribution* and is the limiting distribution of the process of linguistic transmission (given some plausible assumptions about the nature of the transition matrix). The distribution is stationary in the sense that the *probabilities* of any particular language being found do not change, but the particular languages in a population at any point in time may. It can be thought of informally as the time average of languages after the dynamics of iterated learning have settled down. The stationary distribution gives us a way of thinking about the differences between the study of language change and the study of (cultural) language evolution mentioned in section 3. The former looks at how languages move within the stationary distribution. The latter looks at how the stationary distribution itself is formed.

obscure the influence of the prior bias (see, for example, figure 5 which confirms that frequent meaning are far more likely to be irregular despite a prior bias with only a slight and equal preference for regularity across the board).

A more striking result of this model, however, is that for a wide range of values, the actual strength of the prior bias makes *absolutely no difference* to the universal distribution that emerges. Although the nature of the prior bias is clearly important, the degree to which any innate preferences are reflected in the languages that emerge is dependent on such things as the number of examples seen rather than the strength of those innate preferences themselves.

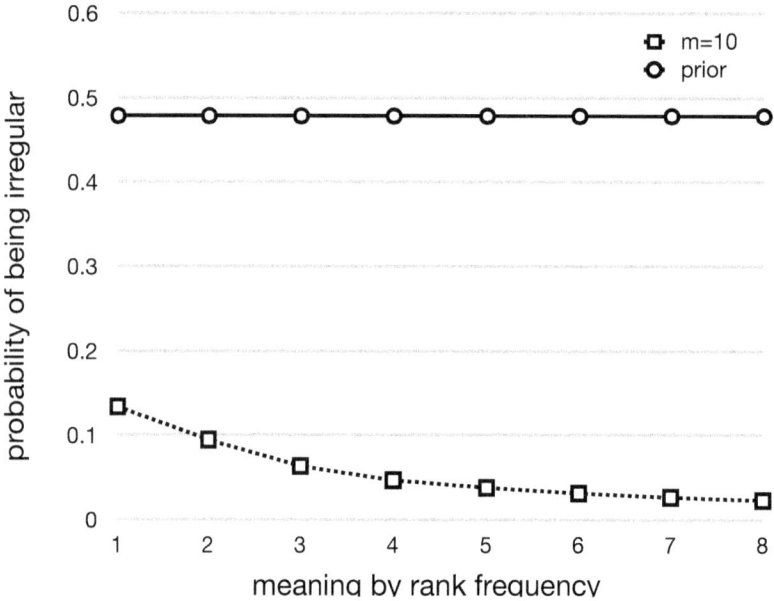

Figure 5. The effect of cultural transmission on an innate bias. The graph shows the probability of a meanings in an abstract model of a language being irregular across meanings with decreasing frequency. The top line shows the expectation of irregularity encoded in the learners' prior learning bias. The lower line shows the actual probability of irregularity that emerges through cultural evolution. (See [Kirby, Dowman & Griffiths, 2007], for more details.)

6   An experimental model: cumulative adaptation without intention

As we have seen, the results from a wide range of formal models lend credence to the principle of linguistic adaptation. Language appears to spontaneously adapt to pressures affecting its own survival through cultural transmission. Of course, there has been some scepticism of the validity of modelling results applied to the evolution of language. For example, Bickerton [2007] complains:

> Powerful and potentially interesting though this approach is, its failure to incorporate more realistic conditions (perhaps because these would be more difficult to simulate) sharply reduces any contribution it might make towards unravelling language evolution. So far, it is a classic case of looking for your car-keys where the street-lamps are. [Bickerton, 2007, p522]

A pressing question is therefore, can this kind of cultural adaptation be observed in real human subjects rather than simulated agents?

Previous experimental work has looked at the emergence of novel systems of communication in groups of experimental subjects. For example, in experiments reminiscent of the board game *Pictionary* Healey et al. [2002] and Fay et al. [2004] show how subjects forced to communicate graphically (and disallowed from writing) can converge on a way of communicating meanings using graphical signals. A particularly fascinating result from this work is an observed transition from the use of icons to communicate in initial stages to a more symbolic mode of communication once shared conventions have been set up. In another experiment, Galantucci [2005] demonstrated that pairs of subjects could converge on a shared symbol system when trying to solve a cooperative computer game with only a graphical means of communication. Selten and Warglien [2007] demonstrate a similar process in a non-graphical paradigm.

These experiments focus on the role of *interactive feedback* in the creation of shared systems of communication. Participants attempt to construct a signalling system and modify it in response to feedback in the form of behaviour or further signalling by the other participant in the exchange. The systems that emerge are a product of a combination of deliberate design and interactive negotiation between interlocutors.

But how good is this as a model of the emergence of linguistic structure? While it cannot be denied that humans are intentional agents who have the potential to design and construct communication systems – indeed these experiments demonstrate this admirably – it remains arguable that the universal structural properties of human languages are the result of such intentional design.

Keller [1994], for example, argues at length that much of human language is best seen as a result of an "invisible hand" process, echoing Smith's [1776] use of the term as a metaphor of the way individuals influence market economics. Keller's point is that language change, although being the result of actions of intentional agents, is not the goal of those agents' intentions. To put it baldly, the shift from OV to VO order in the history of English arose from the actions of speakers of the language and may ultimately have a functional motivation [Hawkins, 1994], but it was surely not the result of individuals deciding to modify the language in such a way to improve its parsing efficiency.

This kind of argument can be applied more broadly to cultural evolution. Many products of human behaviour are the result of intentional design, but some are non-intended consequences of many individuals' actions. It is possible that these non-intended consequences may nevertheless be adaptive – they may show the appearance of design without actually having a designer. The parallels here with biological evolution, where apparent design results not from an intentional Creator, but from the non-local consequence of local selection, has led some to propose studying cultural evolution in similar terms (e.g. [Aunger, 2000]).

Despite huge interest in these theories of cultural evolution, and their relevance to language evolution, there has been as far as we know no previous experimental validation that culturally transmitted behaviour can actually adapt without intentional design. Cornish [2006] and Kirby et al. [2008] set out to rectify this by setting up an analog of the computational models of iterated learning using human subjects rather than simulated agents.

These experiments combine two experimental paradigms: diffusion chain studies and artificial language learning. The former have previously been used among other things (e.g. [Mesoudi et al., 2006b; Bartlett, 1932; Kalish et al., 2007]) to look at whether chimpanzees are able to culturally transmit information about how to open a puzzle box [Horner et al., 2006]. A chain of experimental subjects is set up in which each one observes the performance of the previous subject in the experiment and then in turn produces behaviour that the next subject is able to observe. In this way, the task that a subject faces is in some sense outside the experimenters control (excepting the initial participant in the experiment) because it is ultimately determined by the previous participants' behaviours. The (perhaps surprising) result is that cultural transmission in chimpanzee populations has high fidelity – if a diffusion chain of chimpanzees is initialized with box opening behaviour A then that behaviour will be faithfully transmitted across a number of generations, without a switch to the equally functional opening behaviour B.

Artificial language learning experiments, on the other hand, examine the performance of individuals at learning a particular hand-constructed artificial language (e.g. [Gómez and Gerken, 2000]) with a goal of determining human language learning biases. We can think of this paradigm as mirroring the behaviour of one individual agent in the iterated learning simulations, whereas the diffusion chain experiments are akin to the population model where behaviours are repeatedly transmitted from "adults" to "children".

6.1 The experiment

Subjects in our experiment are treated as if they were participating in a standard artificial language learning task. They are told they are going to be exposed to an "alien" language that they must try and learn. The experiment starts with a random, unstructured, holistic language which is presented to the first subject. After training on this language, the subject is tested and their output recorded. The innovation is the embedding of this task within a diffusion chain: the output of the first experimental subject forms the language that the second subject in the experiment will be trained on, and so on. In this way, we can track how the initially random language changes as it is repeatedly learned and produced by "generations" of participants in the experiment. Crucially, subjects are not aware of the cultural nature of the experiment. They are simply asked to give us back as best they can the language that we have presented to them. In other words, there is no sense that participants in the experiment are trying to improve the language in any way, for example to score well in some collaborative game.

The hypothesis being tested is that there will be cumulative cultural adaptation of the language without intentional design by participants. Accordingly, we expect two things to happen in experiments such as this one:

- the language should become easier to learn;
- and the language should become structured.

If this happens, then insofar as we can say that this was not the result of intentional design on the part of the participants in the experiment, the hypothesis will have been confirmed.

In order to make this kind of iterated learning experiment work, we need to have some way of eliciting language data from subjects. We cannot, for example, simply test subjects recall of strings in the input language through a forced-choice task. This is because we need to generate training data for the next participant. To get round this problem, we trained subjects on stimuli that were a combination of strings of written syllables and simple schematic pictures (corresponding to *signals* and *meanings* respectively). In the testing phase, subjects were asked to produce the correct string of syllables corresponding to each picture in turn, thus providing us with a new training set for the next generation.

Each picture/meaning in the experiment is a coloured shape moving in one of three ways (bouncing, spiralling or sliding). There are three possible shapes (square, circle or triangle) and three colours (red, blue or black), yielding 27 different meanings. The original language is constructed by randomly concatenating, without spaces, 2 to 4 CV syllables from a set of a possible 9. For example, in the original language, a red bouncing square might be labelled "kihemiwi". Although the initial language has these constraints, subjects are free to type any combination of characters they wish in their output at test.

At each generation (i.e. for each participant in the experiment), the input language is divided randomly into a SEEN and and UNSEEN set. Participants are trained a number of times on the SEEN set by being presented with each picture and string in turn on a computer screen. They are then *tested* on the entire SEEN + UNSEEN set of 27 pictures in order that we can gather a complete language. This new language is then divided (randomly again) into SEEN and UNSEEN sets for the next participant (see [Cornish, 2006], for more details).

6.2 Results

The complete results and analysis of this experiment are given in [Cornish, 2006], but we give a brief summary here. In all cases our hypothesis of cumulative adaptation is confirmed.

Firstly, to see if learnability increases, we measured the difference in the strings produced by a subject at generation n with a subject at generation n-1. In the initial stages, the difference was extremely high. This is not at all surprising. After all, we are not only presenting subjects with a random set of strings, but we are asking them to respond with strings for pictures that they have never previously seen. For these unseen examples and the initial random language at least it is impossible to get these right (except by an overwhelming fluke!). Remarkably, however, as the experiment progressed, later generations found it increasingly easy to get strings correct, or near correct. In fact, in some cases after 7 or 8 generations had passed, subjects were getting *every* string correct even those for pictures they had never seen in the training data. In other words, the language evolves culturally to become more learnable.

How does it achieve this feat? Recall we predict that adaptation of the language should lead to structure evolving. This is indeed what happens, but the type of structure depends on how we divide up the data each generation into the SEEN and UNSEEN sets.

In our first experiment, the language was divided evenly into SEEN and UNSEEN, with 14 and 13 pictures in each respectively. The result was quite surprising given previous computational models, but makes a lot of sense in retrospect. The language adapts to be learnable primarily by reducing the number of distinct words. To put it another way, strings become ambiguous with respect to the pictures. The initial random language has 27 distinct words in it (one for each picture), but at the end of the experiment (which ran for 10 generations) the language only has 5 words. This alone does not capture everything that is going on, however, otherwise subjects would still not be able to get all UNSEEN pictures 100% correct as they do for the last three generations in the experiment. To do this, there must be some structure in the mapping from meanings to signals.

A statistical analysis of the language at each stage confirms that this structure exists. Basically, words end up being used for sets of pictures that tend to share features in common. The final language (which is stable for three generations) shows this most clearly:

- *miniku* is used for all bouncing circles
- *tupin* is used for all bouncing triangles
- *tupim* is used for all bouncing squares
- *poi* is used for anything that spirals
- *tuge* is used for anything that slides

What has happened is that word-picture pairs have been generalized in such a way that the language can pass through the learning bottleneck. Even if subjects do not see half of the pictures, they can nevertheless be reliably named.

This is not the kind of result familiar from the computational models reported earlier – structure in the signals themselves does not emerge. What seems to be missing here is any pressure on the language to be *expressive*. Languages with fewer words are clearly more learnable, so adaptation to learnability inevitably reduces the expressive power of the language by introducing what is essentially rampant polysemy and a reduction in the discriminative power of the language. Once the number of words is low enough no further adaptation is necessary since the language passes easily through the learning bottleneck.

For our second experiment, we made a minimal change to the procedure to try and reduce the amount of polysemy that participants (unwittingly) introduce. To do this, we moved any duplicate words from the SEEN set into the UNSEEN set before training each participant. So, if a particular subject had introduced polysemy by using the same word for more than one picture, only one of those word-picture pairs would be provided as training for the next subject.

The result of this small modification is dramatic. Although subjects find the task much harder and perfect transmission is not achieved, the learnability of the language nevertheless increases. However, the type of structure that emerges to make the language learnable is quite different. The strings in the language start to gain internal structure and in some cases clear compositionality emerges with aspects of the meaning being expressed as regular prefixes or suffixes. So, for example, in one of the languages that emerges, a black bouncing circle is named "winekuki" with the prefix "wi-" being largely consistently used to refer to black things, and the suffix "-kuki" being across the board to refer to anything bouncing. In this particular language, the shape is encoded by a complex set of semi-regularities governing the middle syllable and changes to the prefix (see [Cornish, 2006], for the complete set of languages in the experiments).

It is important to reiterate that participants in this experiment are not deliberately constructing a structured system for encoding meanings (as they are in an experiment such as [Selten and Warglien, 2007]). They are attempting as best they can to give us back the language that they were exposed to, idiosyncrasies and all. In fact, some subjects reported that they were not even aware that they were being exposed during the test phase to pictures that they had not seen in training. In addition, the adaptation that occurs is not instantaneous, but gradual and cumulative. The increase in the learnability of the language tends to proceed by small amounts each generation.

This is truly an invisible hand process. The linguistic structure that emerges, which enables the subjects to accurately report the labels for pictures they have never seen, appears to be designed for that purpose, and yet there is no intentional designer. Just as in the computational and mathematical models, the mere fact that language must be passed through a transmission bottleneck causes it to adapt.

7 Conclusions

In this chapter, we have put forward the view that to explain the universal structural properties of language we need to look at language as a complex adaptive system – one in which biologically evolved innate biases on individual learning can be seen as challenges to which a culturally evolving language must adapt. Computational, mathematical and experimental models demonstrate that the process of linguistic evolution on a cultural time-scale is one that has significant explanatory power.

This growing body of work points to a number of conclusions of relevance to linguistics and the study of cultural evolution more broadly:

- biological evolution by natural selection is not the only explanation for adaptive structure in language;
- statistically significant cross-linguistic universals do not necessarily imply strong innate constraints;

- the burden of explaining the constraints on linguistic variation is lifted from a putative biologically evolved innate Universal Grammar;

- the structure of the human language faculty cannot be straightforwardly inferred from the observed structure of human language;

- the appearance of design in human behaviour, including language, does not necessarily require a designer if it is transmitted culturally.

In addition, we hope that we have made a case for attempting to model cultural evolution of language either in simulation or in an experimental setting. For too long explanatory formal frameworks for language structure have focused on the individual and assumed that population effects are unimportant. It is now possible to move beyond these kinds of idealizations and explicitly examine what happens when populations of individuals interact. Work in this area is still in its infancy, but we believe it has the potential to improve our fundamental understanding of why language is structured the way it is.

BIBLIOGRAPHY

[Andersen, 1973] H. Andersen. Abductive and deductive change. *Language*, 49(4):765–93, 1973.

[Aunger, 2000] R. Aunger, editor. *Darwinizing culture: the status of memetics as a science*. Oxford University Press, Oxford, 2000.

[Bartlett, 1932] F.C. Bartlett. *Remembering: A Study in Experimental and Social Psychology*. Cambridge University Press, 1932.

[Batali, 1998] J. Batali. Computational simulations of the emergence of grammar. In J. Hurford, M. Studdert-Kennedy, , and C. Knight, editors, *Approaches to the Evolution of Language: Social and Cognitive Bases*, pages 405–426. Cambridge University Press, 1998.

[Batali, 2002] J. Batali. The negotiation and acquisition of recursive grammars as a result of competition among exemplars. In T. Briscoe, editor, *Linguistic Evolution through Language Acquisition: Formal and Computational Models*, pages 111–172. Cambridge University Press, 2002.

[Bickerton, 1990] D. Bickerton. *Language & Species*. University Of Chicago Press, 1990.

[Bickerton, 2007] D. Bickerton. Language evolution: A brief guide for linguists. *Lingua*, 117(3):510–526, 2007.

[Boyd and Richerson, 1985] R. Boyd and P.J. Richerson. *Culture and the Evolutionary Process*. University of Chicago Press, 1985.

[Brighton et al., 2005] H. Brighton, K. Smith, and S. Kirby. Language as an evolutionary system. *Physics of Life Reviews*, 2(3):177–226, 2005.

[Brighton, 2002] H. Brighton. Compositional Syntax From Cultural Transmission. *Artificial Life*, 8(1):25–54, 2002.

[Brighton, 2003] H. Brighton. *Simplicity as a driving force in linguistic evolution*. PhD thesis, The University of Edinburgh, UK, 2003.

[Briscoe, 2000] E.J. Briscoe. Grammatical acquisition: Inductive bias and coevolution of language and the language acquisition device. *Language*, 76(2):245–296, 2000.

[Cangelosi et al., 2002] A. Cangelosi, A. Greco, and S. Harnad. Symbol grounding and the symbolic theft hypothesis. In A. Cangelosi and D. Parisi, editors, *Simulating the Evolution of Language*, pages 191–210. Springer Verlag, 2002.

[Chomsky, 1975] N. Chomsky. *Reflections on Language*. Pantheon Books, 1975.

[Christiansen, 1994] M.H. Christiansen. *Infinite languages, finite minds: Connectionism, learning and linguistic structure*. PhD thesis, University of Edinburgh, UK, 1994.
[Cornish, 2006] H Cornish. Iterated learning with human subjects: an empirical framework for the emergence and cultural transmission of language. Master's thesis, University of Edinburgh, UK, 2006.
[Croft, 1990] W. Croft. *Typology and Universals*. Cambridge University Press, 1990.
[Croft, 2000] W. Croft. *Explaining Language Change: An Evolutionary Approach*. Longman, 2000.
[de Boer, 2001] B. de Boer. *The Origins of Vowel Systems*. Oxford University Press, 2001.
[Deacon, 1997] T.W. Deacon. The Symbolic Species: The Co-evolution of the Brain and Language. *New York: WW Norton&Co*, 1997.
[Fay et al., 2004] N. Fay, S. Garrod, T. MacLeod, J. Lee, and J. Oberlander. Design, adaptation and convention: The emergence of higher order graphical representations. In *Proceedings of the 26th Annual Conference of the Cognitive Science Society*, pages 411–416, 2004.
[Francis et al., 1982] W.N. Francis, H. Kučera, and A.W. Mackie. *Frequency analysis of English usage: lexicon and grammar*. Boston: Houghton Mifflin, 1982.
[Galantucci, 2005] B. Galantucci. An Experimental Study of the Emergence of Human Communication Systems. *Cognitive Science*, 29(5):737–767, 2005.
[Gómez and Gerken, 2000] R.L. Gómez and L.A. Gerken. Infant artificial language learning and language acquisition. *Trends in Cognitive Sciences*, 4(5):178–186, 2000.
[Griffiths and Kalish, 2005] T.L. Griffiths and M.L. Kalish. A Bayesian view of language evolution by iterated learning. In *Proceedings of the 27th Annual Conference of the Cognitive Science Society*, pages 827–832, 2005.
[Hawkins, 1988] J.A. Hawkins, editor. *Explaining language universals*. B. Blackwell Oxford, UK, 1988.
[Hawkins, 1994] J.A. Hawkins. *A Performance Theory of Order and Constituency*. Cambridge University Press, 1994.
[Healey et al., 2002] P.G.T. Healey, S. Garrod, N. Fay, J. Lee, and J. Oberlander. Interactional context in graphical communication. In *Proceedings of the 24th Annual Conference of the Cognitive Science Society*, pages 441–446, 2002.
[Heine and Kuteva, 2002] B. Heine and T. Kuteva. On the evolution of grammatical forms. In A. Wray, editor, *The Transition to Language*, pages 376–397. Oxford University Press, 2002.
[Hoekstra and Kooij, 1988] T. Hoekstra and J.G. Kooij. The innateness hypothesis. In J.A. Hawkins, editor, *Explaining Language Universals*, pages 31–55. B. Blackwell Oxford, UK, 1988.
[Horner et al., 2006] V. Horner, A. Whiten, E. Flynn, and F. de Waal. Faithful replication of foraging techniques along cultural transmission chains by chimpanzees and children. *Proceedings of the National Academy of Sciences*, 103(37):13878–13883, 2006.
[Hurford, 1990] J.R. Hurford. Nativist and functional explanations in language acquisition. In I.M. Roca, editor, *Logical Issues in Language Acquisition*, pages 85–136. Foris, Dordrecht, 1990.
[Hurford, 2000] J.R. Hurford. Social transmission favours linguistic generalization. In J.R.H. Chris Knight and M. Studdert-Kennedy, editors, *The Evolutionary Emergence of Language: Social Function and the Origins of Linguistic Form*, pages 324–352. Cambridge University Press, 2000.
[Kalish et al., 2007] M.L. Kalish, T.L. Griffiths, and S. Lewandowsky. Iterated learning: Intergenerational knowledge transmission reveals inductive biases. *Psychonomic Bulletin & Review*, 14(2):288–294, 2007.
[Keenan and Comrie, 1977] E. Keenan and B. Comrie. Noun phrase accessibility and universal grammar. *Linguistic Inquiry*, 8(1):63–99, 1977.
[Keller, 1994] R. Keller. *On Language Change: The Invisible Hand in Language*. Routledge, 1994.

[Kirby and Hurford, 2002] S. Kirby and J.R. Hurford. The emergence of linguistic structure: An overview of the iterated learning model. In A. Cangelosi and D. Parisi, editors, *Simulating the Evolution of Language*, pages 121–148. Springer Verlag, 2002.

[Kirby et al., 2004] S. Kirby, K. Smith, and H. Brighton. From UG to universals: Linguistic adaptation through iterated learning. *Studies in language*, 28(3):587–607, 2004.

[Kirby et al., 2007] S. Kirby, M. Dowman, and T.L. Griffiths. Innateness and culture in the evolution of language. In *Proceedings of the National Academy of Sciences*, volume 104, pages 5241–5245. National Acad Sciences, 2007.

[Kirby et al., 2008] S. Kirby, H. Cornish, and K. Smith. Cumulative cultural evolution in the laboratory: an experimental approach to the origins of structure in human language. Forthcoming, 2008.

[Kirby, 1994] S. Kirby. Adaptive explanations for language universals: a model of Hawkins' performance theory. *Sprachtypologie und Universalienforschung*, 47:186–210, 1994.

[Kirby, 1997] S. Kirby. Competing motivations and emergence: explaining implicational hierarchies. *Language Typology*, 1(1):5–32, 1997.

[Kirby, 1999] S. Kirby. *Function, Selection, and Innateness: The Emergence of Language Universals*. Oxford University Press, 1999.

[Kirby, 2000] S. Kirby. Syntax without natural selection: How compositionality emerges from vocabulary in a population of learners. In C. Knight, editor, *The Evolutionary Emergence of Language: Social Function and the Origins of Linguistic Form*, pages 303–323. Cambridge University Press, 2000.

[Kirby, 2001] S. Kirby. Spontaneous evolution of linguistic structure-an iterated learning model of the emergence of regularity and irregularity. *Evolutionary Computation, IEEE Transactions on*, 5(2):102–110, 2001.

[Kirby, 2002a] S. Kirby. Learning, bottlenecks and the evolution of recursive syntax. In T. Briscoe, editor, *Linguistic evolution through language acquisition: Formal and Computational Models*, pages 173–203. Cambridge University Press, 2002.

[Kirby, 2002b] S. Kirby. Natural Language From Artificial Life. *Artificial Life*, 8(2):185–215, 2002.

[Kirby, 2007] S. Kirby. The evolution of meaning-space structure through iterated learning. In C. Lyon, C. Nehaniv, and A. Cangelosi, editors, *Emergence of Communication and Language*, pages 253–268. Springer Verlag, 2007.

[Mesoudi et al., 2006a] A. Mesoudi, A. Whiten, and R. Dunbar. A bias for social information in human cultural transmission. *British Journal of Psychology*, 97(3):405–423, 2006.

[Mesoudi et al., 2006b] A. Mesoudi, A. Whiten, and K.N. Laland. Towards a unified science of cultural evolution. *Behavioral and Brain Sciences*, 29(04):329–347, 2006.

[Nowak et al., 2002] M.A. Nowak, N.L. Komarova, P. Niyogi, et al. Computational and evolutionary aspects of language. *Nature*, 417:611–617, 2002.

[Oudeyer, 2006] P.Y. Oudeyer. *Self-Organization in the Evolution of Speech*. Oxford University Press, 2006.

[Pinker and Bloom, 1990] S. Pinker and P. Bloom. Natural language and natural selection. *Behavioral and Brain Sciences*, 13(4):707–84, 1990.

[Selten and Warglien, 2007] R. Selten and M. Warglien. The emergence of simple languages in an experimental coordination game. *Proceedings of the National Academy of Sciences*, 104(18):7361–7366, 2007.

[Smith et al., 2003] K. Smith, S. Kirby, and H. Brighton. Iterated Learning: A Framework for the Emergence of Language. *Artificial Life*, 9(4):371–386, 2003.

[Smith, 1776] A. Smith. *An Inquiry into the Nature and Causes of the Wealth of Nations*, London: W. *Strahan and T. Cadell*, 1776.

[Smith, 2002] K. Smith. The cultural evolution of communication in a population of neural networks. *Connection Science*, 14(1):65–84, 2002.

[Smith, 2005] A.D.M. Smith. The Inferential Transmission of Language. *Adaptive Behavior*, 13(4):311–324, 2005.

[Sperber, 1996] D. Sperber. *Explaining Culture: A Naturalistic Approach*. Blackwell Publishers, 1996.

[Steels et al., 2002] L. Steels, F. Kaplan, A. McIntyre, and J. Van Looveren. Crucial factors in the origins of word-meaning. In A. Wray, editor, *The Transition to Language*. Oxford University Press, 2002.

[Steels, 2003] L. Steels. Evolving grounded communication for robots. *Trends in Cognitive Sciences*, 7(7):308–312, 2003.

[Teal and Taylor, 1999] T. Teal and C.E. Taylor. Compression and adaptation. In D. Floreano, J.D. Nicoud, and F. Mondada, editors, *Advances in Artificial Life*, pages 709–719. Springer, 1999.

[Tonkes, 2001] B. Tonkes. *On the Origins of Linguistic Structure: Computational models of the evolution of language*. PhD thesis, University of Queensland, Australia, 2001.

[Vogt, 2005] P. Vogt. The emergence of compositional structures in perceptually grounded language games. *Artificial Intelligence*, 167(1-2):206–242, 2005.

[Wray, 1998] A. Wray. Protolanguage as a holistic system for social interaction. *Language and Communication*, 18(1):47–67, 1998.

[Zuidema, 2003] W. Zuidema. How the poverty of the stimulus solves the poverty of the stimulus. In S. Becker, S. Thrun, and K. Obermayer, editors, *Advances in Neural Information Processing Systems 15: Proceedings of the 2002 Conference*. MIT Press, Cambridge, MA, 2003.

Simon Kirby
Language Evolution and Computation Research Unit, University of Edinburgh, Edinburgh, UK.
simon@ling.ed.ac.uk

Kenny Smith
Cognition and Communication Research Centre, Northumbria University, Newcastle, UK.
kenny.smith@unn.ac.uk

Hannah Cornish
Language Evolution and Computation Research Unit, University of Edinburgh, Edinburgh, UK.
hannah@ling.ed.ac.uk

Natural Languages as Collections of Resources[1]

ROBIN COOPER AND AARNE RANTA

1 Natural languages and formal languages

The view of natural languages as formal languages played a significant role in the development of linguistics in the second half of the twentieth century. The view of languages as sets of strings underlay the early development of generative transformational grammar. The following famous quotation from Montague's [1974] 'Universal Grammar' represents a cornerstone of work on formal semantics since the seventies:

> There is in my opinion no important theoretical difference between natural languages and the artificial languages of logicians; indeed I consider it possible to comprehend the syntax and semantics of both kinds of languages within a single natural and mathematically precise theory.

Formal semantics involves the treatment of interpreted formal languages which may be regarded as sets of pairs of string and meanings.

Chomsky [1980] and in other work makes clear that he does not regard natural languages as formal languages, or that at least to regard them in terms of string sets is at best missing the point of linguistic theory and at worst dealing with an incoherent notion. In his view, speakers of a natural language have acquired particular individual instantiations of universal principles. It is the nature of the principles and the parameters involved in instantiating them which are of interest for linguistic theory, not the nature of a string set corresponding to external public language, which may not be consistent since each speaker will have acquired their own individual grammar. While the view we propose in this paper is somewhat different to Chomsky's, we share with him a focus on the formal characterization of the resources available to a speaker of a natural language, rather than a characterization of a set of

---

[1] This work was supported by Vetenskapsrådet project 2005-4211 *Library-based Grammar Engineering*, http://www.cs.chalmers.se/~aarne/GF/doc/vr.html

strings (or string-meaning pairs) which are to be regarded as grammatical in the language.

In this paper we will first discuss the advantages and disadvantages of regarding natural languages as formal languages (section 1.1). We will then (section 1.2) propose a view on which natural languages are rather to be regarded as collections of resources, a toolbox which can be used for constructing languages in the formal sense. This view arose from work on the Grammatical Framework, an implemented system for the construction of small application grammars based on general resources for natural languages and we will give a brief characterization of the system in section 2. Finally, we will speculate on how our view could be extended to accommodate linguistic innovation (section 3).

1.1 Are natural languages formal languages?

The view of natural languages as formal languages was a tremendously productive abstraction which enabled us to apply twentieth century logical techniques to the characterization of human linguistic ability. Without it we would be able to say very little that is mathematically precise about the structure of language and its interpretation. It has provided great insight into the nature of language and has provided a foundation on which a great deal of computational natural language processing has been built. The view of natural languages as formal languages has provided a rich vein of research which has led to important theoretical and practical results which should not, we believe, be abandoned.

However, there are problems with the view of natural languages as formal languages and such problems have sometimes been addressed either by abandoning adherence to the formal language view or by regarding the problems as properties of language use which are beyond the purview of a formal theory. Here are what seem to be the two main types of problem, relating respectively to the formal views of languages as sets of strings and sets of string-meaning pairs:

grammaticality Native speakers of a language do not have robust judgements about grammaticality which support the simple view of a language as a set of strings. Rather, there appear to be degrees of grammaticality. Something that appears to be ungrammatical in one context can be judged to be grammatical in another context. Speakers can adapt the language to new situations and phenomena and this adaptation can lead to the "bending" of grammaticality judgements.

meaning Speakers do not consistently use words and phrases with a fixed range of interpretations as would be suggested by a theory of meaning based on model theoretic interpretation. Rather they adapt meaning to the subject matter they are describing and negotiate meaning dynamically during the course of a dialogue. This can be something as apparently simple as using the same proper name to refer to different individuals or as complex and subtle as discussing the nature of abstract concepts such as democracy, love or theoretical notions such as meaning or gravity. A great deal of human discourse, it seems, involves not simply discussion of issues of truth given a fixed set of meanings, but rather discussion of meta-issues concerning the interpretation of given terms.

How can we construct a theory which addresses these kinds of problems while maintaining the insights and precision that we have gained from the view of natural languages as formal languages? We present our proposal in section 1.2.

1.2 Natural languages as collections of resources

Our proposal is to move from the view of natural languages as languages in the formal sense to a view of them as a collection of resources (a "toolbox") which can be used to construct such languages. The idea is that speakers of natural languages are constantly in the process of creating new language to meet the needs of novel situations in which they find themselves. The resources of the natural language provide the means to create formal languages, allowing us to exploit the insights of the formal language view of natural languages. However, a natural language is not limited to being regarded as a single formal language. A corpus of natural language data is not required to be consistent either in terms of grammaticality or in terms of meaning since it represents output based on a collection of related grammars rather than a single grammar. This may be true even for a very small corpus (e.g. consisting of a single dialogue) since it is quite often the case that speakers will adjust their grammar to suit the needs of what is being talked about or to match the usage of other speakers.

This view may sound like it is opening the way to linguistic chaos and that it may make it very difficult to formulate any kind of precise and testable linguistic theory. We believe that the Grammatical Framework, described in section 2, provides the beginnings of a precise formulation of such a theory. Currently, the Grammatical Framework says nothing about linguistic innovation or change, but in section 3 we will speculate on some ways in which we could progress to such a theory.

2 The Grammatical Framework

GF is a grammar formalism based on constructive type theory [Martin-Löf, 1984]. It is structured in the same way as *logical frameworks* (LF): there is a relatively simple and general core formalism, inside which specific formalisms can be defined by sets of declarative judgements. The idea was first implemented in Edinburgh LF [Harper *et al.*, 1993]. In this "framework for defining logics", all questions of variable bindings, hypothesizing logics", all questions of variable bindings, hypothesis management, proof checking, and proof search are once and for all implemented on the framework level, and the user can take these mechanisms for granted when defining her own logic or mathematical theory.

In addition to the implementation advantages, the *framework idea* is motivated by a certain philosophy of mathematics, proper to constructivism. In this philosophy, there is no such thing as a universal theory of mathematics, to which everything else can be reduced. In many schools of classical mathematics, Zermelo-Fraenkel set theory plays such a role. But if the framework idea is followed, mathematics consists of many systems and is open for the creation of new ones. The unifying layer is very thin: it consists of general principles of reasoning and structure, upon which each theory can build its system of mathematical objects and axioms governing them.

In the philosophy of language, the framework idea can be recognized in the thinking of later Wittgenstein [1953]. In this line of thinking, *language* is not a system formally defined once and for all, but a set of *language games*, each with their own rules. Extended to the level of words, this thinking says that the *meaning of a word* is not a definite object given once and for all, but the totality of its uses in different language games, which are at most related by a *family resemblance*.

2.1 Abstract and concrete syntax

With no special commitment to the constructivist philosophy, GF was implemented as a logical framework, which provides what we called *abstract syntax*. An abstract syntax in GF (as in LF) is a system of types and functions, which together define a *semantic model* of some domain we want to reason about, or write a grammar for. To this LF ingredient, GF adds a *concrete syntax*, which is a mapping from the semantic objects of the abstract syntax into the strings of some language.

To give a very simple example, let us consider the abstract syntax modelling spoken communication with an MP3 player. This syntax is a part of a dialogue system developed within the European TALK project[2] and is described in more detail by Perera and Ranta [2007].

An abstract syntax defines *categories*, which classify objects in the domain. In the MP3 grammar, we have (among other things), actions performed by the player, playlists that are manipulated, and objects, such as songs and artists, which are included in playlists and possibly played:

---

[2] http://www.talk-project.org/

```
cat Action ; Playlist ; Object ; Song ; Artist ;
```

An abstract syntax also defines *functions*, which are used for constructing objects in the domain - called *abstract syntax trees*. Here are functions for constructing the action to add an object to a playlist, the action to create a new playlist, and the action to play an object:

```
fun
  add_object_to_playlist : Playlist -> Object -> Action ;
  create_playlist : Action ;
  play : Object -> Action ;
```

In the concrete syntax, it is defined how the semantic objects are *linearized*. This is done compositionally, i.e. so that each abstract syntax fun rule has a corresponding lin rule:

```
lin
  add_object_to_playlist x y = "add" ++ x ++ "to" ++ y ;
  create_playlist = "create" ++ "a" ++ "playlist" ;
  play x = "play" ++ x ;
```

From a set of linearization rules, both generation and parsing algorithms can be derived [Ranta, 2004].

2.2 Resource grammar libraries

One advantage of the abstract/concrete distinction is that one abstract syntax can be equipped with many concrete syntaxes. Thus GF in general supports *multilingual grammars*, where the semantic model defined in the abstract syntax acts as an *interlingua*. Thus a French version of the MP3 grammar is defined by the concrete syntax

```
lin
  add_object_to_playlist x y = "ajouter" ++ x ++ "à" ++ y ;
  create_playlist = "créer" ++ "une" ++ "liste" ++
                    "de" ++ "lecture" ;
  play x = "jouer" ++ x ;
```

A general experience from GF is that interlingua-based translation works very well in a domain that is delimited enough to support the formalization of a semantically motivated abstract syntax [Ranta, 2006]. A very different domain on which the idea has been used on a larger scale is mathematical exercises in the WebALT project [Strotmann et al., 2005]. In both the MP3 and the mathematics application, six languages are included.

However, writing a concrete syntax soon becomes an arduous task, requiring the grammarian - who is often a domain expert rather than a linguist - to solve demanding linguistic problems. For instance, in the German version of the MP3 grammar, the objects treated in actions must be inflected in different cases, which becomes particularly complex in the presence of determiners and adjectives (for instance, in *add the previous song to the current playlist*). Returning strings in linearization is no longer sufficient, but we need *records* with *features* and, possibly, discontinuous constituents. All these constructs are provided by GF, but writing grammars correctly is still demanding.

The solution to this problem has been the creation of *resource grammar libraries*. These libraries are grammars based on general syntactic structures, rather than domain-specific semantic structures. The categories in a resource grammar are familiar to linguists: sentence, noun phrase, verb phrase, etc. The functions are syntactic combination rules such as

```
mkImp : V3 -> NP -> NP -> Imp
```

which builds an imperative phrase (`Imp`) from a three-place verb (`V3`) by providing its two `NP` complements. This function can now be used in the linearization of an action to add an object to a playlist:

```
add_object_to_playlist x y = mkImp add_V3 x y
```

The constant `add_V3` is defined in each language as a verb appropriate for this function. For instance, in German we use

```
add_V3 = mkV3 (prefixV "hinzu" (regV "fügen"))
              accPrep zu_Prep
```

This rather complex-looking definition hides an even larger complexity, e.g. the complete inflection of the verb *fügen* expressed by the resource function `regV`, the management of the verb prefix *hinzu* in different combinations, and the forms of the complements triggered by the accusative case for the first complement and the preposition *zu* for the second.

Thus resource grammars are an important practical asset, and the experiment reported by Perera and Ranta [2007] confirmed that it is possible to achieve a division of labour between linguists who write these libraries and domain experts who use them in applications [Ranta, 2007]. The same libraries are used in the WebALT project, which shows that linguistic resources are domain-independent.

What is the semantic model formalized by the abstract syntax of a resource grammar? A word that could be used for it is *linguistic ontology*. It is a system of linguistic structures, which are manifested in many different domains and can be put into new, unanticipated uses. It is the resource grammar that formalizes the unifying structure of *English*, or *German*, which is then put into different uses in different "language games".

3 Towards a theory of linguistic innovation

GF is a grammar engineering application and as such does not present a linguistic theory. However, it suggests a view of natural languages as collections of resources which is importantly different from at least one standard twentieth century view of language based on the analogy between natural languages and formal languages. In this section we sketch some of the components which would need to be integrated into this GF view in order to obtain a theory of linguistic innovation.

3.1 Agent-related resources

GF, as a grammar development system, provides a facility for utilizing grammar resources developed as libraries for a given natural language. This idea needs to be adapted to a theory of agents with individual linguistic resources. While human agents who speak the same natural language have similar linguistic resources, they are not identical and are influenced by the linguistic experience of the agent. This much is generally assumed in linguistic theory. Where GF differs from the standard assumption in linguistic theory that the available resource is a grammar of the language is that in GF the resources are available to the agent to construct an appropriate grammar for a given domain or application. At the moment GF provides facilities for a programmer to construct such grammars. It provides no learning capabilities for an agent to construct such a grammar on the basis of its resources and linguistic needs.

However, it does provide some hints about what steps might be involved in the acquisition of new grammar. An agent confronted with an innovative use (i.e. one that is not covered by the resource grammar available to it) related to a particular expression of abstract syntax can be compared to a GF grammar writer who needs to relate an expression of abstract syntax to a natural language expression in the concrete syntax which is not covered by the resource grammar for that language. There are three choices available. The first and simplest is to relate the abstract syntax expression to an unanalyzed string in the way that we presented in section 2.1 before we introduced resource grammars. This is the quickest fix and is particularly appropriate for a grammatical construction that is not going to be used anywhere else in the system. It does not involve any linguistic analysis. The second option is useful if you notice that a particular construction is going to be used in several places in your application. In this option you can define a syntactic operation within your application grammar. An advantage of doing this is that the new syntactic construction you have defined will be limited to the small grammar you are defining and you do not have to take responsibility for a potential overhaul of the resource grammar where your adjustment to the grammar might have far-reaching and unforeseen consequences elsewhere in the grammar. If, however, you feel that the construction you need is a general construction which will be used in future application grammars as well then you should really consider the third possibility, that is, adding to the resource grammar (or asking your resource grammar expert to make the appropriate addition).

These programming options suggest a learning strategy. An agent which is exposed to an innovative construction in some particular domain, may, on hearing the construction for the first time, not analyze it but simply relate a string of words to the meaning that it appears to have. However, noticing similar strings may lead the agent to make a local linguistic analysis related to that domain (possibly related to a single speaker). If the agent is exposed to the construction in different domains and in connection with different speakers then the agent will be encouraged to "promote" the construction to the level of the resources and make a general adjustment to their resources available for processing input in arbitrary domains. Interesting empirical questions associated with this are where the thresholds lie between these strategies. Are the thresholds purely in terms of numbers of exposures, or also numbers of speakers and numbers of domains? Do different linguistic agents have different values for the thresholds (that is, are more susceptible to influence by other speakers)? Is an agent with lower thresholds a more efficient language learner than one with higher thresholds – that is, is it more efficient to change your grammar or resource immediately on noticing new data or to collect data first and adjust on the basis of a larger amount of data?

3.2 Lexical semantics

GF does not provide any semantics in its resource grammars. It eschews any kind of general semantic theory. The idea is that semantics is expressed locally in each application grammar by relating the resources to the abstract syntax of the given application. This idea is of deep importance for the view of language we wish to suggest. We do not think that natural languages are like formal languages in the sense that they come along with a fixed interpretation. Rather natural languages provide the tools for creating languages *ad hoc* with interpretations appropriate to the purposes at hand.

However, an adequate theory of language would have to place constraints on the kind of creativity which GF currently offers the programmer. The grammatical resource places constraints on the syntax of words but not otherwise on what kind of meaning they can be associated with in a given application. This is perfectly sensible for a grammar development tool since one can rely on the programmer to know enough of the language to choose appropriate words for given meanings in the domain. But speakers of a natural language choose interpretations for words which, while they may not be identical in each circumstance, are sufficiently related to their interpretation in other circumstances in order to make communication possible. We do not, for example, say *close* when we mean *open* even though *open* may mean many different things in connection with files, connections, shows, boxes and so on. Speakers are influenced by the interpretations words have had in other linguistic circumstances they have been involved in. Part of their resource for the language is a characterization of the kind of meaning that may be associated with a word and it is this they call on when they choose a word for a particular interpretation in a given domain or when they try to interpret the use of a word by another speaker in a given domain. Thus the resource must contain information about lexical semantic interpretation. But it is not, as with a formal language, a precise specification of the interpretation of a given word, but rather a set of constraints indicating the kind of meaning the word can be associated with (or has been associated with in the speaker's past experience). In order to build a theory which will account for this we need a theory of meaning that is rich enough to allow for a similarity measure on meanings. Perhaps such a theory might involve giving an interpretation to abstract syntax so that interpretation across different domains can be compared. One approach to a theory of innovation in lexical interpretation using record types is suggested in [Cooper, 2007]. Using record types to represent meaning provides enough structure to compare meanings and formalize the modification of meanings in novel situations. However, there are still a number of open questions concerning the role of such record types in GF. GF uses record types in concrete syntax, in a similar way as feature structures are used in other formalisms. In the kind of semantics and modelling of unification-based formalisms with structure sharing described in [Cooper 2005a, 2005b, 2008], we need to generalize them to *dependent record types*, where the types of some fields may depend on the values of other fields. Such types have not yet been implemented in GF.

3.3 Coordination

Speakers coordinate their language in given situations so that their usage is similar, a fact that is discussed by a number of papers in the current volume (e.g. [Healey, this volume; Larsson, this volume]). This kind of coordination is closely related to notion of microsocial speech accommodation in sociolinguistics which is discussed by [Sharma *et al.*, this volume]. This can be particularly important if a speaker recognizes an utterance which is in some way innovative with respect to the resources the speaker has available. An important part of a theory based on GF would be a way of learning grammar on the basis of input and even adjusting the resource if it does not cover the input. This would mean that we not only have dynamic grammar construction on the basis of resources but also dynamic resources which change as the agent is exposed to new linguistic situations. An interesting route to explore would be one that relates this view to the kind of exemplar theory discussed in [Jäger, this volume]. Given that we are assuming that speakers construct grammars on given occasions on the basis, as far as possible, of available resources, we could try to build an exemplar theory where grammars are taken as the exemplars. This might give us a measure of the fitness of grammars which could govern which novel aspects of grammars are accepted into the resource grammars.

3.4 Potential for grammar engineering

The prize of working this out is not only a theory of linguistic evolution and change but also the possibility of building machines that learn language as they use it.

BIBLIOGRAPHY

[Chomsky, 1980] Noam Chomsky. *Rules and Representations*. Columbia University Press, New York, 1980.

[Cooper, 2005a] Robin Cooper. Austinian truth, attitudes and type theory. *Research on Language and Computation*, 3:333–362, 2005.

[Cooper, 2005b] Robin Cooper. Records and record types in semantic theory. *Journal of Logic and Computation*, 15(2):99–112, 2005.

[Cooper, 2007] Robin Cooper. Copredication, dynamic generalized quantification and lexical innovation by coercion. In *Proceedings of GL2007, Fourth International Workshop on Generative Approaches to the Lexicon*, 2007. available from http://www.ling.gu.se/~cooper/records/copredinnov.pdf.

[Cooper, 2008] Robin Cooper. The abstract-concrete syntax distinction and unification in multilingual grammar. In Joakim Nivre, Mats Dahllöf, and Beáta Megyesi, editors, *Resourceful Language Technology: Festschrift in Honor of Anna Sågvall Hein*, number 7 in Studia Linguistica Upsaliensia, pages 49–60. Uppsala University, 2008.

[Harper et al., 1993] R. Harper, F. Honsell, and G. Plotkin. A framework for defining logics. *Journal of the Association for Computing Machinery*, 40(1):143–184, 1993.

[Healey, this volume] P. G. T. Healey. Interactive Misalignment: The Role of Repair in the Development of Group Sub-languages. In R. Cooper and R. Kempson, editors, *Language in Flux: Dialogue Coordination, Language Variation, Language Change and Evolution*. Kings College Press, this volume.

[Jäger, this volume] G. Jäger. Language evolution and George Price's "General Theory of Selection". In R. Cooper and R. Kempson, editors, *Language in Flux: Dialogue Coordination, Language Variation, Language Change and Evolution*. Kings College Press, this volume.

[Larsson, this volume] S. Larsson. Formalizing the Dynamics of Semantic Systems in Dialogue. In R. Cooper and R. Kempson, editors, *Language in Flux: Dialogue Coordination, Language Variation, Language Change and Evolution*. Kings College Press, this volume.

[Martin-Löf, 1984] Per Martin-Löf. *Intuitionistic Type Theory*. Bibliopolis, Naples, 1984.

[Montague, 1974] Richard Montague. *Formal Philosophy: Selected Papers of Richard Montague*. Yale University Press, New Haven, 1974. ed. and with an introduction by Richmond H. Thomason.

[Perera and Ranta, 2007] N. Perera and Aarne Ranta. Dialogue system localization with the dialogue system localization with the GF resource grammar library. In *Proceedings of the ACL Workshop on Grammar-Based Approaches to Spoken Language Processing (SPEECHGRAM)*, 2007.

[Ranta, 2004] Aarne Ranta. Grammatical Framework: A type-theoretical grammar formalism. *Journal of Functional Programming*, 14(2):145–189, 2004.

[Ranta, 2006] Aarne Ranta. Type theory and universal grammar. *Philosophia Scientiae*, Cahier spécial 6 (Special Issue on Constructivism):115–131, 2006.

[Ranta, 2007] Aarne Ranta. Modular grammar engineering in GF. *Research on Language and Computation*, 5(2):133–158, 2007.

[Sharma *et al.*, this volume] D. Sharma, J. Bresnan, and A. Deo. Variation and change in the individual: Evidence from the Survey of English Dialects. In R. Cooper and R. Kempson, editors, *Language in Flux: Dialogue Coordination, Language Variation, Language Change and Evolution*. Kings College Press, this volume.

[Strotmann *et al.*, 2005] A. Strotmann, W. Ng'ang'a, and O. Caprotti. Multilingual access to mathematical exercise problems. In *Electronic Proceedings of the Internet Accessible Mathematical Computation Workshop, ISSAC 2005*, Beijing, 2005. Chinese Academy of Science.

[Wittgenstein, 1953] Ludwig Wittgenstein. *Philosophical Investigations*. Blackwell, Oxford, 1953.

Robin Cooper
Department of Linguistics, University of Gothenburg, Göteborg, Sweden.
cooper@ling.gu.se

Aarne Ranta
Department of Computer Science, Chalmers University of Technology and University of Gothenburg, Göteborg, Sweden
aarne@cs.chalmers.se

Formalizing the Dynamics of Semantic Systems in Dialogue

STAFFAN LARSSON

1 Introduction

Semantic change happens both in the long term (over years and decades) and in the very short term (in a single dialogue)[1]. In addition, semantic change can occur either globally in a language such as Swedish or English, or more locally in specific institution- or activity-specific sub-languages, in social communities, or even between pairs (dyads) of speakers.

As an example, take the discussion in [Clark and Clark, 1979] of "porch" as a verb, as e.g. in "he porched the newspaper". This is an example of an innovative use of an existing word, whose meaning thus changes (in this case, by being extended), provided that the innovation is understood and accepted by the other dialogue participants on concrete occasions of use. This may either be unproblematic (if the other speakers understand and accept the innovative use) or may involve explicit negotiation of the appropriateness of using "porch" in this way. The resulting semantic change may either be limited to a specific dialogue (thus amounting to a "local convention"); it may spread over a community and eventually become part of the language as it is represented in dictionaries; or it may become part of a more limited subcultural/activity-specific sub-language, e.g. the jargon used by U.S. mailmen.

As a further example, an exploratory study of a Map Task dialogue (below) indicates that dialogue participants (henceforth, DP's) coordinate on an ad-hoc vocabulary and associated concepts (meanings) to enable information exchange, and that ad-hoc vocabularies can be cobbled together from a heterogeneous mix of "micro-vocabularies" borrowed from various other (a priori unrelated) domains.

To account for these observations, I outline a formal account of how the meanings of words[2] can change as a result of their use in dialogue. This

---
[1]The work presented here was funded by the Faculty of Arts, University of Gothenburg, and by the project "Semantic Coordination in Dialogue" (The Bank of Sweden Tercentenary Foundation project P2007-0717).

[2]Although this account is intended to cover not only words but also other expressions

account has two main parts: (1) a semantic part in the form of an abstract account of *semantic plasticity* intended to capture formally how meanings can be modified (updated), and (2) a pragmatic account of *semantic negotiation* in dialogue, intended to capture how meanings are negotiated in dialogue and how such negotiations are related to semantic plasticity.

2 Background

This section presents the theoretical and empirical background and motivation for the theory proposed in this paper.

Formal semantics [Portner and Partee, 2002] gives precise analyses of meaning and compositionality, and formal pragmatics gives detailed accounts of how the "common ground" [Clark and Brennan, 1990] is dynamically updated in dialogue [Traum and Larsson, 2003]. However, these research areas typically assume that meanings are static and unchanging during the course of a dialogue, and have not paid much attention to the dynamics of meaning.

In the last two decades, several psycholinguists have begun turning their attention to lexical and semantic coordination in dialogue [Clark and Wilkes-Gibbs, 1986; Garrod and Anderson, 1987; Pickering and Garrod, 2004] and the dynamics of language use in limited groups [Brennan and Clark, 1996; Healey, 1997], and have provided evidence that linguistic conventions can emerge during the course of a dialogue or sequence of dialogues. Preliminary informal and semi-formal analyses have been presented, but the psycholinguistic tradition is not primarily concerned with developing comprehensive formal accounts of their findings. And as observed earlier, these are phenomena that traditional formal semantics and pragmatics are ill-equipped to deal with, because of their static view of meaning.

Some relevant computational work is being done [Steels and Belpaeme, 2005; Briscoe, 2002] on emergent vocabularies and category formation, proving that it is possible to simulate the dynamics of language and meaning in computers. However, this work has not yet addressed the wide variety of strategies for meaning negotiation available to human speakers, nor attempted to provide a comprehensive formal semantics (independent of, e.g. specific learning algorithms).

Thus, a general, detailed, empirically substantiated, and formal account of how linguistic meaning is negotiated and coordinated on a dialogue game micro-level (word-by-word, utterance-by-utterance) is still lacking. The work reported here is a first step towards such an account.

(phrases, syntactic categories, and other linguistic elements), "word" is frequently used instead of "linguistic expression".

3 Vocabulary in a Map Task dialogue

In the Map Task corpus[3], a GIVER explains a route, provided on the giver's map, to a FOLLOWER who has a similar (but slightly different) map but with no route marked. A map contains landmarks portrayed as labelled line drawings. In a route-giving task like that recorded in the Map Task corpus, expressions referring to landmarks, compass directions etc. can be a priori expected as a kind of "prototype" devices for talking about maps. A typical utterance may look as follows[4]:

(1) GIVER: right **a camera shop**, right, head due **south** ... from that just ... **down** for about **twelve centimetres**, have you got **a parked van** at the bottom ?

Here, we may note two expressions expressing direction ("south", "down"), one expressing a distance ("twelve centimetres") and two referring to landmarks ("a camera shop", "a parked van"). A further example:

(2) GIVER: go round the left hand side of the camera shop ... in between **the edge of the page** and the camera shop.

Whereas the previous expressions were completely expected given the general direction-giving task, the reference to an absolute position using "the edge of the page" is perhaps less expected. Clearly, this is a consequence of the DP's talking about a (paper) map rather than e.g. about some actual terrain.

(3) GIVER: so you're ... you're going diagonally sort of north ... northeast ... it's not it's it's a sort of **two o'clock** almost **three o'clock** ... from the allotments ... over

Here, we have GIVER referring to map directions using the expressions "two o'clock" and "three o'clock". This is most likely an everyday variant of the practice of English-speaking pilots of using "o'clock" for directions[5]. Let's look at a final excerpt:

(4) GIVER: right, you go ... down the side of the camera shop right for about twelve centimetres ... and do a sort of **a 'u' shape** ... for and

---

[3] http://www.hcrc.ed.ac.uk/maptask/maptask-description.html
[4] The following excerpts are taken from Map Task dialogue q4nc4, available at the Map Task web site.
[5] Note the use of a hedging "sort of" before "two o'clock", which seems to indicate that the speaker is slightly unsure as to whether the following expression is quite appropriate. A similar observation is made by [Brennan, 2000] (p. 11): "[h]edges seem to be one way of marking that a referring expression is provisional."

the bottom of the 'u' shape should be about three centimetres long, right do you know what i'm meaning
... GIVER: you've worked it out already , eh we're doing **a 'u' shape** round the parked van but it's a sort of three cent– see if you imagine a 'u' right ... **the stems of the 'u' the ... vertical bits** are sort of three centimetres between

First, a trajectory is referred to using the expression "a 'u' shape". This trajectory is then (or so it appears) reified as an imagined 'u'-shape on the map, now acting more akin to a landmark with a concrete (if invisible) shape, size and even component parts ("the ... vertical bits"; "the stems of the 'u' ").

4 Micro-vocabularies used in Map Task dialogue

Based on the above excerpts (and others from the same dialogue), we can provide a very tentative inventory of referring expressions used by GIVER and FOLLOWER in the Map Task dialogue. DP's refer to distances, absolute and relative locations, directions, and trajectories. Below, we list the sub-types of expressions used for each basic class.

- distances on page, in centimetres ("about twelve centimetres")
- absolute locations
  – landmarks ("the camera shop")
  – page edges ("the edge of the page"; "at the bottom"; "the far right-hand side")
  – typography on page ("the words 'yacht club'")
  – (imagined) letter shapes ("the bottom of the 'u' shape"; "the stems of the 'u' the ... vertical bits")
- relative locations
  – relative to landmark ("left hand side of (landmark)")
  – relative to sheet of paper ("the other side of the page")
- directions
  – compass directions ("head due south")
  – left, right, up, down, diagonally, etc.
  – clock directions ("sort of two o'clock")
- trajectories
  – imagined/drawn lines ("a straight line up the ...")
  – letter shapes as trajectories ("do sort of a 'u' shape")

Now, how can we account for this diversity in the range of linguistic expressions used in a simple direction-giving dialogue?

5 Interleaving resource registers

In this section, a basic terminology is proposed, intended to form a basis for a formal account of what we see happening in dialogues such as the one quoted above.

5.1 Perspectives

In the Map Task dialogue, the DP's need to coordinate on a way of talking about the map. What the above excerpts show is that there are several ways of talking about a map; this is also shown in the Maze Game experiments [Garrod and Anderson, 1987; Healey, 1997] where DP's alternative between an abstract "coordinate system" perspective on a maze ("Go to the fourth row down and the second from the right"; "Six three"), and more concrete perspectives involving e.g. corridors ("Go forward, then turn left at the junction") or shapes ("the bit sticking out on the right"). A way of talking about X can be said to involve *taking a perspective*[6] on X and selecting a vocabulary associated with that perspective. Taking a perspective P on subject matter X in dialogue involves an analogue - "talking about X as P" - e.g. talking about directions on a map as clock arms. Different perspectives have different advantages and disadvantages; for example, an abstract perspective is compact but error-prone; a clock perspective on directions may e.g. enable shorter utterances. One plausible reason for interleaving and switching several perspectives and associated vocabularies thus seems to be that it increases the efficiency of communication.

5.2 Resource and ad-hoc registers

A language can be regarded as consisting of a multitude of activity-specific "language games" involving *registers*[7]. This term will be used here to denote *activity-specific semantic systems* ("micro-languages"), each consisting minimally of a set of linguistic signs, i.e. linguistic expressions and associated concepts (meanings)[8]. In dialogue, registers may be used as *resources* which can be borrowed or appropriated into a new activity and adapted to the domain at hand. Putting it differently, an *ad-hoc register* is assembled to be able to talk about some subject matter from one or more perspectives. In the map-task dialogue, several different resource registers are introduced and ac-

---

[6]This terminology follows [Clark, 1997]. Garrod and Anderson [1987] and Healey [1997] instead talk about adopting "description types".

[7]The term "register" is borrowed from [Halliday, 1978]. In general, a register (in the linguistic sense) is a subset of a language used for a particular purpose or in a particular social setting.

[8]A *compositional* register will more generally contain *mappings* between expressions and meanings.

cepted[9]. Often, both introduction and acceptance are implicit, but sometimes verbal signals (including feedback) are used to manage semantic coordination. For example, one could imagine the expression "sort of" being used (perhaps only indirectly, by expressing doubt that the adjacent term is appropriate) to signal introduction of new register.

As mentioned, in the Map Task dialogue we find some resource registers that can be regarded as "standard" or "default" ways of talking about maps, whereas others are more unexpected. First, the standard map register subsumes (1) a *landmarks* register provided to DP's as pictures and text on map, (2) a *compass directions* register, and (3) a *(metric) distance* register. The non-standard parts of the ad-hoc register include:

- *clock* register: map directions as clock hands "two o'clock" etc.
- *sheet-of-paper* register perspective: map as a sheet of paper edges of page distances on page relations between pages (e.g. "opposing page")
- *letter shape* register perspective: Viewing map as a piece of paper where letter shapes can be drawn letter shapes ("a 'u' shape") parts of letter shapes ("stems")

5.3 Appropriating and interleaving registers

To describe the dynamics of registers in the above dialogue, we can say that the clock, sheet-of-paper and letter-shape registers are appropriated into the map task activity, where it is *interleaved* with landmark, compass direction, and metric distance registers to form an ad-hoc register[10]. This involves adapting the meanings associated with resource register vocabularies to the current situation.

6 Meaning potentials

To describe how linguistic expressions can be interactively (in dialogue) appropriated into a new activity, we need an account of semantics which (1) allows several activity-specific meanings for a single expression, and (2) allows open and dynamic meanings which can be modified as a consequence of language use.

The received view in formal semantics [Kaplan, 1979] assumes that there are abstract and context-independent "literal" meanings (utterance-type meaning;

---

[9] Often, several resource registers are used in a single phrase, as e.g. in "in between the edge of the page and the camera shop".

[10] This "interleaving strategy" can be compared with the "switching strategies" evident in maze game experiments [Healey, 1997; Garrod and Anderson, 1987], where speakers switch between perspectives (description types). Presumably, both interleaving and switching are possible.

Kaplan's "character") which can be regarded formally as functions from context to content; on each occasion of use, the context determines a specific content (utterance-token meaning). Abstract meanings are assumed to be static and are not affected by language use in specific contexts. Traditional formal semantics is thus ill-equipped to deal with semantic coordination, because of its static view of meaning.

In the present account, we explore the possibility that the idea of "meaning potentials" may offer a more dynamic view of meaning. The term originates from "dialogical" approaches to meaning [Recanati, 2003]. On the "dialogical" view, language is essentially dynamic; meaning is negotiated, extended, modified both in concrete situations and historically. Interaction and context are essential for describing language, and there is a general focus on the context-dependent nature of meaning. Linguistic expressions have meaning potentials, which are not a fixed and static set of semantic features, but a dynamic potential which can give rise to different situated interpretations. Different contexts exploit different parts of the meaning potential of a word.

In the account of meaning potential presented in these pages, the term *semantic plasticity* refers specifically to the dynamic aspect of meaning potentials. This will be central to our account of how activity-specific abstract[11] meanings are updated and gradually change as a consequence of use[12].

7 Towards a formalization of semantic plasticity

To describe in more detail how DP's coordinate on registers (e.g. when adapting a resource register to a new domain), we need a dynamic account of meanings and registers allowing incremental modifications (updates) to semantic systems. We also need a description of possible dialogue strategies for register coordination. Describing this process *formally* requires formalizing the dynamics of registers and meaning potentials, and the dialogue protocols involved in negotiating semantic systems. In this section, I will take some initial steps towards this goal by sketching a formal account of semantic plasticity.

To keep the theoretical framework general, it intentionally leaves open the issue of semantic representation (formulae of first-order logic, semantic features, semantic vectors, neural nets, etc.) and the kinds of learning mechanisms used in linguistic coordination. The main purpose of the formal semantic component of the theory is (at the current stage at least) not to champion one semantic theory over another. Instead, I want to provide an abstract and general semantic framework which can be connected to the pragmatic account of

---

[11] I use "abstract meaning" to refer to utterance-type meanings, either activity-specific or activity-independent.

[12] Note that "dynamic semantics" [Groenendijk and Stokhof, 1988] is not dynamic in this sense, as it follows traditional formal semantics in assuming a static mapping between words and meanings.

semantic negotiation to describe the interactive conditioning of usage patterns.

The proposal here is to regard the meaning of a linguistic expression or word to depend on previous uses of that word[13] . This makes it possible to model how meanings change as a result of using language in dialogue. The basic idea is that speakers have internalized (potentially complex) dispositions, or *usage patterns*, governing the use of specific words. These dispositions depend, among other things, on observations of previous situations where the word in question has been used, and on specific generalizations over these situations.

Semantic plasticity is described in terms of updates to individual usage patterns associated with words triggered by observations of their use in dialogue. When a usage pattern for a word c is sufficiently coordinated (shared) within a community, we can talk about c as having a meaning potential. Meaning potential is thus construed as emerging from processes of interactive coordination of usage patterns. By modelling plasticity of usage patterns of individuals, we thus indirectly model semantic plasticity in a linguistic community.

That a usage pattern connected to an expression is "sufficiently coordinated" in a community means, roughly, that speakers and hearers are able to use that expression to exchange information sufficiently to enable them to achieve their shared and private goals. For example, in the Map Task dialogues an expression is sufficiently coordinated when DP's are able to make use of it in successfully carrying out the route-giving tasks assigned to them.

7.1 Usage sets and usage patterns

To get a handle on semantic plasticity, a *usage-set*[14] S_c^A will be posited for each language user A and word c , containing all situations[15] where A has observed a use (token) of c. Formally, this can be written as follows:

(5) $\quad S_c^A = \{s \mid A \text{ has observed a use of } c \text{ in situation } s\}$.

The usage set should be regarded merely as an abstract theoretical entity. Again, similar suggestions have been made before:

> Semantic potential is defined in terms of a set of source-situations. A source-situation is a situation that a speaker has learned to as-

---

[13]This idea is not new. Its origins can be traced back to the idea that "meaning is use" [Wittgenstein, 1953].

[14]An alternative term is *situation-collocation*.

[15]It is important to point out that the notion of "situation" I am are using here is an abstract one; the reason is that I want to keep the framework general. In more concrete instantiations of this abstract framework, the notion of a situation will be specified based on the activity in which an agent acts and the requirements on the agent in this activity, as well as the representations and sensory-motor machinery of the agent. As a simple example, in the work of Steels and Belpaeme [2005] the situation is limited to a colour sample, perceived by a robot through a camera and processed into a representations of colours in the form of three real-valued number.

sociate with a term because during learning the speaker has seen the term legitimately applied to that situation. [Bezuidenhout, 2002]

I assume that A generalizes over S_c^A to produce a usage pattern (or usage disposition) $[c]^A$. In cognitive terms one can think of the usage pattern as the "memory trace" of observed uses of c by A.

7.2 Situated meanings and interpretations

On each occasion of use of c in situation s, c has a specific situated (utterance-token) meaning, formally written as $[c]_s$, which derives partly from the shared abstract utterance-type meaning (meaning potential) $[c]$ and partly from s. The subjective counterpart of a situated meaning is a *situated interpretation*, written as $[c]_s^A$ for an agent A; this is the interpretation that A makes of c in s based on A's usage pattern $[c]^A$. A situated meaning $[c]_s$ arises in a situation when DP's make sufficiently similar situated interpretations of c in s.

7.3 Appropriate and non-appropriate uses

I will assume that new uses of a word c can be classified as *appropriate* or *inappropriate* given an existing usage pattern[16] for c[17]. The formal notation which will be used to express that a use of c in situation s is appropriate with regard to A's usage pattern for c is $[c]^A \vdash s$. Correspondingly, $[c]^A \nvdash s$ means that s is not an appropriate situation in which to use c given $[c]^A$[18].

On the whole, if a token of c uttered in a situation s is consistent with $[c]^A$, A is likely to understand c and to judge s to be an appropriate situation of use of c. However, it is important to leave open the possibility that a DP may not understand, or understand but reject, a token of c even if this token of c in the current situation is appropriate with respect to A's usage pattern for c. Similarly, a DP may choose to use a word in a situation where she judges it

---

[16] It may be thought that appropriateness should be defined in terms of collective meaning potentials rather than individual usage patterns, to make sense of talk of "incorrect use of words." However, I believe that such talk is better regarded as one of many strategies for explicit negotiation of meanings, which always occurs in concrete situations and between individual DP's with their respective usage patterns. A theoretical notion of correct or incorrect use of words (independent of individual usage patterns) runs into several problems, such as defining how many DP's must share a usage pattern in order for it to be deemed "correct." This does not mean we cannot make sense of talk of incorrect and correct use of words; it only means that regard such notions primarily as devices in negotiations of shared meanings.

[17] In general, appropriateness is not necessarily a Boolean property, but rather a matter of degree. This is a simplification in the current formalization.

[18] The exact method of deciding whether a new token is appropriate or not will depend on the specific kinds of representations, learning algorithms, and measures of similarity that are assumed (or, in an artificial agent, implemented).

inappropriate given previous uses; This can be referred to as a *creative use*, in contrast to *conservative uses* which are appropriate given previous uses.

7.4 Usage-pattern updates

It follows from the definition of $[c]^A$ that whenever A observes or performs a use of c, S_c^A will be extended, and so the usage pattern $[c]^A$ may change. This is a *usage pattern update*. Prima facie, there are many different possible kinds of ways that a usage pattern may be modified, depending on assumptions regarding semantic representation.

Usage-pattern updates can be distinguished according to several dimensions. An initial rough distinction can be made between *reinforcements* and *revisions*.

If a use of c in situation s is consistent with A's usage pattern for c, i.e. c is appropriate in s ($[c]^A \vdash s$), there is no drastic change; the previous disposition is reinforced by extending $[c]^A$ with A's situated interpretation of c in s, $[c]_s^A$. This will be written formally as $[c]^A \circ_= [c]_s^A$. However, if the current use of c is not consistent with usage disposition ($[c]^A \nvdash s$), there will be a relatively drastic revision of the disposition (formally, $[c]^A \circ_* [c]_s^A$).

We may also want to be able to distinguish between updates based on positive (successful communication) and negative evidence (failed communication). This gives us four different possible update operations:

- $\circ_=^+$: reinforce with positive evidence
- $\circ_=^-$: reinforce with negative evidence
- $\circ_*^+$: revise with positive evidence
- $\circ_*^-$: revise with negative evidence

7.5 Situation-types and structured meaning potentials

To account for how registers can be appropriated (borrowed) from one activity (e.g. telling the time) to another (e.g. direction-giving) we need a formalization which allows new meanings of existing words to be created as a result of observed novel (at least subjectively) language use. Meaning potentials, in addition to being dynamic, can also be *structured*, and thus allow for different contexts to exploit different meaning potential *components*.

I will use *situation-type* as a general term for contexts, activities, institutions etc. where words take on specific meanings. A register, or "micro-language", is the lexicon used in a situation-type, pairing the words used (vocabulary) with meanings (what can be talked about; ontologies; coordinated usage patterns) in the situation-type[19]

In general, a situation-type may be associated with several registers (corresponding to different perspectives on the situation-type), each providing a

---

[19]This terminology builds on (and modifies slightly) that of [Halliday, 1978].

mapping from a vocabulary to (abstract) meanings specific to the situation-type. Conversely, the meaning potential for a word is often structured into several situation-type-specific components.

Above, it has been established that $[c]^A$ is agent A's usage pattern for word c, and that $[c]^A_s$ is the interpretation that agent A makes of c in s; this interpretation is a function of s and $[c]^A$. This notation will now be extended with $[c]^A_\alpha$ - an agent A's situation-type-specific usage pattern component for c in situation-type α. In general, any aspect of the utterance situation-type may activate usage pattern components. A structured meaning potential exists in a linguistic community with coordinated structured usage patterns. A component of structured meaning potential for c in situation-type α is written as $[c]_\alpha$.

As a simple example inspired by the Map Task dialogue above, the meaning potential ["two o'clock"] can be described as structured into

- ["two o'clock"]$_{clock}$, where *clock* stands for an activity type involving telling the time; this meaning potential component can be paraphrased "02:00 AM or PM"

- ["two o'clock"]$_{dir-giv}$, where α has been assigned a situation type index corresponding to direction-giving activities; this meaning potential component is paraphraseable as "east-northeast direction"

7.6 Interpretation and update involving structured usage patterns

A token c_s of a word c in situation s is interpreted by B as $[c]^B_s$. If $[c]^B$ is a complex usage pattern, some component of $[c]^B$ must be selected as the abstract meaning to be used for contextual interpretation. Now, assume that situation s is classified by B as being of situation-type α. This triggers a component of $[c]^B$ - the *activated usage pattern component* $[c]^B_\alpha$.

In this case, $[c]^B_\alpha$ is a likely candidate for which part of $[c]$ gets updated. (If B is not able to find a relevant usage pattern component, B may create a new ad-hoc component, which can be updated during the dialogue. This pattern may or may not be retained afterwards; it may be assimilated into some existing component of $[c]$, or the start of a new usage pattern component.)

Let's take an example. Assume the usage pattern ["two o'clock"] is structured into ["two o'clock"]$_{clock}$ and ["two o'clock"]$_{dir-giv}$, as above. Now assume we get the following utterance:

(6) GIVER: "sort of two o'clock"

Because the activity is direction-giving, FOLLOWER activates the usage pattern component ["two o'clock"]$^{follower}_{dir-giv}$. FOLLOWER then instantiates the component ["two o'clock"]$_{dir-giv}^{follower}$ to arrive at a situated interpretation ["two o'clock"]$_s^{follower}$ (roughly, a 60 degree angle on FOLLOWER's map). Insofar as ["two o'clock"]$_{dir-giv}^{follower} \vdash s$, we get a reinforcing update ["two o'clock"]$_{dir-giv}^{follower} \circ_=^\pm$ ["two o'clock"]$_s^{follower}$.

8 Semantic coordination

This section sketches a framework for modelling *negotiation of meaning in dialogue*, i.e. the social processes (dialogue games) involved in the explicit and implicit negotiation of meaning in dialogue, and their relation to the cognitive processes (semantic updates).

After discussing the basic devices available to speakers for conducting semantic negotiation, I will give examples of how the theory sketched above can be used to analyze short dialogue excerpts in terms of semantic updates. As yet, the theory does not include a taxonomy of dialogue moves involved in semantic negotiation, and therefore the analysis does not include dialogue moves; instead, utterances are analyzed directly in terms of their associated semantic updates. Coming up with a general taxonomy of such moves and their associated updates is a major future research goal.

I assume (provisionally) three basic devices available to dialogue participants for negotiating (and, typically, achieving coordination of) linguistic resources: feedback, explicit negotiation, and accommodation. "Negotiation" is used here in a weak sense of "interactive achievement of coordination".

8.1 Feedback

Feedback [Allwood, 1995; Clark, 1996] involves signals indicating perception, understanding, and acceptance of utterances in dialogue, as well as failure to perceive or understand; clarification requests; and rejections. It is well known that feedback governs that coordination of the dialogue gameboard ("informational coordination"); however, it also guides coordination of language use ("language coordination").

Corrective feedback [Clark, 2003] is common in adult-child interaction. Below is an example; A is the child, B the adult, and as part of the common ground there is a topical object in the situation s visible to both A and B. Assume also that A is not familiar with the word "panda"[20].

(7)   A: Nice bear
      B: Yes, it's a nice panda

A's initial situated understanding of "bear" will here involve various aspects of the topical object that appear relevant to A, e.g. that it looks like (has

---

[20]This is a made-up example; similar examples from real adult-child interactions can be found in [Clark, 2003].

certain physical characteristics in common with) previous animals that people have called "bear" in the presence of A.

In Example 7, B rejects this use of "bear" by providing negative feedback in the form of a correction (however, B also gives positive feedback accepting the assertion that the focused object (animal) "is nice". After B's utterance, A will produce a situated interpretation of "panda", $[\text{"panda"}]_s^A$. According to the principle that "speakers assume that any difference in form signals a difference in meaning" [Clark, 2003], A will try to detect a difference between bears and pandas (such as colour); presumably this will be part of A's situated interpretation of "panda" which is used to revise (or in this case, create). In our theory, the semantic updates resulting from this dialogue are:

- $[\text{"bear"}]^A \circ_*^- [\text{"bear"}]_s^A$
- A creates a new usage pattern $[\text{"panda"}]^A$
- $[\text{"panda"}]^A \circ_*^+ [\text{"panda"}]_s^A$

The first update revises $[\text{"bear"}]^A$ with s as negative evidence; this should make it less likely that A will use "bear" in similar situations in the future. It is possible that A's updates will reflect an inference that a panda is a kind of bear. In any case, what A has learnt is that it is more appropriate to use "panda" than to use "bear" in situations similar to s. As for the second update, perhaps this new usage pattern will be based on $[\text{"bear"}]^A$; this amounts to an assumption that pandas are similar to bears. The third update adds s as positive evidence of a use of "panda".

8.2 Explicit negotiation

Explicit negotiation is the overt meta-linguistic negotiation of the proper usage of words, including e.g. cases where explicit verbal or ostensive definitions are proposed (and possibly discussed). Although semantic negotiation typically has the goal of coordinating language use, it may in general be both antagonistic and cooperative.

Steels and Belpaeme [2005] investigate the effect of social linguistic interaction on learning and coordination of colour categories. Robot agents play a language game of referring to and pointing to colour samples. The language system of an individual agent is modelled as a set of categories in the form of neural nets that respond to sensory data from colour samples, and a lexicon connecting words to categories.

This is clearly a case of semantic plasticity and semantic negotiation, as categories are updated as a result of language use. Semantic negotiation here takes the form of explicit and cooperative negotiation. There is also an asymmetry with respect to the roles within each game; one agent is speaker and the other is the hearer. The interaction follows a predefined "guessing game" script; essentially, a language game of guessing and ostensive definition. The situation, as perceived by the agents, is a set of objects (colour samples), where one is the *topic* object.

Below is a possible interaction between two agents playing the guessing game, and the corresponding updates in terms of the model presented in this paper.

The context is O a set of object (colour samples), $O = \{o_1, \ldots, o_N\}$ where one object o_t is the topical object. The speaker (A) knows which object is the focus object but the hearer (B) does not. The goal of the game is for B to correctly identify o_t from O based on the interaction with A. A will first utter the word (here: "wabaku") that A associates with o_t, i.e. the word associated to the semantic category (in the form of a neural network) that uniquely discriminates o_t. In terms of the theory outlined in these pages, I identify the neural network with the usage pattern, which for the speaker is ["wabaku"]^A.

(8) A: wabaku

B now looks up "wabaku" in its own lexicon and finds an associated semantic category ["wabaku"]^B. B then produces a situated interpretation ["wabaku"]^B_s, namely (given the architecture of agents in this experiment) B's sensory impression of an object (o_g) that B (in this example) is able to uniquely pick out from the context using the semantic category (neural network) ["wabaku"]^B.

(9) B: (points at object o_g)

A then gives feedback to check whether this interpretation is correct. Unfortunately, B has made a wrong guess, which leads to negative feedback and a correction:

(10) A: (feedback indicating rejection of B's answer)

   A: (points to topic object o_t)

B will now produce a new situated interpretation ["wabaku"]$^{B'}_s$ to be (the sensory impression from) object o_t. As a consequence of this game of semantic negotiation, B will then revise its usage pattern (neural network) ["wabaku"]^B by adjusting it to better match this new situated meaning; in our theory[21].

- ["wabaku"]^B $\circ^+_*$ ["wabaku"]$^{B'}_s$

---

[21] It seems that negative evidence is not used in this case; in our notation this would amount to the update ["wabaku"]^B $\circ^-_*$ ["wabaku"]^B_s.

Note that accommodation is not an option in this game. One reason for this is that the context is not rich enough to allow the hearer to infer the intended referent in problematic situations without consulting the speaker.

8.3 Accommodation

In linguistics, *accommodation* can be taken generally to refer to adaptations to the behaviour of other DP's. For example, one may adapt to the presuppositions of an utterance of "The King of France is bald" by modifying the dialogue gameboard to include the existence of a king of France. For the purposes of the current account, the notion of accommodation will be extended beyond the dialogue gameboard, to include changes in the language system.

Upon hearing a word c in new situation s, A's reaction (the kind of feedback A gives) partly depends on $[c]$, but crucially, A's behaviour is not *determined* by $[c]$. This means that A can understand, and may choose to accept, uses of c that deviate from $[c]$; this is a case of accommodation. For understanding to be possible here, it is necessary that the hearer has access to contextual cues in the utterance situation that makes it possible to make a reasonable guess at the meaning of this token of c. Similarly, A's own future uses of c partly depend on $[c]$ but not determined by $[c]$. Thus, A can use c in ways that deviate from $[c]$. Also, A can correctly understand words that she does not use herself[22].

Assuming a semantics which allows new uses of a word c to be classified as appropriate or inappropriate given an existing usage pattern for c, we can construct a simple table of the possible outcomes of a limited class of meaning negotiation games. This class is limited to cases where either a usage is understood and accepted (successful uses), or is rejected or not understood (unsuccessful uses). In the latter case, explicit negotiation of the meaning and proper usage of c may well occur; this table shows a subset of the cases where this does not happen, i.e. the negative feedback (regarding understanding or acceptance) is the last word on the matter (for the time being).

For each word c used in an utterance u, the addressee (here, B) in a dialogue is (usually) expected to react if he thinks c was inappropriately used. If B is able to construct a situated interpretation $[c]_s^B$ (which may involve more or less effort) but finds this use inappropriate ($[c]^B \not\vDash s$), this may be due to a mismatch between s (as perceived by B) and $[c]^B$. B may now reject this use of c explicitly using negative feedback, or quietly alter $[c]^B$ ($[c]^B \circ_*^+ [c]_s^B$) so that this use of c can be counted as appropriate after all. The latter process we may call usage accommodation, or meaning accommodation.

As an example, take the (made-up) dialogue (11) where A uses "porch" in

---

[22]However, it seems unlikely that anyone could correctly use a word that she does not understand.

	$[c]^A \vdash s$	$[c]^A \nvdash s$
$[c]^B \vdash s$	default case $[c]^A \circ^+_= [c]^A_s$ $[c]^B \circ^+_= [c]^B_s$	unnoticed creative $[c]^A \circ^+_* [c]^A_s$ $[c]^B \circ^+_= [c]^B_s$
$[c]^B \nvdash s$	accommodated conservative $[c]^A \circ^+_= [c]^A_s$ $[c]^B \circ^+_* [c]^B_s$	accommodated creative $[c]^A \circ^+_* [c]^A_s$ $[c]^B \circ^+_* [c]^B_s$

Table 1. Possible outcomes of speaker A successfully using c, addressed to hearer B in situation s.

a situation s to mean approximately "successfully throw onto a porch". We assume that B is not familiar with this use (and thus $[\text{"porch"}]^B \nvdash s$) but that this is a common usage for A (and thus $[\text{"porch"}]^A \vdash s$).

(11) A: On my paper round this morning I porched all the papers without getting off my bike!

B: Congratulations.

In this case, B is able to create a situated interpretation $[\text{"porch"}]^A_s$ by using contextual cues, world knowledge, commonsense background, and the ability to reason by analogy and metaphor. Also, B chooses to accept this novel use of "porch" and provides feedback displaying understanding and acceptance (and possibly other attitudes as well). This thus counts as a case of accommodated conservative use in Table 1, and as a consequence (or so our theory predicts) the corresponding updates are made. Other cases are of course also possible. For example, if B had not been able to understand A's use of "porch", or if B had understood it but not accepted it, explicit negotiation would be expected.

8.4 Accommodation of complex meaning potentials

Let us now have a look at a further example of semantic coordination, this time based on the Map Task dialogue, where meaning accommodation leads to updates to complex usage patterns.

Assume, as before, that we get the following utterance in a Map Task dialogue in a situation s:

(12) GIVER: "sort of two o'clock"

In contrast to the example in Section 7.6, we now assume that FOLLOWER is *not* familiar with the "direction-giving" use of "two o'clock". More precisely, ["two o'clock"]^{follower} only contains ["two o'clock"]$^{follower}_{clock}$, so ["two o'clock"]$^{follower} \nvdash s$.

By analogical reasoning using contextual features, FOLLOWER is nevertheless able to correctly understand A's utterance and arrives at a contextual interpretation ["two o'clock"]$^{follower}_{s}$.

Now, since ["two o'clock"]$^{follower} \nvdash s$, FOLLOWER will need to revise ["two o'clock"]^{follower} by creating a new activity-specific usage pattern component ["two o'clock"]$^{follower}_{dir-giv}$. We get an overall update ["two o'clock"]$^{follower} \circ^{+}_{=}$ ["two o'clock"]$^{follower}_{s}$ which can be decomposed as two updates. First, creation of ["two o'clock"]$^{follower}_{dir-giv}$, and then updating with the situated interpretation: ["two o'clock"]$^{follower}_{dir-giv} \circ^{+}_{=}$ ["two o'clock"]$^{follower}_{s}$. After this update, we have ["two o'clock"]$^{follower} \vdash s$, i.e. the novel (for FOLLOWER) use of "two o'clock" by GIVER has been accommodated.

9 Kinds of coordination in dialogue

On our view, two kinds of coordination happen in everyday human-human dialogue. *Informational coordination* has successfully been studied using the concepts of dialogue games and updates to a shared dialogue gameboard. One of the goals of the research presented here is to extend this approach to describing *language coordination* (and more specifically, semantic coordination) in terms of the dynamics of updates to language systems.

The framework sketched here aims at describing all kinds of semantic coordination. In the "two o'clock" example given above, coordination is essentially a matter of mapping an expression ("two o'clock") to a pre-existing meaning (denoted in the compass directions register as "east-northeast"). For this kind of coordination, some version of traditional formal semantics may suffice, provided it is extended with a dynamic mapping between linguistic expressions and their meanings.

However, in other cases the dynamics go beyond word-meaning mappings. Specifically, to account for cases where an expression is used to denote a *new* concept, such as "the 'u'-shape" above, we need to describe the dynamics of *concept creation*. Similarly, existing concepts may be affected by their use in dialogue, e.g. by subtly modifying values of usage-governing conceptual features by small increments. For example, in [Steels and Belpaeme, 2005], concepts are represented as neural nets which are updated by small adjustments to network weights, according to a standard back-propagation algorithm.

These dynamics, which I refer to as *concept-level* dynamics, are an important motivation for the introduction of meaning potentials. They are also our main reason for believing that traditional formal semantics will not suffice to account for semantic coordination.

To deal with concept-level dynamics in a general way, one will probably need to keep track of of semantic features connected to expressions in the lexicon [Pustejovsky, 1991] and allow these feature matrices to be updated as a result of semantic negotiation and coordination subdialogues. Work in this direction may benefit from ideas put forward by [Gärdenfors, 2000], as well as in work on machine learning [Mitchell, 1997] and Latent Semantic Analysis [Landauer and Dumais, 1997]. One version of formal semantics which seems promising for the illumination of concept-level dynamics is the record-type theoretic approach which Cooper has been developing [Cooper, 2005a, 2005b]. This formal approach allows for both underspecification or uncertainty of meaning by the use of types of meaning and also a structured approach to meaning analysis which allows for modification of meaning in a way which is not possible, for example, in the classical formal semantics analysis of meaning as functions from contexts to intensions.

10 Semantic dynamics and dialogue systems

As we have seen above, vocabularies (and associated meanings) in human-human dialogue are dynamic and changeable. By contrast, a prominent problem in current dialogue systems is that the user must adapt to a static pre-programmed vocabulary. This is related to what Brennan [2000] calls the "vocabulary problem" in spoken dialogue systems. A solution to this problem, quite compatible with what has been proposed here, is sketched by Brennan:

> A system could begin a dialogue with a large (an inefficient) vocabulary, in order to allow a user to propose terms. Negotiation - either implicit or explicit - of mappings [...] would be necessary early in the dialogue[.] ... the system would maintain a discourse model of currently active conceptualizations, terms, and mappings to rapidly narrow down the vocabulary its speech recognizer expected. [Brennan, 2000]

Allowing dialogue systems (and other language technologies) to coordinate with users on language use would clearly be beneficial. Relatively simple instances of this would include switching between predefined vocabularies, as well as adding new words to the interpretation lexicon and assigning them a predefined meaning. To do this in interaction with the user would require the system to be able to follow common protocols for coordination of language use. A more complex version is to keep track of of semantic features connected to words in the lexicon [Pustejovsky, 1991] and allow these feature matrices to be updated as a result of semantic negotiation and coordination subdialogues.

Here's an example of the kind of dialogue that can be envisaged between a user and a city navigation system.

(13) U: What's the nearest cafe?

S: Danny's deli is just north of your current location. [*using compass + distance register*]

U: uh. I don't know where that is!

S: Turn to face the church. Walk straight ahead for one block, then make a right turn and walk 50 meters. [*using blocks, buildings and streets register*]

U: Oh it's on High Street? [*user switches to street-name ontology*]

S: No. It's on South Bridge, number 45 [*using street-name ontology*]

U: Sorry, I don't know where South Bridge is.

S: Danny's deli is on Clerk Street, near the bridge in the city centre [*using slightly different street-name ontology; South Bridge and Clerk Street are different sections of the same street, but the whole street is sometimes referred to as Clerk Street*]

U: Sorry, I don't get it

S: Turn to face the church and walk along Meadow street towards the north, then at the junction to Clerk Street make a right turn and walk along Clerk Street for about 50 meters until it changes name into South Bridge, then continue on South bridge until you reach number 45. [*combining several registers in one utterance*]

This dialogue shows many of the characteristics of dialogues from the Maze Game experiments [Garrod and Anderson, 1987; Healey, 1997], as well as the Map Task dialogue in Section 3, including switching between and interleaving various registers in response to communication difficulties.

11 Conclusion

To account for the observed dynamics of semantic systems in dialogue, this paper has sketched a formalization of the notion of meaning potential, in the form of dynamic structured usage patterns which are shared within a linguistic community through a process of semantic coordination in dialogue. This process can be described as updates to structured usage patterns resulting from language use. Some basic mechanisms of coordination - feedback, explicit negotiation, and accommodation - have also been outlined.

This paper presents preliminary work aiming towards a unified theoretical account of semantic coordination. Apart from developing the theory and the formal framework further, an important goal is to extend the coverage of this theory by further empirical studies, and to start implementing strategies for semantic coordination in practical dialogue systems.

BIBLIOGRAPHY

[Allwood, 1995] Allwood, Jens 1995. An activity based approach to pragmatics. Technical Report (GPTL) 75, Gothenburg Papers in Theoretical Linguistics, University of Göteborg.

[Bezuidenhout, 2002] Bezuidenhout, Anne L. 2002. Truth-conditional pragmatics. In Tomberlin, James E., editor 2002, *Philosophical Perspectives 16: Language and Mind, 2002*. Blackwell Publishers, Oxford. 105–134.

[Brennan and Clark, 1996] Brennan, S. E. and Clark, H. H. 1996. Conceptual pacts and lexical choice in conversation. *Journal of Experimental Psychology: Learning, Memory and Cognition* 22:482–493.

[Brennan, 2000] Brennan, S. E. 2000. The vocabulary problem in spoken language systems. In Luperfoy, S., editor 2000, *Automated spoken dialog systems*. Cambridge, MA: MIT Press. To appear.

[Briscoe, 2002] Briscoe, E. J., editor 2002. *Linguistic Evolution through Language Acquisition: Formal and Computational Models*. Cambridge University Press.

[Clark and Brennan, 1990] Clark, H. H. and Brennan, S. E. 1990. Grounding in communication. In Resnick, L. B.; Levine, J.; and Behrend, S. D., editors 1990, *Perspectives on Socially Shared Cognition*. APA.

[Clark and Clark, 1979] Clark, E. V. and Clark, H. H. 1979. When nouns surface as verbs. *Language* 55(4):767–811.

[Clark and Wilkes-Gibbs, 1986] Clark, H. H. and Wilkes-Gibbs, D. 1986. Refering as a collaborative process. *Cognition* 22:1–39.

[Clark, 1996] Clark, H. H. 1996. *Using Language*. Cambridge University Press, Cambridge.

[Clark, 1997] Clark, Eve V. 1997. Conceptual perspective and lexical choice in acquisition. *Cognition* 64(1):1–37.

[Clark, 2003] Clark, E. V. 2003. *First language acquisition*. Cambridge: Cambridge University Press.

[Cooper, 2005a] Cooper, Robin 2005a. Austinian truth, attitudes and type theory. *Research on Language and Computation* 3(4):333–362.

[Cooper, 2005b] Cooper, Robin 2005b. Records and record types in semantic theory. *J. Log. and Comput.* 15(2):99–112.

[Gärdenfors, 2000] Gärdenfors, Peter 2000. *Conceptual Spaces: The Geometry of Thought*. MIT Press, Cambridge, MA, USA.

[Garrod and Anderson, 1987] Garrod, Simon C. and Anderson, Anthony 1987. Saying what you mean in dialogue: a study in conceptual and semantic co-ordination. *Cognition* 27:181–218.

[Groenendijk and Stokhof, 1988] Groenendijk, J. A. G. and Stokhof, M. J. B. 1988. Context and information in dynamic semantics. In *Working models of human perception*. Academic Press.

[Halliday, 1978] Halliday, M.A.K 1978. *Language as Social Semiotic: The Social Interpretation of Language and Meaning*. Baltimore: University Park Press.

[Healey, 1997] Healey, P.G.T. 1997. Expertise or expertese?: The emergence of task-oriented sub-languages. In Shafto, M.G. and Langley, P., editors 1997, *Proceedings of the 19th Annual Conference of the Cognitive Science Society*. 301–306.

[Kaplan, 1979] Kaplan, D. 1979. Dthat. In Cole, P., editor 1979, *Syntax and Semantics v. 9, Pragmatics*. Academic Press, New York. 221–243.

[Landauer and Dumais, 1997] Landauer, Thomas K and Dumais, Susan T. 1997. A solution to Plato's problem: The latent semantic analysis theory of the acquisition, induction and representation of knowledge. *Psychological Review* 104:211–240.

[Mitchell, 1997] Mitchell, Tom M. 1997. *Machine Learning*. McGraw-Hill, New York.
[Pickering and Garrod, 2004] Pickering, Martin J. and Garrod, Simon 2004. Toward a mechanistic psychology of dialogue. *Behavioral and Brain Sciences* 27(02):169–226.
[Portner and Partee, 2002] Portner, P and Partee, B. H., editors 2002. *Formal Semantics: The Essential Readings*. Malden, Mass.
[Pustejovsky, 1991] Pustejovsky, J. 1991. The generative lexicon. *Computational Linguistics* 17(4):409–441.
[Recanati, 2003] Recanati, Francois 2003. *Literal Meaning - The Very Idea*. Cambridge University Press.
[Steels and Belpaeme, 2005] Steels, Luc and Belpaeme, Tony 2005. Coordinating perceptually grounded categories through language: A case study for colour. *Behavioral and Brain Sciences* 28(4):469–89. Target Paper, discussion 489-529.
[Traum and Larsson, 2003] Traum, David and Larsson, Staffan 2003. The information state approach to dialogue management. In Smith, Ronnie and Kuppevelt, Jan, editors 2003, *Current and New Directions in Discourse & Dialogue*. Kluwer Academic Publishers.
[Wittgenstein, 1953] Wittgenstein, Ludwig 1953. *Philosophical Investigations*. Basil Blackwell Ltd.

Staffan Larsson
Department of Linguistics, University of Gothenburg, Göteborg, Sweden.
sl@ling.gu.se

'All that he endeavoured to prove was': On the emergence of grammatical constructions in dialogual and dialogic contexts

ELIZABETH CLOSS TRAUGOTT

1 Introduction

In the present paper[1] I discuss some of the kinds of evidence we can find in historical texts for the emergence of grammatical constructions, and the kinds of discourse contexts in which these changes may have arisen. My particular example is the development of the WH- and ALL-"pseudo-clefts", as in *What/All I said was X, What/All I did was X*. In the course of this discussion I also aim to provide an example of the ways in which combining the insights of grammaticalization and construction grammar can help account for micro-changes in morphosyntax (for some earlier studies with similar objectives, see [Bergs and Diewald, forthcoming; Traugott, 2008, forthcoming; Trousdale, forthcoming(a), forthcoming(b)]).

I start with some background assumptions and terminology (section 2). In section 3, I sketch out the development of ALL- and WH-pseudo-clefts, and discuss in which discourse contexts each construction appears to have arisen. Section 4 outlines what the dual perspectives of grammaticalization and construction grammar suggest not only for the pseudo-clefts but for the emergence of constructions in general.

2 Some background assumptions and terminology

Here I introduce the distinctions that I am assuming between innovation and change (2.1), and between "dialogual" and "dialogic" contexts for language use (2.2). I also outline the views of grammaticalization and construction grammar relevant for this paper (2.3).

---

[1] Many thanks to Ruth Kempson for comments and to Scott Schwenter and Graeme Trousdale for ongoing discussion of the issues. Ulrich Detges, Amanda Patten, and Richard Waltereit made several helpful comments on an earlier draft. Liz Coppock and Harry Tily helped me access some of the electronic databases. To all my deepest appreciation.

2.1 Innovation and language change

I assume that language change arises in language use [Milroy, 2003; Croft, 2000], i.e. in "practices of speaking" [Andersen, 2006, p65]. It starts as an ad hoc innovation by an individual in the speech (or writing) situation, but counts as a change only when the innovation is adopted by others [Weinreich et al., 1968].

A further assumption is that innovations may occur throughout a language user's life-time, not only prior to puberty.[2] While more radical morphosyntactic innovations leading to structural changes may be privileged in early child language acquisition, some occur later, though at a less rapid rate (see [Bergs, 2005]). Innovations are made by speakers as well as hearers, that is, in production as well as perception. In language change there is normally no intention to change some aspect of language [Keller, 1994]. What speakers and addressees intend is to negotiate common ground (see [Clark, 1996; Croft, 2000]) and achieve certain ends such as getting each other to listen, exchange information, or to behave in certain ways, but not normally to change the language.

Negotiation of common ground is central to my view of discourse analysis.[3] I will be adopting not only a primarily neo-Gricean information-structure-based approach to the data in question (see [Traugott, 2004]), but also a more interactional approach (see e.g. [Mann and Thompson, 1992; Ford, 1994]).

2.2 Dialogual and dialogic discourse contexts

The focus of this volume is dialogue. The term can be understood in two ways. One is general speaker-hearer interaction, in which participants negotiate meanings through alignment, and accommodation (see [Larsson, this volume]). The second is more narrowly understood as turn-taking involving consecutive patterns of the type in (1) (see [Sacks et al., 1974]):

(1) A: Current speaker selects next speaker.
     B: Next speaker (selected or self-selected) takes a turn.
     A: First speaker continues.

Since in historical work we are dealing with written texts, we need to think not only of a Speaker-Addressee (SP-AD) dyad, but also of a Writer-Reader (W-R) dyad. We may combine these as SP/W-AD/R. Unless we are to restrict ourselves entirely to represented conversations, we also need to think of SP/W

---

[2] Contrast the Chomskyan generative position that language change is grammar change (see [Kiparsky, 1968]), with the concomitant assumption that a change is a change in the individual child's grammar. The two points of view are discussed in [Croft, 2000, pp42–63]) and [Hopper and Traugott, 2003, 1993, pp43–50].

[3] Not all interaction is cooperative, or seeks to achieve common ground; however, distinctly non-cooperative interactions are not evidenced in my data.

as negotiating meaning through dynamic, interactive, discourse expressed by one individual (the writer, represented narrator, etc.).

Recently, as researchers in historical pragmatics have sought to identify contexts in which particular changes occurred, there has been considerable interest in turn-taking as a context for the development of micro-changes, as well as negotiation of meaning within a turn (see e.g. [Detges and Waltereit, 2003; Detges, 2006]), and this is one of the discourse contexts that I will discuss here. Since it involves interlocutors, it is language-external.

Another context, this time a language-internal one, that I will be discussing is dialogicity.[4] As has long been recognized, especially in work associated with [Roulet, 1984] and [Ducrot, 1984, 1996] (see also more recently, e.g. [Schwenter, 2000; Nølke, 2006]), discourses may be relatively homogeneous in orientation (i.e. closely aligned toward some argumentative conclusion), or multiply perspectivized, in both cases either within or across turns.[5] Multiply perspectivized expressions may be said to be "dialogic" or "polyphonic". In the work cited above, attention is paid to expressions that code multiple perspectives, for example *but* vs. *and*, or focus particles like *only* within a clause. Here, however, I will be concerned primarily with prior contexts that either include such expressions and/or are intended to be contesting, and therefore introduce multiple perspectives.

Historically there are two issues to consider here. One is that cross-linguistically expressions that code multiple perspectives typically derive from relatively neutral or singly perspectivized expressions (e.g. *but* < *butan* 'on the outside of', see [Nevalainen, 1991]), *only* < 'singly' (see [Brinton, 1998]), *in fact* 'epistemic adverb' < 'in practice' (see [Schwenter and Traugott, 2000]). The other is that such dialogic meanings can be shown in many cases to arise in linguistic contexts where SP/Ws are negotiating non-aligned perspectives, i.e. are presenting opposing arguments to others or to imaginary interlocutors. It is the latter issue that will be the second focus of my attention.

A useful framework within which to discuss dialogual and dialogic contexts is to distinguish numbers of participants and numbers of perspectives invoked. Drawing on Roulet and Ducrot, [Schwenter, 2000] proposed the distinction between monologual-dialogual interaction (this pertains to numbers of interlocutors), and monologic-dialogic perspectives (this pertains the orientation of the speaker's move (alignment or disalignment, as in refutation, counter-expectation, or adversativity)[6] and to the numbers of perspectives in-

---

[4]The terminology can be problematic, e.g. the term "dialogic" is sometimes used to cover both dialogual and dialogic interaction [Ford, 1994; Taavitsainen et al., 2006].

[5]Much of this work ultimately goes back to Bakhtin, see [Holquist, 1981].

[6]Various taxonomies of such moves have been proposed, among them [Mann and Thompson, 1992] where antithesis, concession, and contrast are distinguished, and [Rudolph, 1996], where adversativity and concessions are distinguished.

voked. Treating them as independent parameters allows us to account for the fact that relatively homogeneous or relatively polyphonic perspectives may be taken within or across turns. The intersection of the two dimensions may be modeled simplistically as in Table 1. While Table 1 is based on [Schwenter, 2000], it should be noted that he is primarily concerned with dialogicity within the clause rather than in prior context:

Number of speakers	Number of viewpoints in context	
One: monologual	One: monologual / monologic	Two: monologual / dialogic
Two: dialogual	One: dialogual / monologic	Two: dialogual / dialogic

Table 1. Speakers and viewpoints (based on [Schwenter, 2000, p260])

To date, most of the historical work on interaction in dialogue has been focused on the turn. Over the years some hypotheses have been presented arguing that a particular construction has arisen out of turn-taking in dialogue. For example, in his article on conditionals as topics, Haiman [1978] draws on [Jespersen, 1940, p374] suggestion that conditionals arose out of questions with implied positive answers to account for both the alleged topicality of conditionals, and their tendency to be expressed by forms that are interrogative. Haiman proposes a "mini-conversation" of the type:

(2) A: Is he coming?
     B: (Yes.)
     A: Well then, I'll stay.

which "then functions as the basis for further discussion" [Haiman, 1978, p571]. This assumes that A or some overhearing participant takes the A/B pair and produces a new utterance that combines the pair, and that this combined pair later becomes conventionalized as a new structure in the linguistic system. Whether this kind of alignment and coordination among speakers and hearers actually results in the innovation of conditionals with interrogative forms remains to be tested, to my knowledge.[7]

More recently, seeking to go beyond the rather general (and largely information-structure-based) theory of invited inferencing as a major source of change

---

[7]Rossari and Cojocariu [2007] provide diachronic evidence that questions such as French la raison/la cause? 'the reason/the cause?' (used either dialogually across turns or monologically within a turn) came to be used as routines for introducing explanations and elaborations, but these do not involve the development of complex clauses as in the case of conditionals proposed by Jespersen and Haiman.

(see [Traugott and König, 1991; Traugott and Dasher, 2002]), [Detges and Waltereit, 2003; Detges, 2006; Waltereit, 2006] have discussed the development of discourse markers like Italian *Guarda!* 'look' > 'see'/ 'self-selection marker',[8] and of the cliticization of tonic subject pronouns in French and of tonic object pronouns Spanish. They argue that speakers self-select at turns by using attention-getters in "illegitimate" ways, e.g. *Guarda!* when there is nothing to look at, and of tonic clitics when there is no contrast. As the self-selection strategies are used more frequently, and become routinized, the original meanings are lost ("bleached"). The authors emphasize that the forms preexist and propose that it is the implicatures that arise specifically in turn-taking contexts that favor change, while the interactive turn-taking strategy motivates the change. [Waltereit and Detges, 2007] further distinguish turn-taking strategies ("What are we going to do next?") from those negotiating common ground ("What do I believe that you believe concerning the felicity of my speech act?"). They propose that discourse markers are the product of the first strategy, whereas other types of change, such as the development of epistemic uses of adverbs like *in fact* or French *bien* 'surely' have a different, contesting function, and are the product of the second. The distinctions I am drawing between dialogual and dialogic contexts are clearly related to those proposed by Detges and Waltereit in various writings, but my emphasis is on the way in which contesting contexts may give rise to a broader range of expressions than epistemics, and on how they may interact with turn-taking.[9]

Although monologual-dialogic perspectivizing is well attested in older written materials, unfortunately many of these texts do not provide much direct evidence for the self-selection that is the focus of many of Detges' and Waltereit's papers. While they could be identified in spoken corpora collected in the last hundred years or so, and in novels, dramas, etc. that represent such speech, turn-taking that occurs in earlier texts may reflect conversational strategies only indirectly [Culpeper and Kytö, 2000]. Early courtroom trials can be a useful source of dialogue. While contemporary trials are of a largely ritualized nature, with pre-set rules for turn-taking where self-selection is limited, early trials present more oral features, and are more useful for analysis of dialogual turn-taking than might at first be thought (see [Culpeper and Kytö, 2000; Kryk-Kastovsky, 2000].[10] This is because in the seventeenth and eighteenth

---

[8]For similar developments see [Brinton, 2001] on Look!, [Lindström and Wide, 2005] on Swedish Hör du! 'Listen' and other imperatives that have become discourse markers.

[9]Although there is brief mention of the contesting dialogicity of the interaction in passages used in [Detges, 2006] to argue for turn-taking as the strategy leading to obligatory subjects in French, it appears to have been a far stronger motivation than is implied.

[10]Archer [2007] provides a detailed bibliography of Early Modern English courtroom trials as well as an assessment of their value for linguistic analysis. Huber [forthcoming] discusses the Proceedings of the Old Bailey at the end of the Early Modern English and the beginning

centuries defendants did not have defense lawyers to speak for them (and scribes appear to have represented speech fairly well). Basing her analysis on courtroom trials from 1640-1679, Archer [2006] provides figures for initiation, response, and follow-up by judges, defendants, and witnesses, and shows that defendants responded to direct elicitation by following it with another elicitation device almost as frequently as judges. This means that aspects of self-selection are far more likely to occur in early trials than in those of the present day. In what follows I will, draw examples not only from texts with represented dialogue (trials, drama, and narratives) but also from monologual reports.

2.3 Grammaticalization and construction grammar

I will be embedding my discussion of the development of the WH- and ALL-pseudo-clefts in the larger contexts of grammaticalization and construction grammar. Grammaticalization has been defined in various ways (see e.g. [Bisang et al., 2004; Brinton and Traugott, 2005; van Gelderen, 2004; Heine et al., 1991; Hopper and Traugott, 2003; Lehmann, 1995; Roberts and Roussou, 2003]). Here I take grammaticalization to be:

> The change whereby in certain linguistic contexts speakers use parts of a construction with a grammatical function. Over time the resulting grammatical construction may continue to be assigned new grammatical functions. (based on [Brinton and Traugott, 2005, p99])

The developments under consideration in this paper concern an already grammatical construction which involves grammaticalization / constructionalization into another construction without lexical origins (see also [Lehmann, forthcoming][11]), and therefore gives insight into alignments with topic and focus, in this case exhaustive focus patterns.

Some researchers on grammaticalization associate it with a variety of reduction processes (e.g. [Givón, 1979; Lehmann, 1995]), or increasing dependency (e.g. [Haspelmath, 2004]). The assumption is that "grammar" is restricted to "core" structures (syntax, semantics, phonology). However, if one regards grammaticalization as the morphosyntactic change whereby grammatical material is formed, and considers grammar to include "higher" discourse structures, a less reductive perspective can be adopted (see [Tabor and Traugott, 1998]). Himmelmann [2004] suggests that the following three types of expansion are criterial for grammaticalization:

---

of the Modern English period.

[11] In an early version of this paper, Lehmann referred to "grammaticalization without lexical bleaching". In the current version he refers to manipulation of structures "that do not denote anything".

(3) a. Semantic-pragmatic expansion, e.g. when articles arise out of demonstratives they may take on uniqueness functions dependent on the larger situation, including encyclopedic knowledge (*the president*), and may be used in associative anaphoric contexts (cf. *a house – the front door*, where the definite article is licensed by association with *house*); neither of these contexts is available for demonstratives.

   b. Syntactic expansion, e.g. emerging articles develop first in core subject and object argument positions, only later, if ever, in adpositional ones.

   c. Host-class expansion to more parts of speech, e.g. a grammaticalizing form will increase its range of collocations with members of the relevant category (the range of *be going to* expanded from activity to stative verb subclasses when it was reanalyzed from motion with a purpose to futurity).

Like grammaticalization, construction grammar has been defined in various ways (for overviews, see e.g. [Croft and Cruse, 2004; Fried, 2004; Langacker, 2005]. Construction grammar is construed primarily in synchronic terms. Key for our purposes here are the following characteristics (see [Goldberg, 2003, 2006]):

- Form and meaning are paired as equals,
- Grammar is conceived as holistic, i.e. no one level of grammar is "core",
- Grammar is usage-based, i.e. grounded in speakers and utterances,
- Individual constructions are independent but related in a hierarchic system with several levels of schematicity and may intersect.

Importantly, construction grammar assumes that parts of a construction are not assembled on-line. Rather:

[A] construction represents an automated, routinized chunk of language that is stored and activated by the language user as a whole, rather than 'creatively' assembled on the spot. [De Smet and Cuyckens, 2007, p188]

Since construction grammars treat all linguistic elements from morpheme and word to clause as constructions [Goldberg, 2003], grammaticalization intersects only with the development of grammatical constructions [Noël, 2007]. Langacker [2005] has suggested that three factors are crucial in thinking about a grammatical construction: grammatical constructions must be schematic, productive (presumably in terms of tokens, since frequency of use is often mentioned as a criterion, see [Goldberg, 2006]), and not fully compositional (see also [Bybee et al., 1994]).

It is useful to posit for each construction three type levels and one token level to capture similarities and differences between constructions under discussion in terms of schematicity [Traugott, 2008, forthcoming; Fried, forthcoming; Trousdale, forthcoming(a), forthcoming(b)]:

(4) a. Macro-constructions: high-level schemas, e.g. ditransitives,

b. Meso-constructions: sets of similarly-behaving micro-constructions, e.g. *give* Obj Obj2, *send* Obj Obj2, which have prepositional variants with *to*, as distinct from those that have prepositional variants with *for*, e.g. *buy* Obj Obj2,

c. Micro-constructions: individual construction-types, e.g. *give* Obj Obj2 as distinct from *send* Obj Obj2,

d. Constructs: empirically attested tokens of micro-constructions; these are the locus of innovation.

The type levels are meant to characterize "family-resemblances". They may have further sub-types. Most importantly they form networks with other constructions, allowing for partial matches across constructions [Trousdale, forthcoming(a)]. It should be noted that this view of constructions emphasizes the smaller parts out of which a larger construction is constructed (subject to inheritance hierarchies). Some degree of construction-internal accessibility is also assumed, i.e. the "chunk" is not a rigidly fixed entity; if it were, it would not be subject to variation and change. It should also be noted that constructs are characterized in (4d) as the locus of innovation. When such innovations are conventionalized by some set of speakers, a micro-construction emerges, and this is a change.

The term "schema" used above deserves discussion. Focusing on synchronic cognitive systems available to individual language-users or members of a close-knit speech community, Langacker [1987, p371] uses "schema" as an abstraction compatible with all its members, and membership of which "is not a matter of degree". However, in the grammaticalization literature, which focuses on generalizations about shifts of members of categories over time, the term is used very differently. It is equated with general patterns of change (also referred to as "clines"). An item may be more or less prototypical for its category over time and speech communities, and therefore membership of a schema may be more or less prototypical. For example, a number of binominal partitive expressions such as *a bit of, a lot of, a shred of*, and *a deal of*, came over time to have quantifier and degree modifier polysemies, as in *a bit of pie* (partitive) vs. *a bit of a cheat*(quantifier), *a bit prettier* (degree modifier) (see

[Traugott, 2008, forthcoming]). The first expression to undergo this change was *a deal of*. In Old English *dæl* was a member of the category of nominals referring to parts.[12] In Middle English, especially in the context of *great*, it came to be used to express quantity ('amount') rather than 'part' and, in the form *a deal* came to function like adverbial degree modifiers such as *quite, a lot*:

(5) Why can't gentlefolks wroit like Ned Tiller oop at th'Red Lion - printin' loike. It's easier to read, and ***a deal prettier*** to look at. (1863 M. E. Braddon, *Aurora Floyd*, Ch. 22)[13]

By the twentieth century *a deal of* became largely restricted to contexts with a preceding adjective like *good, great*, and especially to *a great deal of money/trouble* and similar formulaic, prefabricated expressions. *A deal of* participated in a general change from binominal partitives such as *a lot of, a bit of, a shred of* to binominal degree modifiers with quantifier readings, but only in a marginal way. Therefore it participated in the schema partitive > quantifier > degree modifier only to a limited extent. In Standard English it never became aligned to the meso- and macro-level degree modifiers and eventually ceased to participate in the quantifier construction except in fixed expressions, whereas *a lot (of)* and *a bit (of)* became well established and underwent changes to adverbial status (for example, they can be used as free adjuncts in response to questions, as can more prototypical degree modifiers like *quite*, and *indeed*).

While schemas of the synchronic type discussed by Langacker may, by hypothesis, be accessible to speakers, diachronic ones cannot, except indirectly (e.g. by drawing inferences from polysemy relationships or age-graded variation). Diachronic schemas are to be understood not as conceptual imprints on the mind but as analysts' generalizations [Andersen, 2001, 2006] concerning steps by which changes from one category to another may emerge over time, subject to general constraints of language acquisition.[14] It is the business of the historian of language to seek out not only individual changes that might be accessible to speakers during their life-times, but also to find general patterns or schemas that, from the perspective of the linguist, can be seen to emerge over generations, centuries, even millennia. As McMahon has said:

> To understand language change as well as we can, we have to deal with two different levels all the time, that of the speaker, and that of the linguistic system ... when it

---

[12]The following approximate periods of the history of English will be referred to: Old English 650-1150, Middle English 1150-1500, Early Modern English 1500-1750, Modern English 1750-1970, Present Day English 1970-.

[13]Thanks to Graeme Trousdale for this example, drawn from a Google search.

[14]This is in contrast to the alleged position that Newmeyer [1998] and Janda [2000] attribute to several proponents of directionality in grammaticalization.

comes to language change, linguists need to stand outside what is going on to understand it. That is what historians are for. [McMahon, 2006, p148, 175]

3 A case study: WH- and ALL-pseudo-cleft constructions

WH- and ALL-pseudo-clefts, as in *What/All I wanted was a Ninja Turtle*, are micro-constructions of considerable interest for several reasons. For one, they involve discourse-structuring of focus elements, and are therefore closely related to information structuring and rhetorical strategizing. Almost all research to date on pseudo-clefts has been on WH-clefts and TH-clefts (the latter will not be discussed here). Some typical (for the most part constructed) examples are:

(6) a. What Martin ate was the banana. (WH-cleft)
     b. What Martin did was (to) dance the mambo. (WH-cleft)
     c. All Martin ate was the banana. (ALL-cleft)
     d. All/*Everything that one has to do is to start training earlier. (ALL-cleft [Kay, 2002, BNC]]))

It is generally agreed that pseudo-clefts share with IT-clefts the following properties (see e.g. [Prince, 1978; Higgins, 1979; Quirk *et al.*, 1985; Delin, 1990; Collins, 1991; Davidse, 2000; Lambrecht, 2001; Huddleston *et al.*, 2002; Miller, 2006; Delin and Oberlander, 2008]:

- Two clauses, one of which is a relative, one of which involves a copula.

- Uniqueness and contrastiveness: elements named by the clefted constituent are construed in terms of an exhaustive, exclusive listing (Martin ate only the banana, not the peach, grapes, etc.); they are dialogic.

- Givenness: some part of the construction (typically the relative) must be given or at least recoverable (Martin ate something).

- Specificational/identifying focus: the complement of the copula is specific and referential (not ascriptive or non-referential) (see Patten 2007, forthcoming for detailed discussion of specificationality); compare (6) with (7):

(7) a. What she did is a shame. (non-referential nominal)
     b. What she did was laughable. (ascriptive adjective)
     c. What he said was laughed at. (ascriptive passive)

d. All/Everything that I command is yours now. (≠ ALL-cleft; ascriptive [Kay, 2002, BNC]])

There are also "reverse clefts" such as:

(8) a. The banana was what Martin ate. (reverse WH-cleft)
b. The banana was all Martin ate. (reverse ALL-cleft)

Depending on their context, these may have a "given-focus" ("topic-comment") or all "focus" structure ([Hedberg and Fadden, 2007], discussing WH-clefts). They therefore are information-structurally different from canonical clefts.

WH- and ALL-clefts differ from IT-clefts in that their focus may be a clause as well as an NP or PP. WH-clefts differ from other clefts in that they can be used cataphorically to introduce an upcoming clause (e.g. *What I am going to talk about is ...*) in contexts such as a lecture where there is an expectation that the speaker will talk about something. More importantly for purposes of this paper, they are often associated with questions, for example, (6a) could be thought of as an answer to the question in (9):

(9) What did Martin eat?

Indeed Den Dikken [2006] rejects the relative clause analysis of WH-clefts, arguing that WHAT is not a free relative but an embedded question.

Most work on pseudo-clefts has been conducted from the point of view of (relatively) formal semantics or of information-structuring. However, investigating WH-clefts from the perspective of interactional conversation, Kim [1995] and Hopper [2001] have suggested that WH-clefts have rather different characteristics than those identified above. Kim argues that in conversation WH-clefts often do not refer to information retrievable from prior context. They are primarily used to express counteractive stance, specifically disagreement with the addressee, or topic-shift. He also argues that they are closely related to left-dislocations. Hopper argues that they play a significant role in turn-taking: WH-clefts are used "to *delay* an assertion for any of a number of pragmatic reasons" (p. 111, italics original). He suggests that, since most examples are not "complete", and do not have a fully developed focus, they are not primarily motivated by the desire to highlight the focus-constituent, as is usually claimed. Basing his analysis on the COBUILD corpus, he says the ideal locus for using the WH-cleft construction is the turn, where the listener's attention must be held, or shortly after, where keeping the floor is important, as in (10).

(10) There's n there don't seem to be a r- real need. And in defence I mean *what snakes or what animals try* <pause> like *what most animals try to do is* if they tha have got a poisonous property is another animal attacks them they give them er a dose of venom... [Hopper, 2001, p115] (italics original)

Hopper suggests that speakers' reasons for using WH-clefts in the data include not only delaying an assertion in order to keep the floor, but also:

> impressing the listener with the "social" significance of something about to be said, and making the listener aware that what follows is part of a considered argument worthy of attention and not a casual comment. [Hopper, 2001, p124]

Similar findings have been made with respect to conversational Brazilian Portuguese [Lilian Ferrari, p.c.] and French [Jullien and Müller, 2007].

Unlike WH-clefts, ALL-clefts have received very little attention, but it is standardly noted that they differ from WH-clefts in being evaluative. *All* is not equivalent to 'everything', but imposes a "below expectation" scalar reading on what follows [Kay, 2002]. It is understood as convertible with *only* (i.e. it is "downward inferential", [Horn, 1996, p18]).

In the one detailed study of ALL-clefts known to me, [Bonelli, 1992], using the COBUILD corpus, argues that they correlate with "change of posture", especially when there is a shift in subject, as in:

(11) a. then, when the call was finished, *all we could hear on lifting was* ... [Bonelli, 1992, p32, COBUILD: 10 Million Corpus]

b. they owed me plenty, but *all I wanted was the right to develop my ideas* [Bonelli, 1992]

Bonelli also identifies the following discourse moves: retrospection (encapsulating prior text), and prospection (pointing to subsequent text, i.e. cataphora) [p32]. With respect to attitudinal standpoint, she identifies "positive attitude" (a course of action is simple, perhaps unimportant and not worth worrying about),[15] negative (evaluating a fact or result as unfortunate, undesirable, or insufficient), and damage limitation (admission, with the suggestion that there were no other alternatives) [p33]. She does not mention correlation with turn-taking. Rather, the functions she identifies often occur within the speech of one individual, and may be embedded in dialogic contexts, as in (11b).

Given these analyses of WH- and ALL-clefts in contemporary speech, it is reasonable to investigate earlier texts to determine whether the same kinds of

---

[15] It is not clear why these are "positive" as opposed to "neutral".

discourse functions can be identified, and to hypothesize about what role they might have had in the development of the constructions, even though our data are written, not spoken. Since WH- and ALL-clefts invoke an exclusive reading, they are semantically dialogic. One question is how this semantic dialogicity arose. The hypotheses that WH-clefts are synchronically related to questions [Den Dikken, 2006], to turn-taking [Hopper, 2001], and to counter-active stance [Kim, 1995] make WH-clefts a particularly interesting site for investigating whether there is evidence that dialogual and/or dialogic contexts were crucial in the development of the construction. The observation that ALL-clefts are downward entailing also raises the question how this characteristic arose.

A search of the MED, OED, and Early Modern English texts shows that the specificational ALL-cleft arose in the second half of the Early Modern English period, around 1600, and the WH-cleft by 1680.[16] This is a period for which we fortunately have a considerable amount of represented dialogue, for example in drama and in trials. I therefore investigated a number of databases, including drama as represented in the LION: Early English Drama database for the two periods Jacobean and Caroline (1603-1660), and Restoration (1660-1700), and trials as represented by the *Old Bailey Proceedings Online* from 1678 to 1743, and the *Old Bailey Speech Set* from 1732-1743.[17] Trials up to August 1731 in the *Proceedings* are summaries reported in the third person, with some first person quotation. Those after that date are reported in first person. Trials in the *Speech Set* are lengthy first person transcripts from which the shorter *Proceedings* were drawn.

Miller [2006] says English is unusual in having IT-, WH- and reverse-WH clefts. He points out that not all languages in the European area have clefts of the IT-type, or this whole set of pseudo-clefts. Indeed, he claims that Finno-Ugric languages, Turkic, Russian, Bulgarian, Serbo-Croation, and Polish have no clefts, and German has no IT-clefts, although most other Western European Indo-European languages have clefts. Old English had equivalents of "NP-focus IT-clefts" with *,æt* or zero but no IT- or pseudo-clefts [Ball, 1994b], nor

---

[16] I searched each file for *all/what I/you/he/she/it/we/they* and for *said/did was*. The latter strings were selected because they were the most frequent verbs found in the earlier development of both cleft constructions, in order to find utterances which might have NP rather than pronominal subjects (none was found). It should be noted that Bonelli restricts the subject to *I, you, we, one*; also she does not use a test for specificationality, and many examples are cut off after the *be*-verb, so her analysis of ALL-clefts is not strictly comparable with the one presented here.

[17] Many thanks to Merja Kytö for introducing me to this database, and to Tim Hitchcock for permission to use it. A corpus for the historical sociolinguistic study of spoken in English in the late seventeenth to early nineteenth centuries, based on the Proceedings of these trials, is under preparation [Huber, forthcoming]. Proceedings of The Old Bailey available to me date from 1678-1805, and those in the Speech Set from 1732-1834. Since I was investigating the period when WH-clefts arose, the earlier texts seemed most useful.

did it have any specificational constructions with the cleft structures of Present Day English. Ball [1994a; 1994b] discusses the development of specificational IT-clefts in Middle English (she calls them "informative-presuppositional"):

(12) The kniht bad speke and seith,
"Vilein, Thou schalt me telle, er that I go.
It is thi king which axeth so".
'The knight commanded him to speak and says: "Villain, you shall tell me before I leave. It is your king who asks this".
(c.1393 Gower, *Confessio Amantis* 3.1244 [Ball, 1994a, p186])

Visser [1963, pp49–50] associates this Middle English development with the shift from relatively free word order to relatively fixed word order with syntactic subject and with changes in the pronominal system (more recent work regards this change as the reanalysis of clitic pronouns as NPs, see e.g. [van Kemenade, 1987]).

In what follows I sketch the histories of the ALL- and WH-constructions, and discuss the discourse contexts in which the developments appear to have occurred. As in other areas of change, constructional emergence can be construed as change either within a construction (intra-constructional change, e.g. developments internal to the Transitive construction, [Trousdale, forthcoming(b)], or from one construction to another (inter-constructional change followed by intra-constructional change, e.g. the development of Partitives into Degree Modifiers, [Traugott, 2008, forthcoming]). A subtype of inter-constructional change is the emergence out of an extant construction or constructions of a new construction that did not exist before as a productive type, followed by intra-constructional change. This is the kind I will be investigating.

3.1 A brief history of ALL-specificational-clefts

Early examples in the database with the string ALL – NP – V – BE – X are ascriptive (13a, b) or purposive (13c, d). In all cases *all* can be understood to mean 'everything':

(13) a. I haue heard as much, and **all** *thou hast said is true.* (1615 Bedwell, *Mohammedes imposturae* [LION: EEBO])

   b. I haue made him happie by training you forth: In a word, **all** *I said was* but a traine to draw you from your vow: Nay, there's no going backe.
   'I have made him happy by drawing you forth: in a word, all I said was only a trick to draw you from your vow. No, there is no going back'. (1606 Chapman, *Monsieur D'Oliue* [LION: EEBO])

   c.   Her nathelesse

Th'enchaunter finding fit for his intents,
Did thus reuest, and deckt with dew habiliments.
For **all** he did, **was** to deceiue good knights.
'Nevertheless, finding her fit for his intentions, the enchanter dressed her again and decked her with appropriate clothes. For everything he did was in order to deceive good knights'. (1590 Spenser, *Fairie Queene* Bk. II [LION: EEBO])

d. I loue thee dearer then I doe my life,
And all I did, was to aduance thy state,
To sunne bright beames of shining happinesse.
(1601 Yarrington, *Two Lamentable Tragedies* [LION: EEBO])

There are also some strings that might be "reverse" ALL-clefts prior to 1600;[18] here *all* means 'only':

(14) a. *Candidus.* Why crau'st thou then my Verse, & dost anothers bowndes inuade?
Siluanus. I reaue ('deprive') thée not thy Muse, ...
But ***to thy Musicke for to lende an eare, is all I craue.***
'C. Then why do you crave my verse, and invade another's territory?
S. I don't deprive you of your Muse ... but to your music to bend an ear is all I crave'. (1567 Baptista, *Eglogs* [LION: EEBO]; this text is a translation)

b. But happinesse I had not as I thought,
... things begunne in ioy, were parting sad,
And yet ***that present ioy was all I had,***
In recompence of all my trau'll and paine.
'But I didn't have happiness as I thought I would ... things begun in joy turned sad at parting, and yet the joy of the moment was all I had in recompense for all my work and pain'. (1597 Lok, *Ecclesiastes* [LION: EEBO])

Note (14a) is a complex example with a topicalization paraphrasable as 'All I crave is for to lende an ear to thy Musicke'. If examples in (14) are reverse clefts, they are structurally different from early "canonical" ALL-clefts in that the verbs used are different: *crave* and *have*, whereas those of the earliest clefts are *say* and *do*, as illustrated in (15) below.

Around 1600 we begin to find ALL NP V BE X strings with the pseudo-cleft meaning: *all* means 'only', not 'everything', and the focus is understood to be

---

[18] Thanks to Mirjam Fried for suggesting investigation of the reverse clefts.

exhaustive and specificational, i.e. dialogic. The NP is a personal pronoun (*it* was, however, not found in the data). Most occur with a verb of speaking, usually *say* (15a, b), some with *do* plus infinitive marker (15c):

(15) a. [The nymph Melliflora kisses Faunus]
Faunus thought oft Loues fire for to display,
Desire was bolde, but Shamefastnesse said nay.
If he began to come but somewhat neare her,
His body quak't as though his heart did feare her,
All that he said was, Nimph when you are at leasure, Faine would I speak, he might haue spoke his pleasure ...
(1600 Weever, *Faunus* [LION: EEBO])

b. [A "confutation" between a Jesuit (S.R.) and Bell]
Our slanderous and rayling Iesuite, reporteth my wordes in this manner; for saith *Bell*) it is a thinge proper to God, to make something of nothing in al cases, and at al times. So then, **all that I said was this;** (viz) **That though man can at sometime in some cases, make one thing of another; yet to make of nothing something, is proper to GOD alone, neither is man able to performe the same.** (1608 Bell, *The Jesuits Antepast* [LION: EEBO]) (Note *so then*, and orientation to a conclusion contrary to that of the Jesuit; the referent of *all* is anaphoric, the focus repeats a prior statement with minor modification)

c. there is no possibilitie of overthrowing the new election which shalbe made when the place is voyd, and if it be so allready, or shalbe so, **all you can doe is to do some good for the tyme to come,** which if you can doe conveniently, and without much trouble, it wilbe woorth your labour... Further then this I see not to be done. (1624 Oliver Naylor to John Cousin [ICAME:CEECS])

Say often appears in the formula *all I can say*, as in (16). Whether in this formula or not, the verb of speaking in the ALL-clefts is followed directly by a finite clause (15a, 16a), or indirectly by the deictic *this* (15b), (16b) or the quotative *viz* (15b).[19] This means that virtually all ALL-clefts in the seventeenth century have a clausal focus.

(16) a. *Medloc.* [on bees] But as a bow continually bent, doth lose his strength: so Salomon wisheth that in hauing found hony, we

---

[19]'Viz', short for videlicet that is to say', is a quotative grammaticalized in legal texts and restricted to writing according to [Moore, 2006].

should but eate that is sufficient, lest other wise it fall out, we vomit it vp....

Malcon. And **all I can say is**, **Wisedome wil be iustified of her Children*, when **Follie will not depart from a foole, though he were brayed in a morter with a pestell.* (1608 Clapham, *Errour on the Left* [LION: EEBO])

b. What have you to say concerning the cause of the flowing and ebbing of the Sea?
Answ. To that, **all I can say is this**, that Aristotle himselfe for all his cunning was so perplexed in following that doubt, that he died for griefe because he could not understand it aright. (1635 Person, *Varieties* [LION: EEBO])

The clearest examples of the ALL-cleft construction include those used in negative contexts like (17a) (they block an 'everything' reading, and trigger an 'only/nothing but' or 'below expectation' reading), and clauses with *do* + bare Verb (17b):[20]

(17) a. But as for my self he doth me notorious wrong, I did not mention any Principles of Vnity in this place, nor so much as dream of them, ... **All I said was this, That we doe not separate from other Churches, but from their Accidentall Errours.** (1658 Bramhall, *Schisme Garded* [LION: EEBO])

b. When any bow'd to me with Congees (= ceremonious bow) trim, **All I could do, was stand and laugh at him**. (1681 Baxter, *Poetical fragments* [LION: EEBO])

Examples like (17b) show that by the later part of the 17C the ALL-cleft construction had become conventionalized and morphosyntactically differentiated from the purposive string of the same abstract form. ALL-clefts with *do* do not have a purposive reading when V is modalized by *can/could*. By hypothesis, *to* in the originally purposeful constructions with *do* (13c, d) was reanalyzed as an infinitive marker in the context of modalized *do*. Having no semantic significance, *to* could be treated as optional (bare infinitives were, however, not the norm until the end of twentieth century).

Later developments of the ALL-cleft include use with gerundive complements after *do* (18), with *it* and full NP subjects, and with NP and PP focal elements.[21]

---

[20] Heine [2002] and Diewald [2002] call such unambiguous contexts "switch contexts" and "isolating contexts", respectively.

[21] When the use of it and full NP subjects and of NP and PP focal elements occurred, remains to be investigated; they appear to be largely nineteenth century developments.

(18) What I did I was driven to, as any one can see. It takes a real shock to make the average Familey wake up to the fact that the youngest daughter is not the Familey baby at seventeen. ***All I was doing was furnishing the shock***. If things turned out badly, as they did, it was because I rather overdid the thing. (1917 Rinehart, *Bab: A Sub-Deb* [UVa])

Assuming that the origin of the ALL-pseudo-cleft was in ascriptive and purposive clauses like those in (13), there was:

(19) a. Semantic-pragmatic expansion in that:
- the string ALL PRO V BE X is now polysemously used for semantically dialogic specificational focus constructions as well as for semantically monologic ascriptive and purposive constructions,
- *all* is assigned downward inferential meaning,

b. Syntactic expansion, as illustrated by use of bare infinitives after *do*, and of gerundives,

c. Host class expansion, in that more Vs come to be used. At first, V is mainly a verb of saying or *do*; later we find statives, e.g. *desire, know, mean, want*. Other expansions include those of the subject to full NPs and of the focal element to NPs and PPs.

These changes are clear cases of grammaticalization in Himmelmann's [2004] sense, albeit grammaticalization without lexical bleaching. Likewise, they are clear cases of constructionalization, since the new pseudo-cleft is understood holistically.

3.2 Discourse contexts for the development of specificational ALL- clefts

I turn now to evidence that can be gleaned from the data for discourse contexts for the development of ALL- clefts. The first question is what kinds of contexts would have allowed for the semantic reanalysis of ascriptive and purposive constructions into specificational clefts. In the case of ALL-clefts, everything that one person says or does may not be enough for some other person or may be interpreted as mistaken/inadequate. This is because of the quantificational meaning of *all*. In (20) Henry V explicitly discusses this dilemma:

(20) More will I do;
Though ***all that I can do is*** nothing worth,
Since that my penitence comes after all,
Imploring pardon. (1599 Shakespeare, *Henry V* IV.i.319 [UVa])

In (20) we see two perspectives interwoven dialogically: that of the person referred to, and that of the speaker:

(21) By all which your Honours may perceive, how he hath falsly traduced the Commissioners of the Navie, ... and **all he drives at, is by his unjust aspersions to bring the Parliament and them at ods,** that so he might accomplish his own ends. (1646 mscb [ICAME: Lampeter])

From the perspective of the subject (*he*), everything he does is for the purpose of causing discord. From the perspective of SP/W, however, what he does is cause conflict (note the tense difference here), and is to be evaluated negatively (*falsly* and *unjust* are grounded in SP/W, not *he*, since he would not have characterized his own remarks as 'false' or 'unjust').

All the examples in (14) (reverse constructions) and (15) (canonical constructions) occur in dialogic and at least partially contesting contexts. If the subject is third person, SP/W typically evaluates an individual's action, conveying counter-expectation (the 'everything' was not as much as could be expected, not good enough), as in (15a) and (22a). In the case of first person subjects, the speaker typically complains (everything they said or did was misunderstood, undervalued, or did not meet their own expectations), as in (15b) and (15b):

(22) a. The Trial was very tedious; a Cloud of Witnesses being called on either Side ... But there being a Parson in Dod's Company, and he charged for being aiding and abetting, he discover'd where his Haunts were, so that the same Night he was taken. **All that he endeavoured to prove, was, That there was no former Malice between them**; so that upon my Lord Chief Baron Mountague's summing up the Evidence, the Jury gave in their Verdict, That he was guilty of Manslaughter. (12th July 1682, Trial of Robert Dod [BAILEY: s1682071216820712001])

b. There was no possibility of my leaving the Army to fetch her out of that Convent ... I never could obtain Leave to be absent, but remain'd most part of the Winter there; **all I could do was to order some Soldiers, that went for France, to call at Charleville,** but I never heard from them since. (1697 Evremont, *Female Falsehood* (translation) [LION: EEBO])

Since dialogicity is in the context, it is not necessarily semanticized at this stage. To establish semanticization of the dialogicity we need to look for examples that occur independently of dialogic contexts. These include use at turns. In the data ALL-clefts are rarely found at a turn, except in the formulaic expression *all I can say* in (16). (23) is a relatively late example from the Old Bailey trials of the ALL-cleft used by the speaker to initiate a turn:

(23)   Sarah Clayton. I happened to go that Night to see what a-Clock it was, by Mrs Burges's Dial ... I saw him go into the same House, and speak to a Woman, - ...
Alexander Watson. ***All I know of the Matter,*** my Lord and Gentlemen of the Jury, ***is this. On Tuesday I saw this Moody walking about our Court, with his Hat on;*** - I live in Windsor Court over against Mrs Burges's. -(Jan. 1740, Trial of Sarah Burges and Ann Hill [BAILEY: s17400116-84174001160001])

We can hypothesize that semanticization of dialogicity occurred in the early part of the eighteenth century. Here and in other uses at turns they mainly express unwillingness or inability to give information.

ALL-clefts occur in contexts what are "given" or "recoverable" in the sense that the prior context indicates that the subject was saying or doing something, or was attempting or expected to do so. However, in most cases the most important function appears not to be to fill an open proposition, but rather to highlight an upcoming statement as salient, and impose an exhaustive reading on it. This is particularly clear in the case of (15b). Here the focus, *That though man can at sometime in some cases, make one thing of another; yet to make of nothing something, is proper to GOD alone...*, is only a minor reformulation of what Bell a few lines quoted himself as saying: *as man can in some cases at some time make one thing of another; so in all cases, at all times, to make something of nothing, is proper to God alone.*

We may conclude that ALL-clefts arose as discourse moves of the type Bonelli [1992] identified for Present Day English, namely retrospection (referring back to given or recoverable contexts), although the salience of the focus may suggest prospection (or forward, cataphoric orientation) as well. Bonelli regards "change of posture" as a major characteristic of ALL-clefts. Understood strictly as switch-reference (which is what she intends), this does not appear to have been a significant factor in their development. However, understood more broadly as dialogicity, it is unquestionably crucial in their development.

With respect to attitudinal standpoint, from the beginning ALL-clefts conveyed what Bonelli identifies as "negative attitude". There are no examples of what she calls "positive attitude" ("evaluating a course of action as very simple") or the related "damage limitation". Interestingly, she lists "damage limitation" first under attitudes [Bonelli, 1992, p23], but no clear examples of this appear in the historical data until the nineteenth century (an early example is (24)). They appear to be largely associated with the progressive, as in all *I am saying is*,[22] and their absence in the Early Modern English data is therefore not surprising, given that progressive examples are rare at that period.

(24) "...Tell me, do you never relax from this very correct behaviour?" "I do not pretend people in general are without imperfections," Charlotte said stiffly. "***All I am saying is that goodness and foolishness are so often combined to such an extent that it is sometimes impossible to separate them on a short acquaintance.***" (1817 Austen, *Sanditon* [UVa])

In sum, ALL-clefts arose in dialogic contexts. Only ALL-clefts in the formula *all I can say is* are dialogual in the sense of being associated with question and answer, or any other kind of turn-taking. The contesting, adversative meaning of the original context, though often still present, has essentially become semanticized into the construction, so that even out of context, *all* in ALL-constructs with the appropriate syntax are understood as meaning 'only', not 'everything'. This has also occurred in expressions like *albeit, although, all the same, after all*.

3.3 A brief history of WH-specificational-clefts

Prior to around 1680 the only examples in database with the structure WHAT – NP – V – BE – X are of the ascriptive and purposive types in (25):

(25) a. Weigh well my words, and perswade thy selfe, that ***what I haue said is true***. (1631 Mabb, *Spanish Bawd* I [LION: English Prose Drama]) (ascriptive adjective)

b. I am ty'd to nothing In this businesse, ***what I doe is meerely recreation***, Not constraint. (1630 Middleton, *Chaste Maid* [ICAME: Helsinki ceeduc3a]) (non-referential nominal)

c. his hate to you unjustly, did not grow so fast, as my esteeme waranted by vertue, since ***what you did, was in defence,*** both of your Prince and Countrey. (1639 Carlell: *Arviragvs and Philicia* II [LION: English Prose Drama]) (reason adverb)

d.   Shal. Will you, upon good dowry, marry her?

---

[22]In some present-day contexts it has political significance deriving from John Lennon's All we are saying is give peace a chance. The discourse origins of this anti-Vietnam War slogan include covert contesting of the FBI's attempt to deport Lennon on grounds of his being a potential terrorist: 'No, we are not advocating violence, all we are saying is give peace a chance' (U.S. v. John Lennon 2006).

Slen. I will do a greater thing than that, upon your request, cousin, in any reason.

Shal. Nay, conceive ('understand') me, conceive me, sweet coz. ***What I do is to pleasure*** ('please') **you,** coz. Can you love the maid? (?1597 Shakespeare, *Merry Wives of Windsor* I.i.250 [LION: Shakespeare]) (purposive)

(26) illustrates some possible reverse-clefts prior to 1680. Like the possible reverse ALL-clefts in (15), they have verbs that are atypical of the canonical clefts (which have mainly verbs of saying and *do*, as in (26) below):

(26) a. Some things *I haue,* which here I will not show;
Some things *I want,* which you shall neuer know: ...
That, which to treat of, I now purpose (therefor,)
Is what I neither haue, nor want *('lack'),**nor care for**.*
(1621 Wither, *Wither's Motto* [LION: EEBO])

b. There remaineth yet a third [objection], which may be answered ... Who will forbid them to supply in such a case, that by a voluntary and arbitrary forme, which the Church could not provide for in a set forme? And ***this is what I intended to say of this argument***. (1642 Mede, *Diatribae* [LION: EEBO])

A few WH-Left-dislocations are also found in the data. Most have indefinite (non-given or inferrable) *what(soever)* (27a) but some are definite/referential (27b). (27b) follows several stanzas representing the speech and describing the actions that are the referents of *what*):

(27) a. Christ was conceiued for vs, ... & ***whatsoeuer*** *he did, he did it for our profite.*
"Christ was conceived for us ... and whatever he did, he did it for our profit' (1581 Baker, *Lectures on Christian Faith* [LION: EEBO])

b. For ***what*** *he spake, for you he spake it*, Dame,
And ***what*** *he did, he did himself to saue.*
(1596 Spenser, *Fairie Queene*, VI,2.13.5-6)[23]

WH-Left-dislocations were rare in Early Modern English (and had been in decline from Middle English on, see [Pérez-Guerra and Tizón-Couto, forthcoming]. All the same, examples like (27b) may have served along with other specificational constructions, such as specificational IT-clefts, WH-clefts, and ALL-clefts as partial models for the new construction which emerged toward the

---

[23]Thanks to Carol Kaske for introducing me to this example.

end of the seventeenth century. As mentioned above, Kim [1995] sees a close relationship between WH-clefts and WH-left-dislocations in contemporary English.

Early examples of the WH-specificational cleft with a definite focus element include:

(28)   a.   Good Lord! Sir *Anthony*, you need not be so purty (*pretty* = 'proper'); **what I say, is the Discourse of the whole City**, how lavishly you let him live, and give ill Examples to all young Heirs. (1685 Behn, *City-heiress* I.i [LION: English Prose Drama])

       b.   If it be objected that I preached to separate Congregations; my Answer is, That I preach'd only to some of many Thousands that cannot come into the Temples, many of which never heard a Sermon of many years. And **what I did, was only to preach to such as could not come to our Churches.** (1697 Baxter, *Mr. Richard Baxter's Last Legacy* [LION: EEBO])

In the case of WH-clefts, NP focal elements appeared early (e.g. (28a)), unlike in the case of ALL-clefts, but were rare. None of the historical databases used show syntactic expansion to bare verbs after *do* within the Early Modern English period. This is apparently a twentieth century phenomenon. The first example I have found so far is (29a)); the parenthetical (*Mr. Werner said*) and the light verb *let* are suggestive of a possible entry-point for the construction.

(29)   a.   Werner said yesterday that operations continued through the weekend. **What he did,** Mr. Werner said, **was let manual laborers go home Tuesday for some rest.** (1961 Keat, *Baltimore Sun* [ICAME-Brown])

       b.   **What an impro of this kind does is confront the actors with a situation where they have to act truthfully.** (1991 *So You Want to Be an Actor* [BNC])

Nevertheless, in general, the WH-clefts followed the same line of structural development as the ALL-clefts. Overall, Himmelmann's criteria for grammaticalization are met. Semantic-pragmatic expansion is clear: the examples in (28) are specificational, not ascriptive or purposive as in (25). In so far as WH-clefts eventually came to have a bare infinitive after *do*, they participated in syntactic expansion, and in so far as they came to be used with NP subjects and more Vs, they participated in the normal types of host-class expansion that grammaticalizing constructions typically undergo. As in the case of ALL-clefts, they illustrate grammaticalization without lexical bleaching and the development of a micro-construction.

3.4 Discourse contexts for the development of WH-clefts

Like ALL-clefts, WH-clefts arose in contexts where the initial part is given or retrievable. Like ALL-clefts they also appear to be used primarily to highlight the focus as salient, and impose an exhaustive reading on it. But they differ somewhat from ALL-clefts in three other significant respects:

- the extent to which dialogic contexts are involved,
- the preponderance of first person contexts,
- even sparser occurrence at turns.

With respect to the first difference, ascriptive and purposive precursors of ALL-clefts have non-dialogic contexts, while contexts for reverse (14) and canonical (15) ALL-clefts are dialogic. Over time, although ALL-clefts have come to be used in non-dialogic contexts (the dialogicity of their context has been semanticized into the construction), for the most part they continue to occur in contexts of adversativity and refutation. In contrast, contexts for ascriptive, purposive, and reverse-cleft precursors of WH-clefts are all dialogic. Once the WH-cleft arose, most contexts continued to be dialogic, for example in (28a) there is argumentative countering (*Good Lord! ... you need not be so purty; what I say, is the Discourse of the whole City*), as there is in (28b) (*If it be objected ... my Answer is ... And what I did was only to preach ...*). In (30) the context is argumentative reporting on the relationship among various chemicals:

(30) So that I see no reason or necessity, from this Phaenomenon, to assert the existence of Vitriol in the Sand of the Bath ... If any shall affirm this Ochre to be Vitrioline, I have not deny'd it, having formerly supposed it might be Terra Vitrioli, but **what I here question is, whether any Vitrioline saline body, different from the Ochre, be contained in the Sand, or can lye undissolved there.** (1676 [ICAME: Lampeter: scib1676])

But there is no obvious dialogicity in the contexts of (31). (31a) is the beginning of the deposition by Paul Crispin, a shop-keeper and silver-smith who has accused the defendants of stealing a silver dish (the transcriber records Crispin's lisp by substituting 'th' and 'sh' for 's'), and (31b) is the deposition of Mrs. Exton, wife of the owner of the dwelling from which linen was allegedly stolen:

(31) a. *What I have to tha ith thith, I lotht a thilver Dith belonging to Brigadier Churchill, out of my Grate in*

Compton-Thtreet, the Corner of Greek-Thtreet, but I can't tell when, becauth it ish impothible. (June 1733, Trial of Alexander Watson and William Howard [BAILEY:s17330628-441173306280001])

b. I heard a Noise, and came down Stairs, but all the Things were gone: I wash Linnen, and **what I lost was the Property of Mr. Gold.** (May 1736, Trial of Christopher Freeman and Samuel Ellard [BAILEY:s17360505-463173605050])

We may hypothesize that the long association with dialogic contexts, and perhaps the model of ALL-clefts, allowed for semanticization of dialogicity very early.

WH-clefts are favored in the context of first persons (30, 31). In the third person reports of the *Proceedings of Old Bailey*, there are no examples with third person subjects. However, in first person reports, there are several examples, including those in (31). These first-person examples occur at a turn (31a) or shortly after (31b). The first example of a WH-cleft in the first person reports is (32), from the testimony of one of the defendants, Paine, in response to a witness called French. Like (31b) it occurs shortly after the beginning of a turn):

(32) *French.* I keep an Alehouse in Cross-Lane. P - has been at my House in Company with the Prisoners.
Pain. I could have but a short Acquaintance with I - , for I am but just come from Sea. **What I know of him is, that he is a Cooper by Trade, and that when he was taken up, he deny'd that he knew any thing of the Watch.** (Dec 1731, Trial of Samuel Cole and Edward Paine of St. Sepulchres [BAILEY: s17311208-428173112080001])

Nevertheless, WH-clefts were found at turns in only two other trials in the data (August 1740, Trial of Mary Ray, and July 1742, Trial of Stephen Price and John Clark). Most examples prior to the trials do not occur at a turn (see (28b) and (30)). The turn does not appear to be a prime context for the emergence of this construction. Its primary use appears to be identify salient information as part of a narrative of events (or in the case of (30) as part of the development of a research strategy.

It is particularly interesting in light of the fact that (16b) illustrates *all I can say* used in a question-answer pair that there are no WH-clefts used in answer to a question of the type *What did you say/do?* in the data, Most notably, in the Old Bailey trials there are examples of *X asked what it was?*, but WH-clefts do not appear in response. Instead we find answers such as those in (33):

(33) a. *Brown.* What did you say to Mr. Fisher, at Paddington, when he bid you have a Care, or you'd hang yourself?
Curtis. I said, if I knew any Thing of you before, it was the Day before Michaelmas, when you came to our Door with a Couple of Geese, and I shew'd them to my Master. (Dec. 1733, Trial of William Brown and Joseph Whitlock, of Paddington [BAILEY: s17331205-44317331205000])

b. *Q.* What did you do next?
O Bryan. We bound him with a Penny Cord, and turn'd him into the Ditch. (Jan. 1737, Trial of James Ryan, Garret Farrel, and Hugh Macmahon [BAILEY: s17370114-469173701140001])

It appears that at the time of their origin, WH-clefts were used primarily to signal a counter-active stance (see [Kim, 1995]), or to make "the listener aware that what follows is part of a considered argument worthy of attention and not a casual comment" [Hopper, 2001, p124]. However, they are not originally privileged at conversational turns.

In sum, both types of clefts occur at their origins in dialogic contexts. Only ALL-clefts in the formula *all I can say is* are dialogual in the sense of being associated with question and answer, or any other kind of turn-taking. There is no evidence that WH-clefts were construed as related to questions.

4 From micro-construction to macro-construction

The emergence of specificational clefts can be considered an example of the intra-constructional emergence of a new cleft construction with a specific form-meaning pairing out of preexistent building blocks. First there was the development of the IT-cleft drawing on impersonals of the *happen*-class [Ball, 1994b], then the development of the ALL-pseudo-cleft out of ascriptive and purposive, etc. constructions, and that of the WH-cleft out of similar material, micro-construction by micro-construction. It appears that at first ALL-clefts were used exclusively, and WH-clefts almost exclusively with clausal foci. Together they formed a meso-construction separate from IT-clefts by virtue of their clausal complements. IT-clefts in turn came under some circumstances to have clausal foci, and so finally all three came to form a cluster. Amanda Patten (p.c.) has pointed out that while (34a) is ungrammatical, according to her broad construal of the category of IT-clefts, (34b) is grammatical. An earlier example is (34c).

(34) a. *It's that he's an idiot that I don't like him.

b. No, *it's because he's an idiot that I don't like him.*

c. It was the faith and the persistence of Columbus that discovered America and opened the way for the millions who now call it their home. *It is because of these qualities that we honor him to-day; it is because this faith and persistence ended as they did in the discovery of a new world, that to-day his fame is immortal.* (1892 Brooks, *Christopher Columbus* [UVa])

With respect to clefts, we can think of micro- to meso- to macro- constructional changes of IT-, ALL- and WH-clefts as in Figure 1:

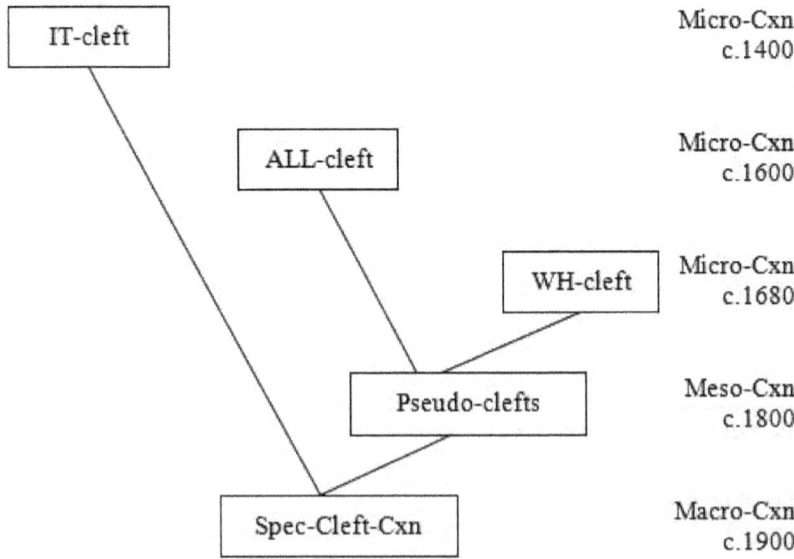

Figure 1. The hypothesized emergence of the specificational cleft macro-construction

While a macro-construction developed early, as soon as multiple clefts came into being, it was not configured in its current form until about 1900.

Patten [2007, forthcoming] questions whether clefts as such should be considered to have a special status, and proposes instead that specification is the overarching concept to be attended to.[24] Patten's argument is that various syntactic strings can be used to express definite descriptions, and clefts are only one type of specificational construction. In clefts the relative clause is

---

[24]Den Dikken [2006], working with a formal syntactic and semantic model, also seeks to connect IT- and WH-clefts to wider specificational functions.

inherently restrictive and contributes to identification of the definite phrase following the copula. However, within the larger domain of specificational constructions, they are presumably only a sub-type. On the assumption that this view is correct, the macro-specificational cleft construction could be regarded as part of an even larger specificational construction. What its history was is a subject for further research.

Working with construction grammar from a historical perspective focuses attention on alignment and matching of micro-constructions with each other, resulting in their incorporation into meso-level constructions, and eventually reconfiguration of macro-constructions. Alignment and matching are analogical processes. The association of new structure with analogy may on first thought appear to be contrary to received practices in grammaticalization. As is well known, Meillet said:

> Tandis que l'analogie peut renouveler le détail des formes, mais laisse le plus souvent intact le plan d'ensemble du système existant, la "grammaticalisation" de certains mots crée des formes neuves, introduit des categories qui n'avaient pas d'expression linguistique, transforme l'ensemble du système". 'While analogy can renew details of forms, but usually leaves the structure of the existing system intact, 'grammaticalization' of certain words creates new forms, introduces categories that had no linguistic expression beforehand, transforms the system as a whole'. [Meillet, 1958, (1912), p133]

Meillet's concern with changes that lead to systemic reconfigurations has resonated with generative interest in "catastrophic" changes in I-language, and parameter-settings (see e.g. [Lightfoot, 1979] and passim). Nevertheless, work on grammaticalization in both parameter-and usage-based research has been largely concerned with initial changes, step-by-step, local realignments—small-scale reanalyses and analogical adjustments that may eventually lead to a major shift. In recent years there has been increasing convergence between formal and functional theories of syntax over grammaticalization ([Fischer, 2007] provides an overview of the different perspectives). Importantly, bringing construction grammar and grammaticalization together provides for partial convergence with Kiparsky's [forthcoming] proposal in terms of constraint-based Optimality Theory and UG that analogical changes are reanalyses at the local level (for fuller discussion see [Traugott, forthcoming]).

Cognitive systems are highly plastic—not only sensitive to frequencies in the linguistic environment as Sharma *et al.*'s OT analysis [this volume] assumes, but also open to experiment and fine-grained local realignments.[25] Each step is a small step and "locally abrupt", whether within or across constructions [Lightfoot, 2005]. This does not, however, deny the correctness of the observation that over time divisions of labor occur, and that prototype, macro-

---

[25] The fine-grainedness of these realignments suggests that it is impossible from a historical perspective to maintain the position Aarts [2004] has put forward that intra-category ("subsective") changes are gradient whereas inter-category ("intersective") changes are abrupt.

constructional constructions lead to strong alignment effects, resulting in the marginalization of non-prototypical members [Denison, 2001]. However, since innovations are always occurring and only some of them become accepted by a speech community, and sometimes only for a short time, categories and especially the more complex meso- or macro- constructions can never be expected to be completely aligned. Emergent structures are essentially unstable in nature [Bybee and Hopper, 2001].

5 Conclusion

In this paper I have shown that some basic assumptions about constructions based on constructed examples may be very specific either to the contemporary linguistic situation, or even to constructed examples. Specifically, I have shown that WH-pseudo-clefts, which are often said to have question-answer properties, do not appear to have them in the early data, at least in so far as they do not normally appear in question-answer turns. It would be worth investigating whether they actually have them in contemporary data of similar genre as were used for the present study. I have also shown that projecting back from conversational data to earlier (admittedly written) data can provide useful questions to explore, but what appears in contemporary conversations may not necessarily have motivated how a construction arose in the first place.

The morphosyntactic changes discussed in this paper suggest that distinguishing dialogic and dialogual (especially turn-taking) contexts is useful in attempting to assess the relative importance of different types of context in which new constructions emerge. This in no way denies the importance of other types of context including the sociolinguistic dynamics behind particular choices [Milroy, 2007], or shifts in cultural values [Wierzbicka, 2006]. Ultimately these and many more issues would ideally contribute to hypotheses about how a particular change occurs, but integration of the various approaches cannot be achieved until the particular components of change are better understood.

The present paper has only scratched the surface of one subset of constructions. To achieve a more fine-grained account of the types of dialogic contexts in which the ALL- and WH-specificational constructions arose, and an assessment of what SP/W attitudes they were used to convey, a quantitative collostructional analysis would be useful such as is modeled in work by [Gries and Stefanowitsch, 2004] for synchronic analysis and by [Hilpert, 2007] for diachronic analysis, if it could be extended to assess inter- as well as intra-clausal distributional preferences.

Sources

BAILEY *The Proceedings of the Old Bailey, London 1674 to 1834* www.oldbaileyonline.org, Tim Hitchcock and Robert Shoemaker, eds. Used by permission of Tim Hitchcock and Magnus Huber; accessed March-September 2007.

BNC *British National Corpus*, www.natcorp.ox.ac.uk

COBUILD *Collins Birmingham University International Language Database*, www.collins.co.uk/Corpus/CorpusSearch.aspx

ICAME ICAME Corpus Collection, nora.hd.uib.no/corpora.html

LION Chadwyck Healey website, lion.chadwyck.com

MED *The Middle English Dictionary*. 1956-2001. Ann Arbor: University of Michigan Press. See also www.hti.umich.edu/dict/med/

UVa University of Virginia, Electronic Text Center, *Modern English Collection*, etext.lib.virginia.edu/modeng/modeng0.browse.html

BIBLIOGRAPHY

[Aarts, 2004]   Bas Aarts. Modelling linguistic gradience. *Studies in Language*, 28(1):1–49, 2004.
[Andersen, 2001]   Henning Andersen. Actualization and the (uni) directionality of change. *Andersen 2001b*, pages 225–248, 2001.
[Andersen, 2006]   Henning Andersen. Synchrony, diachrony, and evolution. *Competing Models of Linguistic Change*, pages 59–90, 2006.
[Archer, 2006]   Dawn Archer. (Re) initiating strategies: Judges and defendants in Early Modern English courtrooms. *Journal of Historical Pragmatics*, 7(2):181–211, 2006.
[Archer, 2007]   Dawn Archer. Developing a more detailed picture of the English courtroom (1640-1760): Data and methodological issues facing historical pragmatics. *Methods in Historical Pragmatics*, pages 185–217, 2007.
[Ball, 1994a]   Catherine N. Ball. Relative Pronouns in "It"-Clefts: The Last Seven Centuries. *Language Variation and Change*, 6(2):179–200, 1994.
[Ball, 1994b]   Catherine N. Ball. The origins of the informative-presupposition it-cleft. *Journal of pragmatics*, 22(6):603–628, 1994.
[Bergs and Diewald, forthcoming]   Alexander Bergs and Gabriele Diewald, editors. *Constructions and Language Change*. Berlin/New York: Mouton de Gruyter, forthcoming.
[Bergs, 2005]   Alexander Bergs. *Social Networks And Historical Sociolinguistics: Studies In Morphosyntactic Variation In The Paston Letters (1421-1503)*. Walter de Gruyter, 2005.
[Bisang et al., 2004]   Walter Bisang, Nikolaus P. Himmelmann, and Björn Wiemer. *What makes grammaticalization?: A look from its fringes and its components*. Berlin; New York: Mouton de Gruyter, 2004.
[Bonelli, 1992]   Elena Tognini Bonelli. 'All I'm Saying Is...': The Correlation of Form and Function in Pseudo-cleft Sentences. *Literary and Linguistic Computing*, 7(1):30–42, 1992.
[Brinton and Traugott, 2005]   Laurel J. Brinton and Elizabeth C. Traugott. *Lexicalization and Language Change*. Cambridge University Press, 2005.

[Brinton, 1998]   L.J. Brinton. The flowers are lovely; only, they have no scent": The evolution of a pragmatic marker". *Anglistentag*, pages 9–18, 1998.
[Brinton, 2001]   Laurel J. Brinton. From matrix clause to pragmatic marker: The history of look-forms. *Journal of Historical Pragmatics*, 2(2):177–199, 2001.
[Bybee and Hopper, 2001]   Joan Bybee and Paul J. Hopper eds. *Frequency and the Emergence of Linguistic Structure*. John Benjamins Pub. Co Philadelphia, PA, 2001.
[Bybee et al., 1994]   Joan L. Bybee, Revere D. Perkins, and Williams Pagliuca. *The Evolution of Grammar: Tense, Aspect, and Modality in the Languages of the World*. University Of Chicago Press, 1994.
[Cain and Russom, 2007]   Christopher M. Cain and eds. Russom, Geoffrey. *Studies in the History of the English Language III: Managing Chaos: Strategies for Identifying Change in English*. Berlin/New York: Mouton de Gruyter, 2007.
[Clark, 1996]   Herbert H. Clark. *Using Language*. Cambridge University Press, 1996.
[Collins, 1991]   Peter C. Collins. *Cleft and Pseudo-Cleft Constructions in English*. Routledge, 1991.
[Croft and Cruse, 2004]   William Croft and D.A. Cruse. *Cognitive Linguistics*. Cambridge University Press, 2004.
[Croft, 2000]   William Croft. *Explaining Language Change: An Evolutionary Approach*. Longman, 2000.
[Culpeper and Kytö, 2000]   Jonathan Culpeper and Merja Kytö. Data in historical pragmatics: Spoken interaction (re) cast as writing. *Journal of Historical Pragmatics*, 1(2):175–199, 2000.
[Davidse, 2000]   Kristin Davidse. A constructional approach to clefts. *Linguistics*, 38(6):1101–1131, 2000.
[De Smet and Cuyckens, 2007]   Hendrik De Smet and Hubert Cuyckens. Studies in the History of the English Language III: Managing Chaos: Strategies for Identifying Change in English. In Christopher M. Cain and Geoffrey Russom, editors, *Competing Models of Linguistic Change*, pages 187–213. Berlin/New York: Mouton de Gruyter, 2007.
[Delin and Oberlander, 2008]   Judy Delin and Jon Oberlander. Cleft constructions in context: Some suggestions for research methodology. Submitted to: Linguistics, draft http://www.fb10.uni-bremen.de/anglistik/langpro/projects/gem/judys_publications/lxpaper.RTF, 2008.
[Delin, 1990]   J. L. Delin. A multi-level account of cleft constructions in discourse. *Proceedings of the 13th conference on Computational linguistics-Volume 2*, pages 83–88, 1990.
[Den Dikken, 2006]   Marcel Den Dikken. Specificational copular sentences and pseudoclefts: A case study. *The Blackwell Companion to Syntax*, pages 62–91, 2006.
[Denison, 2001]   David Denison. Gradience and linguistic change. *Historical Linguistics 1999: Selected papers from the 14th International Conference on Historical Linguistics, Vancouver, 9-13 August 1999*, pages 119–144, 2001.
[Detges and Waltereit, 2003]   Ulrich Detges and Richard Waltereit. Turn-taking as a trigger for language change. Presentation at the panel on Diachronic Micropragmatics of the Romance Languages. *Ninth International Pragmatics Conference (IPra), Toronto*, 2003.
[Detges, 2006]   Ulrich Detges. From speaker to subject. The obligatorization of the Old French subject pronouns. *La Linguistique au Coeur. Valence verbale, grammaticalisation et corpus. Mélanges offerts à Lene Schøsler à l'occasion de son 60e anniversaire. University of Southern Denmark Studies in Literature*, 48:75–103, 2006.
[Diewald, 2002]   Gabriele Diewald. A model for relevant types of contexts in grammaticalization. *New Reflections on Grammaticalization*, pages 103–120, 2002.
[Ducrot, 1984]   Oswald Ducrot. *Le dire et le dit*. Paris: Minuit, 1984.
[Ducrot, 1996]   Oswald Ducrot. *Slovenian Lectures/Conférences Slovènes, Argumentative Semantics/Sémantique argumentative*, 1996.
[Fischer, 2007]   Olga Fischer. *Morphosyntactic Change: Functional and Formal Perspectives*. Oxford University Press, USA, 2007.
[Ford, 1994]   Cecilia E. Ford. Dialogic aspects of talk and writing: because on the interactive-edited continuum. *Text(The Hague)*, 14(4):531–554, 1994.

[Fried, 2004] Mirjam Fried. Construction Grammar: a thumbnail sketch. Construction Grammar in a cross-language perspective, ed. by Mirjam Fried and Jan-Ola Östman, 11-86, 2004.
[Fried, forthcoming] Mirjam Fried. Constructions and constructs: mapping a shift between predication and attribution. *Constructions and language change. Mouton de Gruyter*, forthcoming.
[Givón, 1979] T. Givón. *On understanding grammar*. Academic Press New York, 1979.
[Goldberg, 2003] Adele E. Goldberg. Constructions: a new theoretical approach to language. *Trends in Cognitive Sciences*, 7(5):219–224, 2003.
[Goldberg, 2006] Adele E. Goldberg. *Constructions at Work: The Nature of Generalization in Language*. Oxford University Press, 2006.
[Gries and Stefanowitsch, 2004] S.T. Gries and A. Stefanowitsch. Extending collostructional analysis. *A corpus-based perspective on "alternations", International Journal of Corpus Linguistics*, 9:97–129, 2004.
[Haiman, 1978] John Haiman. Conditionals are topics. *Language*, 54(3):564–589, 1978.
[Haspelmath, 1998] Martin Haspelmath. Does grammaticalization need reanalysis? *Studies in language*, 22:315–351, 1998.
[Haspelmath, 2004] Martin Haspelmath. On directionality in language change with particular reference to grammaticalization. In Olga Fischer, Muriel Norde, and Harry Peridon, editors, *Up and down the cline: The nature of grammaticalization*, pages 17–44. John Benjamins Publishing Company, 2004.
[Hedberg and Fadden, 2007] Nancy Hedberg and Lorna Fadden. The information structure of It-clefts, Wh-clefts and reverse Wh-clefts in English. In Nancy Hedberg and Ron Zacharski, editors, *The Grammar-Pragmatics Interface: Essays in Honor of Jeanette K. Gundel*, pages 49–76. Amsterdam/ Philadelphia: Benjamins, 2007.
[Heine et al., 1991] Bernd Heine, Ulrike Claudi, and Friederike Hünnemeyer. *Grammaticalization: A Conceptual Framework*. University of Chicago Press, 1991.
[Heine, 2002] Bernd Heine. On the role of context in grammaticalization. *New Reflections on Grammaticalization*, pages 83–101, 2002.
[Higgins, 1979] Francis Roger Higgins. *The Pseudo-Cleft Construction in English*. New York:Garland, 1979.
[Hilpert, 2007] Martin Hilpert. *Germanic Future Constructions-A Usage-based Study of Grammaticalization*. PhD thesis, Ph. D. Dissertation, Rice University, 2007.
[Himmelmann, 2004] Nikolaus P. Himmelmann. Lexicalization and grammaticization: Opposite or orthogonal? *What Makes Grammaticalization?: A Look From Its Fringes And Its Components*, 2004.
[Holquist, 1981] Michael Holquist. The Dialogic Imagination: Four Essays by MM Bakhtin. *Trans. Caryl Emerson and Michael Holquist. Austin: U of Texas P*, 1981.
[Hopper and Traugott, 2003] Paul J. Hopper and Elizabeth C. Traugott. *Grammaticalization*. Cambridge University Press, 2003.
[Hopper, 2001] Paul J. Hopper. Grammatical constructions and their discourse origins: Prototype or family resemblance. *Applied cognitive linguistics*, 1:109–129, 2001.
[Horn, 1996] Laurence R. Horn. Exclusive Company: Only and the Dynamics of Vertical Inference. *Journal of Semantics*, 13(1):1–40, 1996.
[Huber, forthcoming] M. Huber. The Old Bailey Proceedings, 1674-1834, forthcoming.
[Huddleston et al., 2002] R.D. Huddleston, G.K. Pullum, et al. *The Cambridge grammar of the English language*. Cambridge University Press New York, 2002.
[Janda, 2000] Richard D. Janda. Beyond "pathways" and "unidirectionality": on the discontinuity of language transmission and the counterability of grammaticalization. *Language Sciences*, 23(2-3):265–340, 2000.
[Jespersen, 1940] O. Jespersen. A Modern English Grammar on Historical Principles, Part V. Syntax, 1940.

[Jullien and Müller, 2007]   Stéphane. Jullien and Gabriele M. Müller. French pseudo-cleft and presentational cleft in French conversation: Two grammatical resources for maintaining the floor. *Tenth International Pragmatics Conference (IPra), Gothenberg, July,* 2007.

[Kay, 2002]   Paul Kay. Patterns of Coining. *Second International Conference on Construction Grammar*, 2002.

[Keller, 1994]   Rudi Keller. *On Language Change: The Invisible Hand in Language*. Routledge, 1994.

[Kim, 1995]   Kyu-hyun Kim. WH-clefts and left-dislocation in English conversation. *Word Order in Discourse*, 1995.

[Kiparsky, 1968]   Paul Kiparsky. Linguistic universals and linguistic change. In Emmon Bach and Robert T. Harms, editors, *Universals in Linguistic Theory*, pages 171–202. New York: Holt, Rinehart and Winston, 1968.

[Kiparsky, forthcoming]   Paul Kiparsky. Grammaticalization as optimization. In Dianne Jonas, editor, *Grammatical Change: Origins, Nature, Outcomes*. Oxford: OUP, forthcoming. http://www.stanford.edu/~kiparsky/.

[Kryk-Kastovsky, 2000]   Barbara Kryk-Kastovsky. Representations of orality in Early Modern English trial records. *Journal of Historical Pragmatics*, 1(2):201–230, 2000.

[Lambrecht, 2001]   Knud Lambrecht. A framework for the analysis of cleft constructions. *Linguistics*, 39(3):463–516, 2001.

[Langacker, 1987]   Ronald Langacker. *Foundations of Cognitive Grammar I: Theoretical Prerequisites*. Stanford: Stanford University Press, 1987.

[Langacker, 2005]   Ronald W. Langacker. Construction Grammars: cognitive, radical, and less so. In Francisco Ruiz de Mendoza Ibáñez and M. Sandra Peña Cervel, editors, *Cognitive Linguistics. Internal Dynamics and Interdisciplinary Interaction*, pages 101–159. Berlin/New York: Mouton de Gruyter, 2005.

[Larsson, this volume]   S. Larsson. Formalizing the Dynamics of Semantic Systems in Dialogue. In R. Cooper and R. Kempson, editors, *Language in Flux: Dialogue Coordination, Language Variation, Language Change and Evolution*. Kings College Press, this volume.

[Lehmann, 1995]   Christian Lehmann. *Thoughts on Grammaticalization*. Munich: Lincom Europa, 1995.

[Lehmann, forthcoming]   Christian Lehmann. Information structure and grammaticalization. In Elena Seoane and María José López-Couso, editors, *in collaboration with Teresa Fanego. Theoretical and Empirical Issues in Grammaticalization*. Amsterdam/Philadelphia: Benjamins, forthcoming.

[Lightfoot, 1979]   David W. Lightfoot. *Principles of Diachronic Syntax. Cambridge Studies in Linguistics London*, 23, 1979.

[Lightfoot, 2005]   Douglas J. Lightfoot. Can the lexicalization/grammaticalization distinction be reconciled? *Studies in Language*, 29(3):583–615, 2005.

[Lindström and Wide, 2005]   J. Lindström and C. Wide. Tracing the origins of a set of discourse particles: Swedish particles of the type you know. *Journal of historical pragmatics*, 6(2):211–236, 2005.

[Mann and Thompson, 1992]   William C. Mann and Sandra A Thompson. Relational discourse structure: a comparison of approaches to structuring texts by 'contrast'. In Shin Ja J. Hwang and Merrifield William R., editors, *Language in Context: Essays for Robert E. Longacre*. Dallas: Summer Institute of Linguistics and the University of Texas at Arlington., 1992.

[McMahon, 2006]   A. McMahon. Restructuring Renaissance English. In Lynda Mugglestone, editor, *The Oxford History of English*, pages 147–177. Oxford/New York: Oxford University Press, 2006.

[Meillet, 1958]   Antoine Meillet. L'évolution des formes grammaticales. *Linguistique historique et linguistique générale*, pages 130–148, 1958. [1912].

[Miller, 2006]   Jim Miller. Focus in the languages of europe. In Giuliano Bernini and Marcia L. Schwartz, editors, *Pragmatic Organization of Discourse in the Languages of Europe. (Empirical Approaches to Language Typology: EUROTYP, 20-8.)*. Berlin/New York: Mouton de Gruyter., 2006.

[Milroy, 2003]   J. Milroy. On the role of the speaker in language change. In Raymond Hickey, editor, *Motives for Language Change*, pages 143–157. Cambridge University Press, 2003.

[Milroy, 2007]   L. Milroy. Off the shelf or under the counter? On the social dynamics of sound changes. *Topics in English Linguistics*, 53:149–171, 2007.

[Moore, 2006]   C. Moore. The use of videlicet in Early Modern slander depositions: A case of genre-specific grammaticalization. *Journal of Historical Pragmatics*, 7(2):245–263, 2006.

[Nevalainen, 1991]   Terttu Nevalainen. *But, only, just: focusing adverbial change in modern English, 1500-1900*. Société néophilologique, Helsinki, 1991.

[Newmeyer, 1998]   Frederick J. Newmeyer. *Language Form and Language Function*. Cambridge, MA/London: MIT Press, 1998.

[Noël, 2007]   Dirk Noël. Diachronic construction grammar and grammaticalization theory. *Functions of Language*, 14(2):177–202, 2007.

[Nølke, 2006]   Henning Nølke. The semantics of polyphony(And the Pragmatics of Realization). *Acta linguistica Hafniensia*, 38:137–160, 2006.

[Patten, 2007, forthcoming]   A. Patten. *Cleft Sentences and Grammaticalization*. PhD thesis, PhD dissertation, Edinburgh University, 2007, forthcoming.

[Pérez-Guerra and Tizón-Couto, forthcoming]   Javier Pérez-Guerra and David Tizón-Couto. On left-dislocations in the history of English: Theory and data hand in hand. In Benjamin Shaer, Philippa Cook, Warner Frey, and Claudia Maienborn, editors, *Dislocated Elements in Discourse: Syntactic, Semantic, and Pragmatic Perspectives*. London: Routledge, forthcoming.

[Prince, 1978]   Ellen F. Prince. A comparison of wh-clefts and it-clefts in discourse. *Language*, 54(4):883–906, 1978.

[Quirk et al., 1985]   Randolph Quirk, Sidney Greenbaum, Geoffrey Leech, and Jan Svartvik. *A Comprehensive Grammar of Contemporary English*. London: Longman, 1985.

[Roberts and Roussou, 2003]   Ian G. Roberts and Anna Roussou. *Syntactic Change: A Minimalist Approach to Grammaticalization*. Cambridge University Press, 2003.

[Rossari and Cojocariu, 2007]   Corinne Rossari and Corina Cojocariu. Constructions of the type la cause/la raison/le prevue+ utterance; Grammaticalization, pragmaticalization or something else, 2007.

[Roulet, 1984]   E. Roulet. Speech Acts, Discourse Structure, and Pragmatic Connectives. *Journal of Pragmatics*, 8:31–47, 1984.

[Rudolph, 1996]   Elisabeth Rudolph. *Contrast: Adversative and Concessive Relations and Their Expressions in English, German, Spanish, Portuguese on Sentence and Text Level*. Walter de Gruyter, 1996.

[Sacks et al., 1974]   Harvey Sacks, Emanuel A. Schegloff, and Gail Jefferson. A simplest systematics for the organization of turn-taking for conversation. *Language*, 50(4):696–735, 1974.

[Schwenter and Traugott, 2000]   Scott A. Schwenter and Elizabeth C. Traugott. Article details Invoking scalarity: The development of in fact. *Journal of Historical Pragmatics*, 1(1):7–25, 2000.

[Schwenter, 2000]   Scott A. Schwenter. Viewpoints and polysemy: Linking adversative and causal meanings of discourse markers. In Elizabeth Couper-Kuhlen and Bernd Kortmann, editors, *Cause-Condition-Concession-Contrast: Cognitive and Discourse Perspectives*, pages 257–281. Berlin/New York: Mouton de Gruyter, 2000.

[Sharma et al., this volume]   D. Sharma, J. Bresnan, and A. Deo. Variation and change in the individual: Evidence from the Survey of English Dialects. In R. Cooper and R. Kempson, editors, *Language in Flux: Dialogue Coordination, Language Variation, Language Change and Evolution*. Kings College Press, this volume.

[Taavitsainen et al., 2006]   Irma Taavitsainen, Juhani Härmä, and Jarmo Korhonen. *Dialogic Language Use*. Helsinki: Société Néophilologique., 2006.

[Tabor and Traugott, 1998] Whitney Tabor and Eliazabeth C. Traugott. Structural scope expansion and grammaticalization. In Anna G. Ramat and Paul J. Hopper, editors, *The Limits of Grammaticalization*, pages 229–272. Amsterdam/Philadelphia: Benjamins, 1998.

[Traugott and Dasher, 2002] E.C. Traugott and R.B. Dasher. *Regularity in Semantic Change*. Cambridge University Press, 2002.

[Traugott and König, 1991] Elizabeth C. Traugott and E. König. The semantics-pragmatics of grammaticalization revisited. In Elizabeth C. Traugott and Bernd Heine, editors, *Approaches to Grammaticalization*, volume 1, pages 189–218. Amsterdam/Philadelphia: Benjamins., 1991.

[Traugott, 2004] Eliazabeth C. Traugott. Historical pragmatics. In L. R. Horn and G. Ward, editors, *Handbook of Pragmatics*, pages 538–561. Oxford/Malden, MA: Blackwell., 2004.

[Traugott, 2008, forthcoming] Eliazabeth C. Traugott. Grammaticalization, constructions and the incremental development of language: Suggestions from the development of degree modifiers in English. In Jaeger Gerhard, editor, *Variation, Selection, Development. Probing the Evolutionary Model of Language Change*, pages 219–250. Berlin/New York: Mouton de Gruyter., 2008, forthcoming.

[Traugott, forthcoming] Eliazabeth C. Traugott. Grammaticalization, emergent constructions, and the notion of "newness". In Anatol Stefanowitsch and Kerstin Fischer, editors, *Konstruktionsgrammatik und grammatische Konstruktionen*, pages 219–250. Berlin/New York: Mouton de Gruyter., forthcoming. Paper presented to the Seventh High Desert Linguistics Society (HDLS), Albuquerque, Nov. 2006.

[Trousdale, forthcoming(a)] Graeme Trousdale. Constructions and grammaticalization and lexicalization: Evidence from the history of a composite predicate construction in English. In Graeme Trousdale and Nikolas Gisborne, editors, *Constructional Explanations in Modern English Grammar*. Berlin/New York: Mouton de Gruyter., forthcoming.

[Trousdale, forthcoming(b)] Graeme Trousdale. Words and constructions in grammaticalization: The end of the English impersonal construction. In Donka Minkova and Susan Fitzmaurice, editors, *Empirical and Analytical Advances in the Study of English Language Change*. Berlin/New York: Mouton de Gruyter., forthcoming.

[van Gelderen, 2004] E. van Gelderen. *Grammaticalization as economy*. Amsterdam; Philadelphia: John Benjamins Pub., 2004.

[van Kemenade, 1987] Ans van Kemenade. *Syntactic Case and Morphological Case in the History of English*. Walter de Gruyter, 1987.

[Visser, 1963] F.T. Visser. *An Historical Syntax of the English Language*, volume 1. Leiden: Brill, 1963.

[Waltereit and Detges, 2007] R. Waltereit and U. Detges. Different functions, different histories. Modal particles and discourse markers from a diachronic point of view. *Journal of Catalan Linguistics*, 2007.

[Waltereit, 2006] Richard Waltereit. The rise of discourse markers in Italian: A specific type of language change. In Kirsten Fischer, editor, *Approaches to Discourse Particles*. Elsevier Science, 2006.

[Weinreich et al., 1968] Uriel Weinreich, William Labov, and Marvin I. Herzog. Empirical Foundations for a Theory of Language Change. In W. P. Lehmann and Yakov Malkiel, editors, *Directions for Historical Linguistics*, pages 95–189. University of Texas Press, 1968.

[Wierzbicka, 2006] A. Wierzbicka. *English: Meaning and Culture*. Oxford/New York: Oxford University Press, 2006.

Elizabeth Closs Traugott
Department of Linguistics, Stanford, CA, USA.
traugott@stanford.edu

Production Pressures, Syntactic Change and the Emergence of Clitic Pronouns[1]

RONNIE CANN & RUTH KEMPSON

1 Introduction

In this paper, we argue that syntactic change can arise from the interaction of syntactic mechanisms and pragmatic constraints on interpretation as the point of departure. The effect of the latter is to narrow down the options available; and the choices made can then get stored as routines for interpretation specific to individual lexical items, subsequently becoming encoded as part of the lexical specification of these forms. This observation is a regular functionalist characterization of grammaticalisation via routinizations associated with language use ([Givon, 1987] and others following). Our contribution is to provide a specification of this for one instance, the development of pre-verbal clitic pronouns in Medieval Spanish from the Latin weak pronouns[2], within a formal framework, and to do so in such a way that we are not merely able to articulate in detail the correspondence between word order effects and clitic distributions, but also to provide an explanation of what are otherwise puzzling gaps in these clitic distributions, such as the Person Case Constraint, which in other frameworks are problematic, and require special stipulation. While the results are tentative in addressing, in this paper, solely pre-verbal clitics, nonetheless the principled account offered for the Person Case Constraint is indicative of the explanatory value of shifting into a dynamic parsing-oriented syntactic perspective.

Our case study is the early positioning and idiosyncratic clustering of pro-

---

[1] This work has been done in conjunction with joint work by the second author and Miriam Bouzouita. Many ideas from this work are reflected in this paper: we wish in particular to thank her not only for help with the Medieval Spanish data, but for forcing us to confront the complexity of the Spanish facts and so refine our account of the Person Case Constraint. We would also like to thank Stelios Chatzikyriakidis for insightful discussions about related but distinct Greek data, and to Eleni Gregoromichelaki, Jieun Kiaer, Andrew Gargett, for helpful input as these ideas have emerged. Thanks also to Rosanna Sornicola for leaving us in no doubt as to the challenges our analysis faces while nevertheless giving very constructive and supportive advice. Normal disclaimers apply.

[2] Throughout we shall use the term "clitic" pronoun co-extensively with 'weak pronoun'. Nothing hangs on this.

nominal clitics in Medieval Spanish and the parallelism between these clitics and earlier Latin scrambling (free constituent-order) patterns. In particular, we argue that the clustering of clitics in a relatively early position in a clausal sequence is a calcified set of reflexes of the mechanisms underpinning scrambling. The theoretical framework in which this account is specified is that of Dynamic Syntax [Kempson *et al.*, 2001; Cann *et al.*, 2005], a framework which enables us to provide an explanation of the Person Case Constraint in terms of general tree-growth principles. The grammar of a language, according to this framework, is a set of parsing actions for building up information in context some of which are general, some of which are specific to individual words and phrases.

We begin our account of the development of the pre-verbal pronominal clitics in Spanish by providing a sketch of Latin scrambling following [Kempson and Kiaer, 2008]. As part of this, we show how cognitive constraints determine what is a prevalent given before new effect in many free word-order languages, and then we show how through routinization, these can come to be lexically encoded with individual weak forms of pronoun as providing a set of triggers all of which determine their relatively early placement. We also show how the processes of construal which the clitic pronouns determine are themselves reflexes of earlier general processes for building up interpretation on line. The result, from a synchronic perspective, is a set of emergent lexical patterns that appear to lack either structural or semantic motivation; the systematicity underpinning these patterns can only be seen to make sense within the diachronic perspective. From a synchronic perspective, then, such phenomena constitute stored macros of actions which a child has to learn in gaining competence in using the clitic pronouns; but this is nevertheless grounded in an ongoing interaction between production processes and the emergent system itself. The further significance of the account is that the diachronic process is seen as involving a feeding relation between general cognitive constraints on usage and articulation of lexical encodings in the core language system, a perspective precluded by standard competence-performance assumptions (though see [Hawkins, 2004]).

2 Background: Clitic and scrambling puzzles

The background against which this account is set is the challenge posed by both clitic clustering and by scrambling phenomena which are normally not seen as related.[3]

---

[3] This observation of parallelism between scrambling and clitic placement has been independently observed by Martins [2002], but given the framework she adopts, her observation cannot be reflected in the analysis she provides.

2.1 Clitic mysteries

The templatic behaviour of clitic clustering is one of the most puzzling syntactic phenomena displayed in natural languages. Right across unrelated language-families, wherever clitic-pronoun systems emerge, they seem resistant to either semantic or syntactic explanation. Yet, despite very considerable lexical idiosyncracy, these systems overall display remarkable similarities, as we shall see, in the RANGE of patterns they make available.

Pronominal clitics are typically weakened quasi-affixal, quasi-pronominal devices, with a characteristic preference for occurring at some relatively early position in a finite clausal sequence, in some languages immediately following some first constituent or word, in other languages immediately preceding the verb. The first of these, the second-position clitic placement (as seen in the Balkan languages, Medieval Spanish, Portuguese, among others), is hosted by a heterogeneous set of categories, commonly including complementisers, *wh* expressions, negation-marker, focused expressions, relative pronouns, verbs (if nothing else precedes), and in some cases conjunction markers[4]:

(1) ... *quien* **te** *algo prometiere* ..
    who 2.CL-IO something would-promise
    'the one who would promise something to you.'
    Data from [Rivero, 1997]

(2) *Quant* **le** *connocio Abdias, homillosle*
    when 3M.CL-DO recognized.3sg Abdias lowered-CL-CL
    'When Abdias recognized him, he bowed for him.'

(3) *Que* **te** *dixo Heliseus?*
    What 2.CL-IO said.3sg Heliseus
    'What did Heliseus tell you?'

(4) *Non* **los** *destroyré [...]*
    not 3.CL-DO will-destroy.1sg [...]
    'I will not destroy them [...].'

(5) *.ij. mios fijos* **te** *dexaré [...]*
    two my sons 2.CL-IO will-leave.1sg [...]
    'My two sons, I will leave you [...].'

---

[4] All illustrations are from 13th century Medieval Spanish; and are taken from a corpus of Medieval Spanish collected by Miriam Bouzouita culled from the *Fazienda de Ultramar*, which dates from around 1230. All Medieval Spanish examples given are from this text unless stated otherwise.

(6) Con   aquellas **se**   aiunto   Salomon [...]
    with   those   CL-REFL   slept.3sg Salomon [...]
    'With those women, Salomon slept (joined himself) [...].'

(7) Oyo**l**   Ruben   [...]
    heard.3sg-CL-DO   Ruben   [...]
    'Ruben heard it [...].'

The environments which act as triggers for early clitic placement are subject to minor variation across languages as to what categories it includes, and resists any unitary syntactic characterization. Out of the languages with this second-position placement of clitics, only some license the interpolation of other expressions between the clitic and the verb, as in (1): Modern Portuguese does not allow such interpolation except very peripherally and Cypriot Greek, otherwise so similar to Medieval Spanish, precludes interpolation altogether. The puzzle, from a syntactic perspective, is what this array of variation can be grounded in: why should clitics occur in these positions, the pre-verbal positioning in particular being a position from which the corresponding full NP is quite generally precluded (precluded, that is, unless the language licenses interpolation)?

Construal of clitics is also puzzling, as, for some clitics, their argument-role is fully determined by their form, but for others it is not. Accusative clitic pronouns in Romance for example are relatively clearcut in indicating a direct-object argument. Dative pronouns on the other hand invariably display variation, with very considerable indeterminacy as to what the intrinsic significance of dative-labelling amounts to. The precise function of the dative case is indeed notoriously hard to pin down, and, despite being the lowest in frequency of all the oblique cases in Latin according to a count of [Hoecke, 1996], is nonetheless reported by him as having been described in the Greco-Latin tradition as dividing into at least ten distinct types, from the marking of direct and indirect objects through to widely varying semantic uses, including possession, advantage, result and 'interest'. He himself provides a characterization of dative construal neutral between these as "grounding the event structure in relation to the speech participants", a weak characterization that is illustrated by examples such as:

(8) an   **tibi**   quisquam   in   curiam
    Q   you.DAT   anyone.NOM.SG   into   senate-house.ACC.SG
    venienti   assurexit?
    coming.DAT.SG   get-up.3SG.PERF
    'Did anyone get up for you (to your benefit) when you came into the senate house?'

Cicero Pis. 26

(9) quid **mihi** Celsus   agit?
     what me.DAT Celsus.NOM.SG do.3.SG.PRES
     'How, pray, is Celsus?' (Lit. 'What to me Celsus does?')

Horace Ep. 1, 3, 15[5]

Following this Latin usage, the first and second dative clitic pronouns in the Romance languages are commonly associated with a large number of distinct construals, the particular range varying from language to language, and even from environment to environment. For example, first and second person clitics have a single form which may variously be construed as reflexive, direct or indirect object, or as ethical-datives, (10).

(10) Testimonias **me**   sed   oy
      witnesses   1.CL-IO be.imp today
      'Be witnesses on my behalf today.'

Yet another aspect of the clitics puzzle is that where there is more than one clitic in a clausal string, they almost invariably cluster together, so that for any statement purporting to restrict the occurrence of the clitic pronoun to immediately following some preceding category of expression or immediately preceding some verbal form, the statement has to be complicated by the fact that another clitic may intervene between it and such a host:

(11) e   ella dixo**gelo**   [...]
      and she   told.3sg.CL-IO.3sg.CL-DO [...]
      'And she told it to him [...].'

(12) ca   ya   non **telo**   mandava matar
      because already not 2.CL-IO.3sg.CL-DO   I-order to-kill
      'because I do not order you any longer to kill him.'

Data from [Granberg, 1988, p132]

Finally, there is the complication that the relative ordering of these clitics may vary between closely related languages and even within a single language without any distinction of interpretation – French pairs of third person clitics occur only in a DO-IO sequence but pairs of third and first/second person clitics occur only in the inverse IO-DO sequence (as in the Spanish example (11)): the basis for such clusterings is thus generally agreed not to have a semantic

---

[5]The phrase *quid agis?* in Latin is generally used for 'How are you?'.

basis. But there is also morphological idiosyncracy, so that a purely phonological explanation doesn't seem appropriate either - in particular restrictions on Spanish clustering differ according as the neutral dative form *se* is construed as ethical dative, indirect object, or reflexive. There is also notorious variation across dialects, with 'leista' effects in which the dative *le* appears to be incorporating accusative uses, but with also 'loista' and even 'laista' dialects in which it is rather the masculine *lo* (or feminine form *la*) which is becoming the form that can cover both direct and indirect object construals. Such rampant variability might seem indicative of homonymy, not worthy of anything other than lexical listing, but this leaves quite unexplained why this type of pattern recurs so regularly across the broad range of clitic systems.

The intransigence of clitic positioning to syntactic, semantic, or phonological explication has led to debates as to whether these clusters interact with syntactic processes at all. In minimalist analyses, variant clitic properties are seen by some as associated with distinct features, hence distinct triggers for movement, inducing movement of the clitic to the requisite checking site [Cardinaletti, forthcoming], others see them as subject only to feature-geometry forms of explanation [Cuervo, 2005], yet others a mixture of the two [Adger and Harbour, 2006] There have been debates over which clitics should have which features, what processes they trigger and, for those that argue for feature geometries, whether there should be rules making reference to concepts of domination displayed on the feature hierarchy [Heap, 2005]. In the majority of cases, the specifications proposed lack independent motivation, and so amount to little more than stipulated invocation of syntactic structure or feature geometry to directly reflect the idiosyncratic orders observed. Cardinaletti's account of the array of idiosyncrasies displayed in Italian [Cardinaletti, forthcoming] involves distinguishing *gli* (the realization of dative *le* when immediately preceding *lo*) as having a +person feature while its alternative realization *le* has only a +number feature without that person feature. Rivero [2007], in addressing cluster properties in association with Spanish psych predicates, defines a newly distinctive mental-state +m feature, whose positing critically provides the necessary count of feature-strength to determine appropriate orderings on which her account depends. Adger and Harbour and others argue over whether there should be binary Participant, Author, and Hearer features over and above other features assigned, and there are debates as to whether Person should be posited as a feature at all ([Anagnostopoulou, 2005] "No", [Rivero, 2007] "Yes" with both overt and covert variants) and over whether features should be binary (the [Adger and Harbour, 2006] account of the problematic morphological gaps posits both binary and non-binary features). Cuervo [2005] defines template positions onto which feature complexes have to be mapped (eschewing a movement-based account), and though noting the problems raised by morphological gaps, provides no account of them. Against these, structural accounts persist: Ormabazal and Romero [2007] for example argue for an agreement-based account, that for any language displaying VP-internal agreement, no more than one such agreement pairing is possible.

In other theoretical frameworks things are little better. In optimality-theoretic frameworks, for example, the set of constraints defined is highly specific to particular clusterings involving for example *PERSONRIGHT*, *PERSONLEFT*, *EDGEMOST(Dat)*, *EDGEMOST(Acc)*, and *PARSE* constraints [Grimshaw, 2001; Legendre, 2003], all defined to allow appropriate flexibility under appropriate conditions; but with the consequence that there is no restriction on possible clusterings, the constraints doing no more than matching the facts. In yet other attempts [Monachesi, 2005; Anderson, 2005], such clustering is taken to motivate the postulation of a morphology component defined as independent of either syntax and semantics, a move which means that lack of independent explanation of the data is turned into a design feature of the grammar. Licensed co-occurrences per language are defined as varying morphological templates onto which the language-sequences have to be mapped, with no attempt in that system to explain why such clustering behaviour should occur.

The overall impression from this increasing wealth of literature devoted to clitics is that there is little indication of anything approaching a principled explanation.

2.2 Word Order Variation

There is an unexpected twist on clitic variability which in this paper we wish to bring out. Clitic sequencing by definition involves sequences of weak pronominal NP expressions, in the Romance languages, in various combinations both before the verb and after it. Such sequencing is redolent of Latin freedom of word order, since in both Latin and in the clitic systems sequenced NP-expressions are presented in combination with the accompanying verb. We shall argue that far from being a trivial observation, this is indeed the source of the explanation.

Latin constituent order variation is syntactically free in simple clauses at least, with NPs able to occur in any order and with any one or more NP able to occur before the verb, or after it. In consequence, there is no apparent indication from the order itself how the various parts are to be semantically combined:

(13) *Catullus Lesbiam amavit*
 Catullus.NOM Lesbia.ACC loved.3.SH.PERF
 'Catullus loved Lesbia.'

 Lesbiam Catullus amavit.

Amavit Catullus Lesbiam.
Amavit Lesbiam Catullus.
Lesbiam amavit Catullus.
Catullus amavit Lesbiam.

It is, of course, the case specifications of the NPs that determine the construal of the arguments they project, relative to the verb, rather than anything intrinsic to the ordering in the string. So it should be no surprise to find variability in order in Medieval Spanish in the one set of nominals, the clitic pronouns, that retain some aspect of the Latin case system which was otherwise entirely lost. Thus, clitic pronouns occur both before and after the verb in Medieval Spanish. The assumption that case determines construal is however only partially true, in that, as with most case-marking systems, much of the Latin case system is syncretic, with only partial determinism of thematic role from the morphological form of the NP-expressions: nominative and accusative forms of nouns are syncretic invariably in the neuter and also regularly in the plural of the consonant stems. In the development of the Romance languages, phonological changes caused massive syncretism within nominal paradigms giving rise in Vulgar Latin to just two or three forms in many cases. For example, the first declension classical forms *rosa, rosam, rosā, rosas, rosarum,* (singular nominative, accusative, ablative and plural accusative, genitive, respectively) are reduced to *rosa* while the late form *rose* stands for the rest of the paradigm, except for the dative/ablative plural. Ultimately, this led to a loss of case distinctiveness amongst the Romance languages (except for Romanian which retains oblique/non-oblique forms in certain declensions) became general for NPs in Medieval Spanish. Syncretism also affected the weak pronominal system so that in medieval Spanish some clitics are not differentiated as to accusative/dative cases, *me* and *te* being obvious examples.

Despite such variable determinism in the case system in Latin, word order freedom extends beyond mere local "scrambling", as constituents can be dislocated even across clausal boundaries:

(14) *Stercilinum   magnum   stude   ut   habeas*
      dunghill.ACC big.ACC ensure.IMP.SG that   have.2.PS.SING
      'See that you have a large dung hill'

Cato De Re Rust. 6

In these classic long-distance dependency constructions, case specifications cannot be seen as contributing anything more than a constraint on their construal, given their arbitrary dislocation from the expression on which they depend.

Nevertheless, despite such flexibility, word order in Latin is very far from being a total free-for-all. Even though more than one constituent can be dislocated and placed at the left periphery, in all cases involving dislocation from an embedded finite clause, there is invariably a restriction that all the constituents so dislocated must be interpreted as local to each other, as in (15, 16):

(15) Ventus   ad   praefurnium   caveto   ne
     wind.NOM   to   furnace-door.ACC beware.IMP   NEG-COMP
     accedat
     come near.3SG
     'Take care that the wind doesn't blow on the furnace door.'

Cato op. cit. 38

(16) digitum   supra   terram   facito   semina
     finger.ACC   above   earth.ACC   make.IMP   seeds.NOM/ACC
     emineant
     project.3PL
     'Make the seeds project a finger above the earth.'

Cato op. cit. 46

This rigid local pairing of NP-expressions receives an echo in the subsequent clitic systems that emerged, with their rigid ordering before the verb, but essential locality with respect to each other.[6] Until quite recently, surface word order had been taken to be a linearization matter to be handled as a surface property not impinging on the structural core of syntax-internal mechanisms. But this leaves unexplained the rigid locality of any two such dislocated expressions relative to each other, a pattern that occurs quite generally with clitic sequences which cannot be split in the same manner as multiple long-distance dependencies.

---

[6] Long-distance scrambling, and its alternant multiple long-distance scrambling, is, in the Japanese literature, generally analyzed as distinct from *wh*-movement, but this assumption depends on theory-specific assumptions on the correspondence between *Move Alpha* and feature-triggering, which scrambling lacks. See Kempson and Kiaer [forthcoming] for an alternative view in which the two are identified. The existence of more than one such expression as a multiple long-distance dependency is highly problematic for all frameworks where long-distance dependency is expressed as a nonlocal relationship between fronted linguistic expression and invisible site. In minimalist explanations, the only way to explain why two or more such moved NPs should be subject to a strict co-argument constraint is either to analyze one of the NPs as adjunct to the other, or to posit empty verb movement or so-called *Remnant Movement*; but all such moves lack justification other than their apparent necessity to yield the facts [Koizumi, 2000; Takano, 2002]. In categorial grammar frameworks, the analogous problem arises that with no local contiguity of the paired argument expressions with the verb they need to be associated with, the only option is to assume a process of verb-union of the paired verb-sequences, but this removes any basis for deciding how to pair up argument expressions and verbs appropriately [Kiaer, 2007].

What we argue is that the patterns attributable to scrambling are indeed reflected in the distribution of medieval Spanish clitics: and we will set out an account that formally defines an explanation in these terms. In informal terms, local scrambling requires constructive use of case [Nordlinger, 1998], with case specifications determining argument role in the presented structure in an on-line way in Latin. Long-distance scrambling, in which an expression can be dislocated arbitrarily far from its dependency site, indicates to the contrary that some case specifications do not perform any such local constructive role, but merely act as some kind of filter on appropriate identification of where they contribute to the overall structure. Multiple long-distance scrambling, in which pairs of such dislocated expressions may occur together at some early position in a string, can be modelled by a mechanism that induces an essentially localized sub-structure, to be resolved in the overall structure as a unit. Finally, parenthetical construals can be available for any expression, so that some expressions can be analyzed as in some sense independent of the structure within which they are contained. It is then the effects of these general mechanisms that underpin what has been seen as requiring clitic template specifications, with the various effects displayed in the distribution of clitics being modelled as a calcification of the sequences of actions which had in the earlier Latin system been induced by these general mechanisms, in different combinations.

An account of scrambling has been argued for in detail elsewhere with respect to Japanese and Korean [Cann *et al.*, 2005; Kempson and Kiaer, 2008]. Our primary aim in this paper is to show how that account can be reapplied to Latin and used to tackle the notorious intransigency of clitic facts as displayed in Spanish to provide a diachronically principled account not merely of clitic positioning, but of the range of variability and clustering that occurs in clitic clusters. We shall by no means solve the full set of clitic mysteries: in particular we do not provide any explanation of the individual stages through which one clitic system might evolve into a subsequent distinct clitic system (see Bouzouita [this volume] for a modelling of how the positioning of the clitic *lo* evolved from Medieval through Renaissance to Modern Spanish). All that we hope to achieve is a demonstration of the potential for a new range of explanations of clitic behaviours which a dynamic perspective offers. The more general significance of the account to be sketched is the fact that syntactic, even morpho-syntactic idiosyncracies, can be explained as resulting from the progressive effect which general cognitive constraints may have over time on an evolving linguistic system. And the analysis will open up a perspective in which case can be analyzed in essentially procedural terms.

3 Towards a Dynamic Syntax of Latin

The novel property of Dynamic Syntax as a syntactic theory is that the concept of structural underspecification and growth of interpretation intrinsic to processing is taken as the core syntactic notion. The syntax of the natural-language system is thus defined as a set of strategies for establishing the interpretation of some string of words in the order in which they appear, reflecting possibilities for choice in on-line parsing. The process involves the incremental development of tree structures representing a semantic interpretation for a string which are decorated by labels that progressively provide the information needed to determine the appropriate interpretation. Generation is defined in exactly the same terms: the very same rules apply in production as in parsing,the only difference between production and parsing being that whereas the parser may not know in advance the interpretation to be constructed, the producer in contrast must do so [Purver and Otsuka, 2003; Purver et al., 2006]. Hence, in generation there is from the outset a 'goaltree' which represents the interpretation to be conveyed, together with a defined constraint that in generation, each update step licensed by the parsing mechanism has to constitute an enrichment towards completing that 'goal tree' (formally a subsumption relation is required to hold between the parse tree and the goal tree [Purver and Otsuka, 2003]).

As the basis of the processing system is parsing, we begin by defining the general parsing strategies used in the framework. The starting point of this process is a tree with just a rootnode and a requirement to construct some propositional formula. The endpoint is a fully decorated binary branching tree structure encoding functor-argument structure of a familiar sort.[7] As figure 1 displays, each completed interpretation is represented as a binary-branching tree whose rootnode is the propositional formula established and its daughter nodes the various sub-formulae that together yield this formula.

The process of tree-growth is the sole basis of syntactic explanation: a sentence is defined to be well-formed just in case there is at least one possible route through that process that leads to a complete propositional tree with no requirements outstanding (see below).[8] Tree growth involves the emergent

---

[7] Fo is a predicate that takes a logical formula as value, Ty a predicate that takes logical types as values, Tn a predicate that takes tree-node addresses as values, e.g. $Tn(0)$ being the rootnode. The $\Diamond$ is a pointer, indicating the node currently under development.

[8] Quantification is expressed in terms of variable-binding term operators, so that quantifying NPs like all other NPs are of type e. The underlying logic is the epsilon calculus, the formal study of arbitrary names, with term-expressions whose internal structure is made up of an epsilon binder, ϵ, a variable, and a restrictor: e.g. $\epsilon, x, Man'(x)$. Since in Latin, nouns project full specification of terms, the structure defined to be projected by *servum* would be a subtree of which the quantifying term is the topnode, dominating a subtree decorated with binder, variable, and restrictor specification. We leave all details on one side.

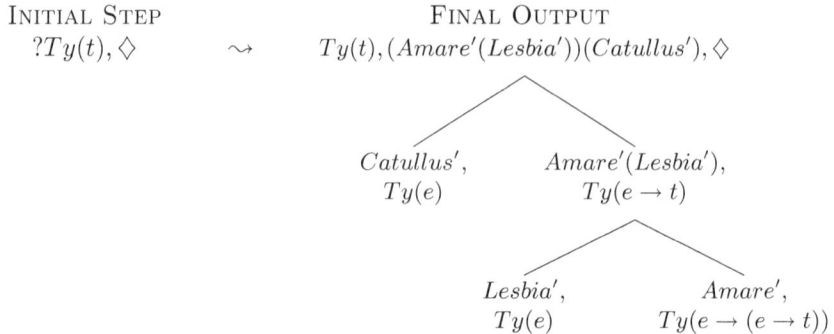

Figure 1. Parsing *Catullus Lesbiam amavit* 'Catullus loved Lesbia.'

unfolding of partial trees, whose node-relations and node-decorations all get progressively specified. Transition steps between partial trees are determined by a combination of general computational actions and lexical actions that are triggered by parsing words in the order in which they are presented in some string, together defining a monotonic process of tree-growth. These computational and lexical actions are expressed in exactly the same terms, that of growth along any of the dimensions associated with decorations on the trees defined by the system. Moreover, both sets of actions are defined using exactly the same vocabulary[9], allowing in principle for computational actions to become associated with particular lexical items and so targets for possible routinization. The only essential differences between computational and lexical actions are that the former are, without exception, optional and not triggered by particular phonological (or orthographic) input, while the latter are so triggered and the actions they determine must be run.

ANY aspect of tree construction or decoration may be partial. Accordingly, tree-relations, tree-decorations, type and formula specifications may all be only partially specified. Central to this process is the concept of requirement $?X$ for any decoration X representing a type, formula or tree-node address. For example, decorations on nodes such as $?Ty(t), ?Ty(e), ?Ty(e \rightarrow t)$ etc. express requirements to construct formulae of the appropriate type on the nodes so decorated; $?\exists \mathbf{x}.Fo(\mathbf{x})$ a requirement to provide a fixed formula specification; and $?\exists x Tn(x)$ a requirement to provide a fixed treenode address. The underpinning formal system is a logic of finite trees (LOFT: [Blackburn and Meyer-Viol,

---

[9]This differs from the theory put forward in Kempson *et al.* [2001] and Cann *et al.* [2005].

1994]) with two basic modalities, $\langle\downarrow\rangle$ and $\langle\uparrow\rangle$, such that $\langle\downarrow\rangle\alpha$ holds at a node if α holds at its daughter, and its inverse, $\langle\uparrow\rangle\alpha$, holds at a node if α holds at its mother. Function and argument relations are distinguished by defining two types of daughter relation, $\langle\downarrow_0\rangle$ for argument daughters, $\langle\downarrow_1\rangle$ for functor daughters (with their inverses $\langle\uparrow_0\rangle, \langle\uparrow_1\rangle$). Domination relations are then definable through Kleene star operators, e.g. $\langle\uparrow_*\rangle Tn(a)$ for some node identified as dominated by treenode $Tn(a)$; a node decorated as $\langle\uparrow_*\rangle Tn(a), ?\exists x Tn(x)$ is a node that though introduced into the emergent tree has not yet been assigned a fixed treenode relation. Such modal statements can be used to formulate modal requirements. These may be general requirements, e.g. the requirements on an introduced proposition-requiring node for an argument-daughter node and a predicate-daughter node: such a node would be decorated with $?Ty(t), ?\langle\downarrow_0\rangle Ty(e), ?\langle\downarrow_1\rangle Ty(e \to t)$. Such requirements constitute subgoals on a wellformed derivation, and are filters on the output.

Requirements may also however be defined as lexically imposed filters on output: and this is the initial basis for modelling case specifications where this is structurally definable. For example, a nominatively marked expression is defined as projecting onto a subject node of the emergent tree an output filter requirement of the form $?\langle\uparrow_0\rangle Ty(t)$ (the requirement that its immediately dominating node be of a formula of type t); an accusatively marked expression projects onto the immediate argument-daughter node of some emergent predicate-requiring node the requirement $?\langle\uparrow_0\rangle Ty(e \to t)$. Thus case specifications, like all other generalizations, are expressed in terms of possible forms of tree growth. And so it is that a range of what in other frameworks are taken to be morphological or syntactic properties can in this framework be expressed as requirements on growth of semantic representation.[10]

Restrictions at the interface of syntax and semantics are also naturally expressible in these terms. An uncontroversial aspect of underspecification of content is that associated with anaphoric expressions, their intrinsic contribution to interpretation being that they provide only some partial specification of any occasion-specific interpretation, the particular value being determined by the context relative to which the uttered expression is understood. In this representational perspective, this is expressed by defining all such context-dependent expressions as projecting an interim place-holding device, adding to the basic *Formula* vocabulary the metavariables **U**, **V**.., each associated with a requirement for a fixed value to be provided either from the context so far accrued in the interpretation process or subsequently from within the

---

[10]The specification of case in these terms is naive in the sense that it assumes that particular cases determine directly the semantic function of the term projected by some noun phrase. This is not generally true (e.g. nominative expressions may be a semantic object in some passive construction while other cases have 'semantic' counterparts). Some effects of this are noted below, but a more sophisticated theory of case in DS remains to be articulated.

construction process. Whatever restrictions there are on the domain within which individual anaphoric expressions have to be construed are also defined in tree-growth terms as constraints on the (sub)-tree within which the values of metavariables have to be found. For example, in the case of reflexives, the value for the projected metavariable has to be found at some node $Tn(a)$ along a path $\langle\uparrow_0\rangle\langle\uparrow_1^*\rangle\langle\downarrow_0\rangle Tn(a)$ from the node being decorated by the reflexive – that is from some co-argument along some unspecified but uninterrupted functor spine. Conversely, metavariables projected by pronouns cannot take such a local value, a constraint expressed as part of the process of substitution (see [Kempson et al., 2001, p97]).

3.1 Scrambling

More controversially, the very same perspective is adopted with what in other frameworks is taken to constitute evidence of either feature passing [Sag et al., 2002] or syntactic movement (e.g. [Hornstein et al., 2005]). Instead of positing morphologically empty sites in a string which are paired with some non-contiguous (left-peripheral) expression as a basis for articulating the contribution of that expression to interpretation of the string, a parsing-based perspective that follows the dynamics of processing of strings in real time is set out as the basis for modelling long-distance dependency, positing underspecification of the tree-relation needed to establish the contribution of the dislocated expression in question to the overall interpretation at the early point in the string at which it occurs. One core mechanism is the license to construct a node dominated by some proposition-requiring node whose tree-relation is not fully specified with respect to that node. This is achieved by a rule of *Adjunction* (read 'star-adjunction') which creates an "unfixed" node with precisely this property, described in the tree-logic language as $\langle\uparrow_*\rangle Tn(a)$ with respect to some treenode $Tn(a)$. The exact role of such unfixed nodes is thus not specified at the point of introduction in the emergent tree structure, but is required to be determined at some later stage in the grammatical process. Such treenode underspecification is characteristically resolved upon parsing a following verb, whose lexical specification induces actions of tree-growth that introduce an array of argument-nodes, with one of which the unfixed node may unify.

There is also a more locally-restricted process of introducing unfixed nodes (*Local*Adjunction*), for which an argument-node is constructed that is also underspecified with respect to some type-t-requiring node but with a tighter constraint that this relation be local to the point from which the underspecified tree relation is constructed. This is characterized on its introduction as having a modality $\langle\uparrow_0\rangle\langle\uparrow_1^*\rangle Tn(a)$ with respect to some treenode $Tn(a)$. This modality specifies that the unfixed node is an argument ($\langle\uparrow_0\rangle$) that is related to an unspecified series of functor nodes to the dominating node ($\langle\uparrow_1^*\rangle$). This has the effect of ensuring strict locality within a single predicate-argument array. Both underspecified tree relations are twinned with a requirement for update ($?\exists\mathbf{x}.Tn(\mathbf{x})$) so that a subsequent fixed tree-node relation must be provided in all wellformed derivations.

A defining property of trees and the nodes they contain is that a node in a tree is uniquely defined by its relation to all other nodes in the containing tree [Blackburn and Meyer-Viol, 1994]. This has a consequence for the tree construction process that there can only be one unfixed node of a type at a time in any partial tree, as all such nodes are characterizable only by their relatively weak modality. This is not a constraint that has to be externally imposed: any duplication of some tree relation simply induces the immediate collapse of any such putative pair of nodes, which invariably leads to an incoherent treenode decoration unless the individual decorations of the duplicated nodes are compatible. This restriction has an important role to play in determining the way unfixed nodes are progressively introduced and updated, and the result, as we shall see, is an account of Latin word order effects covering both *short*- and *long*-distance scrambling.

A common basis for crosslinguistic variation is the minor variation that lexical actions for related categories of expression in the differing languages may display. For example, with its relatively free word order and possibility of pro-drop, the parsing of a Latin verb induces a propositional structure whose argument nodes are decorated with metavariables, capturing the effect of null pronouns in such languages without the assumption that these exist as parts of a *linguistic* string. The left hand side of the following display provides the lexical actions to be carried out by a parse of *amavit* 'loved', with the resulting partial tree shown on the right.[11]

This property is not shared by verbs in non-pro-drop languages whose argument nodes, as projected from the verb, bear the weaker characterization of the requirement $?Ty(e)$, without metavariables, thereby imposing the requirement of morphologically explicit argument expressions.

---

[11] The applicability of specific rules or lexical actions depends on appropriate positioning of the pointer, $\Diamond$, and while there is considerable freedom of the pointer back down a tree in anticipation of further development of nodes, movement of the pointer up the tree is highly restricted, and possible only if the type-requirement on some node has been satisfied, and then, only to the immediate mother node or, in the case of unfixed nodes, to the node from which the underspecified relation was constructed.

(17) *amavit*

IF	$?Ty(t)$
THEN	$\text{put}(Tns(PAST))$;
	$\text{make}(\langle\downarrow_0\rangle); \text{go}(\langle\downarrow_0\rangle)$;
	$\text{put}(Ty(e), Fo(\mathbf{U}_{3sg}), ?\exists \mathbf{x}.Fo(\mathbf{x}))$;
	$\text{go}(\langle\uparrow_0\rangle); \text{make}(\langle\downarrow_1\rangle); \text{go}(\langle\downarrow_1\rangle)$;
	$\text{put}(?Ty(e \to t))$;
	$\text{make}(\langle\downarrow_1\rangle); \text{go}(\langle\downarrow_1\rangle)$;
	$\text{put}(Fo(Amare'),$
	$Ty(e \to (e \to t)), [\downarrow]\bot)$;
	$\text{go}(\langle\uparrow_1\rangle); \text{make}(\langle\downarrow_0\rangle); \text{go}(\langle\downarrow_0\rangle)$;
	$\text{put}(Fo(\mathbf{V}), Ty(e), ?\exists \mathbf{x}.Fo(\mathbf{x}))$
ELSE	Abort

$?Ty(t), Tns(PAST)$

$Ty(e),$
$\mathbf{U}_{3sg}, \quad ?Ty(e \to t)$
$?\exists \mathbf{x}.Fo(\mathbf{x})$

$Ty(e),$
$\mathbf{V}, \quad Ty(e \to (e \to t)),$
$?\exists \mathbf{x}.Fo(\mathbf{x}), \quad Amare'$
$\diamond$

Lexical projection of propositional structures interacts with the construction of nodes by application of Local*Adjunction prior to the parse of some verb, where scrambling effects are driven by constructive use of case.

(18) Lesbiam   Catullus   amavit   Lesbia.
      ACC   Catullus.NOM   love.3SG.PERF
      'Catullus loved Lesbia.'

As noted, case specifications, as defined in lexical entries, are filters on the required output, ensuring that the term projected by some nominal expression is fixed in an appropriate position. However, case-marking may be used constructively to immediately induce an update of the underspecified tree relation, by a step of abduction, that guarantees the ultimate satisfaction of the output filter. The succession of steps required for the processing of (18) begins with the parsing of the accusative noun *Lesbiam* as decorating a locally unfixed node. Abduction proceeds in two steps: from the case constraint $?\langle\uparrow_0\rangle Ty(e \to t)$ on the argument-node to an annotation on the mother of $?Ty(e \to t)$, to ensure that the accusative requirement is satisfied; and then from $\langle\uparrow_1^*\rangle Tn(0)$ to $\langle\uparrow_1\rangle Tn(0)$ to satisfy the tree-node requirement on the functor node.[12]

---

[12] This sequence of steps can apply to all argument relations including subject: the Kleene* intrinsic to defining $\langle\uparrow_*\rangle$ and other operators is satisfied by the empty set, so $\langle\uparrow_0\rangle\langle\uparrow_*^1\rangle Tn(a)$ is true also of the subject relation.

(19)

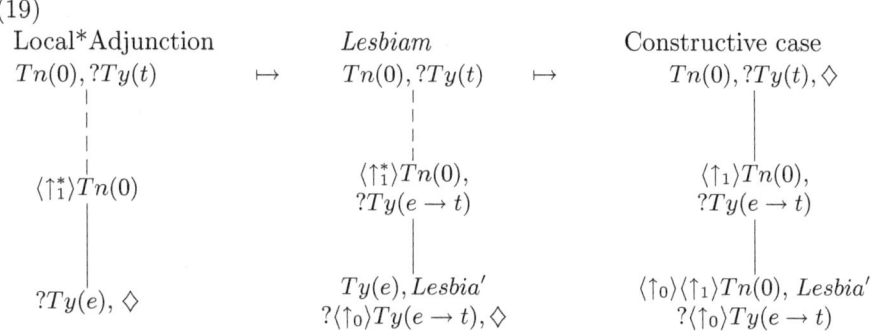

A second step of Local*Adjunction takes place, and the parsing of *Catullus* is then taken to fix the value of the underspecified tree relation $\langle \uparrow_0 \rangle \langle \uparrow_1^* \rangle Tn(0)$ of Local*Adjunction into $\langle \uparrow_0 \rangle Tn(0)$ providing the basis for satisfying the nominative-induced requirement $?\langle \uparrow_0 \rangle Ty(t)$:

(20)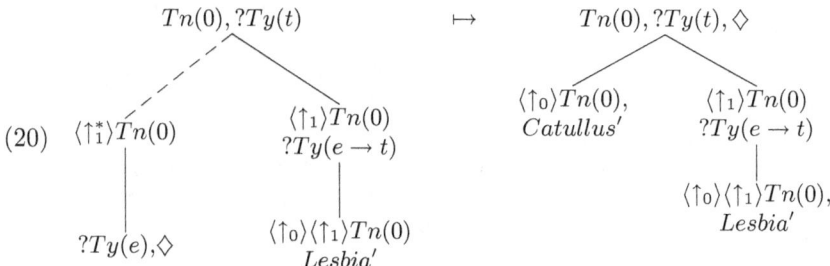

The result is that the relation between the argument node and the dominating node is fixed at the point of parsing the noun phrase, possibly well before the verb is processed. The output-filter restrictions of case-specifications serve thus to induce the update of an unfixed node to a fixed relation as each unfixed node is introduced. The actions of the verb then serve to fill out the remainder of the propositional structure to yield the appropriate output tree. These lexical actions operate exactly as before, giving rise to a duplication in the description of the tree of both subject and object nodes with the already constructed nodes being matched with nodes decorated by metavariables. This duplication of nodes harmlessly collapses into a single description for each affected node because metavariables are not part of the object language of formulae, but merely place-holders for such formulae. The effect of the nodes constructed from parsing the two initial noun phrases is thus to provide values for the metavariables projected by the verb.

The restriction that there can be only one unfixed node at a time remains satisfied, despite the application of procedures to build these nodes twice over. Nothing dictates which of these argument expressions is placed first, so the sequence of actions involving Local*Adjunction followed by a tree-update process reflecting the particular case specification can occur in any order, reflecting the freedom of constituent order which Latin displays.[13] Given the restriction to only one unfixed node of a type at a time, this type of derivation is available only upon the assumption that on-line update of the tree relation is available, so no particular fixing of rule-order application is required: all other derivations will be precluded. And so it is that successful derivations to yield an interpretation of examples such as (18) can be built up incrementally.

This is by no means the only type of tree-growth sequence however. The first expression *Lesbiam* might be taken to decorate an unfixed node introduced through the non-local step of *Adjunction. In this case, by assumption, the case specification serves merely as a filter on update that is not immediately enriched to a fixed position, and in consequence no other unfixed node can be introduced by this step. As a discrete operation, Local*Adjunction nevertheless remains available for the processing of some matrix subject NP that might follow (*Catullus* in (18)). The consequence is that the sequence of strategies for constructing a string-interpretation pairing is by no means unique. Indeed arguably the only major difference in the way *Adjunction and Local*Adjunction apply lies in the fact that immediate case-update to a fixed tree relation cannot take place in the former, because there is no presumption that the term is local to the primary predicate-argument array.

Unlike this alternative derivation of (18), a derivation involving *Adjunction is of course needed essentially for dependencies that are not local.

(14) *Stercilinum   magnum   stude   ut   habeas*
      dunghill.ACC   big.ACC ensure.IMP.SG that   have.2.PS.SING
      'See that you have a large dung hill'

Furthermore, this similarity of processes underpinning long-distance and short-distance scrambling effects provides an immediate explanation for multiple long-distance dependency effects. With both processes involving the building of an unfixed node, we expect the possibility of a feeding relation between *Adjunction and Local*Adjunction, resulting in multiple long-distance dependency. Consider (16), repeated below:

(16) *digitum   supra   terram   facito   semina   emineant*
      finger.ACC   above   earth.ACC   make.IMP   seeds.NOM   project.3PL
      'Make the seeds project a finger above the earth.'

---

[13] Equally, such NPs could be placed after the verb, since both for the application of the actions triggered by the verb and for applicability of Local*Adjunction, the pointer needs to be at the type-t-requiring node. We leave all details about post-verbal clitic placement for another occasion. In rigid verb-final languages, it is the details of tense-specification which ensure finality of the verb: see [Cann *et al.*, 2005]

In the DS account, these data are directly expected. *Adjunction allows the construction of a propositional unfixed node decorated with the requirement $?Ty(t)$. Within in this unfixed propositional domain successive steps of Local*Adjunction may apply to construct partial propositional structures of the sort seen above in the parse of (18), yielding partial trees such as figure 2.[14] In

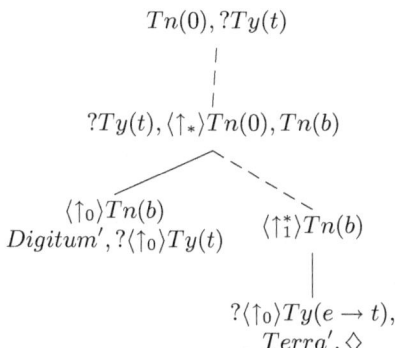

Figure 2. Parsing *digitum (supra) terram*.

this way a sequence of argument nodes can be constructed in which only the last of these remains with its local tree relation not updated. The position of the cluster of argument nodes is then resolved at a subsequent point in the construction process, in (16) with introduction of the propositional complement argument of *facito*, yielding the tree in figure 3).

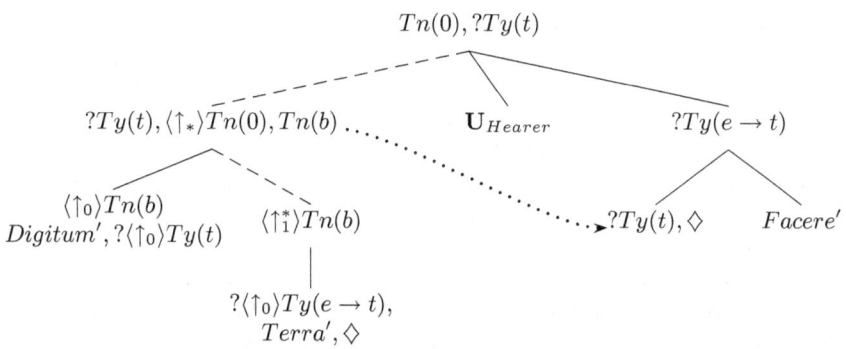

Figure 3. Parsing *digitum (supra) terram facito*.

---

[14]Many details of the analysis are omitted here, including the effect of the preposition *supra*. The essence of the analysis stands, however.

What is notable about such intermediate structures in the present connection is the construction of proposition-requiring structures which, at some intermediate juncture, may contain only an array of argument nodes, as yet lacking the predicate node which is essential to completing that structure. This pattern is strikingly similar to intermediate structure projected from clitic clusters prior to the processing of the verb, given the same left-right perspective on how structures for construal are incrementally built up, as we shall see in due course.

There is one further general tree-construction strategy yet remaining before we have anything approximating to a complete sketch of the mechanisms which the DS framework licenses. There are also mechanisms for building paired structures, where structures are taken to be twinned by being the result of a construction process which ensures the sharing of some term in two such so-called linked trees. This process is defined in DS for construal of relative clauses, clausal adverbials, and also external topic constructions. Such secondary structures have an attendant requirement that the newly introduced proposition-requiring tree have somewhere within it a copy of that term (specified as $?\langle\downarrow_*\rangle Fo(\alpha)$: see [Cann et al., 2005] for details).[15] The significance of

$$\langle L\rangle Tn(0), Fo(\alpha), Ty(e) \qquad Tn(0), ?Ty(t), ?\langle\downarrow_*\rangle Fo(\alpha)$$

Figure 4. Building Link transitions for relative-clause and left-dislocation construal

this process in connection with clitics is that the construction of such twinned structures can always be posited as an available strategy, without there having to be any duplication of two expressions or appropriately construed anaphoric expression in the second structure, as the specification of verbal actions induces a pronoun-style of decoration of the subject node. So in the wake of having constructed such a linked tree providing a term of type e as context for the processing of some subsequent subject specification, the specification of some full propositional structure from a subsequent verb will impose the requirement that one of its arguments be identified with the term provided by that first constructed tree, all without any morphologically explicit anaphoric device. An interpretation for an NP-verb sequence could be constructed using such a sequence of actions, only imposing the relatively weak anaphoric connection between that initially induced structure and the subsequent emergent

---

[15]The process of inducing such pairs of semantic trees is permitted by defining an additional modal operator in the tree logic $\langle L\rangle$, and its inverse $\langle L^{-1}\rangle$; and a rule is defined to yield a transition from an arbitrary node in one tree across a LINK relation to the topnode of a new propositional tree.

propositional structure associated with the following verb that one argument of the verb will be identified with the term projected from that NP. And should that NP be a dative clitic pronoun, it may constitute some additional add-on to the remainder of the clausal sequence, without any further duplication of the information that it provides. Consider how the analysis of (9) might proceed.

(9)   quid   **mihi**   Celsus   agit?
      what   me.DAT   Celsus.NOM.SG   do.3.SG.PRES

'How, pray, is Celsus?' (Lit. 'What to me Celsus does?')

Parsing the interrogative *quid* proceeds via *Adjunction to give an unfixed node and then, since all computational actions are optional, one move could be to construct a node linked to the main propositional node with the requirement to construct a term ($?Ty(e)$). The dative pronoun is parsed and the node is decorated with a metavariable constrained to be substituted by a term that denotes the speaker (figure 5).[16]

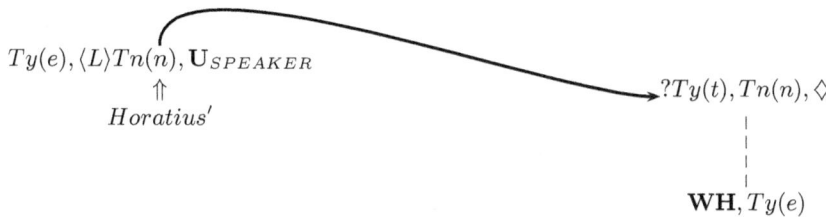

$Ty(e), \langle L \rangle Tn(n), \mathbf{U}_{SPEAKER}$
⇑
$Horatius'$

$?Ty(t), Tn(n), \Diamond$

$\mathbf{WH}, Ty(e)$

Figure 5. Parsing *quid mihi*

By assumption, in this context, the node is not decorated with a case constraint to find a particular function for the term so constructed and the parse of the main clause continues. We end up with a tree like that in figure 6 where the speaker is only tangentially associated with the event denoted by the main verb, allowing, through normal inference driven by relevance considerations, a range of relations to be construed between Horace and what he has said.

The topic-LINK structure will of course give us yet another means of building up interpretation even for simple clausal sequences. In particular, this is applicable to (21) as *praemium* itself lacks any definitive case-marking that might preclude such an opening action-sequence:

---

[16] In this analysis, no term is shared between the linked structure and the main proposition, making it like an analysis of gapless topics in languages like Chinese (see [Wu, 2005]). however, an alternative would be to relate the term that substitutes for the 1st person metavariable with an event variable that is shared between both structures. See [Cann and Wu, 2007] for an analysis of the Chinese *bei* construction along these lines.

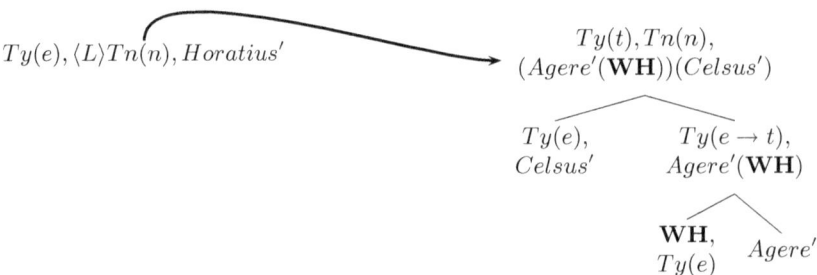

Figure 6. Parsing *quid mihi Celsus agit?*

(21) *Praemium   Xerxes   proposuit*
       a reward   Xerxes   offered
      'Xerxes offered a reward'

Even the parsing of *Xerxes* following the parse of *praemium* can be taken to be the trigger for inducing a transition onto such a linked structure, which the actions associated with *Xerxes* could be taken to decorate (a transition in any case needed for expressions to be construed as in any way parenthetical to the string in which they are contained). The consequence of this flexibility is that there are a number of moves available at any stage of a parse sequence, in particular in the early stages when so little structural specification is as yet determined. There is the availability of building linked structures; there is the possibility of building an unfixed node; and there is the possibility of successively introducing and immediately updating introduced argument node relations. And all these for one and the same string, with one and essentially the same interpretation. Far from this constituting an unwarranted spurious ambiguity, this is an expected side-effect of defining a parsing-directed grammar formalism, demonstrated by Ferreira [1996] to be an advantage in processing, contrary to what might be supposed. Alternative strategies for achieving string-interpretation pairings are anticipated; and this gives a flexibility which is extremely useful in ongoing communication. It means one may be able to understand one's interlocutor without having had to recover exactly the same mode of presentation as them, an advantage which Bouzouita [this volume] exploits to provide a basis for seamless language change.

3.2 Processing pressures, word order and pragmatics

Taking a processing perspective on grammatical structure allows us to consider contextual factors in the definition of well-formed strings within some language and explain pragmatically determined tendencies that may become calcified through processes of language use. General constraints on production and parsing will ensure that speakers and hearers maximize the use of context to cut down the need to search the lexicon for words expressing appropriate meanings or to employ inference to determine what is being conveyed. One clear effect of such pressure to induce variation in word order, whether grammatically marked, as in (e.g.) passive, or not, as in scrambling. Relevance theory, with its tradeoff between cognitive effect and expenditure of effort will tend to encourage the appearance of given material early on in a clause, rather than later. Hence, in Latin, as in all other languages, anaphoric expressions which enable argument terms to be identified independently of processing the verb, often appear early in the clause. Such positioning provides a means of minimizing the search within a given context to establish construal of pronominals as early as possible. In relying on context, speakers/hearers need the search for a substituend to be over as small a domain as possible by general relevance considerations. Accordingly, unless there is reason to the contrary, the position of an anaphoric expression requiring context-identification will be as early as possible in the setting out of propositional structure – quite literally, a minimization of what constitutes the context. This is of course no more than a relevance-based explanation of this well known given-before-new ordering.

However, there is more to be said, as different uses of pronouns in Latin developed into discrete encodings in the subsequent Romance languages of what had been merely different types of usage in the earlier language. In the earlier Latin system, pronouns, like other nominal constituents, could be used either to provide some initial term which constitutes a point of departure for what follows, or to provide a contrast, an update to what follows. From a DS perspective, the first such effect would constitute the projection of a pair of independent linked structures, the second structure to be developed relative to the context provided by the first with a requirement of a shared term in the tree to be constructed. The second type of construal would involve the construction of an unfixed node by *Adjunction, decorating this with the term indicated by the initially placed expression, with anticipation of delay in updating this initially constructed node. Synchronic studies of other languages provide evidence that both such devices are non-canonical and hence characteristically associated with stress or distinguishing intonation as a signal that some non canonical form of construal is required.[17] Of course, we have no direct evidence of stress or prosody for a language such as Latin, but at the very least such contemporary evidence is suggestive:[18]

---

[17]It has been argued in detail by Kempson and Kiaer [2008] in connection with verb-final languages that distinctive intonation is an important determinant of appropriate strategies for build up of the intended form of interpretation, in particular to signal long-distance dependency effects, that depend on departing from the canonical build up of information locally.

[18]The pronouns noted in (22) are taken by Adams [1994] to be illustrative of an emphatic

(22) **A:** ***Tibi***   *ego*   *dem?*   **B:** ***Mihi***   *hercle*
       you.DAT   I.NOM   give.1.SG.SBJ.PRES   me.DAT   by Hercules
uero.
in truth
'**A:** Am I to give it to YOU?' '**B:** Yes, by god, to ME.'

Plautus,Pseud. 626

(22) could be analyzed in DS terms as being associated with the construction of a node introduced by *Adjunction to be decorated by a term representing the hearer.[19] Such a device induces actions that by definition mark an emergent propositional boundary, being associated with introduction of a proposition-requiring node (decorated with $?Ty(t)$) without any decorations other than the imposition of such a requirement. If, in anticipation of explaining the split that occurred between stressed and unstressed uses of pronouns, we turn to what the non-stressed uses of pronouns have in common, it is simply that they will lack this property: they will NOT be associated with those very structural devices which serve to identify some initiation of an emergent propositional structure, they will solely have a regular anaphoric function of context dependence. An interesting example of this occurs in (23) in which a strong pronoun (*ego*) appears immediately before the two weak pronouns (*te, ei*):

(23)   *quod*   *scribis*   *de*   *illo*   *Preciano*
       what   write.2SG.FUT   about   that.ABL.SG   Precianus.ABL.SG
       iure consulto,   ***ego***   ***te***   ***ei***   *non*
       jurist.ABL.SG   I.NOM   you.ACC   him.DAT.SG   not
       desino   *commendare.*
       abandon.1SG.PRES   commend.INF
'Whatever you write about that jurist, Precianus, **I** do not stop recommending you to him.'

Cicero. Ad Fam. 7.8.2

Other linguistic indicators of the emergence of a propositional structure include following focused elements, expressions containing a negative element, complementizers (25), relative pronouns, (24), subordinate temporal adverbials, and verbs (26): indeed this is the only property common to this structurally heterogeneous set (examples culled from [Adams, 1994]):[20]

---

use "often marked by placement of the pronoun at the head of its clause".

[19] The verb is omitted because the predicate, like the structural patterning, is recoverable from the context.

[20] For visibility reasons, we have highlighted in bold the weak pronouns under consideration. Examples of the other types of left-edge identifiers can be found in [Bouzouita and Kempson, 2006; Bouzouita, this volume].

(24) quae **tibi** nulla debetur
     which.NEUT-PL you.DAT no.NEUT-PL is-owed
     'nothing of which is owed to you.'

Cicero, In Act. 1.16

(25) rogo ut **mi** mittas dalabram
     ask.1SG.PRES that me.DAT send.2SG mattock.ACC.SG
     'I ask that you send to me a mattock.'

Terentianus 251.27

(26) delectarunt **me** tuae litterae
     delighted.3PL.PRES me.ACC your letter.NOM.PL
     'I was delighted with your letter.'

Cicero, Ad Fam. 9.16.1

Like their "strong" counterparts, positioning of pronouns under this use will be driven by relevance considerations for these, by assumption, are ever-present. This provides the functionalist underpinnings that explain the weak pronoun usage. What these share is the characteristic that, once an emergent propositional structure is identified by some OTHER expression, they will get placed as closely following as possible, decorating some locally unfixed node duly updated through its case specification, and so, like the strong pronouns, hugging the left edge of any such emergent structure as closely as commensurate with them NOT constituting a stressed/contrastive use.[21]

4 Latin to Medieval Spanish

We now have everything in place to sketch out the assumptions a parsing perspective on grammar formalisms would lead us to expect in the explanation of the emergence of the Romance languages from Latin. Medieval Spanish contains a codification of what had become two phonologically and functionally discrete uses of earlier pronominal forms: strong and clitic. What the clitic pronouns display is two distinct types of property. On the one hand, since they constitute the only remaining reflex of earlier nominal case-marking, their triggers are a direct reflex of the earlier set of environments that yielded pragmatic identification of propositional boundary marking, now encoding this information directly as calcified reflexes of that earlier more liberal system. On the other hand, the structures they severally induce are the retained reflex of the

---

[21] Following [Sperber and Wilson, 1995], if there are specific inferential effects to justify commensurate enlargement of the context to be searched, this would explain the lack of tightness of fit that Adams [1994] notes of weak pronoun positioning in Latin, even assuming that the effects are clause by clause (or "colon" by "colon" to use his terminology).

case dynamics of Latin, with lexically specified actions that yield the types of structural update that had been freely available in the earlier language. Now, however, each individual lexical specification associated with some clitic projects one or more specific sequences of actions, the range of different types of updates available only being seen across the set of clitics as a whole.

4.1 Placement of clitic pronouns: the production pressures

We turn first to explaining the early position in a string at which clitic pronouns cluster; and this is where the production pressures constraining Latin word order come into play.[22] The weak pronouns of Latin, as noted above, occur as close to the left-edge of a clause as possible, but not quite at the edge - they were not the left-edge occurrences as these by definition were the OTHER subset of pronouns which were invariably associated with their decoration of unfixed and linked nodes, with the type of distinctive construal and unreduced stress associated with those strategies. In the subsequent Medieval Spanish system the clitic pronouns share this distribution (for a detailed account see [Bouzouita, 2002, forthcoming; Bouzouita and Kempson, 2006]):

(27) *Esto es el pan de Dios que **vos** da a*
 this be.3SG the bread of God that CL give.3SG to
 comer
 eat.INF
 'This is the bread of God that he gives you to eat.'

(28) *e dizie que **lo** tenie del prior de Sancti*
 and said.3SG that CL had.3SG of-the prior of Saint
 Johannis
 John
 'And he said that he got it from the prior of Saint John.'
 Data from [Granberg, 1988, p46]

(29) *Connocio-**la** Jacob*
 recognized.3sg-CL Jacob
 'Jacob recognized her.'

Such left-peripheral items in Latin may consist of a sequence of NPs [Devine and Stephens, 2006], as in (16) for full noun phrases and (23) for pronominals, a pattern which persists in Medieval Spanish with clitic pronouns:

(30) *Et los dioses **me** quisieron mal e **me lo** quieren*
 And the gods CL wanted.3PL harm and CL CL want.3PL

---

[22]This section is independently reported in [Bouzouita and Kempson, 2006], and represents joint work by Bouzouita and Kempson in conjunction with Cann.

'And the gods wanted to harm me and they still want to.'
Data from [Granberg, 1988, p235]

What is striking about Medieval Spanish is that what had been a purely pragmatically determined distribution in Latin had become encoded, a distribution no longer subject to inferential calculation as to what would constitute an optimal production choice, but a set of categorical restrictions, albeit complex.

4.2 The emergence of clitic pronouns in Medieval Spanish

We do not set out a formal specification of these triggering environments here: this is a primary concern of the Bouzouita paper in this volume, which traces the shift in triggering environments between Medieval Spanish and the present time. We, rather, turn to the actions which arise in these various structural environments which the clitic pronouns severally induce.

One striking property of the Romance clitic systems is that the clitic system that emerged very early on in each Romance language had already in place a complex system displaying the array of variants itemized earlier: the accusative clitic displays a fixed interpretation, the dative clitic displays a large range of interpretations, including an item-specific reflexive clitic itself also with a broad range of uses, and there are also idiosyncratic clitic clusters.[23]

One might justifiably ask how could it be that such complex systems could emerge apparently without some long gestation period. The beginnings of answer comes from the observation that despite notorious idiosyncracies in any one system of clitics, nevertheless, considered as a system, the range of effects displayed in each is strikingly similar. Some clitics fully determine their construal, being associated with a fixed structural configuration, such as the non-syncretic accusative forms, *lo, los*. and their feminine-marked counterparts which signal only direct object function.

(31) *Al   senor   lo   faras.*
      To the gentleman   3sg.CL-DO   you-will do
      'You will do it to/for the gentleman.'
      Data from [Granberg, 1988, p135]

(32) *cuando* **lo**   *ganó*
      When   3sg.CL-DO   he   won
      'When did he win it?'
      Data from [Granberg, 1988, p132]

Other clitics have forms which do not fully determine their case role, with the effect that their contribution to the emergent structure may not be able to be

---

[23]We illustrate with Medieval Spanish, but the phenomenon, though with individual variants, repeats itself in each emergent Romance system.

determined immediately, but only in combination with the verb with which they are associated:[24]

(33) Yo **vos**   defiendo que non vengades   y   màs   et   si
     I 2sg.CL-IO insist   that not you-come and, more, and if
     non ho **vos**   cegaré   et   **vos**   mataré
     not I   2pl.CL-DO I will blind and 2pl.CL-DO I will kill

     I forbid you to come and if not, I will blind you and kill you
     Data from [Granberg, 1988, p235]

In this example, the first occurrence of *vos* is construed as indirect object, the second as direct object; but the morphological input is undifferentiated between these. Then there are the clitic clusters, which occur in the same relative position as the singleton occurrences, sometimes written as a single item, such as *me lo* in (30), above.[25]

Looked at as a whole, taking a step back from the individual heterogeneity, there is striking similarity between this set and the array of patterns which the various word-order and related case-inducing effects of Latin. The pronouns that display immediate fixing of their argument role in the emergent structure can be said to follow the pattern of constructive use of case displayed in the short-scrambling effects of Latin, with the steps of Local*Adjunction and enrichment of that unfixed node to a fully determined role, now lexicalized as a routine. To see this, compare the occurrence and construal of the pronoun *lo* in (31) with the derivation earlier set out for the NPs in (18). In both types of case, the parsing leads to the immediate construction of a fixed structural relation between the argument node and its dominating type-*t*-requiring node. To capture this parallel, all that is required is to analyze the pronoun *lo* as itself inducing the actions otherwise effected by Local*Adjunction plus the subsequent enrichment associated with constructive use of case, hence creating and decorating a fixed argument node immediately dominated by a predicate-requiring node. See Bouzouita [this volume] for detailed specifications of *lo* at different time points, but the following indicates the sorts of ACTION required:[26]

---

[24] Notice in (33) the initial strong pronoun *yo* 'I'.

[25] Notice in passing how, in the first conjunct of (30), it is unclear whether the dative-marked expression is really serving as argument to what is a nominal *mal* or whether it is merely an indicator that "grounds the event structure in relation to the speech participants" as de Jonge's characterization of what the dative intrinsically encodes indicates.

[26] In the lexical specifications, we focus exclusively on the form of update the clitics provide, leaving the complex specification of the environments that trigger these on one side, because, though the actions of the individual clitics and clitic complexes differ, the specification of environments is identical for each. See Bouzouita [this volume] and Bouzouita and Kempson [2006], for details.

(34)

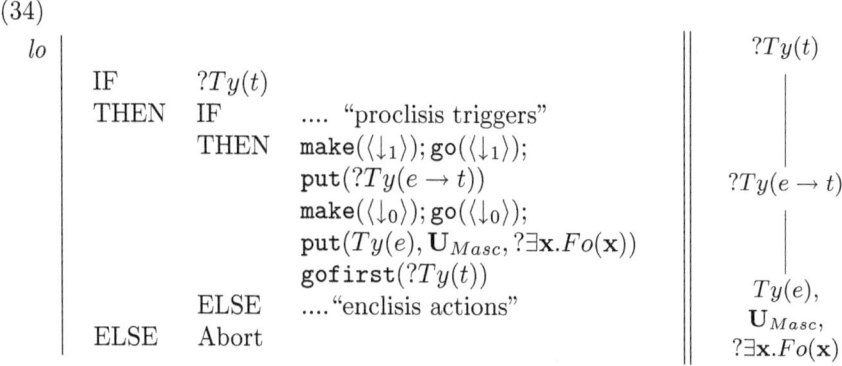

```
lo  | IF     ?Ty(t)
    | THEN   IF      .... "proclisis triggers"
    |        THEN    make(⟨↓₁⟩); go(⟨↓₁⟩);
    |                put(?Ty(e → t))
    |                make(⟨↓₀⟩); go(⟨↓₀⟩);
    |                put(Ty(e), U_Masc, ?∃x.Fo(x))
    |                gofirst(?Ty(t))
    |        ELSE    ...."enclisis actions"
    | ELSE   Abort
```

Secondly, there are the cases where the morphology fails to provide the basis from which a specific argument role can be identified. The first and second person pronouns, and dative specifications more generally are proto-typical cases of this type, illustrated by (33). Arguably, these reflect the failure to establish a fixed node; and we might well thus see these as initiating instead the actions associated with Local*Adjunction:

(35)

```
te  | IF     ?Ty(t), Tn(a)                              ?Ty(t), Tn(a)
    | THEN   IF      "...triggers for proclisis"              |
    |        THEN    make(⟨↓₁⟩); go(⟨↓₁⟩)
    |                put(?Ty(e → t))                     ?Ty(e → t)
    |                make(⟨↓¹_*⟩); go(⟨↓¹_*⟩)                  |
    |                put(⟨↑*_1⟩Tn(a));                         |
    |                make(⟨↓₀⟩); go(⟨↓₀⟩)                      |
    |                put(Ty(e),                          ⟨↑*_1⟩Tn(a)
    |                Fo(U_Hearer),                             |
    |                ?∃xFo(x),)                          Ty(e),
    |                ?∃xTn(x)                            U_Hearer,
    |                gofirst(?Ty(t))                     ?∃xFo(x),
    |        ELSE    "...enclisis actions"               ?∃xTn(x)
    | ELSE   Abort
```

This characterization of *te* is neutral with respect to whether it conveys an object or indirect object construal, reflecting the lack of specification in position along the functor spine of some yet to be specified predicate, exactly in the manner of *Local*Adjunction*.

As we've seen, this only scratches the surface of any account of datives in Spanish, this sequence of actions totally leaving on one side the ethical dative use. However, there is reason to think that a specification of dative-construal in (Medieval) Spanish in terms of ambiguity as between an albeit weak argument-specifier and indication of scenario-perspective is correct: the ethical dative construal, taken over from Latin, can co-occur with another dative form under a distinct type of construal, a pattern quite unlike case specifications in general. Indeed the ethical dative can be added to any independently licensed string. The remainder of the string is then construed as some projection of how the event described pertains to the individual picked out by the dative-marked expression.

(36)   *Pues   que   so   vyera   tonaré   maneba   e*
       given that I-am   old   will turn into.3SG young girl and
       me   *emprenaré*
       CL.1.DAT I will conceive

'Given that I am old, will a young girl turn out and, pray, will I conceive?'
Data from [Granberg, 1988, p174]

With the first and second person pronoun dative forms, this yields an interpretation of how the event described relates to either one of the speech participants, in (36) the speaker perspective being set by use of the dative clitic *me*. As discussed above in relation to Latin (figure 6), this is naturally expressible in DS terms as a reflex of a LINK transition to a node in a tree independent of the predicate-argument structure, with the ethical dative pronoun decorating the node of that quasi-independent structure. Indeed, we can include as part of the actions associated with the form *me* in Medieval Spanish exactly the same actions as induced by the form in Latin, viz.: the decoration of a $?Ty(e)$ node with a first person metavariable just in case that node is a LINK structure:[27]

(37)
me

	IF	$?Ty(e)$				$\langle L \rangle Tn(a)$,	$\widehat{Tn(a)}$,
	THEN	IF	"proclisis"			$\mathbf{U}_{SPEAKER}$	$?Ty(t)$
		THEN	IF	$\langle L \rangle \top$		$Ty(e)$	
			THEN	put($\mathbf{U}_{SPEAKER}$)			
		ELSE	...				

Such an analysis has an immediate benefit: it means that the overall account now has the array of variants the DS framework would lead one to expect appropriately filled out. As part of the set of lexically induced tree relations

---

[27]The parse of the clitic does not here construct a linked node, as this option remains open as a general rule in Medieval Spanish to account for ethical (and other) datives involving full noun phrases.

associated with clitic specifications, we have the induction of a fixed node relation which the clitic pronoun is taken to decorate, the induction of a locally unfixed node relation with the clitic decorating the unfixed node, and the induction of a LINK node relation with the clitic decorating this independent one-node structure.

4.3 Clitic Clusters

There is then one further option that we expect, given Latin as the point of departure. We expect there to be some reflection of the NP-sequencing so characteristic of Latin scrambling. This is immediately suggestive of clitic clusters whose emergence is otherwise unexpected and which match the sequencing effect of building up interpretation from sequences of case-marked NPs by a sequence of actions of *Local*Adjunction* and enrichment to a fixed tree relation; these too are thus no more than part of the expected pattern. All that is needed for their analysis is the lexical specification of a sequence of actions introducing a cluster of argument nodes from a given type-*t*-requiring node, mimicking the result of the composite sequence of actions of Local*Adjunction plus enrichment of tree-relation to yield the appropriate cluster of argument nodes so eminently displayed in any sequence of NPs in a free scrambling language. Putting together the lexical actions associated with parsing *te* and *lo*, given above, would yield the tree structure, in (38).

(38)

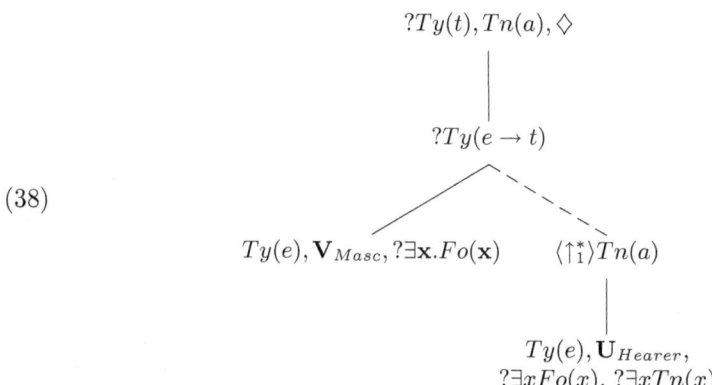

And these correspond precisely to what we would expect from a lexicalised compound specification *te lo*. In this structure, the position of the metavariable projected by *te* remains unfixed and yet in the environment of an immediately subsequent *lo*, all of the forms *te*, *me*, and *se* may only be construed as dative notwithstanding their syncretic form, since the direct object construal is unavailable – that position being duly decorated by a distinct metavariable. Hence, by routinization of the various actions involved, the actual encoding of *te lo* that results would involve construction of a *fixed* pair of indirect-object and direct-object nodes, rather than the actions of Local*Adjunction and some subsequent enrichment. In consequence, the form *te* as a subpart of *telo* has a notably narrower characterization than its independently defined form.[28] The set of lexical actions that are required and the tree they induce are given in (39):

(39) *telo*

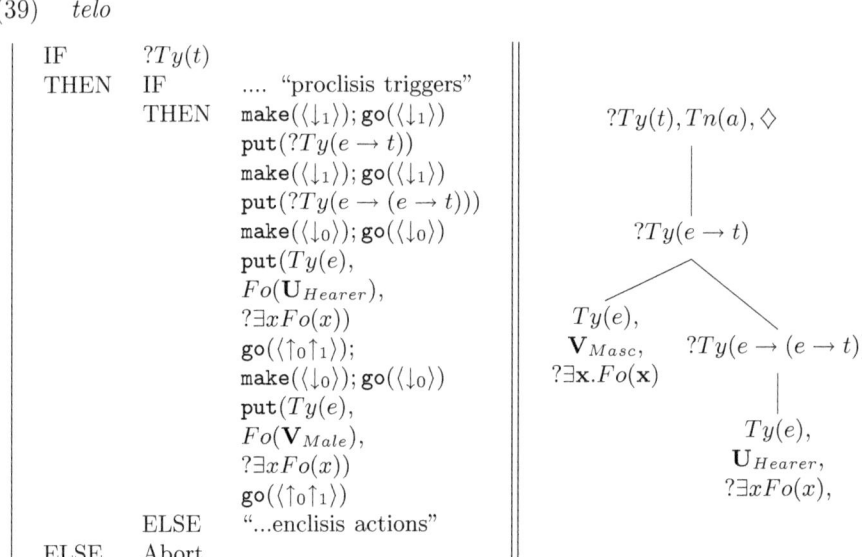

In this macro of actions, the tree relations induced are fully fixed despite the systemic underspecification intrinsic to *te*. This is the proper reflection of the diachronic process that gave rise to the clustered clitic sequence. The encoding of this composite sequence of actions as a cluster takes place via routinization of the most common construal. So the mystery of why such clustered clitic sequences should occur at all, with their fixed locality relative to each other fades away in this processing perspective. They simply form one of an expected range of types of action that became routinized over time in the shift from the freer scrambling system into a more restricted clitic system. As in the earlier Latin system, the construction of such a cluster of argument nodes can be associated with the introduction of an intermediate node from which this sequences of actions takes place, hence allowing the effect of clitic climbing

---

[28]Trivially, this definition could retain the precise sequence of operations used for the individual clitics, involving Local*Adjunction, enrichment, return of the pointer between the actions associated with one clitic and overlapping make, go instructions, but we would take such listing to reduce through reasons of formal economy and the psychological process of routinization.

as displayed in (12). The only difference between these is that in the earlier Latin system, such non-contiguity of paired NPs was not lexically fixed, so in principle could be non-locally established, hence across a complementizer-induced proposition-requiring boundary (subjunctive-marked). In the clitic system, with the shift in actions from being a generally available computational device to a macro of actions for a particular lexically stored sequence, these get restricted to a locally characterizable domain, hence only across a finite-nonfinite sequence of verbs. Note that this pattern parallels that shown in Latin non-finite contexts, as illustrated in (23) above and thus little has apparently changed between the earlier system and Medieval Spanish in this regard.

The range of effects we see displayed in the clitic pronouns of Medieval Spanish is thus broadly the range of effects seen in local scrambling, that is, the strategies associated with local constituent order variation of the Latin system.[29] This is precisely what we would expect in a transition in which the availability of case specifications on a general basis disappears, being replaced by case specifications only within the pronominal system. As noted above, in the DS framework, general computational actions and lexical actions are expressed in exactly the same terms. Lexical actions, like their general counterpart, characteristically induce the construction of nodes in some partial tree in addition to providing decorations for the nodes which the actions associated with the word in question triggers. Thus a shift in tree-update actions from a sequence of general actions to a composite macro of actions associated with an individual word is exactly what one might expect in a shift from general formulation to lexical specification. And in this shift, any one word would normally be associated with only one such sequence of actions (unless its precursor in the source language was ambiguous): and so it is that the various clitic pronouns reflect one or other such action-sequence. Seen in processing terms, the clitic-template phenomenon is thus a freezing of scrambling strategies, hence explicable as a progressive shift, each lexical specification reflecting one of a set of strategies for early NP placement.

Even the existence of interpolation throughout the period of Medieval Spanish is expected, in which the clitic is separated from the verb, as in (1) repeated here:

(1) ... *quien* **te** *algo* *prometiere* ..
  .. who 2.CL-IO something would-promise ..
  'The one who would promise something to you.'

---

[29]The only pattern which is not displayed is the use of case retained simply as an output filter, but as we shall see briefly below, this is illustrated by Greek *me, mou*, where the first person forms for accusative and dative/genitive are symptomatic of the less syncretic system than in Spanish or Italian.

The occurrence of NPs able to occur between clitic (cluster) and verb is precisely what would be expected of a system intermediate between a free-scrambling system and a fully lexicalised one. Such interpolation effects are no more than continuing applicability of computational use of just those actions which are becoming increasingly routinized in association with specific lexical triggers. This is confirmed by the fact that the verb in Medieval Spanish can be ordered after a full sequence of NPs, following the Latin pattern:

(40) la   muger esto   a   su   marido   faze.
     the   wife   this   to   her husband does
     'The wife does this to her husband.'

Or in which interpolation occurs with apparent climbing as in (41), indicating the persistence of abductive strategies in the development of early Spanish:

(41) que   **vos**   mal   quieren   fazer
     that   CL.2PL.DO   harm   they-want   do.INF
     'That they want you to do harm.'

This is all exactly as we would expect. Loss of interpolation could only take place once the association of triggers for clitic construal had become fully encoded, if the expressive power of the evolving system is to be retained. We thus expect the availability of computational actions associated with the construction and update of locally unfixed nodes throughout the period within which this lexicalization shift is taking place.

4.4 The Person Case Constraint

Confirmation of this form of explanation can be gleaned from the novel perspective it provides for addressing the puzzle of what are systematic gaps in available clitic clusterings. Though some gaps are random, some never, or almost never, occur. Most well-known of these are the so-called Person Case Constraint, of which there are two variant forms. Of these, the most widespread is that construal of either first and second person forms as an accusative can never co-occur with third person dative, a restriction which holds in all the Romance languages as long as we keep distinct the various usages of the dative clitic as ethical, reflexive, and impersonal. Thus, though there are occurrences of first or second person construed as dative followed by third person accusative in Medieval Spanish, just as in other Romance languages, as in (30) above and (42) below, there is no reported occurrence of construal of either as accusative, with dative third person:

(42) agora   quiero   **uos**   **lo**   descubrir
     now   want1.SG   youPL   it   revealINF

'Now I want to reveal it to you.'
Data from [Granberg, 1988, p176]

The lack of first or second person accusative forms with a third person dative is a puzzling gap if such clitic forms are thought to be a mere listing of possible morphological forms. There is also a further restriction displayed by a subset of these languages: that first and second person pronominal forms should not co-occur.[30] In this case, the restriction is less definitive, and indeed even in modern Spanish, a long way further down the historical chain, such examples are wellformed, a problem which we return to:

(43)   **Te**   **me**   *recomendaron.*
      you   me   they-recommend
      'They recommended you to me.'

[Modern Spanish]

(44)   ... **te**   **me**   *deje*   *ver*
      you   me   let   see
      '(may God) let you see me'

Such gaps are mysterious, apparently lacking either syntactic or semantic explanation; and they have been taken to be diagnostic of the need for a separate morphology component in which such restrictions can at least be defined [Anderson, 2005; Monachesi, 2005]. Indicative of the fact that this is not simply a matter of lack of need to express relations between human participants, they can all be side-stepped by realizing one of these arguments as a strong pronoun or full NP:[31]

(45)   *Se*   *de*   **nos**   **te**   *non*   *partes..*
      If   from   us   CL-DO   not   depart....
      'If you do not leave us' Data from [Rivero, 1997]

(46)   *Con*   *el*   *so*   *manto*   *a*   *amas*   **las**   *cubrió*
      With   the   his   mantle   to   both   them$_{ACC}$ he-covered
      'He covered both with his mantle.'

---

[30]This is not the situation in Latin:

i.   *qui*   *me*   *tibi*   *fecerit*   *hostem*
    who.NOM.SG   me.ACC   you.DAT   make.3SG.PERF   enemy.ACC

'who would make me an enemy to you.'   Lucan DBC 1.

[31]This phenomenon is notably redolent of the Bantu restriction that there can ever be only one object clitic, construable either as direct or indirect object, which, equally, is not a restriction on the numbers of argument nodes that are licensed, but a restriction merely a restriction on whether these can be realized by weakened clitic/agreement-marking mechanisms: see [Marten et al., forthcoming].

In all such cases, the phenomenon is lost a little in the free translation, but, more literally, in (45), the string is construed as 'If from us you do not part yourself...'.

In the face of the various challenges which these clustering facts present, many authors settle for a discrete morphological form of explanation, not characterizing the phenomenon within the syntactic domain at all (see e.g. [Nevins, 2007; Rivero, 2007]).

Such arguments are potentially embarrassing for the DS framework too, as they threaten the very strong DS claim that grammar design needs no more than the articulation of the process of mapping from phonological specification of individual word (cluster) onto semantic representation. However, the DS framework has a natural explanation to offer for such gaps, with one additional assumption about dative-case specification. This is the assumption that dative marked nominals are underspecified with respect to the semantic function they perform: direct object, indirect object, reflexive, adjunct (ethical and other semantic uses). Thus, of necessity, they must be under-specified with respect to their structural relation within any predicate-argument structure.

With this assumption that dative construal involves an underspecification of any tree relation, all variants of the Person Case Constraint fall into place: both morphological gaps follow from the tree-logic restriction that there can be no more than one underspecified tree relation of a type at any point in the tree-growth process. Let us take the more comprehensively satisfied restriction first, the preclusion of any co-occurrence of first or second case specifications as accusative with a third person specification as dative (the so-called strong form of the Person Case Constraint: [Bonet, 1995; Nevins, 2007; Ormabazal and Romero, 2007]). Recall that there was no need of stipulation that there should be only one unfixed node of a type at a time: in all putative cases where more than one such underspecified tree-relation might be introduced, they collapse as undifferentiatable, with all cases where the resulting treenode decoration is inconsistent being necessarily debarred. This is precisely the scenario which these morphological gaps present. Given the analysis of dative as intrinsically underspecified as to whether the node being decorated is a direct or indirect object (or a semantically weak adjunct), the syncretic first and second person forms will be predicted not to co-occur with any such form, irrespective of order, since they too have a form that fails to discriminate between the various argument roles they can satisfy. Upon an analysis of tree growth that reflects this underspecification both must be taken to decorate an unfixed node. Neither 1st or 2nd person markers could accordingly ever be constructed together with a third person dative marker, let alone be constructed sufficiently often to get routinized into a stored clustered form: both are defined as inducing the construction of a locally unfixed node without any case basis for inducing appropriate update ahead of the verb.

Their lack of co-occurrence is immediately predicted. The encoding of clitic sequences might itself specify fixed tree-relations for the paired nodes, but, since these arise from routinizations of earlier general processes, there is no possibility of these becoming established as lexical clusters, if those clusters cannot be produced. Hence their lack of occurrence in the established clitic system. It is not the occurrence of these syncretic forms construed as indirect object with an accusative third person form which is problematic. Indeed, it is not the specific construals of these pronouns that provide the appropriate explanation for the oddity of the precluded forms. It is the fact that these forms, being syncretic, are associated with inducing only the building and decorating of some locally unfixed argument-relation, and so cannot co-occur with a dative or any other case-specification which is itself associated with inducing exactly the same weak tree relation.

This explanation should, without doubt, carry over to anticipate equally that co-occurrence of first and second person pronouns should also be impossible. Surprisingly, however, many cases are fully acceptable in Modern Spanish and they occurred albeit rarely in Medieval Spanish also:

(47)   No   *te*   *me*   acerques
       Not CL   CL   come-closer
       'Don't come closer to me.'

[Mod.Spanish]

(48)   y   *te*   *me*   devuelven   vivo
       and   you   me   bring-back   alive
       'and may he bring you back to me alive
       (may he bring you back alive for my benefit).'

Examples like these are widespread, and have been taken by some to indicate that this restriction is no more than a reflection of the fact that declarations involving ditransitives in which both participants described are human are not common as scenarios, hence with no reflection in the clitic clusterings that emerged.

However, it is notable that there are several strategies for construal available in principle for analyzing such clitic sequences, only one of which threatens to involve the precluded multiplication of unfixed tree relations. On the one hand, the occurrence of *te* in (47) could be taken to decorate a node in an independent linked structure, in a manner similar to that suggested above with respect to the ethical dative. With Spanish being a pro-drop language no other morphologically explicit expression would be needed to yield the appropriate copy of the term in question as subject of the predicate *acerques*.

It has independently been noted by Hoecke [1996] that ethical datives and argument-construal of datives merge seamlessly into one another, in particular for all first and second person clitic pronouns, since all first and second person specifications by definition constitute specification of the speech participants and their relation to the event described, which is the hallmark of the ethical dative. Analogously, though not involving a subject construal, (48) could be taken as having the first-person pronoun *me* decorate a linked structure, so that the action of bringing back the hearer alive is presented as being to the benefit of the speaker, a clear illustration of the closeness of ethical datives and argument construal. We accordingly expect examples such as (47)-(48) to be wellformed at all stages of Spanish, despite the preclusion by the system of two unfixed nodes of a type at a time. More generally, since all the dative clitics, first, second and third person, all allow ethical dative construals, on this account, we expect all combinations to be wellformed, even though not perhaps occurring often enough to have become a stored, routinized pairing.[32]

There is yet a further form of explanation for the rare cases of co-occurring first and second person clitics that can be observed in Medieval Spanish, as indicated by the scribal transcription of the pair of clitics in (49) below:

(49) Qui-***d***   ***nos***   dio   pro   alcalde?
      Who-CL.2.SG.DO CL.1.PL.IO gave.3.SG as   mayor?
      'Who gave you to us as mayor?'

Notice the phonological cliticization of the second person on the *wh* form, suggesting a different form of explanation. This is that it is the *wh* expression plus its enclitic which form a cluster, these being the result of an early step of *Adjunction feeding the building of clustered subject and object argument nodes associated with that first unfixed node, exactly as in the multiple long-distance dependency forms such as (16). Under this derivation, the subsequent occurrence of *nos* will be able unproblematically to decorate a node locally unfixed with respect to the root, even though the ultimate position of the first cluster is itself not resolved until the verb is parsed. Indeed, we would anticipate that systematic exceptions to the Person Case Constraint might arise according as the parsing of the string does not treat the sequence of clitics as clustered together, but as in potentially different domains, as in this example, given the analysis to be provided for the left-peripheral *wh* expression.

The explanation of the Person Case Constraint as a consequence of formal properties of trees and tree growth has the marked bonus of being in terms

---

[32]This form of analysis might also apply to explain why nominative case marking, even where syncretic with other cases, quite generally fails to display any Person Case Constraint affects. We do not however explore nominative marking in this paper, given the subject-pro-drop property of Latin and Spanish.

of a strong structural restriction, hence one that would be expected to apply on a broad cross-linguistic basis. It should be noted, moreover, that it is the flexibility of a parsing-based system which makes such an explanation possible: there is very generally more than one possible sequence of steps available for establishing a string-interpretation pair. Indeed, as is argued for in detail in Bouzouita [this volume], this is what makes seamless diachronic change possible.[33]

However, this account is not problem-free; it might be said to fall into the trap of identifying case-underspecification with structural underspecification, equating gaps in a paradigm with syncretism. As pointed out by Adger and Harbour, accounts which turn on case syncretism as reflecting relative weakness of specification are at best insufficient, since the same restriction is displayed in clitic systems with no syncretism in the clitic forms. In particular, this is displayed by Greek, with its distinct nominative/genitive forms for both first/second person subject and object marking. Yet, as it turns out, such examples buttress the DS account, for they illustrate the one further type of tree growth that the DS system leads us to expect. So far, we have itemized the induction of an unfixed argument node subject to immediate enrichment, the induction of a linked structure, and the building of sequences of locally unfixed nodes from an intermediate node. But we haven't had an instance analogous to the core mechanism underpinning long-distance dependency, which is the specification of case as decorating an unfixed node which does NOT induce immediate update. But this is the scenario provided by Greek, which Adger and Harbour cite as problematic for syncretism-based accounts for the Person Case Constraint. In these cases, the morphological specification for direct and indirect object arguments is distinct. If however, we assume that one of the options for tree growth that might get calcified is precisely such a non-constructive use of case, then we have the basis for analyzing Greek, while also getting the bonus, finally, of completing the picture of possible calcification updates that clitic systems might reflect. For, upon such an analysis, the morphologically distinctive forms would nevertheless be subject to the Person Case Constraint precluding their occurrence either with each other or with the dative on exactly the same grounds as the syncretic forms: their decoration of an unfixed node would preclude their co-occurring in a string with any other form which induced the same relatively weak structural relation. So one type of problem isn't a problem for the analysis at all - to the contrary, it buttresses it.

---

[33] It is of course relatively hard on this set of assumptions to establish lack of wellformedness: to be ungrammatical, there must be no possible derivation for which an appropriate string-interpretation pairing can be established (see [Cann et al., 2007] for an account of wellformedness within the DS framework).

Thus though the account of the data offered is far from comprehensive, the strength of the cross-linguistic explanation it provides suggests it may nevertheless provide the best explanation currently available, stemming from general principles of the parsing-directed base system and uncontroversial assumptions about the atrophying of a case-rich system.

5 Summary

Overall, we have set out a framework for characterizing scrambling effects in language that explains syntactic limitations these display in virtue of the ongoing process of building up interpretation along a time-linear perspective. We then characterized the templatic, highly idiosyncratic distributions of medieval Spanish clitics in terms of various routinizations of these general processes, to yield a putative basis for why such complex systems could arise in such a short span of time. The complexity is no more than is to be expected from routinizations set up to accommodate the regularly recurring sequences of computational actions licensed in the earlier system. What we have not provided is a step-by-step account of the fine structure whereby the syntactic changes indicated took place, electing, rather, to look at the type of update which the various case specifications induce. Since such an account is a necessary condition for any robust account of syntactic change, the account set out here has done no more than set out preliminaries for a detailed specification of the diachronic sequence. Indeed, Bouzouita [this volume] uses this general perspective to provide a detailed account of the diachronic development of one such Spanish clitic, *lo*, detailing transitions from the mixed medieval Spanish placement of clitics placement through to the modern Spanish distribution (in which *lo* along with other clitics in finite clauses immediately precedes the verb). Nevertheless we have set out an outline of how clitic pronouns could have emerged from the clitic-lacking system of Latin. The account is one which not only provides a basis for formulating the puzzling heterogeneity of any individual clitic system, but also provides a principled explanation for the Person Case Constraint, an explanation which any account of clitic placement needs if it is to be more than a stipulatory list. The more general significance of the account is how substance can be given to the functionalist claim that syntactic change can emerge from purely pragmatic pressures on construal without jeopardizing the commitment in the explanation to formal modelling of the processes involved.

BIBLIOGRAPHY

[Adams, 1994] J. Adams. Wackernagel's law and the position of unstressed personal pronouns in Classical Latin. *Transactions of the Philological Society*, 92:103–178, 1994.

[Adger and Harbour, 2006] D. Adger and D. Harbour. The person case constraint. *Syntax*, 4, 2006.

[Anagnostopoulou, 2005] E. Anagnostopoulou. Strong and weak person restrictions: a feature checking analysis. In L. Heggie and F. Ordonez, editors, *Clitics and affixation*, pages 199–235. Benjamins, 2005.

[Anderson, 2005] S. Anderson. *Aspects of the theory of clitics*. Oxford University Press, Oxford, 2005.

[Blackburn and Meyer-Viol, 1994] P. Blackburn and W. Meyer-Viol. Linguistics, logic and finite trees. *Bulletin of Interest Group of Pure and Applied Logics*, 2:2–39, 1994.

[Bonet, 1995] E. Bonet. Feature structure of Romance clitics. *Natural Language and Linguistic Theory*, 13:607–647, 1995.

[Bouzouita and Kempson, 2006] M. Bouzouita and R. Kempson. Clitic placement in old and modern Spanish: a dynamic account. In O. Nedergaard Thomsen, editor, *Competing Models of Linguistic Change*. John Benjamin, 2006.

[Bouzouita, 2002] M. Bouzouita. *Clitic Placement in Old and Modern Spanish*. Msc, Kings College London, 2002.

[Bouzouita, this volume] M. Bouzouita. At the Syntax-Pragmatics Interface: Clitics in the History of Spanish. In R. Cooper and R. Kempson, editors, *Language in Flux: Dialogue Coordination, Language Variation, Language Change and Evolution*. Kings College Press, this volume.

[Bouzouita, forthcoming] M. Bouzouita. *Clitic Placement in the History of Spanish*. PhD, King's College London, forthcoming.

[Cann et al., 2005] R. Cann, R. Kempson, and L. Marten. *The Dynamics of Language*. Elsevier, Oxford, 2005.

[Cann et al., 2007] R. Cann, R. Kempson, and M. Purver. Context wellformedness: the dynamics of ellipsis. *Research on Language and Computation*, 5, 2007.

[Cann and Wu, 2007] R. Cann and Y. Wu. The 'bei' construction in Chinese: a dynamic approach. *MS, University of Edinburgh/University of Hong Kong*, 2007.

[Cardinaletti, forthcoming] A. Cardinaletti. On different types of clitic clusters. In K. Demuth and C. de Cat, editors, *The Romance-Bantu Connection*. Benjamin, forthcoming.

[Cuervo, 2005] M.C. Cuervo. Clitics: three of a perfect pair. MIT generals paper, 2005.

[Devine and Stephens, 2006] J. Devine and L. Stephens. *Latin Word Order: Structured Meaning and Information*. Oxford University Press, Oxford, 2006.

[Ferreira, 1996] V. Ferreira. Is it better to give than to donate: syntactic flexibility in language production. *Journal of Memory and Language*, 35:724–755, 1996.

[Givon, 1987] T. Givon. *On Understanding Grammar*. Academic Press, New York, 1987.

[Granberg, 1988] R. Granberg. *Object pronoun position in Medieval and Early Modern Spanish*. PhD thesis, UCLA, 1988.

[Grimshaw, 2001] J. Grimshaw. Optimal clitic position and the lexicon in romance clitic systems. In G. Legendre, J. Grimshaw, and S. Vikner, editors, *Optimality Theoretic Syntax*, pages pp.205–240. MIT Press, Cambridge, Mass, 2001.

[Hawkins, 2004] J. Hawkins. *Efficiency and Complexity in Grammars*. Cambridge University Press, Cambridge, 2004.

[Heap, 2005] D. Heap. Constraining optimality: Clitic sequences and feature geometry. In L.Heggie and F.Ordó nez, editors, *Clitic and Affix Combinations: Theoretical perspectives*, pages pp.81–102. Benjamin, Berlin, 2005.

[Hoecke, 1996] van Hoecke, W. The Latin dative. In W. van Belle and Langendonck W. van, editors, *The Dative: Volume I Descriptive Studies*, pages 3–38. Benjamins John, Amsterdam, 1996.

[Hornstein et al., 2005] N. Hornstein, J. Nunes, and K. Grohmann. *Understanding Minimalism*. Cambridge University Press, Cambridge, 2005.

[Kempson and Kiaer, 2008] R. Kempson and J. Kiaer. Japanese scrambling and the grammar-parser correspondence. In H. Hoshi, editor, *Language, Mind and Brain: Perspectives from Linguistics and Cognitive Neuroscience*. Kuroshio, Tokyo, 2008.

[Kempson et al., 2001] R. Kempson, W. Meyer-Viol, and D. Gabbay. *Dynamic Syntax*. Blackwell, Oxford, 2001.

[Kiaer, 2007] J. Kiaer. *Processing and Interfaces in Syntactic Theory: The case of Korean*. PhD, KCL London, 2007.

[Koizumi, 2000] M. Koizumi. String-vacuous overt verb raising. *Journal of East Asian Linguistics*, 9:227–85, 2000.

[Legendre, 2003] G. Legendre. What are clitics? evidence from Balkan languages. *Phonological Studies*, 6:89–96, 2003.

[Marten et al., forthcoming] L. Marten, R. Kempson and M. Bouzouita. Concepts of structural underspecification in Bantu and Romance. In C. de Cat and K. Demuth, editors, *The Bantu Romance Connection*. John Benjamin, Amsterdam, forthcoming.

[Martins, 2002] A-M. Martins. The loss of IP-scrambling in Portuguese: Clause structure, word order variation and change. In D. Lightfoot, editor, *Syntactic Effects of Morphological Change*. Oxford University Press, Oxford, 2002.

[Monachesi, 2005] P. Monachesi. *A Study of Romance Clitics*. Oxford University Press, Oxford, 2005.

[Nevins, 2007] A. Nevins. The representation of third person and its consequences for person-case effects. *Natural Language and Linguistic Theory*, 25:273–313, 2007.

[Nordlinger, 1998] R. Nordlinger. *Constructive Case*. CSLI, Stanford, 1998.

[Ormabazal and Romero, 2007] J. Ormazabal and J. Romero. The Object Agreement Constraint. *Natural Language and Linguistic Theory*, 25:315–347, 2007.

[Purver and Otsuka, 2003] M. Purver and M. Otsuka. Incremental generation by incremental parsing: tactical generation in dynamic syntax. In *Proceedings of the 9th ACL Workshop on generation*, pages 79–86, 2003.

[Purver et al., 2006] Matthew Purver, Ronnie Cann, and Ruth Kempson. Grammars as parsers: Meeting the dialogue challenge. *Research on Language and Computation*, 4(2-3):289–326, 2006.

[Rivero, 1997] M. L. Rivero. On Two Locations for Complement Clitic Pronouns: Serbo-Croatian, Bulgarian, and Old Spanish. *Parameters of Morphosyntactic Change*, 170–206, 1997.

[Rivero, 2007] M. L. Rivero. Oblique subjects and person restrictions in Spanish: a morphological approach. In R. D'Alessandro, S. Fischer, and G. Hrafnbjargarson, editors, *Agreement restrictions*. de Gruyter, 2007.

[Sag et al., 2002] Ivan Sag, Thomas Wasow, and Emily Bender. *Syntactic Theory: A Formal Introduction*. CSLI Publications, Stanford, 2002.

[Sperber and Wilson, 1995] D. Sperber and D. Wilson. *Relevance: Communication and Cognition (2nd editn)*. Blackwell, Oxford, 1995.

[Takano, 2002] Y. Takano. Surprising constituents. *Journal of East Asian Linguistics*, 11:243–301, 2002.

[Wu, 2005] Y. Wu. *The dynamic syntax of left and right dislocation: a study with special reference to Chinese.*. PhD thesis, Ph. D. Dissertation, University of Edinburgh, 2005.

Ronnie Cann
Linguistics and English Dept., University of Edinburgh, United Kingdom.
ronnie@ling.ed.ac.uk

Ruth Kempson
Philosophy Department, King's College London, United Kingdom.
ruth.kempson@kcl.ac.uk

At the Syntax-Pragmatics Interface: Clitics in the History of Spanish

MIRIAM BOUZOUITA

1 Introduction

This paper[1] tries to contribute to a better understanding of the diachronic changes in clitic placement with respect to the finite verb in the history of Spanish (13th -20th c.).[2] Additionally, it uses this clitic account as a case study to argue that it is essential for a grammar formalism to consider (i) the interdependency of syntax, semantics and pragmatics, and (ii) the time-linear processing aspect of parsing and production in order to obtain a better understanding of language change. The framework chosen for this study is the Dynamic Syntax grammar formalism (DS; [Kempson et al., 2001; Cann et al., 2005]), in which syntax is seen as the progressive construction of semantic representations, following the dynamics of parsing, hence a left-to-right process.

Firstly, I examine in detail clitic placement with respect to the finite verb for various stages in the diachronic development of object clitics: namely, for Medieval (13th -14th c.), Renaissance (16th c.) and Modern Spanish (20th c.). Secondly, synchronic accounts are presented within the DS framework for each of these periods. The diachronic changes are then set out in order to outline the progressive shift from a clitic system with a pragmatic basis to one in which the position of the clitic pronoun is determined by the verbal mood which the clitic appears with. Medieval Spanish (MedSp) presents a notoriously complex set of clitic patterns. What I shall show is that, in this stage of the evolving Spanish system, it is the process whereby semantic content is constructed

---

[1]This paper reports preliminary results from my doctoral research. I would like to thank Ruth Kempson, Ronnie Cann, Lutz Marten, Eleni Gregoromichelaki, Stelios Chatzikyriakidis and Jieun Kiaer for helpful input at various stages, Concepción Company for providing me with an electronic version of her corpus (*DLNE*) and Andrés Enrique Arias for giving me access to the facsimile of *Faz*. Further, I would like to acknowledge the financial support provided by the Arts and Humanities Research Council, the School of Humanities of King's College London and the Mexican Secretaría de Relaciones Exteriores. Normal disclaimers apply. This paper is a revised and extended version of Bouzouita 2007, 2008

[2]I will use throughout this paper the labels clitic and weak pronoun as pre-theoretical notions. The terms proclisis and enclisis are used to denote preverbal and postverbal placement respectively.

for the left-peripheral constituents that affects the syntactic positioning of these weak pronouns in finite verb clauses. Furthermore, I shall show that the availability of more than one strategy, which is endemic to parsing, provides a basis for explaining syntactic intra-speaker variation between pro- and enclisis within one environment. I shall go on from there to argue that what had initially been a pragmatic basis for MedSp clitic placement became lexically encoded for the clitics due to a routinization process [Pickering and Garrod, 2004], thereafter side-stepping any such pragmatic reasoning. Once this was in place, a production/parsing mismatch between speakers could arise, due to the availability of a number of strategies. The immediate consequence of any such mismatch on the hearer's part with respect to the processing of the clitic would have to involve some reanalysis of the lexical entry of the clitic whose preverbal placement thereby became interpreted as unrestricted, lacking the limitations of the former system. The result is a spread of proclitics in Renaissance Spanish (RenSp) across those environments that previously allowed only postverbal clitics. A second reanalysis subsequently takes place as enclitics became increasingly associated with imperatives, resulting eventually in the Modern Spanish system (ModSp) in which the position of the clitic is determined by the mood of the accompanying verb.

2 Clitic Placement in Medieval Spanish

To illustrate the extent of the syntactic variation found in the MedSp clitic system, I shall first briefly sketch some of its main characteristics. MedSp clitics occur in a complex disjunction of environments and in two discrete positions, preverbal (but not necessarily immediately adjacent to the verb, allowing a phenomenon known as 'interpolation') and immediately postverbal:[3]

(1) Que **te** dixo Heliseus?
    what CL said.3SG Heliseus
    'What did Heliseus tell you?' (*Faz.*: 134)

(2) Oyo**l** Ruben
    heard.3SG-CL Ruben
    'Ruben heard it.' (*Faz.*: 51)

Some environments fully determine which of these two positions is selected, but other environments allow variation, notably the subject position.

(3) e el conde respondio**l** que
    and the count replied.3SG-CL that

---

[3] For visual clarity, the clitics under consideration have been highlighted in bold and are glossed as CL while the constituents preceding the weak pronouns that influence their positioning, and the interpolated items have been underlined and bracketed respectively.

'And the count replied him that [...].' (*Luc.*: XVI)

(4) <u>El conde</u> **le** pregunto   commo
     the count   CL   asked.3SG   how

'The count asked him how [...].' (*Luc.*: V)

Unlike in ModSp, there seems to be a restriction precluding sentence-initial clitic pronouns, the so-called Tobler-Mussafia Law. Moreover, unlike in Classical Latin or Ancient Greek, Spanish interpolation can only occur with preverbal clitics:[4]

(5) Et   esto <u>que</u> **te** [yo] [agora] mostrare   aqui
     and this that   CL   I   now   will-show.1SG here

'And this that I will now show you here.' (*Gen.Est.I*: 324 apud [Sánchez Lancis, 1993, p327])

The predominant position in main clauses is postverbal: in my corpus only 26% (647/2464) of proclisis is registered (see Table 2, section 2.3). In non-root clauses, on the other hand, the most frequently encountered clitic position is proclitic, with clitics occurring after relative pronouns, complementisers and subordinating conjunctions:[5]

(6) no   quiero   <u>que</u> **me** sirbas   en balde
     not want.1SG   that   CL   serve.2SG   in vain

'I don't want you to serve me in vain.' (*Faz.*: 48)

(7) <u>Quant</u> **le** connocio   Abdias
     when   CL   recognized.3SG   Abdias

'When Abdias recognized him [...]' (*Faz.*: 121)

(8) Di   a fijos de Israel   <u>que</u> prenda**nse**   unos   blagos
     tell.2SG   to sons of Israel   that   take.3PL-CL   some   sticks

'Tell the sons of Israel that they find themselves some sticks.'(*Faz.*: 86)

Given this lack of variation in subordinate clause clitic placement, in what follows, I shall focus primarily on the change in root clause clitic distributions, where we shall see that an initially complex disjunctive set of environments

---

[4]Although I will not give analyses for this phenomenon here, I shall relate its existence and disappearance with other syntactic changes that occurred in the history of Spanish (see section 5, and [Bouzouita, 2007; Bouzouita, forthcoming]).

[5]There are a few exceptions, most explicable as mimicking direct speech or as syntactic calques from Latin. For more details on variation in non-root clauses, see [Bouzouita, forthcoming; Castillo Lluch, 1996, pp142–196; Granberg, 1988].

triggering clitic placement progressively simplifies.[6] As part of this, we shall see that clitics in imperative verb contexts in the earlier system have a very similar distribution to their non-imperative counterparts, only evolving towards a placement system based on verbal mood later on.

2.1 Non-imperative Contexts

The MedSp clitic environments in root clauses can be grouped into (i) exclusively proclitic constructions, (ii) exclusively enclitic constructions and (iii) variation constructions, which license both pro- and enclisis ([Nieuwenhuijsen, 1999, 2002, 2006; Elvira, 1987] inter alia).

Exclusively Proclitic Constructions

Some constructions retained exclusive preverbal clitic placement throughout the history of Spanish, namely those in which the clitic is immediately preceded by one of the following five left-peripheral constituents:

(i) *Wh*-ELEMENT

(9) <u>Quien</u> **te** fyzo rey?
    who   CL made.3SG king

   'Who made you king?' (*Faz.*: 107)

(10) <u>Por que</u> **nos** faze   el Criador esto?
     why   CL   does.3SG the Lord   this

   'Why does the Lord do this to us?' (*Faz.*: 55)

(ii) NEGATION[7]

(11) <u>Non</u> **los** destroyré
     not   CL   will-destroy.1SG

   'I will not destroy them.' (*Faz.*: 77)

(12) <u>Nunca</u> **se** allegó   al   rey
     never   CL   adhered.3SG to-the king

   'He never adhered to the king.' (*EG*: f.57v apud [Granberg, 1988, p131])

---

[6]It should be highlighted that this simplification is only visible at the formal level and not at the data level, considering that in RenSp, for instance, more environments show variation in comparison to MedSp.

[7]Only Gessner [1893, p37] and Eberenz [2000, p172] report enclitic cases in negation environments. For a discussion of these examples, some of which contain transcription or scribal errors, see [Bouzouita, forthcoming].

(13)   &   <u>ni**l**</u>   prestaron   armas   nin   auer
       and   nor-CL   lent.3PL   weapons   nor   good
       'Nor did they lend him weapons nor goods.' (*Gen.Est.IV,CDE* s.v. *nil*)

(iii) NON-COREFERENTIAL COMPLEMENT NP

(14)   <u>Tal gualardon</u>   **me**   dyo   el   Criador
       such prize   CL   gave.3SG   the   Creator
       'Such a reward did the Lord give me.' (*Faz.*: 102)

(15)   <u>A to linnaje</u>   **la**   daré
       to your lineage   CL   will-give.1SG
       'To your lineage I will give it.' (*Faz.*: 81)

(iv) PREPOSITIONAL COMPLEMENT[8]

(16)   e   <u>de todas vuestras ydolas</u>   **vos**   mondaré
       and   of all   your   idols   CL   will-purify.1SG
       'And of all your idols I will rid you.' (*Faz.*:171)

(v) PREDICATIVE COMPLEMENT

(17)   <u>Dia [de] angunstia ed aquexadura</u>   **nos**   es   est
       day of anguish and distress   CL   is.3SG   this
       'This is a day of anguish and distress for us.' (*Faz.*: 155)

(18)   <u>Huecas</u>   **las**   faras
       empty   CL   will-make.3SG
       'You will make them hollow.' (*Faz.*: 82)

---

[8]Nieuwenhuijsen [1999, pp56-57; 2002, p362; 2006, pp1362-1363] regards the prepositional complement environment as one which admits both pro- and enclisis. However, her examples, given in (i)-(ii) (personal communication), are more appropriately analyzed as adjuncts, being fully optional.

(i)   e   <u>por amor de su mugier</u>   pusol   nombre   Libira
      and   out-of love for his wife   gave.3SG-CL   name   Libira
      'Out of love for his wife, he named her Libira.' (*EE*:12)

(ii)   E   el   rey   <u>con grand miedo</u>   acogiose   a   vn   nauio
       and   the   king   with great fear   took-refuge.3SG-CL   to   a   ship
       'And the king, with great fear, took refuge in a ship.' (*Hist.Troy.*: XI)

Many studies, like Nieuwenhuijsen (e.g. [Castillo Lluch, 1996; Elvira, 1987, p71; Gessner, 1893, pp37-38]) fail to recognize the prepositional complement environment as a strictly proclitic one exactly because they don't distinguish adverbial complements from adjuncts.

Strict Enclitic Constructions

On the other hand, there are some constructions that occur with enclitic pronouns in MedSp:[9] (i) when the verb appears sentence-initially (ii) when in a paratactic root clause also with the verb in initial position, and (iii) with a contrastive coordination marker such as *pero/mas* 'but':

(i) VERB IN SENTENCE-INITIAL POSITION

(19) *Enbio**l***   Juda un cabrito
      sent.3SG-CL Juda a   little goat
      'Juda sent her a little goat.' (*Faz.*: 52)

(20) *Miembra**t***   quando   lidiamos   cerça   Valençia   la   grant
      remember.3SG-CL   when   fought.1PL near   Valencia   the   great
      'Do you remember when we fought near the great city of Valencia?'
      (*Cid*: 3315 apud [Fontana, 1993, p133])

(ii) VERB IN PARATACTIC ROOT CLAUSE[10]

(21) *Alli en Gaza(r) fo Sampson luengos tienpos;*   *conta**lo***   *Libre*
      there in Gaza was.3SG Samson long times   tell.3SG-CL   Book
      Judicum
      of-the-Judges
      'Samson stayed there in Gaza for a long time; the Book of Judges tells this.' (*Faz.*: 207)

(iii) CONTRASTIVE COORDINATION (PERO/MAS)

(22) *nin* *so* *nombre* *non* *me* *dixo*   *mas* *dixo**m***
      nor   his   name   not   CL   told.3SG   but   told.3SG-CL
      'Nor did he tell me his name but he told me [...].' (*Faz.*:207)

---

[9] See [Bouzouita, forthcoming] for a list of potential counterexamples.

[10] As reported in [Bouzouita, 2007, p56], one counterexample was registered in my corpus, given in (iii), reproduced here as punctuated by Lazar [1965]:

(iii) *murio (lo mala) [de] mala muert en Judea;*   *lo*   *comieron*   *gusanos.*
       died.3SG of bad death in Judea;   CL   ate.3PL   maggots
       'He died horribly in Judea; the maggots ate him.' (*Faz.*: 203)

However, it may be the case that the punctuation is as follows: *murio (lo mala) [de] mala muert; en Judea lo comieron gusanos*, in which the semi-colon is placed before the PP. In this case, the pronoun position is not unusual, as we shall see when discussing adverbial environments. The facsimile of this text reveals that this alternative is indeed a valid possibility considering there is also a punctuation mark present before the PP. Accordingly, this example cannot be considered a counterexample. See [Bouzouita, forthcoming] for more details.

(23) ovo   muy grand pesar pero dixoles   que
    had.3SG very great grief but   told.3SG-CL that
    'He had a lot of grief but he told them that [...].' (*Luc.*:XLVI)

Variation Constructions

There is additional complexity, in virtue of there being environments in which variation between proclisis and enclisis occurs:

(i) SUBJECTS (whether pronominal or nominal)

(24) e   ella dixogelo
    and she   told.3SG-CL-CL
    'And she told it to him.' (*Faz.*: 47)

(25) Yo vos enbiaré
    I   CL   will-send.1SG
    'I will send you.' (*Faz.*: 67)

(26) santo domingo   fizolo
    saint Dominic   did.3SG-CL
    'Saint Dominic did it.' (*Luc.*: XIV)

(27) Sant Mate   lo   testimonia
    saint Matthew   CL   testify.3SG
    'Saint Matthew attests it.' (*Faz.*: 97)

Several authors have claimed that the variation in clitic placement in subject environments can be explained on the basis of phonological pauses, more specifically, that if there is a phonological pause between the left-peripheral subject and the verb, the clitic will appear postverbally (e.g. [Ramsden, 1963, pp80-83; Staaff, 1907, p626]). However, this explanation fails to explain the existence of proclitic examples in which the subject is followed by a relative clause or an apposition (or by the combination of the aforementioned), as in (28) and (29):

(28) Estas bestias grandes que son .iiii. reyes se   levantaran
    these animals big   that are.3PL four kings CL   will-stand-up.3PL
    'These big animals which are four kings will stand up.' (*Faz.*: 181)

(29) El Dios de mio padre Abraam e de Ysaac, el Sennor que dixo
    the God of my father Abraham and of Isaac, the Lord who said.3SG
    'tornat a tu tierra o nacist'   me   aya   merced
    return.2PL to your land where born.2SG   CL   have.3SG mercy

'May the god of my father Abraham and of Isaac, the Lord who said 'Return to the land where you were born' have mercy on me.' (*Faz.*: 50)

Granberg [1999; 1988, pp200-213] proposes a relationship between emphasis and clitic placement in subject environments: proclisis is found after emphatic subjects and enclisis is the absence of such emphasis. Martins [2003] more generally argues that all the variation constructions in both MedSp and Medieval Portuguese appear to be emphatic when a preverbal clitic is present and neutral otherwise. Although Granberg's hypothesis seems broadly apposite for the subject environment, it does not straightforwardly extend to all variation environments, in particular in the case of adverbials, as we shall see shortly.

(ii) ADVERBIALS

These unsurprisingly are heterogeneous, with clitics appearing both in enclisis or in proclisis, some consistently with preverbal positions, such as *siempre* 'always' (30), others, e.g. *agora* 'now', allowing variation (31)-(32):[11]

(30)   &   *siempre* **los** uencio
       and   always   CL   defeated.3SG

'And he always defeated them.' (*Est.Esp.II, CDE* s.v. *siempre los*)

(31)   et   *agora* prí**so***lo*
       and   now   took.3SG-CL

'And now he took him.' (*EE*: 108 apud [Granberg, 1988, p176])

(32)   *Agora* **me** quieres   fer   matar
       now   CL   want.2SG   make   kill

'Now you want to have me killed.' (*Faz.*: 122)

It is the adverbial environment with *siempre* that is problematic for Martins' view that variation in clitic positioning invariably is correlated with emphasis on the preceding constituent (or lack of it); and cross-linguistic evidence from Modern Galician corroborates the lack of any such straightforward correspondence with emphasis: [Álvarez Blanco *et al.*, 1986, p190] (apud [Granberg, 1988, p184]), for instance, state that emphatic readings are rare, although possible, for those adverbs that always trigger proclisis.

---

[11] I do not aim to give an exhaustive account of the adverbial environment here but a mere overview of the possible variation patterns. For an extensive account on clitic placement after left-peripheral adverbials, I refer the reader to [Granberg, 1988, pp155-194; Castillo Lluch, 1996, pp232-247].

(iii) VOCATIVES

Although some (e.g. [Barry, 1987]) have claimed that vocatives require enclisis, proclisis is also option, when the vocative is the imperative subject (see section 2.2).[12] However, no unambiguous proclisis examples have been encountered for the non-imperative environments.

(33) <u>O mio Sennor</u>,   priegot   que
      Oh my Lord   beg.1SG-CL   that
      'Oh my Lord, I beg you that [...].' (*Faz.*: 121)

(iv) CO-REFERENTIAL OBJECT NPS

Despite the predominance of enclisis in Clitic Left Dislocation/Hanging Topic Left Dislocation (CLLD/HTLD) constructions as in (34), proclisis has also been attested, to wit when the left-peripheral constituent contains the indefinite pronoun or adjective *todo(s)* 'all' or *am(b)os* 'both', as in (35)-(36):

(34) <u>al rey</u>   mataron**le**   en   so   lecho   sos   syervos
      ACC-the king   killed.3PL-CL   in   his   bed   his   slaves
      'The king, his slaves killed him in his bed.' (*Faz.*: 159)

(35) Levo   cativo   el   rey   de   Babilonia   al   rey
      brought.3SG   captive   the   king   of   Babylon   ACC-the   king
      Joachin   e   a   sue   madre,   a   sus   mugieres   e   a
      Joachim   and   ACC   his   mother   ACC   his   wives   and   ACC
      sos   vassallos   e   todos   los   mayores   de   toda   su   tierra;
      his   vassals   and   all   the   elders   of   all   his   land;
      <u>todos</u>   **los**   cativo
      all   CL   captured.3SG
      'The king of Babylon captured king Joachim, his mother, his wives, his vassals and all the elders of all his land, he captured them all [...].' (*Faz.*: 160)

(36) con   el   so   manto   <u>a amas</u>   **las**   cubrió
      with   the   his   cape   ACC both   CL   covered.3SG
      'With his cape he covered them both.' (*Cid2*: 2807 apud [Ramsden, 1963, p86])

Although Granberg's [1988; 1999] hypothesis of a correspondence between emphatic subjects and proclisis cannot be extended to the adverbials environment, as suggested by Martins [2003], it seems plausible to assume that left-peripheral constituents in CLLD/HTLD constructions that appear with proclitic

---

[12]It is indeed difficult to distinguish in MedSp command contexts between imperative subjects and vocatives.

pronouns, are pragmatically salient in some sense, in view of examples such as (35) where the quantifier *todos* 'all' clearly bears emphatic stress (it summarizes an extensive list of people who got captured by the king of Babylon). As we shall see later, imperative verb contexts show a similar pattern.

(v) COORDINATION[13]

Despite the predominance of enclisis with *e(t)/y* 'and', as in (37), preverbal placement is possible if a preceding conjunct contains a proclisis-inducing element in what appears to be a parallelism or alignment effect, as in (38)-(39).

(37) Sonno   Joseph un suenno e   contolo   a sos
     dreamt.3SG Joseph a dream and told.3SG-CL to his
     ermanos
     brothers
     'Joseph had a dream and he told it to his brothers.' (*Faz*.: 50)

(38) Yot   acreceré   e   te muchiguaré
     I-CL will-enlarge.1SG and CL will-multiply.1SG
     'I will enlarge and multiply you.' (*Faz*.: 58)

(39) Por   esto que dizie,   lo firio   Phashur, fijo
     because-of this that said.3SG CL wounded.3SG   Phashur son
     de Hymer, e   lo metio   en cepo
     of Hymer, and CL put.3SG in trap
     'Because of what he said, Phashur, son of Hymer, injured him and trapped him.' (*Faz*.: 167)

Proclisis in the first conjunct is not however a prerequisite for the occurrence of preverbal clitics in subsequent conjuncts as (40)-(41) demonstrate. What is necessary is the occurrence of a proclisis-inducing element in a preceding conjunct, which in the following examples are the adverbs *por esto* 'because of this' and *alli* 'there'. But any such parallelism is in any case not obligatory, as illustrated in (42):

(40) por   esto bendixo   Dios al   dia septimo el
     because-of this blessed.3SG   God to-the day seventh and-CL
     sanctiguo
     consecrated.3SG
     'Because of this, God blessed the seventh day and consecrated it.' (*Faz*.: 76)

---

[13] I will not discuss disjunctive constructions as I did not encounter any examples in my corpus. Similarly, other studies, such as Castillo Lluch, [1996, p113] and Granberg, [1988, pp252-254] lament the scarcity of relevant data. Accordingly, I will leave this issue aside.

(41) alli   convertio   sant Peydro a   Cornelius Centurio
     there   converted.3SG   saint Peter   ACC Cornelius Centurio
     e   **lo** babtizo
     and   CL   baptised.3SG

   'There Saint Peter converted Cornelius Centurio and baptised him.'
   (*Faz.*: 125)

(42) El   Criador te   fizo   rey   e   diot   las
     the   Creator CL   made.3SG   king   and gave.3SG-CL   the
     mugieres de   to   enemigo e   de   to   sennor en   to
     women   of   your   enemy   and of   your   lord   in   your
     poder
     power

   'God made you king and gave you the wives of your enemy and of
   your lord.' (*Faz.*:141)

(vi) NON-ROOT/ABSOLUTE CLAUSES

Again though an absolute clause construction (more colloquially, a clausal adjunct) or a non-root clause will generally be followed by postverbal clitics, as exemplified in (43) and (44), my corpus contains a few exceptions to this: namely, when the subordinating element of the preceding non-root clause is *antes que* 'before that', as in (45):

(43) <u>andando el muy sin reçelo,</u>   vio**lo**   el   Raposo
     walking he very without suspicion   saw.3SG-CL   the fox

   'While he was walking without any suspicion, the fox saw him.'(*Luc.*: XII)

(44) <u>quant le vyo,</u>   dixo**l**
     when CL saw.3SG   said.3SG-CL

   'When he saw him, he told him [...].' (*Faz.*: 122)

(45) <u>antes que saliestes del vientre</u>   **te**   santigué
     before that left.2SG of-the belly   CL   blessed.1SG

   'Before you were born, I blessed you.' (*Faz.*: 165)

According to Leavitt (apud [Granberg, 1988, p139]), the preverbal placement in (45) can be explained as a consequence of adverbial force of *antes*.[14]

---

[14][Granberg, 1988, p141] also mentions other exceptions which can be explained with this notion of adverbial force, namely those non-root clauses which occur with *assy como* 'considering'. For a detailed overview of the first attestations of a change for this syntactic environment, I refer the reader to this work [Granberg, 1988, pp136-146].

However, a quick search in the online *CDE* reveals that *antes que* clauses also occur with postverbal clitics:

(46) <u>antes que el emperador muriesse</u>   perdono**le**
      before that the emperor died.3SG   forgave.3SG-CL

   'Before the emperor died, he forgave him.' (*GranCon.*,*CDE* s.v. *antes que*)

On the face of it, then, environments that license both pro- and enclisis positioning seem an ineliminably heterogeneous set, yet each primarily displays enclisis.

2.2 Imperative Contexts

Although some (e.g. [Barry, 1987, p215]) claim that only the enclitic ordering is found with imperative verbs in MedSp, it has been noted that proclisis is also attested in these contexts. I shall show here that clitics occur in essentially the same positions with respect to the verb, irrespective of it being imperative or not, so whatever systematicity there is to the complex distribution patterning needs to be seen as carrying over to these imperative constructions.[15] Here I shall illustrate less comprehensively.

Imperative examples with preverbal pronouns have been found for all the exclusively proclitic constructions except for those that commence with a *wh*-element: negation (47)-(49), non-coreferential complement NPs (50), prepositional and predicative complements (51)-(52):

(47) <u>No**l**</u>   fagas   mal
      not-CL   do.2SG   hurt

   'Don't hurt him.' (*Faz.*: 49)

(48) <u>Nunca</u>   **te**   metas   o   puedas   auer   malandança
      never   CL   put.2SG   where   can.2SG   have   misfortune

   'Never put yourself in a unfortunate situation.' (*Luc.*: XXXIV)

(49) <u>Ni</u>   **los**   adores   <u>ni</u>   **los**   sirvas
      neither   CL   adore.2SG   nor   CL   serve.2SG

   'Neither adore them nor serve them.' (*Faz.*: 75)

(50) <u>A vuestros [fijos]</u>   **lo**   recontat
      to your children   CL   tell.2PL

   'Tell it to your children.' (*Faz.*: 186)

---

[15]I classified sentences containing wishes, as in (54), (59) and (60), in the imperative clitic environments although wish contexts always appear with preverbal clitics, except if the verb occurs as the first constituent. For more details on the behaviour of clitics in these contexts, see [Bouzouita, forthcoming].

(51) <u>A las cosas çiertas</u>   **vos**   comendat
 to the things certain   CL   entrust.2PL
 'Confide in certainties.' (*Luc.*: VII)

(52) <u>Testimonias</u> **me** sed   oy
 witnesses   CL   be.2PL   today
 'Be my witnesses today.' (*Faz.*: 200)

Then, as expected on the non-imperative pattern, postverbal clitics are found in verb-initial constructions (53)-(54), paratactic root clauses (55), and constructions with contrastive coordination (56):

(53) <u>Sacad**la**</u>   fuera
 take.2PL-CL   out
 'Take her out.' (*Faz.*: 52)

(54) <u>Vea**lo**</u>   Dios
 see.3SG-CL   God
 'May God see it.' (*Faz.*: 65)

(55) <u>Andat e matemos**le**</u>,   echemos**le**   en   aquel   pozo
 walk.2PL and kill.1PL-CL   throw.1PL-CL   in   that   well
 'Walk and let's kill him, let's throw him in that well.' (*Faz.*: 51)

(56) <u>mas</u> da**les**   a   comer   e   a   bever
 but   give.2SG-CL   to   eat   and   to   drink
 'But give them to eat and drink.' (*Faz.*: 126)

As we might now expect, this close parallelism of distribution carries over to the variation constructions, as illustrated, for instance, for the adverbials in (57)-(59).

(57) <u>Agora</u> da**nos**   rey
 now   give.2SG-CL   king
 'Now give us a king.' (*Faz.*: 104)

(58) E   vos   Sennor   Conde   Lucanor   <u>siempre</u>   **vos**   guardat
 and   you   Lord   Count   Lucanor   always   CL   be-careful.2SG
 'And you, Count Lucanor, always be careful [...].' (*Luc.*: XIII)

(59) <u>Asy**m**</u>   faga   Dios
 like-this-CL   make.3SG   God
 'May God treat me like this.' (*Faz.*: 126)

The situation for the subject and vocative environments is slightly more complicated. Only preverbal clitics have been encountered in wish contexts with a left-peripheral subject, as shown in (60), whereas variation is observed for non-wish imperative contexts, as in (61)-(62). The parallelisms between the imperative vocatives, on the one hand, and the non-imperative subject and CLLD/HTLD cases, on the other hand, deserve somewhat more comment. Firstly, the vocatives in these imperative contexts can be regarded as imperative subjects based on several criteria. To begin with, they have a similar semantic role as the declarative/non-imperative subjects. More specifically, while non-imperative subjects can be agents, the vocatives in these imperative contexts can be described as *intended agents* i.e. the agents designated by the utterers of these clauses to carry out the given command [Jensen, 2003, p155]. Furthermore, both agree in number with the verb. Recall further that, for the non-imperative subject environments, we concluded that there exists some correlation between the emphasis of the subject and the placement of the subsequent clitic (see section 2.1): namely, enclisis is found with unemphatic subjects while proclisis appears with emphatic ones. Similarly, this pattern arises in vocative environments with imperative verbs since vocatives that don't seem to be emphasized, as for instance in (61), appear with postverbal pronouns whereas others which do seem to bear emphatic stress, such as (62)-(64), trigger proclitic placement.[16]

(60) <u>Dios</u> **te** aya   merced, myo fijo
     God   CL have.3SG mercy   my   son
     'May God have mercy of you, my son.' (*Faz.*: 56)

(61) <u>Rey</u>, salva**m**
     king save.2SG-CL
     'King, save me.' (*Faz.*: 126)

(62) <u>Madre, plena de gracia, reina poderosa, tú,</u> **me** guia   en ello
     Mother, full of grace, mighty queen, you   CL guide.2SG in this
     'Mother, full of grace, mighty queen, you, guide me through this.'(*BMlg.*: 46c-d)

---

[16]Because my corpus did not contain any vocative examples with proclisis, I consulted *BMlg.* and *SDom.* by Berceo and *LPal.* by López de Ayala since Gessner [1893, p43] cites an example from each of them. A quick search for the personal pronoun *tú* in these texts reveals that proclisis in the vocative environment is not uncommon as I encountered in total 37 different cases. The search for occurrences with *am(b)os*, as in (64), on the contrary, did not give any results. Searching in the *CDE* reveals that proclitic vocative examples are not restricted to poetry only as examples can also be found in the *Gen.Est.IV* and the *Est.Esp.II*, which are historiographical texts.

(63) <u>Tú</u>, **me** libra   Señora
     You CL free.2SG Lady
     'You free me Lady.' (*LPal.*: 3871)

(64) <u>Rachel e Vidas, amos,</u> **me** dat   las manos
     Rachel and Vidas both   CL give.2PL the hands
     'Rachel and Vidas, both, give me your hands.' (*Cid3*: 106)

With regards to the parallelism with the CLLD/HTLD cases, it is striking that most of the preverbal vocative examples encountered contain invocations (to God, the Virgin Mary, etc.) in which the personal pronoun *tú* 'you' appears as the last vocative in a list of several epithets. Consider for instance (62). This example contains an invocation to the Virgin Mary, who gets addressed with several epithets, such as mother and mighty queen, which characterize different aspects attributed to her.[17] These epithets are then followed by the personal pronoun *tú* which then seems to 'summarize' in a sense the previous epithets as it does not refer to just one aspect of her.[18] The same also applies for example (64) which contains as the final vocative the indefinite pronoun *amos* 'both', compromising as such the previous vocatives *Rachel e Vidas*. Recall that we concluded for CLLD/HTLD environments with the indefinite pronoun *todos* 'all', as in example (35), that this pronoun bears emphatic stress since this left-peripheral pronoun summarizes a list of people who got captured. Likewise, we can deduce that these vocatives which also occur with preverbal clitics and 'summarize' previous vocatives/epithets, are emphatic.

As regards the CLLD/HTLD constructions, again the determining factor seems to be emphasis, with enclisis found whenever the left-peripheral constituent seems to be unemphatic, as in (65), whereas proclisis arising with emphatic CLLD/HTLD constituents such as *todos* 'all' in (66).

(65) e   la cosa graf que non podran judgar   adugan**la**   a
     and the thing serious that not will-can.3PL judge bring.3PL-CL to
     ty
     you

---

[17]Most of these examples contain this figure of speech, known as a merism, which is commonly used in biblical poetry and by which an entity is referred to by a conventional phrase that enumerates several of its parts, or which lists several synonyms for the same referent.

[18]Notwithstanding this, proclisis after the personal pronoun *tú* is not obligatory as the following clearly illustrates:

(iv) e   <u>tu</u>, di**la**   a nos
      and you tell.2SG-CL to us
      'And you, tell it to us.' (*Faz.*: 209)

'And the serious things that they won't be able to judge, bring them to you.' (*Faz.*: 74)

(66) <u>todos</u> **los** metet   a   espada et <u>todos</u> **los** matat
     all   CL   put.2PL to   sword and all   CL   kill.2PL

'Put them all on your swords and kill them all.' (*EE*: 374, 36a apud [Castillo Lluch, 1996, p226])

2.3 Data Summary

In sum, we have seen that MedSp clitic placement in main clauses can be classified into the three groups: (i) exclusively proclitic environments, (ii) exclusively enclitic environments, and (iii) variation environments, with no major differences between non-imperative and imperative verb contexts, as shown in Table 1. The significance of this is that what emerges later as a categorial distinction between imperative and non-imperative environments is a relatively late basis for differentiation. Preverbal clitics are recorded exclusively in a disjoint set of environments: when the clitic is preceded by a left-peripheral (i) *wh*-element, (ii) negation marker, (iii) non-coreferential complement NP, (iv) prepositional or (v) predicative complement. Conversely, the postverbal pronoun position is attested for those environments in which the verb is located in a sentence-initial or paratactic position, or in which the contrastive coordination marker *pero/mas* 'but' precedes the verb. The variation environments, again with no significant differences found between imperative and non-imperative contexts vis-a-vis clitic placement, range over yet a further somewhat heterogeneous set: (i) left-peripheral subjects, (ii) adverbials, (iii) vocatives[19], (iv) coordination markers *et/y*, (v) object NPs that are co-referential with the clitic (CLLD/HTLD), and (vi) non-root/absolute constructions. The possibility of assigning a principled syntactic basis for such a heterogeneous set of distributions seems remote. This constitutes a challenge for any attempt to formally model the synchronic system or, more ambitiously, provide a diachronic account for a sequence of such systems. What underlying pattern could indeed be recovered from these disparate distributions?

---

[19] As seen in section 2.2, variation is only attested for the command environments.

Table 1: Clitic Placement in 13th and 14th c. Medieval Spanish

	Non-imperatives		Imperatives	
	Proclisis	**Enclisis**	**Proclisis**	**Enclisis**
Wh-word	X	-	-	-
Negation	X	-	X	-
Complement NP	X	-	X	-
Prepositional complement	X	-	X	-
Predicative complement	X	-	X	-
Verb	-	X	-	X
Paratactic root clause	-	X	-	X
Pero/mas 'but'	-	X	-	X
Subject	X	X	X	-*
Adverbial	X	X	X	X
Vocative	-	X	X	X
Coordination	X	X	X	X
Object NP (CLLD/HTLD)	X	X	X	X
Non-root/absolute clause	X	X	X	X

*: Wish contexts only

As Table 2 shows, the overall predominant clitic position in MedSp root clauses is the postverbal one: 75% of all 13th c. cases and 68% of all 14th c. examples exhibit this placement, despite there being systematic exceptions in certain syntactic environments. Furthermore, enclisis can be considered as the default position which can be overridden in certain circumstances [Bouzouita, 2007, p53]. We saw, for instance, that for the coordinate constructions preverbal placement seems only possible if a preceding conjunct contains a proclisis-inducing element, such as e.g. a subject, a *wh*-element, etc. Proclitic CLLD/HTLD contexts, on the other hand, only arise in the presence of a left-peripheral *todo(s)* 'all' or *am(b)os* 'both' which seem to bear emphatic stress. We also concluded that the imperative vocative environment shows that there exists a correlation between the emphasis of the left-peripheral element and the placement of the subsequent clitic, as do the subject and CLLD/HTLD contexts. However, this principle cannot be extended to the adverbial environments. Enclisis also seems to be the default position whenever a non-root/absolute clause precedes the matrix clause, unless this non-root clause contains the subordinating element *antes que* 'before that'. We shall see later on that a unified account can be given for all these environments.

Table 2. Percentage of Proclisis in 13ᵗʰ and 14ᵗʰ c. Medieval Spanish

	Total	13ᵗʰ c.	14ᵗʰ c.
Wh-word	100% (41/41)	100% (41/41)	-
Negation	100% (207/207)	100% (168/168)	100% (39/39)
Complement NP	100% (24/24)	100% (18/18)	100% (6/6)
Prepositional compl.	100% (14/14)	100% (10/10)	100% (4/4)
Predicative compl.	100% (6/6)	100% (6/6)	-
Verb	0% (0/336)	0% (0/335)	0% (0/1)
Paratactic root cl.	0% (0/34)	0% (0/33)	0% (0/1)
Pero/mas 'but'	0% (0/10)	0% (0/3)	0% (0/7)
Subject	66% (172/259)	69% (114/165)	62% (58/94)
Adverbial	64% (147/228)	70% (119/170)	48% (28/58)
Vocative	0% (0/17)	0% (0/14)	0% (0/3)
Coordination	2% (24/1155)	2% (23/997)	1% (1/158)
Object NP	27% (9/33)	19% (5/27)	67% (4/6)
Non-root/absolute cl.	3% (3/100)	8% (3/39)	0% (0/61)
Total	26% (647/2464)	25% (507/2026)	32% (140/438)

Additional evidence that corroborates enclisis as the default MedSp clitic position, even though able to be overridden, is provided by those cases in which a proclisis-triggering constituent follows other constituents that would normally occur with postverbal clitics, as exemplified by the following:[20]

(67) *[Mas] non **los** seruen todos*
 but not CL serve.3PL all
 'But not all serve them.' (*Luc.*: Prólogo)

(68) *[sos castiellos] a espada **los** metras*
 his castles to sword CL will-put.2SG
 'His castles you will siege them.' (*Faz.*: 133)

(69) *[a los ricos e al ganado gruesso] no **los**
 ACC the rich and ACC-the livestock fat not CL
 quiso matar*
 wanted.3SG kill
 'The rich and the fat livestock, he didn't want to kill them.' (*Faz.*: 106)

---

[20] The constituents that override the enclitic norm have been underlined whereas those that appear with postverbal clitics when not preceded (or followed) by other constituents have been bracketed.

(70) [Sus decimas e sus primycias]   <u>fidel myentre</u> **las** dava
    his tithes and his duties on first fruits   faithfully   CL   gave.3SG
    'His tithes and duties on first fruits, he paid them faithfully.' (*Faz.*: 114)

In example (67), for instance, the contrasting coordination marker *mas* 'but', which occurs always with postverbal clitics if not preceded by other elements, is followed by a negation adverb *non*, which overrides the default enclitic positioning. Similarly, in examples (68)-(70), the left-dislocated NPs that are co-referential with the following clitics, are followed by proclisis-inducing elements: to wit, the prepositional complement *a espada* 'to sword', the negation adverb *no* 'no' and the manner adverb *fidel myentre* 'faithfully'.

Although proclisis-inducing constituents can override the enclitic norm, the opposite does not hold. In other words, proclisis-inducing constituents need not immediately precede the clitic in order to be able to influence its positioning with respect to the verb. In (71)-(72), for instance, the vocative *sennor conde (lucanor)* is preceded by the adverb *agora* which is capable of inducing preverbal placement (see also (31)). Although proclisis has been recorded with imperative vocatives, no unambiguous attestations exist for the non-imperative contexts (see section 2.1). Accordingly, I conclude that the proclitic placement is very likely to be due to the adverb and not the vocative.[21]

(71) <u>Agora</u>, [sennor conde], **vos** he   dicho el mio consejo
    now   lord count   CL   have.1SG said the my   advice
    'Now, Count, I have given you my advice.' (*Luc.*: Quinta Parte)

(72) <u>Agora</u>, [sennor conde lucanor], **vos** he   contado
    now   lord count Lucanor   CL   have.1SG told
    'Now, Count Lucanor, I have told you [...].' (*Luc.*: XLVIII)

3 Clitic Placement in Renaissance Spanish

3.1 Novel Proclisis Cases

As we saw previously, the overwhelming majority of MedSp clitic cases exhibit enclisis in finite main clauses. When we turn to Renaissance Spanish (RenSp),

---

[21] As I commented elsewhere [Bouzouita, 2007, pp52-53], these examples show that the strict string-linear methodology for identifying the different clitic environments is problematic as it presupposes that only the constituent immediately preceding the clitic can influence its placement (e.g. [Nieuwenhuijsen, 1999, 2002, 2006]). In view of this, I adopted a more DS-oriented approach whereby only the elements of the tree to which the clitic pronoun contributes are considered relevant, and not necessarily the entire sentential sequence (see [Cann and Kempson, this volume] for the concept of linked structure and [Bouzouita, forthcoming] for more details).

we see evidence of change, which started taking place in the 15th c. ([Arias Álvarez, 1995; Eberenz, 2000, p133; Nieuwenhuijsen, 1999, ch. 5] inter alia).

Table 3. Clitic Placement in 16th c. Renaissance Spanish

	Non-imperatives		Imperatives	
	Proclisis	Enclisis	Proclisis	Enclisis
Wh-word	X	-	-	-
Negation	X	-	X	-
Complement NP	X	-	X	-
Prepositional complement	X	-	X	-
Predicative complement	X	-	X	-
Verb	X	X	X	X
Paratactic root clause	X	X	X	X
Pero/mas 'but'	X	X	X	X
Subject	X	X	X	-*
Adverbial	X	X	X	X
Vocative	X	-	X	X
Coordination	X	X	X	X
Object NP (CLLD/HTLD)	X	X	X	X
Non-root/absolute clause	X	X	X	X

*: Wish contexts only

Table 4. Percentage of Proclisis in 16th c. Renaissance Spanish

	16th c.
Wh-word	100% (1/1)
Negation	100% (33/33)
Complement NP	100% (11/11)
Prepositional complement	100% (5/5)
Predicative complement	-
Verb	20% (3/15)
Paratactic root clause	100% (1/1)
Pero/mas 'but'	25% (1/4)
Subject	100% (67/67)
Adverbial	96% (73/76)
Vocative	100% (1/1)
Coordination	62% (31/50)
Object NP (CLLD/HTLD)	100% (17/17)
Non-root/absolute clause	38% (8/21)
Total	83% (252/302)

As Table 3 demonstrates, in 16th c. RenSp proclisis is also found in those very environments that had in MedSp been strictly enclitic: (i) those which contained a sentence-initial verb, (ii) a preceding paratactic root clause and (iii) those with a contrastive coordination marker *pero/mas* 'but', as exemplified respectively in (73)-(74), (75)-(76) and (77)-(78) for both non-imperative and imperative contexts.

(73) **Se** <u>dize</u> publicamente que
      CL says.3SG publicly that
      'Publicly it is being said that [...].' (*DLNE*: 1529.9)

(74) **Le** <u>deis</u> allá por él quarenta o çinquenta pesos
      CL give.2SG there for him forty or fifty pesos
      'Give him there forty or fifty pesos.' (*HDO*: IX, 14)

(75) *Asi mismo ha reçibido de Alonso Davila muchos cohechos speçial*
      likewise has.3SG received of Alonso Davila a-lot-of harvests especially
      en çierta compañia deflhazienda que tienen, **le** *haze   pagar*
      in certain company of estate that have.3PL CL makes.3SG pay
      las costas
      the costs
      'Likewise he received a lot of harvests from Alonso Davila, especially from a certain estate that they have, it makes him pay the costs.' (*DLNE*: 1529.9)

(76) *I ansí en esto como en todo lo demás que le tocare*
      and so in this as in all the rest that CL would-touch.3SG
      i vos le podáis hazer plazer lo hazed
      and you CL can.2SG do pleasure CL do.2SG
      'And so in this as well as in all the rest that concerns him and in which you could please him, do it.' (*HDO*: VI, 1)

(77) <u>pero</u> **se** hazen   ocho o diez géneros de atole
      but CL make.3PL eight or ten types of atole
      'But eight or ten types of *atole* are made.' (*Prob.Secr.*, *CORDE* s.v.*pero*)[22]

(78) <u>mas</u> **los** *rompan   luego*
      but   CL break.3PL afterwards
      'But break them afterwards.' (*ARC, CDE* s.v.*mas los*)

---

[22] *Atole* is a Mexican corn-starch based hot drink.

Examples (73) and (74) also show that in 16th c. RenSp the Tobler-Mussafia Law is no longer rigidly enforced, despite a clear preference for postverbal placement still remaining, as shown in Table 4 (see also [Arias Álvarez, 1996, p131]). Table 3 and 4 also reveal that nothing changed for the exclusively proclitic constructions compared to 13th and 14th c. MedSp. The variation environments, however, show an increase in the use of preverbal positioning, in spite of enclisis still remaining an option.

The higher frequency of proclisis for the variation environments in 16th c. RenSp is not simply due to a higher occurrence of those preverbal cases also found in MedSp, such as for instance coordination cases in which a preceding conjunct contains a proclisis-inducing constituent. For, as (79) and (80) exemplify respectively for the non-imperative and imperative coordination cases, RenSp can feature preverbal clitics despite lacking a proclisis-triggering constituent in a preceding conjunct:

(79) Y   porque   les suelo   reprehender, han   huido mjs
     And   because CL   use-to.1SG   tell-off   have.3PL fled   my
     sermones e   se van   a   banquetes cada   domingo
     sermons   and CL go.3PL   to feasts   every Sunday

   'And because I usually tell them off, they have fled my sermons and they go to parties every Sunday.' (*DLNE*:1529.7)

(80) A   buestro padre   y   madre   le   podes   dezir que   por
     to   your   father and mother   CL   can.2SG   tell   that due
     amor de Dios, que   me perdonen;   y   **le** da   mis
     love of God   that CL forgive.3PL and CL   give.2SG   my
     encomiendas
     greetings

   'To your father and mother, you can tell them that they for the love of God forgive me, and give them my greetings.' (*DLNE*:1574.44)

Similarly, for the CLLD/HTLD cases, we find proclitic cases that do not contain an emphatic *todo(s)/am(b)os*, as in (81)-(82) (see also [Bouzouita, 2007, p58; Keniston, 1937, p93]):

(81) <u>a otro</u>   **le** hazen   esclavo porque   hurtó   diez
     ACC other   CL   make.3PL   slave   because stole.3SG ten
     maçorcas de *maiz*
     cobs   of maize

   'Another one, they made him a slave because he stole ten cobs of maize.' (*DLNE*: 1525.1)

(82) <u>Al señor mi hermano</u>   **le**   diga   que
to-the gentleman my brother   CL   tell.2SG   that
'My brother, tell him that [...].' (*DLNE*: 1572.40)

And, for the preceding non-root/absolute clause environment, proclitic cases equally occur without the subordinating element *antes que*, that had previously been the trigger for proclisis:

(83) <u>Y porque tan bien acostunbrados a la carne humana,</u>   **les**   es
And because so good used to the meat human   CL   is.3SG
más   dulçe
more   sweet

'And because they are so used to [eating] human meat, they find it sweeter.' (*DLNE*: 1525.1)

(84) <u>Y trayendolos,</u>   **os**   venj [sic]   lo   más   presto   que
And bringing them   CL   come.2SG   the   more   fast   that
pudieredes
can.2SG

'And bringing them along, come the fastest you can.' (*DLNE*:1571.38)

Accordingly, the relatively restricted conditions under which proclisis was licensed in the MedSp variation environments no longer restrict preverbal placement in RenSp. In other words, the preverbal distribution is spreading. Observe as well that again no substantial differences have been found between clitic placement in non-imperative environments and imperative ones.

4   Clitic Placement in Modern Spanish

It should not be concluded from the previous that enclitic placement was on the wane. On the contrary, in ModSp, both proclitic and enclitic placement are retained. However, the circumstances which license this syntactic intra-speaker variation differ significantly from those found in earlier periods. Whereas in MedSp and RenSp pre- and postverbal positioning is attested both in imperative and non-imperative finite verb contexts, in ModSp the only available option for clitics in non-imperative environments is proclisis, as shown in (85)-(86). Notice also that, unlike in MedSp, ModSp does not have a restriction on sentence-initial clitics. Enclitic placement became restricted to imperative contexts, as exemplified in (87)-(88) and shown in Table 5, indicating that clitic placement in ModSp seems to be determined in some sense by the mood of the associated verb. Syntactic variation in clitic positioning is still observed in the imperative contexts. Notwithstanding this, this variation is not unrestricted but seems to depend on the syntactic environment, as shown in (87)-(90).

(85) ¿**Te** hacían   muchas   preguntas?
      CL made.3PL a-lot-of questions
      'Did they ask you a lot of questions?' (*Habla*: 2.30)

(86) *¿Hacían**te** muchas preguntas?
      made.3PL-CL a-lot-of questions
      Intended: 'Did they ask you a lot of questions?'

(87) Cuénta**me** cómo es
      tell.2SG-CL how is.3SG
      'Tell me how it is.' (*Habla*: 2.26)

(88) ***Me** cuenta cómo es
      CL tell.2SG how is.3SG
      Intended: 'Tell me how it is.'

(89) No **me** hables
      not CL talk.2SG
      'Don't talk to me.' (*Habla*: 2.22)

(90) *No hábles-/hábla-**me**
      not talk.2SG-CL
      Intended: 'Don't talk to me.'

Table 5. *Clitic Placement in 20th c. Modern Spanish*

	Non-imperatives		Imperatives	
	Proclisis	**Enclisis**	**Proclisis**	**Enclisis**
Wh-word	X	-	-	-
Negation	X	-	X	-
Complement NP	X	-	-	X
Prepositional complement	X	-	-	X
Predicative complement	X	-	-	X
Verb	X	-	-	X
Paratactic root clause	X	-	-	X
Pero/mas 'but'	X	-	-	X
Subject	X	-	X*	-*
Adverbial	X	-	X*	X
Vocative	X	-	-	X
Coordination	X	-	X*	X
Object NP (CLLD/HTLD)	X	-	-	X
Non-root/absolute clause	X	-	-	X

*: Wish contexts only

Table 6. Percentage of Proclisis in 20th c. Modern Spanish

	20th c.
Wh-word	100% (49/49)
Negation	100% (99/99)
Complement NP	100% (5/5)
Prepositional complement	100% (6/6)
Predicative complement	-
Verb	77% (115/150)
Paratactic root clause	82% (47/57)
Pero/mas 'but'	73% (11/15)
Subject	100% (101/101)
Adverbial	91% (170/186)
Vocative	-
Coordination	95% (79/83)
Object NP (CLLD/HTLD)	100% (24/24)
Non-root/absolute clause	91% (21/23)
Total	91% (727/798)

5 Diachronic Changes

5.1 Towards a Verb-Centered Clitic System

In sum, we have seen that syntactic variation in clitic positioning is observed not only in MedSp but also in RenSp and ModSp. This syntactic variation does not manifest itself in each of these clitic systems in the same way. This might be taken to suggest that different principles underly each of these clitic distributions; however, these are not categorically discrete distinctions.

Table 7. Percentage of Proclisis per Verbal Mood

	MedSp		RenSp	ModSp
	13th c.	14th c.	16th c.	20th c.
Non-imperatives	25% (446/1771)	32% (130/410)	88% (215/244)	100% (723/723)
Imperatives	24% (61/255)	36% (10/28)	64% (37/58)	5% (4/75)
Total	25% (507/2026)	32% (140/438)	83% (252/302)	91% (727/798)

As regards the diachronic changes, enclisis, the most frequently encountered position for MedSp clitics in root clauses, was only gradually replaced by proclisis in the non-imperative contexts, leading to ModSp in which enclisis is no longer a valid option for these environments. The imperative environments underwent a similar shift towards proclisis up until RenSp. Table 7 illustrates this diachronic shift in clitic placement throughout the history of Spanish per verbal mood (imperatives vs. non-imperatives). Recall also that RenSp clitics had in both imperative and non-imperative contexts a similar distribution, as did MedSp. Notwithstanding this, Table 7 shows that in RenSp proclisis was more prevalent for the non-imperative cases considering that 88% (215/244) of non-imperatives exhibit proclisis while only 64% (37/58) of imperative cases display this positioning. Similarly, [Keniston, 1937, p97] notes that for 16th c. imperatives 'the postposition of the pronoun becomes more and more the rule'. In other words, even though RenSp imperative and non-imperative environments exhibit the same syntactic variation (see Table 3), enclisis was used more frequently in imperative contexts in comparison with the non-imperative ones. This difference becomes even greater in ModSp – 100% (723/723) and 5% (4/75) respectively –, where enclisis is the only possible clitic position for commands (except for negative commands).[23] In sum, we can conclude that the ModSp clitic system, unlike the MedSp one, is a verb-centered clitic system with the distribution of clitics determined by the mood of its associated verb [Wanner, 1996].

5.2 Interpolation

Confirmation that the Spanish clitics shifted towards a verb-centered system comes also from the loss of interpolation. In ModSp, clitics have to be adjacent to the verb. Recall that in the MedSp clitic system, on the other hand, this was not the case for preverbal clitics. In MedSp, interpolated constituents can be found both in root and non-root clauses, as illustrated in (91) and (92) respectively (contra [Chenery, 1905]). Nonetheless, most examples proceed from non-root contexts given that in MedSp proclisis is found overwhelmingly in these environments whereas postverbal placement prevails in the root ones (see Table 7).[24]

(91)   Ont   *me*   [yo]   loo   mucho   de   la   tu   amor
       thus   CL   I   praise.1SG   a-lot   of   the   your   love
       'Thus I praise your love a lot.' (*Faz.*: 43)

---

[23] For more detailed information on clitic placement in the period from the 16th c. till 20th c., I refer the reader to [Bouzouita, forthcoming]. See also [Keniston, 1937; Parodi, 1979; Rubio Perea, 2004] for the 16th c., [Lesman St. Clair, 1980] for the 17th c., [Buffum, 1927] for the 19th c. and [Armijo Canto, 1985; Armijo Canto, 1992] for the 16th - 19th c. period.

[24] As regards the range of possible interpolating constituents, I refer the reader for MedSp to [Castillo Lluch, 1996, 1998; Chenery, 1905], and for RenSp to [Eberenz, 2000]. See [Bouzouita 2007, 2008, forthcoming] for DS analyses of interpolation.

(92) Et   esto que **te** [yo] [agora] mostrare   aqui
      and this that CL   I   now   will-show.1SG here

'And this that I will now show you here.' (*Gen.Est.I*: 324 apud [Sánchez Lancis, 1993, p327])

(93) **Le** [yo] daré
      CL   I   will-give.1SG

'I will give her [...].' (*Corbacho*: 264 apud [Company Company, 1985-6, p96])

Interpolation examples are also found in RenSp, despite no preceding initial triggering expression, as illustrated in (93). This example, which dates from 1438, displays novel preverbal placement along with interpolation. This seems to indicate that the appearance of sentence-initial clitics predates the loss of interpolation.[25] In my view, this observation is critical to understand the diachronic changes in Spanish clitic placement. In consequence, the view that Spanish only started allowing sentence-initial clitics once the clitic formed a complex unit with the immediately following verb (e.g. [Meyer Lübke, 1897], see also [Nieuwenhuijsen, 1999, p116, p149], summarized by the syntactic re-bracketing in (94), is simplistic and needs to be reformulated as in (95) since the former conflates different changes.[26] More specifically, (94) suggests that sentence-initial clitics are allowed only once interpolation is lost. However, examples such as (93) indicate that there was an intermediate step (X) + CL + (X) + V, as shown in (95), in which the occurrence of proclisis no longer depends on the preceding constituent nor is there necessary verbal adjacency.

(94) $[X + CL] + (X) + V \ > \ (X) + [CL + V]$

(95) $[X + CL] + (X) + V \ > \ (X) + CL + (X) + V \ > \ (X) + [CL + V]$

I acknowledge that examples such as (93) are rare. However, I do not find this surprising in view of the following. Firstly, the occurrence of interpolation decreases sharply after the 14th c. [Eberenz, 2000, p166]. Secondly, interpolation is hardly found in root clauses even in the 13th and 14th c., a period in which interpolation is relatively frequent in non-root clauses [Chenery, 1905; Castillo Lluch, 1996, 1998; Sánchez Lancis, 1993]. In consequence, the low occurrence of examples such as (93) is expected.

---

[25] The first uncontroversial indications that the restriction on sentence-initial unstressed pronouns is disappearing date from the beginning of the 15th c. (1438). The last known interpolation examples, on the other hand, are from the end of the 16th c. (1594) [Keniston, 1937, p101; Rini, 1990, pp362-363].

[26] Both (94) and (95) are syntactic representations and thus do not represent phonological cliticization.

It must be pointed out that, despite the existence of interpolation, the prevalent pattern is for the verb and not some interpolated constituent to immediately follow the clitic pronoun, even in MedSp ([Wanner, 1996] inter alia). [Castillo Lluch, 1996, pp310-314], for instance, registers for her corpus of MedSp – the period at which the use of interpolation is at its height – 53 interpolation cases out of a total of 245 complement clauses that could have displayed this phenomenon. In other words, only 22% of these examples exhibits interpolation (calculation is mine). As we shall see later on, the fact that the clitic pronoun is mostly followed by the verb will influence the diachronic development of Spanish clitic placement.

6 Dynamic Syntax Analyses

The accounts to be given for the MedSp, RenSp and ModSp clitic systems adopt the Dynamic Syntax framework (DS; [Kempson *et al.*, 2001; Cann *et al.*, 2005]).[27] DS is a grammar formalism that reflects the dynamics of parsing, with syntax defined as the incremental growth of semantic trees following the time-linear parsing/production process. These semantic trees represent a possible interpretation of the natural language string. Once the processing process is completed, the top node of the tree is decorated with some propositional formula and each daughter node with some sub-term of that formula, representing a predicate-argument structure. Various processing strategies i.e. different ways of building up semantic content for a natural language string, are made available. More specifically, DS licenses the construction of (i) fixed nodes, (ii) unfixed nodes, which represent structural underspecification (or functional uncertainty) and which can be constructed locally or non-locally, and (iii) linked structures, i.e. trees that are hooked together and often share semantic content (see [Cann and Kempson, this volume] for more details in connection with Latin). Moreover, as a set of strategies for parsing, the grammar standardly makes available more than one sequence of strategies for parsing a string with little or no difference in content associated with the distinct output structures. For example, in parsing a pro-drop language with case such as Latin, there are three strategies available for the parsing of a subject expression, as was displayed in [Cann and Kempson, this volume]. The subject expression may be parsed following the strategy available for parsing all argument expressions, which is to (i) construct an unfixed node merely indicating argumenthood, (ii) decorate it as indicated by the nominal, and (iii) then use case to immediately fix the structural relation as that of subject. The second strategy is to take that subject expression as providing a context relative to which the reminder is interpreted, that is in DS terms to build a linked structure decorated solely

---

[27] For a short introduction to DS, I refer the reader to [Cann and Kempson, this volume, section 3].

with information provided by the subject expression and use that structure as the point of departure for constructing an independent tree containing a proposition with subject agreement indicating the identification of that term with the already presented context. Finally, there is also the possibility of taking the subject expression to decorate a node initially constructed as unfixed that is not immediately updated, but rather is identified as subject only subsequent to parsing the verb, this decision to fully determine its role in the propositional structure at only this very late stage as the means of achieving a non-backgrounding/contrastive effect.

6.1 Medieval Spanish

In this section, I shall argue that it is the availability of these different strategies for processing the constituents preceding the clitics MedSp that govern clitic placement (extending analyses proposed in [Bouzouita, 2007; Bouzouita, 2008; Bouzouita and Kempson, 2006]. We shall see that preverbal placement is found after a disjunct set of triggers, to wit, whenever a negation marker, a tense marker, or a constituent that can be represented as structurally (syntactically) underspecified i.e. an expression decorating an unfixed node, precedes the weak pronoun. This cluster of triggers will thus be stored as part of the clitic pronoun's lexical specification. Postverbal pronouns, on the other hand, appear in the absence of these triggers, a complementary cluster of restrictions.

Strict Proclitic Constructions

More specifically, recall from section 2 that the various MedSp root clause environments in which only preverbal clitics occur are those with (i) a *wh*-word, (ii) a negation adverb, (iii) a non-coreferential complement NP, (iv) a prepositional or (v) a predicative complement. From a DS perspective, these environments, all except negation, share a structural property, that of involving an unfixed node.[28] Thus, after the starting point of the parse, **Adjunction* may construct an unfixed node which can then be decorated by one of these left-peripheral elements once its lexical actions have been processed, as illustrated in Figure 1 for a *wh*-question, such as example (9). A similar analysis can be given for the left-peripheral non-coreferential complement NPs, prepositional and predicative complements. Accordingly, these environments can also be analyzed as involving the introduction of an unfixed node, which the left-peripheral complement will then annotate, to be subsequently fixed within the emergent tree.

---

[28] Negation remains without formal characterization in DS. In view of this, I shall use the feature [NEG +] to mark the presence of a negation operator.

Figure 1. Parsing a Wh-Word

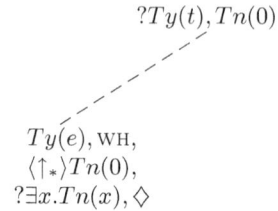

$?Ty(t), Tn(0)$

$Ty(e), \text{WH},$
$\langle\uparrow_*\rangle Tn(0),$
$?\exists x.Tn(x), \Diamond$

The DS analyses for non-root clauses also involve unfixed nodes, except for the complement clauses (see [Gregoromichelaki, 2005] for more details).

Strict Enclitic Constructions

The analyses for the strict postverbal constructions, on the other hand, do not involve structural underspecification nor do the complement clauses. Recall that the MedSp environments that always appeared with postverbal pronouns are those in which the verb appears in an absolute sentence-initial or paratactic position, or those constructions with *pero/mas* 'but'. These latter, for instance, are analyzed as different $Ty(t)$-trees between which a link relation has been established (without requirement for a copy of a formula). Once *pero/mas* introduces the linked structure, constructed as a quasi-independent tree linked only anaphorically, the verb is parsed and its lexical actions give the full subject-predicate template, decorate the subject-argument node with a metavariable (e.g. **U**) and then place the pointer at the newly constructed object-argument node decorated with the requirement $?Ty(e)$, as exemplified in Figure 2 for example (22). The postverbal pronoun can then decorate this fixed object node.

Figure 2. Parsing 'mas dixo-'

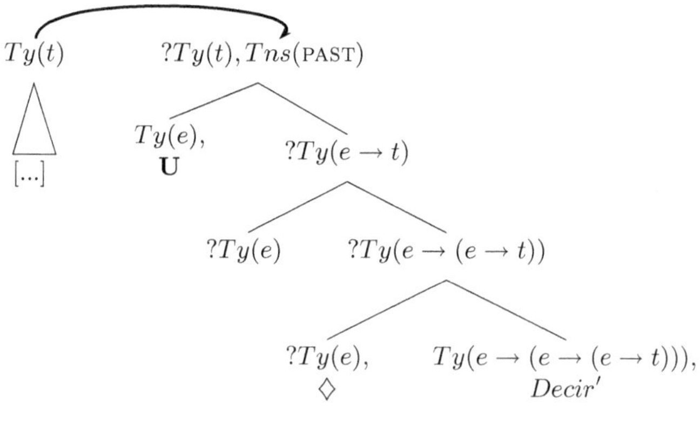

$Ty(t) \quad\quad ?Ty(t), Tns(\text{PAST})$

$[\ldots] \quad\quad Ty(e), \mathbf{U} \quad\quad ?Ty(e \rightarrow t)$

$?Ty(e) \quad\quad ?Ty(e \rightarrow (e \rightarrow t))$

$?Ty(e), \Diamond \quad\quad Ty(e \rightarrow (e \rightarrow (e \rightarrow t))), Decir'$

Observe that in these analyses the postverbal clitics pattern with postverbal complement NPs both only decorating a fixed argument node within the tree (see also [Rivero, 1991; Bouzouita, 2008; Bouzouita, forthcoming]). The analyses for the other two strict postverbal constructions are very similar as, in these, the lexical specifications of the verb will also build the full subject-predicate structure and leave the pointer at the (in)direct object node. The only difference is that, unlike the *pero/mas* constructions, these do not involve linked structures.

Variation Constructions

We can now see that, with alternative processing strategies being presumed to be available, variation in clitic placement is expected, given its sensitivity to particular parsing choices. More specifically, the analyses of certain left-peripheral expressions involve the construction either of an unfixed node (triggering preverbal placement), or of fixed nodes with/without linked structures (triggering postverbal positioning). Preverbal subjects, for instance, can be represented in subject-pro-drop languages such as Spanish, as decorating a (locally) unfixed node or a $Ty(e)$-linked structure with a requirement for a shared formula, since the lexical specifications of the verb decorate the subject node with a metavariable as an anaphoric placeholder, exactly as though a morphologically expressed pronoun were present.

Figure 3. Parsing Possibilities for Left-Peripheral Subjects

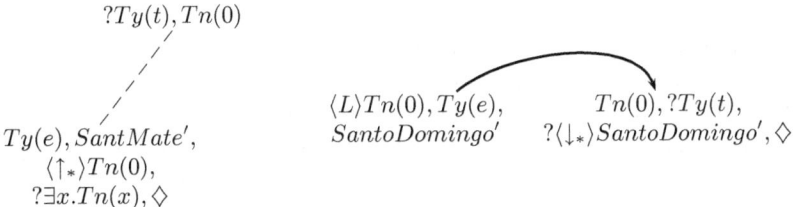

Relative to this first alternative, if the subject is then processed as decorating an unfixed node, this unfixed node will merge later on in the parse with the subject node which the verb introduced and annotated with a metavariable, as shown on the left-hand side in Figure 3 for the left-peripheral subject *Sant Mate* 'Saint Matthew' in (27). Relative to the second alternative, if the subject is parsed/produced as a $Ty(e)$-linked structure, the subject metavariable introduced by the verb will duly be replaced by a term that is identical to whatever decorates the linked structure, fulfilling its requirement for a shared term, as illustrated on the right-hand side in Figure 3 for example (26).

The same alternative strategies are expected to be available for the left-peripheral constituents in other variation constructions. The intra-speaker variation between preverbal and postverbal clitic placement within the same syntactic environment is thus expected; and, equally, the heterogeneous positioning in these environments does not pose a problem. More generally, MedSp clitic placement seems indeed to be regulated by different processing strategies used for the constituents preceding the clitics. Preverbal placement is encountered when a negation marker, a tense marker or a constituent decorating a left-peripheral unfixed node, precedes the unstressed pronoun. Postverbal weak pronoun positioning, on the contrary, occurs in the absence of these triggers.

Lexical Characterization of Clitic Pronouns

Now that the various clitic environments have been examined and their respective analyses introduced, I shall discuss the lexical characterization of the MedSp clitic. We saw in section 2.1 that Granberg [1988], for instance, observed that pragmatic considerations were at the basis of the MedSp subject environments, as the appearance of preverbal pronouns is associated with a focus reading of the preceding subject. I go further by claiming that the whole MedSp clitic system can be seen as a consequence of the encoding of a pragmatically driven strategy, as we shall see shortly (see also [Bouzouita, forthcoming; Cann and Kempson, this volume; Kempson and Cann, 2007]). As has been noted in the literature, Latin weak pronouns occur close to the left-edge of a clause ([Adams, 1994; Devine and Stephens, 2006; Janse, 2000] inter alia). Moreover, they follow a structurally heterogeneous set of categories, very similar to the triggers for occurrence of MedSp unstressed pronouns (e.g. following negative expressions, verbs etc.). In my view, the positioning of these Latin weak pronouns can be explained in terms of minimizing production costs. As in all other languages, Latin anaphoric expressions enable argument terms to be identified independently of the verb and often appear early in the clause. In relying on context, speakers/hearers need the search for a substituend to be over as small a domain as possible, by general relevance considerations minimizing cognitive cost [Sperber and Wilson, 1995]. Accordingly, unless there is reason to the contrary, the position of an anaphoric expression requiring context-identification is as early as possible in the setting out of propositional structure - quite literally, a minimization of what constitutes the context (see also [Bouzouita, forthcoming; Cann and Kempson, this volume; Kempson and Cann, 2007]). It is this relevance-driven distribution that became calcified in the lexical specification of the clitic pronoun through a routinization process. Being phonologically weak, clitics need some other expression to co-occur with, unlike their strong-pronoun counterparts. This other expression must involve the initiation of a new propositional domain in order that the clitic itself will occur as close as possible to the domain within which its antecedent is to be found (the relevance-based constraint). It is the requirement for this structural trigger and the actions inducing an early tree relation for the clitic to decorate that becomes routinized, itself a means of ensuring processing economy [Pickering and Garrod, 2004, p181]. The most well-known examples of routines are the non-productive ones such as idioms (e.g. *kick the bucket*), whereby the component words get stored as a complex in the lexicon. In the lexical entry for the MedSp clitic, it is the pragmatic basis of weak pronoun placement that got stored in the lexicon: the requirement of its structural trigger, and the actions inducing the tree node for it to decorate. Accordingly, the once fully pragmatic basis for determining the tree growth process associated with the unstressed pronouns got replaced with a sequence of tree growth actions specific to the individual (clitic) pronouns. MedSp clitic distribution is then no longer determined simply by pragmatic reasoning itself as this has got shortcut by the presence of such a lexically stored sequence of actions. An immediate consequence of this routinization process is that the pragmatic basis can atrophy and eventually vanish, as happened in the period between MedSp and RenSp, a matter I shall return to in due course. Another consequence of this routinization is that the lexical encoding of the clitic is highly disjunctive, the only property held in common by the different triggers for clitic placement being that they all reflect confirmation that an emergent propositional boundary has definitively been established. As Figure 4 illustrates, the lexical entry of the MedSp accusative clitic *lo* reflects this lexical calcification of the earlier pragmatic basis since preverbal pronouns can only be constructed in the presence of a negation marker, an unfixed node or a requirement for a tense marker whereas the postverbal ones only occur in the absence of such triggers.[29]

It should be noted that both preverbal and postverbal accusative clitics are taken to annotate fixed object nodes.[30] The nodes decorated by the postverbal clitics have been introduced by the lexical specification of the verb, as discussed earlier (see Figure 2). Those being annotated by proclitics, on the other hand, have been constructed by the lexical entry of the weak pronoun itself due to the lexical calcification of the accusative case in Old Romance. The self-evident complexity of the disjunctive form is what then gets progressively simplified, as we can now see with a characterization of the RenSp *lo*.

---

[29]This account assumes that complementisers annotate the $?Ty(t)$-node of the complement clause with a requirement for a tense marker ($?\exists x.Tns(x)$). No such assumption is necessary for the other non-root clauses if one adopts [Gregoromichelaki, 2005]'s account, which involves the construction of an unfixed node.

[30]Not all clitics involve the construction of a fixed argument node. In leísta dialects, for instance, the clitic *le* will be taken to introduce and annotate a locally unfixed node due to its case ambiguity (see also [Bouzouita, forthcoming]).

Figure 4. Lexical Entry of Medieval Spanish Accusative Clitic 'lo'

P	IF	$?Ty(t)$,		
R		$Tn(a)$		
O	THEN	IF	$[NEG+] \lor$	} Negative marker
C			$(\langle\downarrow_*\rangle Fo(\alpha), ?\exists x.Tn(x)) \lor$	} unfixed node
L			$?\exists x.Tns(x)$	} Tense requirement
I		THEN	$make(\langle\downarrow_1\rangle\langle\downarrow_0\rangle)$,	
S			$go(\langle\downarrow_1\rangle\langle\downarrow_0\rangle)$,	
I			$put(Fo(\mathbf{U}), Ty(e)$,	
S			$?\exists x.Fo(x)$,	
			$[\downarrow]\bot, ?\langle\uparrow_0\rangle Ty(e \to t))$	
		ELSE	ABORT	
E	ELSE	IF	$?Ty(e), \langle\uparrow\rangle\top$	
N		THEN	IF	$(\langle\uparrow_0\rangle\langle\uparrow^1_*\rangle(?Ty(t) \land [NEG+])) \lor$
C				$(\langle\uparrow_0\rangle\langle\uparrow^1_*\rangle(?Ty(t) \land \langle\downarrow_*\rangle(Fo(\alpha),$
L				$?\exists x.Tn(x)))) \lor$
I				$(\langle\uparrow_0\rangle\langle\uparrow^1_*\rangle(?Ty(t) \land \langle\uparrow\rangle\top))$
S			THEN	ABORT
I			ELSE	$put(Fo(\mathbf{U}), Ty(e), ?\exists x.Fo(x)$,
S				$[\downarrow]\bot, ?\langle\uparrow_0\rangle Ty(e \to t))$
		ELSE	ABORT	

6.2 Renaissance Spanish

In RenSp, recall, a much freer use of proclisis is found. This can be faithfully reflected in the DS characterization.

Figure 5. Lexical Entry of Renaissance Spanish Accusative Clitic 'lo'

P	IF	$?Ty(t), Tn(a)$		
R	THEN	$make(\langle\downarrow_1\rangle\langle\downarrow_0\rangle)$,		
O		$go(\langle\downarrow_1\rangle\langle\downarrow_0\rangle)$,		
C		$put(Fo(\mathbf{U}), Ty(e)$,		
L.		$?\exists x.Fo(x)$,		
		$[\downarrow]\bot, ?\langle\uparrow_0\rangle Ty(e \to t))$		
E	ELSE	IF	$?Ty(e), \langle\uparrow\rangle\top$	
N		THEN	IF	$(\langle\uparrow_0\rangle\langle\uparrow^1_*\rangle(?Ty(t) \land [NEG+])) \lor$
C				$(\langle\uparrow_0\rangle\langle\uparrow^1_*\rangle(?Ty(t) \land \langle\downarrow_*\rangle(Fo(\alpha),$
L.				$?\exists x.Tn(x)))) \lor$
				$(\langle\uparrow_0\rangle\langle\uparrow^1_*\rangle(?Ty(t) \land \langle\uparrow\rangle\top))$
			THEN	ABORT
			ELSE	$put(Fo(\mathbf{U}), Ty(e), ?\exists x.Fo(x)$,
				$[\downarrow]\bot, ?\langle\uparrow_0\rangle Ty(e \to t))$
		ELSE	ABORT	

The major change between lexical specification for *lo* in MedSp and RenSp is the loss of proclisis constraints, while retaining the disjunctive specification constraining enclisis placement. A notable property of this lexical entry is its disjunctive nature, with a cluster of triggering environments. This is strikingly redolent of the clustering property of lexical meanings as they emerge in semantic change environments (see [Larsson, this volume]). This lexical entry reflects directly the fact that all MedSp exclusively enclitic environments in the intervening period acquired the possibility of also licensing preverbal pronouns (see section 3). As this specification shows, this was due to a relatively small change in the lexical entry of the weak pronoun: the so-called proclisis triggers that were present in MedSp (the presence of a negation marker, an unfixed node or a tense requirement) are dropped from the RenSp characterization, as shown in Figure 5. The immediate result of the loss of these triggers is the occurrence of proclisis in substantially more environments: RenSp clitics can appear preverbally as long as there is a $?Ty(t)$-requirement. Note however that the same does not apply to the occurrence of enclitics, as these restrictions remain unchanged. The diachronic shift from using predominantly enclisis to proclisis is thus modelled in this account as the simplification of the lexical characterization of the clitic pronoun. Perhaps surprisingly, the effect of this lexical simplification is not a more simplified distribution, as what emerges is a greater number of environments in RenSp that exhibit syntactic variation.

There remains the question why this simplification in the lexical entry occurred. Recall that DS regularly makes available more than one strategy for interpretation: for the variation environments in particular, (i) the strategy of building a pair of linked structures, with the left-peripheral NP decorating that first linked tree as an independent structure, and, in addition, (ii) the strategy of inducing the construction of an unfixed node for that left-peripheral expression to decorate. Recall also that once routinization took place in MedSp, the original pragmatic motivation underpinning weak pronoun placement gradually disappeared, as it had been shortcut. With no pragmatic basis or intonation cues present, there is then nothing to determine which of these two processing strategies to select. Accordingly, a processing mismatch between speaker and hearer is then plausible for these variation environments. In particular, the change could have happened because dialogue exchanges are never algorithmically determinable. The left-peripheral subject in a sentence containing a preverbal clitic, for instance, can be produced relative to a strategy for building and annotating an unfixed node, as in the left-hand side of Figure 3 (see [Purver et al., 2006] for a DS characterization of generation). The hearer, on the other hand, can parse this subject as annotating a $Ty(e)$-linked structure, as in the right-hand side of Figure 3. Once the preverbal clitic has been heard, the hearer has two processing choices: (i) they can access the lexical entry for MedSp clitics and notice that the left-peripheral subject should have been parsed as an unfixed node due to the occurrence of this preverbal pronoun and consequently choose to parse this subject as an unfixed node instead or (ii) they can ignore this MedSp lexical entry and infer that proclitic pronouns are allowed after linked structures since that is how they just parsed the left-peripheral subject. In the latter option, the hearer will have effectively reanalyzed the lexical entry for the weak pronoun as given in Figure 5. In other words, a production-parsing mismatch in the variation environments could accordingly have led to the inference that there are no conditions on the occurrence of preverbal pronouns. Once the hearer has made such a move, and indeed has done so on a recurrent basis, this reanalysis could be used as the basis for a production decision, thereby confirming a shift of analysis in the system itself. Notice further that this production-parsing mismatch, restricted to taking place in variation environments only, led to the reanalysis of the weak pronoun's lexical entry, hence affecting all the other environments as well. Furthermore, such a reanalysis can only take place once the original pragmatic reasoning behind weak pronoun placement vanished and with it its specific intonation patterns. Such atrophying has been attributed to the routinization process whereby the pragmatic considerations becoming lexically calcified. Importantly, this reanalysis does not affect interpolation which is still observed in RenSp; it only affects the Tobler-Mussafia pattern. In other words, while the restriction on sentence-initial weak pronouns is loosened, verbal adjacency is still not required in RenSp.

6.3 Modern Spanish

As mentioned in section 5.2, despite the existence of interpolation, the verb and not some interpolated constituent follow most frequently the MedSp preverbal clitic pronoun. This pattern becomes even more widely used once the occurrence rate of interpolation decreases after the 14th c. [Eberenz, 2000, p166]. This predominance of the verb following the clitic pronoun is all that is needed to provide the grounds for a second step of routinization, whereby the actions of the clitic get stored alongside information on the following verb, as shown in Figure 6. In other words, a second reanalysis takes place whereby the positioning of the clitic becomes associated with the mood of the verb, as seen in ModSp, where enclisis in finite contexts is now only allowed with imperative verbs (by the feature IMP). When comparing Figure 5 and 6, one will notice that, apart from this imperative feature another small change took place in the lexical entry of the clitic: to wit, two 'negative triggers', previously present in the enclisis part, vanished. These two negative triggers prevented in MedSp and RenSp postverbal clitics from appearing after tense markers or unfixed nodes.

Figure 6. Lexical Entry of Modern Spanish Accusative Clitic 'lo'

P	IF	$?Ty(t), Tn(a)$	
R	THEN	$make(\langle\downarrow_1\rangle\langle\downarrow_0\rangle),$	
O		$go(\langle\downarrow_1\rangle\langle\downarrow_0\rangle),$	
C		$put(Fo(\mathbf{U}), Ty(e),$	
L.		$?\exists x.Fo(x),$	
		$[\downarrow]\bot, ?\langle\uparrow_0\rangle Ty(e \rightarrow t))$	
E	ELSE IF	$?Ty(e), \langle\uparrow\rangle\top,$	
N		$\langle\uparrow_0\rangle\langle\uparrow_1\rangle IMP$	
C		THEN IF	$\langle\uparrow_0\rangle\langle\uparrow_*^1\rangle(?Ty(t) \wedge [NEG+])$
L.		THEN	ABORT
		ELSE	$put(Fo(\mathbf{U}), Ty(e), ?\exists x.Fo(x),$
			$[\downarrow]\bot, ?\langle\uparrow_0\rangle Ty(e \rightarrow t))$
		ELSE ABORT	

Dating this second routinization is not that straightforward. However, we saw that the appearance of novel proclisis cases predates the loss of interpolation, as exemplified by example (93) in section 5.2. In consequence, we can conclude that the reanalysis whereby the proclisis triggers get lost predates the completion of the routinization process which results in a system in which the clitic positioning is determined by the mood of the verb along which it appears. Once again, a cognitive economy measure seems to be responsible for one of the diachronic changes observed in Spanish clitic placement.

7 Conclusion

In conclusion, I have argued that MedSp clitic placement is governed by different processing (producing/parsing) strategies i.e. different ways of building up semantic content. More specifically, preverbal placement is observed when the clitic is preceded by a negation marker, a tense marker or a structurally underspecified constituent, whereas postverbal pronouns are precluded from arising after these triggers but occur in all other environments (fixed nodes/linked structures). Accordingly, MedSp placement is no longer governed by pragmatic considerations but by different processing (producing/parsing) strategies since the original pragmatic underpinning became routinized i.e. lexically calcified in the weak pronoun characterization in order to create a processing shortcut. Furthermore, syntactic variation between preverbal and postverbal clitic positioning within one and the same syntactic environment is expected since different processing strategies are made available for any one sequence of words to be parsed. Accordingly, we can conclude that processing factors contribute to the syntactic intra-speaker variation observed in the MedSp clitic system.

As concerns the diachronic changes, a diffusion of preverbal pronouns was observed in RenSp as those environments that were previously strictly postverbal started using preverbal pronouns as well. This was attributed to a reanalysis of the lexical characterization of the clitic pronoun: namely, the loss of restrictions on the occurrence of preverbal pronouns. Additionally, once the pragmatic reasoning behind clitic placement vanished (due to routinization), the various processing strategies could have played a role in this diachronic change since their availability within one syntactic environment makes a processing mismatch between speaker and hearer possible. On the assumption that the routinization process has consolidated into a fixed encoding, any such processing mismatch would have to result in a reanalysis of the lexical entry of the clitic pronoun, which if buttressed by further use would lead to loss of restrictions on preverbal placement. We can thus conclude that routinization – the cognitive shortcuts whereby whole chunks of pragmatic or computational actions become lexically stored – played an important role in the syntactic changes that occurred between MedSp and RenSp. Similarly, routinization is responsible for the second reanalysis which led to the ModSp system, in which the clitic position becomes associated with the mood of the verb, since the actions of the clitic got stored alongside information on the following verb.

More generally, it has been shown that it is essential to take into account (i) the interdependency of syntax, semantics and pragmatics, and (ii) the time-linear processing aspect of parsing and production in order to obtain a better understanding of language change in view of the following. Firstly, the pragmatic basis for the syntactic variation in weak pronoun placement, already present in Latin, became lexically encoded for the MedSp clitics, which led to the fade-out of this pragmatic basis (and its associated intonation patterns). Accordingly, the diachronic changes in clitic placement in the history of Spanish cannot be fully understood if one does not take into account the intertwinement of syntax, semantics and pragmatics. Secondly, we saw that a subsequent production-parsing mismatch could have given rise to the reanalysis of the lexical entry of the clitic, whose preverbal placement became interpreted as not having any restrictions in RenSp, resulting thus in the spread of proclisis across other environments. In other words, the diachronic account given here does not only take into consideration the fact that the possible interpretation(s) of a natural language string is/are built up progressively but, more importantly, is based on the assumption that a processing mismatch can result in a reanalysis, without having a complete breakdown in communication since both speaker and hearer will end up with the same semantic interpretation of the string in question. Such a processing mismatch is possible due to the availability of various processing strategies for the same string. Accordingly, the availability of various processing strategies also played a role in the diachronic changes observed in Spanish clitic placement.

Sources

ARC = Saint Juan of Ávila (1499-1569) , *Avisos y reglas cristianas ... compuestas ... sobre aquel verso de David : audi, filia ...*, BVMC, Alicante, 1999.
http://www.cervantesvirtual.com/FichaObra.html?Ref=1535

BMlg. = Gonzalo de Berceo (1195-1253?), *Milagros de Nuestra Señora*, BVMC, Alicante, 2005.
http://www.cervantesvirtual.com/FichaObra.html?Ref=13691

BVMC = *Biblioteca Virtual Miguel de Cervantes*,
http://www.cervantesvirtual.com/

CDE = *Corpus del Español*,
http://www.corpusdelespanol.org/

Cid = Anonymous (12th c.), *Poema de Mio Cid*, edition of C. Smith, Cátedra, Madrid, 1987.

Cid2 = Anonymous (12th c.), *Cantar de Mio Cid*, edition of R. Menéndez Pidal, Espasa Calpe, Madrid, 1946.

Cid3 = Anonymous (12th c.), *Cantar de Mio Cid*, BVMC, Alicante, 2003.
http://www.cervantesvirtual.com/FichaObra.html?Ref=10379\
&portal=68

Corbacho = Alfonso Martínez de Toledo (1398-1470?), *Arcipreste de Talavera o Corbacho*, edition of J. González Muela, Castalia, Madrid, 1970.

CORDE = *Corpus Diacrónico del Espannol*,
http://corpus.rae.es/cordenet.html

DLNE = C. Company. *Documentos lingüísticos de la Nueva España: Altiplano central*. Universidad Nacional Autónoma de México, Mexico, 1994.

EE = Alfonso X el Sabio (1252-1284), *Primera Crónica General de España [Estoria de España]*, edition of R. Menéndez Pidal, Gredos, Madrid, 1977.

EG = Anonymous (1243-1271), *Estoria de los godos*, BNC Ms. 302.

Est.Esp.II = Alfonso X el Sabio (1252-1284), *Estoria de España II, MC*, Escorial Monasterio X-I-4.

Faz. = Almeric, Arçidiano de Antiochia (begin 13th c.), *La Fazienda de Ultra Mar* = [Lazar, 1965]

Gen.Est.I = Alfonso X el Sabio (1252-1284), *General Estoria I*, edition of A.G. Solalinde, Centro de Estudios Históricos, Madrid, 1930.

Gen.Est.IV = Alfonso X el Sabio (1252-1284), *General Estoria IV, MC*, Roma Vaticana Urb lat 539.

GranConq. = Anonymous (13th c.), *Gran Conquista de Ultramar, MC*, Salamanca Giesser 1503-06-21.

Habla = J. M. Lope Blanch. *El habla de la Ciudad de México*. Universidad Nacional Autónoma de México, Mexico, 1971.

HDO = J. M. Lope Blanch. *El habla de Diego de Ordaz: contribución a la historia del español americano (2nd edition)*. Universidad Nacional Autónoma de México, Mexico, 1998.

Hist.Troy. = Leomarte (mid 14th c.), *Sumas de Historia Troyana*, edition of A. Rey, *Revista de filología española*, Anejo XV, Madrid, 1932.

LPal. = Pedro López de Ayala (1378-1403), *Libro de Palacio, BVMC*, Alicante, 2004.
http://www.cervantesvirtual.com/FichaObra.html?Ref=383

Luc. = Don Juan Manuel (1330-1335), *Libro del conde Lucanor, MC*, BNC Ms. 6376.

MC = Electronic Texts and Concordances of the Madison Corpus of Early Spanish Manuscripts and Printings. Prepared by John O'Neill. Hispanic Seminary of Medieval Studies, Madison/New York, 1999. CD-ROM.

Prob.Secr. = J. de Cárdenas (1591), *Primera parte de los problemas y secretos maravillosos de las Indias*, re-published by CILUS, Salamanca, 2000.

SDom. = Gonzalo de Berceo (1195-1253?), *Vida de Santo Domingo de Silos*, *BVMC*, Alicante, 2005.
http://www.cervantesvirtual.com/FichaObra.html?Ref=516

BIBLIOGRAPHY

[Adams, 1994] J. Adams. Wackernagel's Law and the Position of Unstressed Personal Pronouns in Classical Latin. *Transactions of the Philological Society* 92: 103–178, 1994.
[Álvarez Blanco et al., 1986] R. Álvarez Blanco, X. L. Regueira, and H. Monteagudo. *Gramática Galega*. Editorial Galaxia, Vigo, 1986.
[Arias Álvarez, 1995] B. Arias Álvarez. Colocación de los pronombres átonos en el 'Libro de los gatos'. In A. González, L. Von der Walde and C. Company (eds), *Palabra e imagen en la Edad Media*, 113–125. Universidad Nacional Autónoma de México, Mexico, 1995.
[Arias Álvarez, 1996] B. Arias Álvarez. El orden de colocación de los clíticos pronominales durante la primera mitad del siglo XVI. *Revista de Humanidades* 1: 128–137, 1996.
[Armijo Canto, 1985] C.E. Armijo Canto. *Colocación de los pronombres átonos lo, la, le durante los siglos XVI al XIX en documentos mexicanos*. Licenciatura Dissertation, Universidad Nacional Autónoma de México, Mexico, 1985.
[Armijo Canto, 1992] C.E. Armijo Canto. Colocación de los pronombres átonos lo, la, le durante los siglos XVI al XIX en documentos mexicanos. In L. Traill (ed.), *Scripta philologica: in honorem Juan M. Lope Blanch*, vol. 1, 213–260. Universidad Nacional Autónoma de México, Mexico, 1992.
[Barry, 1987] A.K. Barry. Clitic Pronoun Position in Thirteenth-Century Spanish. *Hispanic Review* 55: 213–220, 1987.
[Bouzouita and Kempson, 2006] M. Bouzouita and R. Kempson. Clitic Placement in Old and Modern Spanish: a Dynamic Account. In O. Nedergaard Thomsen (ed.), *Competing Models of Linguistic Change*, 253–268. John Benjamins, Amsterdam/Philadelphia, 2006.
[Bouzouita, 2007] M. Bouzouita. Processing Factors in Syntactic Variation and Change: Clitics in Medieval and Renaissance Spanish. In J. Salmons and S. Dubenion-Smith (eds), *Historical Linguistics 2005: Selected papers from the 17th International Conference on Historical Linguistics, Madison, 31 July - 5 August 2005*, 51–71. John Benjamins, Amsterdam/Philadelphia, 2007.
[Bouzouita, 2008] M. Bouzouita. Modelling Syntactic Variation. *Diálogo de la lengua* 1, 15-39, 2008. http://www.dialogodelalengua.com/articulo/numero1.html
[Bouzouita, forthcoming] M. Bouzouita. *The Diachronic Development of Spanish Clitic Placement*. PhD Dissertation, King's College London, forthcoming.
[Buffum, 1927] M.E. Buffum. The Post-Positive Pronoun in Spanish. *Hispania* 10.3: 181-188, 1927.
[Cann et al., 2005] R. Cann, R. Kempson, and L. Marten. *The Dynamics of Language*. Elsevier, Oxford, 2005.
[Cann and Kempson, this volume] R. Cann and R. Kempson. Production Pressures, Syntacic Change and the Emergence of Clitic Pronouns. In R. Cooper and R. Kempson, editors, *Language in Flux: Dialogue Coordination, Language Variation, Language Change and Evolution*. Kings College Press, this volume.
[Castillo Lluch, 1996] M. Castillo Lluch. *La posición del pronombre átono en la prosa hispánica medieval*. PhD Dissertation, Universidad Autónoma de Madrid, 1996.
[Castillo Lluch, 1998] M. Castillo Lluch. La interpolación en español antiguo. In C. García Turza, F. González and J. Mangado (eds), *Actas del IV Congreso Internacional de Historia de la Lengua Española*, vol. I, 409–422. Universidad de la Rioja, Logroño, 1998.
[Chenery, 1905] W. Chenery. Object-Pronouns in Dependent Clauses: a Study in Old Spanish Word-Order. *Publications of the Modern Language Association* 20: 1–151, 1905.
[Company Company, 1985-6] C. Company Company. Los futuros en el español medieval. Sus orígenes y su evolución. *Nueva Revista de Filología Hispánica* 34.1: 48–108, 1985-6.
[Devine and Stephens, 2006] J. Devine and L. Stephens. *Latin Word Order: Structured Meaning and Information*. Oxford University Press, Oxford, 2006.
[Eberenz, 2000] R. Eberenz. *El español en el otoño de la Edad Media: sobre el artículo y los pronombres*. Gredos, Madrid, 2000.
[Elvira, 1987] J. Elvira. Enclisis pronominal y posición del verbo en español antiguo. *Epos* 3: 63–79, 1987.

[Fontana, 1993] J. Fontana. *Phrase Structure and the Syntax of Clitics in the History of Spanish*. PhD Dissertation, University of Pennsylvania, 1993.
[Gessner, 1893] E. Gessner. Das spanische Personal-pronomen. *Zeitschrift für romanische Philologie* 17: 1–54, 1893.
[Granberg, 1988] R. Granberg. *Object Pronoun Position in Medieval and Early Modern Spanish*. PhD Dissertation, University of California, Los Angeles, 1988.
[Granberg, 1999] R. Granberg. Clitic Position in Thirteenth-Century Spanish: Sentences with Preverbal Subject. *La corónica* 27.2: 89-113, 1999.
[Gregoromichelaki, 2005] E. Gregoromichelaki. *Conditionals in Dynamic Syntax*. PhD Dissertation, King's College London, 2005.
[Janse, 2000] M. Janse. Convergence and Divergence in the Development of the Greek and Latin Clitic Pronouns. In R. Sornicola, E. Poppe and A. Shisha Ha-Levy (eds), *Stability, Variation and Change of Word-Order Patterns over Time*, 231–258. John Benjamins, Amsterdam/Philadelphia, 2000.
[Jensen, 2003] B. Jensen. Syntax and Semantics of Imperative Subjects. In A. Dahl, K. Bentzen and P. Svenonius (eds), *Nordlyd: Proceedings of the 19th Scandinavian Conference of Linguistics*, 31.1: 150–164, 2003.
[Kempson et al., 2001] R. Kempson, W. Meyer-Viol, and D. Gabbay. *Dynamic Syntax*. Blackwell, Oxford, 2001.
[Kempson and Cann, 2007] R. Kempson and R. Cann. Dynamic Syntax and Dialogue: Preliminaries for a Dialogue-driven Account of Syntactic Change. In J. Salmons and S. Dubenion-Smith (eds), *Historical Linguistics 2005: Selected papers from the 17th International Conference on Historical Linguistics, Madison, 31 July - 5 August 2005*, 73–103. John Benjamins, Amsterdam/Philadelphia, 2007.
[Keniston, 1937] H. Keniston. *The Syntax of Castilian Prose: the Sixteenth Century*. University of Chicago Press, Chicago, 1937.
[Larsson, this volume] S. Larsson. Formalizing the Dynamics of Semantic Systems of Dialogue. In R. Cooper and R. Kempson, editors, *Language in Flux: Dialogue Coordination, Language Variation, Language Change and Evolution*. Kings College Press, this volume.
[Lazar, 1965] M. Lazar. *La Fazienda de Ultra Mar: Biblia Romanceada et Itinéraire Biblique en Prose Castillane du XIIe Siècle*. Universidad de Salamanca, Salamanca, 1965.
[Lesman St. Clair, 1980] A. Lesman St. Clair. *El pronombre átono en la prosa española del siglo XVII*. PhD Dissertation, University of Maryland, 1980.
[Martins, 2003] A.-M. Martins. From Unity to Diversity in Romance Syntax: Portuguese and Spanish. In K. Braunmüller and G. Ferraresi (eds), *Multilingualism in European Language History*, 201-233. John Benjamins, Amsterdam/Philadelphia, 2002.
[Meyer Lübke, 1897] W. Meyer Lübke. Zur Stellung der tonlosen Objektspronomina. *Zeitschrift für romanische Philologie* 16: 313–334, 1897.
[Nieuwenhuijsen, 1999] D. Nieuwenhuijsen. *Cambios en la colocación de los pronombres átonos en la historia del español*. PhD Dissertation, University of Groningen, 1999. http://elies.rediris.es/elies5/
[Nieuwenhuijsen, 2002] D. Nieuwenhuijsen. Variación de la colocación de los pronombres átonos en el español antiguo. *Zeitschrift für romanische Philologie* 118: 360–375, 2002.
[Nieuwenhuijsen, 2006] D. Nieuwenhuijsen. La colocación de los pronombres átonos. In C. Company (ed.), *Sintaxis histórica del español*, vol. 2, 1337-1404. Fondo de Cultura Económica & Universidad Nacional Autónoma de México, Mexico, 2006.
[Parodi, 1979] C. Parodi. Orden de los pronombres átonos durante el primer cuarto del siglo XVI en el español novohispano. *Nueva revista de filología hispánica* 28: 312–317.
[Pickering and Garrod, 2004] M. Pickering and S. Garrod. Towards a Mechanistic Psychology of Dialogue. *Behavioral and Brain Sciences* 27: 169–226, 2004.
[Purver et al., 2006] M. Purver, R. Cann, and R. Kempson. Grammars as Parsers: Meeting the Dialogue Challenge. *Research on Language and Computation* 4.2-3: 289–326, 2006.
[Ramsden, 1963] H. Ramsden. *Weak-Pronoun Position in the Early Romance Languages*. Manchester University Press, Manchester, 1963.

[Rini, 1990]   J. Rini.   Dating the Grammaticalization of the Spanish Clitic Pronoun. *Zeitschrift für romanische Philologie* 56.3-4: 350–370, 1990.
[Rivero, 1991]   M. L. Rivero. Clitic and NP Climbing in Old Spanish. In H. Campos and F. Martínez-Gil (eds), *Current Studies in Spanish Linguistics*, 241–282. Georgetown University Press, Washington D.C., 1991.
[Rubio Perea, 2004]   E. Rubio Perea. La posición del pronombre personal átono en un manuscrito del siglo XVI: 'las ordenanzas de Canena' 1544. *Interlingüística* 15.2: 1207–1216, 2004.
[Sánchez Lancis, 1993]   C. Sánchez Lancis. La interpolación de complementos entre el pronombre personal átono y el verbo en español medieval. In G. Hilty (ed.), *XXe Congrès international de linguistique et philologie romanes*, vol. 2, 323–334. Francke Verlag und Basel, Tübingen, 1993.
[Sperber and Wilson, 1995]   D. Sperber and D. Wilson. *Relevance: Communication and Cognition (2nd edition)*. Blackwell, Oxford, 1995.
[Staaff, 1907]   E. Staaff. Contribution à la syntaxe du pronom personnel dans le 'Poème du Cid'. *Romanische Forschungen* 23: 621-635, 1907.
[Wanner, 1996]   D. Wanner. Second Position Clitics in Medieval Romance. In A. L. Halpern and A. M. Zwicky (eds), *Approaching Second. Second Position Clitics and Related Phenomena*, 537–579. CSLI, Stanford, 1996.

Miriam Bouzouita
Philosophy Department, King's College London, London, United Kingdom.
miriam.bouzouita@kcl.ac.uk

Variation and change in the individual: Evidence from the Survey of English Dialects[1]

DEVYANI SHARMA, JOAN BRESNAN, ASHWINI DEO

Theoretical idealizations of language as a homogeneous object have long been challenged by attestations of extensive variation in language—both synchronic and diachronic. One response has been to reject such idealizations, and to describe language as 'an object possessing orderly heterogeneity', in which 'nativelike command of heterogeneous structures is not a matter of multidialectalism or 'mere' performance, but is part of unilingual linguistic competence' [Weinreich et al., 1968] henceforth WLH [pp100–101].

Under their implementation of this view, WLH propose an ordered set of questions for the investigation of language change, three of which are particularly closely linked:

> *The Constraints Problem:* "If one's observations of languages are tied together by a broader theoretical structure,... all the more challenging and meaningful becomes the search for 'optimization' tendencies in language change." [p127]

> *The Transition Problem:* "We find that the theory of language change can learn more from so-called transitional dialects than from 'core' dialects. Indeed, it stands to gain by considering every dialect as transitional... The transition or transfer of features from one speaker to another appears to take place through the medium of bidialectal speakers, or more generally, speakers with heterogeneous systems characterized by orderly differentiation." [p184]

> *The Embedding Problem:* "The changing linguistic structure is itself embedded in the larger context of the speech community,

---

[1]**Source note:** Sections 1–5.3 of this article have been reprinted from: Joan Bresnan, Ashwini Deo, and Devyani Sharma (2007), 'Typology in variation: A probabilistic approach to *be* and *n't* in the Survey of English Dialects' (*English Language and Linguistics* 11:2, pp301–346), with kind permission from Cambridge University Press. The introduction, section 5.4, and section 6 of this article include new material provided by Sharma.

in such a way that social and geographic variations are intrinsic elements of the structure." [p185]

WLH thus anticipate that universal constraints, transitional stages, and socio-geographic embedding together account for an individual's linguistic state, predicting that variation within a single grammar will bear a close resemblance to variation across grammars.

The Transition (microsocial) Problem and the Embedding (macrosocial) Problem have been addressed extensively in sociolinguistics. At the microsocial level, unconscious speech accommodation in interaction reduces dissimilarities and has been shown to be a fundamental property of individual speech variation [Giles and Powesland, 1985; Coupland, 1984, p160]. At the macrosocial level, diffusion of variants proceeds through groups in both geographical and socio-hierarchical space, based on frequency of interaction [Trudgill, 1983; Kerswill, 2002, p196; Labov, 2001, p506]. These two levels of social processes are unified in the sociolinguistic finding that 'variation within the speech of a single speaker derives from the variation which exists between speakers' [Bell, 1984, p151].

The Constraints Problem has been addressed separately, in typological studies, but has rarely been formally integrated with the sociolinguistic insights outlined above. The locus of such a unified view would be in a reworked theory of how individual grammars can be sensitive to both typological and socio-geographic constraints.

In general, syntactic theory has been slow to adopt heterogeneity as a property of grammars. However, recent developments in Optimality Theory [Boersma and Hayes, 2001; Anttila, 1997a; van Oostendorp, 1997; Nagy and Heap, 1998, a.o.] have problematized the assumption that the variation phenomena—variable outputs for the same input—must be external to formal grammatical theory. In the framework of Stochastic Optimality Theory (Stochastic OT; [Boersma, 1997, 1998, 1999a; Boersma and Hayes, 2001]), for example, it is expected that variable outputs across dialects and within individual speakers should be constrained by the same kinds of typological generalizations that are found crosslinguistically. Typological variation across languages is explained in OT by means of language-particular rankings of universal constraints, and variation across dialects should thus derive from the same typological space. In Stochastic OT, the noisy evaluation of candidates reranks constraints by temporarily perturbing their ranking values along a continuous scale; this inherent variability in grammars may lead to either categorical or variable grammars depending on the environment a speaker is exposed to. In this framework, therefore, both dialectal variation and individual variation sample the typological space of possible grammars.

We propose here that Stochastic OT offers a natural, unified treatment of

WLH's three problems of language change. The data for the present study come from individual patterns of variation in subject-verb agreement with affirmative and negative *be* extracted from the *Survey of English Dialects* (SED, [Orton et al., 1962–71]). We show that individual variability in the data shows striking structural resemblances to patterns of inter-dialectal, or categorical, variation, suggesting that individual and group variability can be captured by the same set of constraints on language, with rates of variability or categoricity finely calibrated by the frequency of exposure to different grammars.

1 Background

1.1 Previous work

A number of studies have examined verb agreement patterns in nonstandard varieties of English [Ihalainen, 1991; Cheshire, 1991, 1996; Cheshire et al., 1993; Schilling-Estes and Wolfram, 1994; Anderwald, 2001, 2002, 2003]. Many of these studies have observed a reduction of variation with plural (vs. singular) subjects and negative (vs. affirmative) sentences.[2]

Leveling of distinctions in paradigms of *be* with plural subjects is widespread, and is also instantiated in Standard English, which assigns the form *are* to all plural subjects. Cheshire [1991] observes that in many nonstandard dialects of English leveling across number and person results in either the present tense -*s* suffixed form of verbs or the suffixless form of verbs generalizing across verbal paradigms. Trudgill and Chambers, [1991, p52], Cheshire et al., [1993, p73], and Trudgill, [1999, p104] also observe that the negative counterparts of present tense *be* paradigms in many modern nonstandard dialects of British English have reduced distinctions and employ just one form, *ain't*, for the negative present tense of both auxiliary *be* and auxiliary *have*. In many of these varieties, this single form covers all subject persons and numbers, despite the fact that the affirmative paradigm for these two auxiliary verbs retain person and number distinctions. Schilling-Estes and Wolfram [1994, p287] note that some nonstandard varieties of American English that have leveling of *be* distinctions in the past tense also restrict this leveling to negative sentences.

These patterns of dialect variation have recently been related to typological markedness [Kortmann, 1999; Anderwald and Kortmann, 2002; Anderwald, 2003]. Studies in typology have shown that contrasts are often categorically neutralized across languages in marked contexts, and many of the grammatical contexts in which British dialects exhibit leveling correspond to marked

---

[2] Another type of leveling in *be* inventories involves a reduction of variation in past tense marking relative to present tense marking [Cheshire et al., 1993, pp71–72; Schilling-Estes and Wolfram, 1994, p280; Trudgill, 1999, p106; Anderwald, 2003, p520]. We restrict the present study to present tense inventories, but the pattern of leveling in past tense would be straightforwardly subsumed under the analysis here, as past tense morphology can also be seen as marked in ways similar to plural and negative morphology.

grammatical categories: plural number, negation, and past tense.

Our goals in this study are twofold: first, we aim to verify whether variation in affirmative and negative leveling in English dialects does indeed reflect more general typological patterns, and if so, why; second, we offer a unified formal analysis of variable leveling in the grammars of dialects as well as of individuals using a probabilistic model.

Following a description of the data extraction methodology used, we first present a summary of all categorical affirmative and negative *be* paradigms (inter-speaker variation) and present an analysis of this space of variation. Next, we present a summary of all variable affirmative and negative *be* paradigms (intra-speaker variation) and offer a stochastic OT analysis of individual variation. As the data do not include frequency distributions, they do not make full use of the stochastic OT apparatus; however we adopt stochastic OT as a useful conceptual and theoretical model of localized, individual variation.

1.2 Data Extraction from *The Survey of English Dialects*

Although *be* variation is attested in many varieties of English, the dialects of England may exhibit the widest variety of *be* inventories [Schilling-Estes and Wolfram, 1994, p277], and this was our motivation for selecting the *Survey of English Dialects* [Orton et al., 1962–71] as a data source.

We should note that the *SED* was compiled during the 1950s (first published in 1962 for the University of Leeds) and thus constitutes a relatively old data source. Some studies have attempted to relate *SED* findings to more recent survey work. For instance, Cheshire *et al.* [1993] compare the *SED* to The Survey of British Dialect Grammar (conducted 1986–1989) and Anderwald [2003] briefly compares the *SED* to the British National Corpus (completed in 1994). The primary finding of both comparisons is that selected features which were originally regional have spread to many urban areas and now constitute a set of generalized nonstandard urban British dialect features, while other traditional regional features are being lost. As we are specifically concerned with the typological range of possible paradigms of *be*, a slightly earlier stage of regional variation is no less appropriate for study than a more contemporary one, and as the *SED* offers explicit and organized detail of over 300 individual grammatical systems along with their regional groupings, it lends itself particularly well to an examination of intra- and inter-group variation.

The questionnaire data in the *SED* are organized by county and survey question, but also include an index of individual respondents for each set of responses to a given question. To extract partial grammars for each individual, we entered all of the responses to questions that elicited present tense forms of the verb *be* into a database, collapsing the fine-grained phonetic variations in pronunciation recorded in the transcriptions into an orthographic representation of distinct morphosyntactic forms (see Appendix A for a list of the relevant *SED* questions).

In the construction of this database, we coded for construction type (interrogative/tag/declarative, with/without ellipsis, affirmative/ negative), predicate type, subject person, subject number, region, and site/speaker. Figure 1 shows the regional divisions used in the *SED* and Appendix B gives a list of abbreviations used for these regions. Assuming a 'grammar' to be a set of construction types used by an individual, the total number of individual grammars present in the *SED* is 312.[3]

For the present study we used a subset of each grammar, restricting our attention to affirmative declarative constructions and their synthetic negation counterparts and excluding from the present analysis other forms of positional variation such as *wh*-, yes/no, or tag question formation. In order to isolate individual partial grammars for declarative clauses, we sorted the data by respondent and construction type.

Some speakers in the *SED* have fixed paradigms for *be* with pronominal subjects and these speakers comprise the set of invariant inventories. Other speakers give multiple answers for a single subject type, and these individuals form the group of variable inventories. We classified speakers with identical paradigms, whether invariant or variable, as sharing a single inventory. Each inventory discussed in the paper thus represents the grammar of an individual speaker or a group of speakers from whom the same input/output pairs were elicited.

Because of systematic gaps in the *SED* survey questionnaires, the following subject types were the maximum possible data extractable for a given speaker:

Affirmative declarative:	singular:	1sg, 2sg, 3sg
	plural:	1pl, 3pl
Negative declarative:	singular:	1sg, 3sg
	plural:	3pl

Aside from these intrinsic constraints on the *SED* data, we were obliged to impose two additional criteria on the initial data set in order to ensure a reliable basis for comparison of dialect systems. Dialect inventories were only included for analysis if (a) the inventory had a complete set of affirmative and synthetic negative forms recorded and (b) each combined affirmative and

---

[3] Individual data points in the *SED*, e.g. Sr5, usually represent responses by one individual; however, in a few cases they represent the composite responses of two or three demographically similar individuals from a single locality. It would be slightly more accurate to refer to these points as localities rather than individuals, but as we are discussing regions as well, we retain the term 'individual' in referring to distinct data points collected in a given region.

Figure 1. Counties of England.

synthetic negative paradigm was attested in an identical form for at least two speakers.

According to the first criterion, any speaker with an incomplete affirmative or negative paradigm was omitted. For the affirmative part of speakers' *be* paradigms, this simply applied to speakers for whom a form had not been recorded by the fieldworker in one or more of the cells. The criterion is slightly more specific in the case of speakers' negative paradigms. The *SED* includes either synthetic negation such as *isn't* or *ain't*, analytic negation such as *'m not* or *'s not*, or both synthetic and analytic forms. The hypothesis in the present paper regarding leveling only applies to synthetic forms, as the claim pertains to overloading of a single lexical form with multiple semantic features such as negation, person and number. As analytic negation such as *am not* or *'m not* reserves separate morphemes for the marking of nominal features and negation, leveling is not predicted for such constructions. Based on this reasoning, speakers for whom only analytic negation or incomplete synthetic negation had been recorded in the *SED* were excluded, as we could not verify what synthetic negation forms they would favor for different subject types. This first criterion reduced the total number of individuals included in the study to 216.

The second criterion was designed to isolate patterns in the *SED* data that are reliably systematic. In the present paper we are primarily interested in systematic and stable dialect paradigms, and although stochastic OT grammars can model a certain degree of noise and instability which is evident during periods of massive constraint re-ranking, they can also model the stable systems that speakers may ultimately converge on and they make typological predictions about these. As we are interested in the typology of stable dialect paradigms, we sorted all the *SED* speakers into groups that shared affirmative *and* synthetic negative paradigms and omitted speakers that had unique or idiosyncratic paradigms, treating their data as less reliable. As a result, the subset of data analyzed includes all speakers who share their affirmative and negative declarative paradigms with at least one other speaker.

The only exception to the second criterion is the inclusion of two invariant inventories that are represented by only one speaker each in the *SED*: Kent (speaker K7) and Sussex (speaker Sx5). We include these two inventories as other research in these regions has shown evidence of these two paradigms having once been robust systems.[4]

---

[4]Support for the existence of the all-*be* paradigm of Sx5 and the *I are* paradigm of K7 comes from dialect literature as well as the *SED*. A number of early texts support the view that invariant *be* existed in the Somerset area for all subject types ([Elworthy, 1877, p55; Barnes, 1863, p24; Hewett, 1894, p3; Wilson, 1913, p30]; all references cited in [Ihalainen, 1991, p104]). Richard Coates [p.c., August 4, 2004] similarly suggests that the regional dialect in Sussex and neighboring regions had an all-*be* paradigm that began to be replaced

The total number of speakers remaining after both selection criteria were applied was 119. These speakers were separated into two groups: speakers with invariant affirmative paradigms (89 total) and speakers with variable affirmative paradigms (30 total).

Additional methodological considerations include the analysis of contracted forms and of null forms. Where contracted forms are provided by speakers in addition to full forms (e.g. *am, 'm* or *is, 's*), the contracted form is treated as an allomorph of the full form, rather than as a distinct dialect variant of *be*. Similarly, the paired set *'r*, ϕ occurred in some paradigms, and here ϕ is also treated as a reduction of *'r* rather than as a completely distinct null form of *be*.[5] Where a contracted form is clearly not an allomorph of another variant in its cell within a paradigm, e.g. non-1-sg *'m* (Figure 22), it is included in the analysis as a distinct form.

2 Inter-speaker variation in affirmative and negative declaratives

This section presents all *be* paradigms in the *SED* which are instantiated in more than one speaker, have complete data sets for affirmative and synthetic negation paradigms, and are invariant. The paradigm tables in Figures 2–8 present affirmative and synthetic negative paradigms, listing at the top of the table all individual *SED* respondents who exhibit the pattern, e.g. Db6. Slight differences in lexical form for a speaker are given in parentheses following the speaker index. The figure headings separate tables according to the type of leveling in the affirmative paradigm. When the affirmative paradigm is identical but the negative paradigm is distinct, two separate tables are listed, both are under the general heading that describes their affirmative pattern (e.g. Derbyshire and Cornwall).[6]

---

in the 19th century by more general vernacular forms and gradually came to be largely limited to stylized dialect writing. Evidence of the earlier robustness of the all-*be* paradigm also comes from the fact that several *SED* speakers other than Sx5 do in fact exhibit the all-*be* pattern but have additional variants and thus are either included as variable systems (Bk3, O3) or excluded due to their having unique systems (Sx1, Sx3, Brk1, Brk4, Ha7, O2, So1). The *I are* system of K7 is similarly cited as an attested, once robust system in Kent and Surrey [Gower, 1893, vi; Trudgill, 1999, p106]. Additional evidence of its wider distribution comes from its presence in the paradigms of other *SED* speakers as well, who also either had to be classed as variable due to the presence of other variants (K3, Bd1, Bd2, Bd3, Sr2, Sr4) or excluded due to their having unique paradigms (K1, K4).

[5] The null form is not treated as a distinct form because it does not occur independent of reduced *'r* and it is not generally attested as an independent verbal form in British dialects [Wolfram, 2000, p54].

[6] Regional names assigned to inventory tables are somewhat arbitrary and are based on their representation among *SED* respondents. For instance, Devon, Somerset, and Sussex have significant overlaps in their *be* patterns, and the all-*be* pattern we refer to as 'Sussex' has sometimes been described as characteristic of Somerset as well. These regional names

Figure 2. All person distinctions in singular

Derbyshire: Db1(thee),Db6(thee),Db7,St1,Y22(she)

(I) am	(we) are	(I) amnt	
(thou) art			
(her) is	(they) are	(her) isnt	(they) arent

Cornwall: Co5,Co7

(I) am	(we) are	(I) arent	
(thee) art			
(she) is	(they) are	(she) isnt	(they) arent

Figure 3. Leveling of first person

Devon: D2,D6,Do3(we),Co1,So13(we)

(I) be	(us) be	(I) baint	
(thee) art			
(her) is	(they) be	(her) isnt	(they) baint

Wiltshire: Gl4,W2,W4,W5(she),W6(isnt),W8(she,isnt)

(I) be	(we) be	(I) baint	
(thee) beest			
(her) is	(they) be	(her) aint	(they) baint

A striking aspect of the data is that the same abstract paradigm is sometimes instantiated with different morphs. For instance, Devon and Wiltshire share the same abstract paradigm, as do Kent and Somerset. Similarly, the complete loss of all agreement contrasts is leveled to the form *be* in the Sussex inventory, but parallel systems using *am*, *are*, and *is* have also been reported, although we did not find these in our data: *I/you/she/we/you/they am here, I/you/she/we/you/they are here, I/you/she/we/you/they is here* [Trudgill, 1999, p98]. Past tense in West and East Midlands shows a similar loss of all agreement contrasts, again with a different morph performing the leveled function: *I were singing. So were John. Mary weren't singing.* [Cheshire et al., 1993, p80]. These abstract parallels in dialect systems are unlikely to be explicable in terms of simple sound changes ('accidental homonymy' in

---

should therefore be treated simply as tags for inventories rather than accurate geographical delineations.

Figure 4. Leveling of second person

Northumberland: Nb1,Y26(thou)

(I) am (we) are	(I) amnt
(you) are	
(she) is (they) are	(she) isnt (they) arent

Norfolk: Nf1-2,Nf5,Nf9-13,Sf2,Ess1,L6(isnt), Nf3(isnt),Nf6(isnt),St4(ina)

(I) am (we) are	(I) arent
(you) are	
(she) is (they) are	(she) aint (they) arent

Suffolk: Sf1,Sf3-5,Nf4,MxL2,Lei1-2,Lei4-6,Lei8, Ess2-3,Ess5,Ess8-9,Ess11-13,Hu1-2,K5,Ha4, Sr1,Sr3,M6,C1-2,L14-15,R1-2,Hrt1-2,Nth2-4

(I) am (we) are	(I) aint
(you) are	
(she) is (they) are	(she) aint (they) aint

Figure 5. Leveling of first and second person

Kent: K7

(I) are (we) are	(I) aint
(you) are	
(she) is (they) are	(her) aint (they) aint

Somerset: So12

(I) be (we) be	(I) baint
(you) be	
(she/her) is (they) be	(she) baint (they) baint

Hampshire: D8,So6,Ha2,Ha5,Bk5(aint3sg)

(I) be (us) be	(I) baint
(you) be	
(her) is (they) be	(her) isnt (they) baint

Figure 6. Leveling of first and third person

Berkshire: Brk1,Brk2,W7

(I) be	(us) be	(I) baint
(thee) beest		
(her) be	(they) be	(her) baint (they) baint

Figure 7. Leveling of person but not number

Yorkshire: Y2,Y6,Y13,Y24,La1,Cu2

(I) is	(we) are	(I) isnt
(thee/thou) is		
(she) is	(they) are	(she) isnt (they) arent

Carstairs-McCarthy [1987, p91] and Kusters' [2003, p27] terminology). They are better understood in terms of changes at the paradigmatic level in the system for expressing semantic content. Therefore we distinguish between the inventory of specific forms and the inventory of abstract contrasts; it is the latter that this paper is concerned with.

Nevertheless, it is worth noting in passing that the choice of lexical forms is affected by regular sociohistorical processes. Figures 2–8 show that certain forms, such as *be* and *ain't*, are quite widespread. While *be* is an archaic form and is being replaced in some regions by newer forms [Trudgill, 1999, p106], *ain't* is commonly cited as one of several supralocal non-standard features currently spreading across parts of the British Isles, replacing more regional forms. The use of this latter type of non-standard urban form tends to be determined more by social class than region [Hughes and Trudgill, 1987; Coupland, 1988; Cheshire et al., 1993], and the resulting leveling has often been associated with "a reduction of marked, socially heavily stigmatised, highly localized, or minority forms in favour of unmarked, less stereotyped, supralocal, majority variants" [Britain, 2002, p35]. A number of social and historical factors are thus instrumental in the processes of selection and adoption of particular forms.

We emphasize that these processes are not the focus of the present study; our focus rather is on the typological range of possible abstract contrasts revealed by paradigms of specific morphs. Three key observations can be drawn from the data in Figures 2–8 regarding abstract systems of contrasts and leveling of

Figure 8. Leveling of person and number

Sussex: Sx5

(I) be	(we) be	(I) baint	
(you) be			
(she) be	(they) be	(she) baint	(they) baint

distinctions:

Observation 1:
There are 0–3 person distinctions made in the singular;
There are 0 person distinctions made in the plural; therefore
⇒ Person distinctions are levelled in the plural.

Observation 2:
Regardless of whether verb forms are leveled, pronominal subjects do not undergo leveling.

Observation 3:
The negative paradigms never express more information about person or number than their corresponding affirmative paradigms, and they frequently express *less*, as illustrated in Figure 9.

Figure 9. Leveling in negation

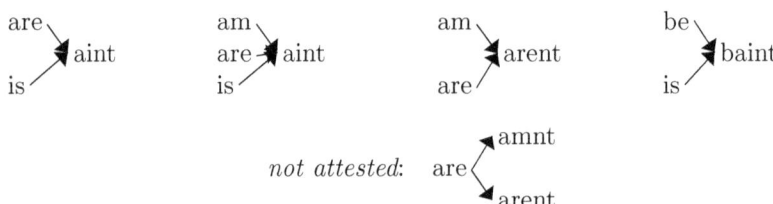

Thus we find that the type of paradigm in Figure 10—with leveling of *be* forms in the first person in the affirmative but with no leveling in the first person in negation—is not attested.

Figure 10. Paradigm unattested in the *SED*

	(I) are (we) are	(I) amnt	
*	(you) are		
	(she) is (they) are	(her) isnt	(they) arent

3 Optimality Theory analysis of leveling

We now turn to the framework we use for formally analyzing the surveyed inventories. In the present section we restrict the analysis to conventional OT, and in the later discussion of individual variation we introduce the stochastic component.

3.1 Optimality Theory

An OT grammar can be viewed as a function from INPUT s to OUTPUT s. We take the morphosyntactic INPUT to be language-independent content drawn from the space of possible lexical and grammatical contrasts and the OUTPUT to consist of language-specific forms with varying expressions of that content. INPUTs are fully specified for person and number features. Candidate expressions for each INPUT are generated by GEN and evaluated according to an EVAL function. Given a set of ranked violable constraints hypothesized to be present in all grammars, the EVAL function defines the OUTPUT to be the candidate which best satisfies the highest ranked constraint on which it differs from its competitors [Grimshaw, 1997a; Prince and Smolensky, 2004].[7]

The overall structure we assume for syntactic expressions in OT is shown in Figure 11. The INPUT is represented here as an abstract specification of semantic features, while the candidate set comprising the OUTPUT is represented by pairings of c(categorial)-structures and f(feature)-structures in correspondence. This conception of INPUT and OUTPUT draws on a mathematically and empirically well-understood representational basis, OT-LFG (see [Bresnan, 2000, 2001a, 2001b, 2001c, 2002; Kuhn, 2000, 2001, 2002, 2003; Clark, 2004]).[8]

We assume that the INPUT is an underspecified f-structure which semanti-

---

[7]Note that Stochastic OT as a framework does not require that constraints be universal and/or innate, and in fact Boersma's theory of functional phonology [1998] is a well articulated alternative.

[8]In Figure 11 the customary attribute-value notation is used in which $+feature$ is rendered $[feature \quad +]$ [Johnson, 1988]. The verb forms paired with each f-structure actually consist of an abstract characterization of word class properties, such as V^0 or I^0, and a language-particular pronunciation, such as *is*; the choice of phonological representations is outside the scope of our study.

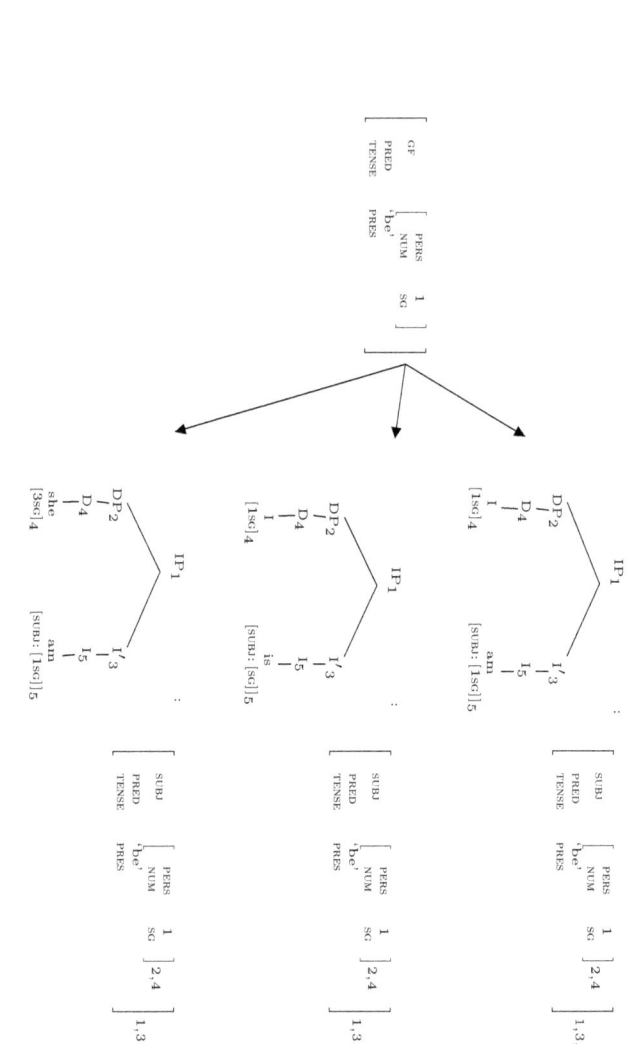

Figure 11. OT Grammar of English Subject-Verb Agreement

cally subsumes the candidate f-structures, an assumption justified by considerations of decidability and learnability [Kuhn, 2002, 2003]. The INPUT feature structure contains only semantically relevant features; thus GF (for 'grammatical function') denotes any argument of the predicator BE and does not specify syntactic role.[9] GEN provides additional purely grammatical features as well as particular argument realizations (SUBJ, for example) to the candidate analyses, which thus contain the INPUT. The terminal string of the c-structure consists of fully inflected words which represent morpholexical choices to be optimized against the candidate f-structure. The lexical choices of the sentence are optimized in parallel, so that in Figure 11 both the subject pronoun and the verb must be optimized against the given features [1SG] belonging to the SUBJ argument of the candidates. Lexical choices may be unfaithful to the INPUT to varying degrees.[10]

Since the candidate feature structures are all semantically subsumed by the input in this model, the lexical optimizations can be carried out against the candidate f-structure, which in general contains the input together with

---

[9] As observed in [Bresnan, 2000], an underspecified f-structure is a formal representation of the idea that the OT INPUT for syntax is an argument structure with annotations of additional semantically relevant information [Legendre et al., 1993; Grimshaw, 1997a]. One advantage of this formalization is the availability of generation and parsing algorithms, recursive enumeration of the candidate set, a formal constraint language, and other useful computational and mathematical properties [Kuhn, 2002, 2003]. Another advantage is the typological expressiveness of the theory of representations [Bresnan, 2001a].

[10] In a feature-logic basic theory of syntactic representation such as this, the formalism may be viewed as a feature checking system which is output oriented ('declarative') rather than derivational ('procedural'). The basic workings of the system of feature-structure comparison are as follows. The numerical subscripts coindexing the tree nodes and feature structures show the correspondence relations between the two parallel structures, which follow from general principles of tree-to-feature-structure correspondence [Bresnan, 2001b; Kuhn, 1999]. For example, the feature structures associated with the I nodes in these particular trees are indexed by 5, which is identified with the index of I' (=3) and IP (=1) by a principle that identifies the f-structures of heads with those of their mothers. Similarly, the feature structures of the D nodes are indexed by 4, which is identified with the index of DP (=2) by the same head principle. The DP and IP f-structures are related by the specifier principle, which says here that f-structure 5's SUBJ has f-structure 2 as its value. (Other principles apply to the exocentric and nonconfigurational constructions found in many languages: see [Bresnan, 2001a; Nordlinger, 1998])

In faithfulness evaluations, the lexical feature structure of a terminal node is compared with the f-structure corresponding to (coindexed with) its preterminal node in the c-structure. By the syntactic correspondences in Figure 11 just discussed, this comparison will hold for the f-structures of the phrasal projections of these terminals (IP in the case of *am, is*, and DP in the case of *I, she*). By the uniqueness principle, which states that every f-structure attribute must have a unique value, the verb's inner agreement feature structure [1SG] in [SUBJ [1SG]]$_5$ can be inferred to correspond to the subsidiary f-structure 4 (=2) in the sentential feature structure, which also corresponds to the lexical feature structure of the subject pronoun. For more details of the LFG representational basis adopted here, see [Bresnan, 2001a] and references.

purely grammatical features provided by GEN. More precisely, then, the faithfulness constraints will relate the morpholexical f-structures of the c-structure terminals to the global feature structures of the candidates. Again, different lexical optimizations (for example, those for the subject pronoun and for the verb) may proceed in parallel and degrees of faithfulness to pronominal INPUT information and to verbal INPUT information may vary.

3.2 Analysis for Observation 1: Leveling in plural

Observation 1 noted that all of the varieties of English surveyed here show loss of person distinctions in the plural. This leveling in the plural in British dialects reflects a more general, cross-linguistic markedness pattern [Greenberg, 1966, pp28–29; Croft, 2003, p126], though there are exceptions (see n. 14). For the reasons given above (absence of explanation in terms of simple sound changes, presence of the same abstract leveling pattern in very different inventories of forms), we represent leveling by changes in the inventories of expressions of abstract semantic contrasts.

To model these contrasts, we assume that each form of *be* is represented by *the intersection of person and number values of all of the cells of the paradigm it occurs in.* The examples listed in (1) illustrate this mapping between semantic content and lexical form.

(1)   Yorkshire ⇒

	SG	PL
1	is	are
2	is	
3	is	are

Yorkshire Feature Values

	SG	PL
1	[SG]	[PL]
2	[SG]	
3	[SG]	[PL]

Derbyshire ⇒

	sg	pl
1	am	are
2	art	
3	is	are

Derbyshire Feature Values

	sg	pl
1	[1 SG]	[PL]
2	[2 SG]	
3	[3 SG]	[PL]

Wiltshire ⇒

	SG	PL
1	be	be
2	beest	
3	is	be

Wiltshire Feature Values

	SG	PL
1	[ ]	[ ]
2	[2 SG]	
3	[3 SG]	[ ]

Somerset ⇒

	SG	PL
1	be	be
2	be	
3	is	be

Somerset Feature Values

	SG	PL
1	[ ]	[ ]
2	[ ]	
3	[3 SG]	[ ]

A possible alternative would be to assume perfect faithfulness between the input and the candidates' morphosyntactic features is maintained, as in (2).

(2)

Yorkshire ⇒	SG	PL
1	is	are
2	is	
3	is	are

Yorkshire Feature Values	SG	PL
1	[1SG]	[1PL]
2	[2SG]	
3	[3SG]	[3PL]

This approach would posit extensive, arbitrary homonymy, and would deprive us of a means for explaining the extension and retraction of forms by feature neutralization and generalization which recurs across the dialect varieties and is a common typological feature of languages [Greenberg, 1966, pp28–29; Croft, 2003, p126]. We assume that our paradigms are not based on arbitrary homonymy and instead we allow candidate feature structures to be unfaithful to the input via underspecification.

Examples of morphosyntactic faithfulness violations [Grimshaw, 1997b, pp193–4; 2001] are Romance clitic inventories where number and gender features "float" onto adjacent clitics in certain circumstances [Bonet, 1995]. When the divergence between the form and content of the candidate is contextually restricted, as in the Romance example, the output alternates between a faithful form and an unfaithful form that replaces it in limited circumstances. The contentful features of the input are thus only contextually neutralized, and are still transparent in most output forms.

In the Yorkshire grammar, the use of *is*[3SG] in non-3SG contexts similarly implies that the form satisfies other, higher-ranked constraints. Morphosyntactic faithfulness violations will produce such divergences between form and content. However, the Yorkshire grammar gives us absolute (context-free) neutralization of person features in the output, such that the candidate's person feature could be opaque in every context of its use.[11] In this situation 'remorphologization' or 'lexicon optimization' of the system may occur, i.e. although the set of candidates is technically unconstrained, the lack of evidence for the speaker/learner of person distinctions in the Yorkshire system can induce a 'rewriting' of input feature values in the output, replacing the candidate's unfaithful features with a more faithful, and therefore meaningful, analysis. This leads to generalization of the lexical form through remorphologization of its syntactic features as simply bearing a [SG] value.

---

[11] Because our data set, like our constraint set, is small and incomplete, we cannot of course be certain that there are not relevant alternations elsewhere in the grammar. Indeed, the "Northern Rule" affecting verb agreement when a subject pronoun is adjacent would be relevant in some Yorkshire inventories. All of our *SED* inventory verbs come from sentences with pronoun subjects.

We will see below how remorphologizing can arise through continuous constraint reranking in a stochastic OT grammar. The point of interest here is that gradual changes on the continuous ranking scale can give rise to apparently categorical changes in content—without any derivational operations or procedures. This approach also allows inflectional changes to arise from morphosyntactic feature simplification independently of phonological erosion [Kusters, 2000].

In the same way the analysis of *are* as a general form lacking PERS and NUM features may be the result of historical remorphologization of an earlier more specific plural form. In the Yorkshire and Derbyshire/Cornwall inventories, *are* is restricted to the plural. But elsewhere in our data *are* generalizes into the singular column of the paradigm, expressing the second person or both second and first persons.

The generalization or spread of a form in the *be* paradigm can proceed in the present theory by (the OT equivalents of) either feature deletion or, less commonly, feature change. The generalization of *are* across both number and persons in some dialects requires the deletion analysis, under which it lacks both PERS and NUM values. Although we do not have clear instances of this in the present data, a lexical form can also undergo feature change, such that it becomes specialized to a new person and/or number value.

The constraint set

In OT there are two broad types of constraints: faithfulness constraints, which compare a candidate to the input, and markedness constraints, which assess the well-formedness of the candidate in terms of its featural complexity. Markedness constraints penalize complex or 'difficult' structures, and so tend to erode contrasts. Faithfulness constraints, by contrast, require that features of the input content be preserved in the output expression; they thus serve the communicative function of expressing contrasts in content, protecting content against the eroding effects of markedness constraints on forms. A particular language harmonizes these conflicting constraints by prioritizing (ranking) them.

Different faithfulness constraints may be instantiated for various morphosyntactically defined domains; this is called 'positional faithfulness' in phonology [Urbanczyk, 1995; Benua, 1995]. English has three inflectional classes for present-tense verbs (*be*, modal verbs, and lexical verbs), for which there are three families of separately rankable faithfulness constraints [Bresnan, 2000, 2002]. We will be concerned here mainly with faithfulness in the domain of *be*. The faithfulness constraints that follow are thus implicitly indexed to this domain.

The faithfulness constraints in (3) ensure the expression in the output of person and number features in the input.[12] This faithfulness may be achieved in different grammars by either fusional or non-fusional forms. Each of these constraints represents a family of more specific constraints. For instance, EXPRESS (PERSVALUE) includes EXPRESS (1), EXPRESS (2), and EXPRESS (3).

(3) Non-fusional faithfulness:

EXPRESS (NUMVALUE), EXPRESS (PERSVALUE)

Fusional faithfulness:

EXPRESS (PERSVALUE, NUMVALUE)

If we consider the sample input in (4), candidate 1 violates both the non-fusional constraints — EXPRESS (NUMVALUE) and EXPRESS (PERSVALUE) — and the fusional constraint EXPRESS (PERSVALUE, NUMVALUE). Candidate 2, by contrast, satisfies the non-fusional constraint EXPRESS (NUMVALUE), but violates the non-fusional constraint EXPRESS (PERSVALUE) as well as the fusional constraint EXPRESS (PERSVALUE, NUMVALUE).

(4) example input: $\begin{bmatrix} \text{NUM} & \text{SG} \\ \text{PERS} & 2 \end{bmatrix}$

candidate 1: *be*: $\begin{bmatrix} \text{NUM} & \\ \text{PERS} & \end{bmatrix}$

candidate 2: *is*: $\begin{bmatrix} \text{NUM} & \text{SG} \\ \text{PERS} & 3 \end{bmatrix}$

The two markedness constraints in (5), again indexed to the domain of the verb *be*, impose restrictions on the featural complexity of candidates regardless of their input features. We interpret these as constraints to avoid informational density. Thus, although candidate 2 in (4) satisfies faithfulness to number, in doing so it violates *NUM. By contrast, candidate 1 violates all faithfulness constraints, but satisfies both markedness constraints.[13]

(5) Avoid informational density: *PERS, *NUM

---

[12]These constraints differ somewhat from those in the preliminary study by Bresnan and Deo [2001] which were based in part on [Grimshaw, 1997b, 2001]. The present constraints are conceptually preferable in postulating word class differences in faithfulness to agreement values rather than arbitrary markedness differences among person values.

[13]Of course, derivational operations of feature deletion and rewriting are not involved when candidates 'omit' input features; rather, these are epiphenomenal consequences of the parallel optimization of candidates that may diverge from the given input in various ways.

Increased leveling in plurals, as evidenced in the present data and in typological studies, can be captured by constraint subhierarchies, within which the relative rankings are fixed across languages, either extrinsically [Prince and Smolensky, 2004; Aissen, 1999; Kager, 1999] or by use of constraint semantics [de Lacy, 2002]. The relevant subhierarchy for the present study is shown in (6).

(6)   EXPRESS (PERSVALUE, SG) ≫ EXPRESS (PERSVALUE, PL)

The fixed ranking of constraints within this subhierarchy allows us to capture the cross-linguistic generalization that languages exhibit fewer distinctions among plural forms than singular forms in verbal agreement inventories.[14] The subhierarchy in (6) expresses the observation that, because plurality is a marked feature, it is universally dispreferred to mark plurality in addition to another feature, such as a person feature. In other words, there is a preference to highlight the marked status of plurality at the cost of other features.

A markedness constraint such as *PERS may intervene at any point in a constraint subhierarchy. As a result, the expression-constraint subhierarchy in (6) sets up implicational structures that permit leveling of plurals before singulars, but not the reverse. This effect is shown in (7).[15]

(7)   *PERS ≫ EXPRESS (PERSVALUE,SG) ≫ EXPRESS (PERSVALUE,PL)
      EXPRESS (PERSVALUE,SG) ≫ *PERS ≫ EXPRESS (PERSVALUE,PL)
      EXPRESS (PERSVALUE,SG) ≫ EXPRESS (PERSVALUE,PL) ≫ *PERS

A secondary observation that can be made with regard to the present data is that there are 'column generalizations' leveling person distinctions within a single number category—the Yorkshire system has column generalizations for both SG and PL and Derbyshire has a column generalization for PL—but there are no 'row generalizations' leveling number distinctions within a single person category. This distinction is illustrated in (8).

---

[14]This is sometimes said to be a general property of Germanic, but in modern Icelandic, and in Old Icelandic as well to a lesser extent, in most paradigms there is only one person distinction in the singular—1st against 2nd and 3rd, or 1st and 3rd against 2nd person—while 1st, 2nd, and 3rd person are distinguished in the plural [Wouter Kusters, p.c., April 6, 2001]. Thus, we can only provisionally interpret the constraint subhierarchy in (6) as universal, pending detailed study of the relevant grammars.

[15]See [Kager, 1999] for further exemplification of this type of factorial typology.

(8) Column Generalizations

	sg	pl
1	a	b
2	a	b
3	a	b

Row Generalizations (not attested)

	sg	pl
1	a	a
2	b	b
3	c	c

The faithfulness constraints EXPRESS(PERSVALUE) capture 'row forms'. In the analysis of our data, these constraints are always ranked below constraints favoring the expression of number. They are consequently inactive in grammars of all our varieties, and the candidates they select—with person/number values of [1], [2], [3]—are always suboptimal. For expository simplicity, we omit these inactive constraints and candidates, as well those that would produce person contrasts in the plural. We do not, however, structure this secondary observation as a general typological property of language. There is plenty of evidence that these constraints can be active, leading to leveling of number distinctions within a single person category (as occurs in the future and the present progressive in Bengali, for instance).

Constraint ranking and dialect outputs

In this section we present a simplified OT account of constraint rankings, omitting details of stochastic evaluation which are assumed to be part of the grammar; we later elaborate on the mechanism of stochastic evaluation in relation to variable inventories. Here, we present detailed constraint rankings for three invariant dialect systems—Yorkshire, Derbyshire, and Suffolk—to illustrate the varied outcomes of constraint reranking. Aspects of each of these three analyses extend to all the other systems of contrast and neutralization in Figures 2–8.

Yorkshire

The constraint ranking for Yorkshire *(is, is, is, are, are)* levels the expression of all person contrasts, both in the singular and in the plural. In Figure 12,[16]

---

[16] Note that in this and subsequent tableaux the candidate set forms 'is', 'art', etc. are merely convenient mnemonic tags for the feature structure which is the actual input.

we see that the high rank of *PERS disfavors the selection of any candidate bearing person features, regardless of whether the input is singular or plural. However, the relatively high rank of EXPRESS(SG) and EXPRESS(PL) favors the choice of lexical forms indexed for SG when a SG input is involved and PL when a PL input is involved, as opposed to the selection of a completely underspecified form such as *be* [ ].

Figure 12. Tableaux of a Yorkshire Grammar

input: [1SG]	*PERS	EXP(SG)	EXP(PL)	EXP(PERSVALUE,SG)	*NUM	EXP(PERSVALUE,PL)
'am': [1SG]	*!				*	
☞ 'is': [SG]				*	*	
'are': [PL]			*!		*	*
'are': [1PL]	*!		*		*	*
'be': [ ]			*!		*	
'am': [1]	*!		*		*	

input: [2SG]	*PERS	EXP(SG)	EXP(PL)	EXP(PERSVALUE,SG)	*NUM	EXP(PERSVALUE,PL)
'am': [1SG]	*!			*	*	
☞ 'is': [SG]				*	*	
'are': [PL]			*!		*	*
'are': [1PL]	*!		*	*	*	*
'be': [ ]			*!		*	
'am': [1]	*!		*		*	

input: [1PL]	*PERS	EXP(SG)	EXP(PL)	EXP(PERSVALUE,SG)	*NUM	EXP(PERSVALUE,PL)
'am': [1SG]	*!		*		*	*
'is': [SG]			*!		*	*
☞ 'are': [PL]					*	
'are': [1PL]	*!				*	
'be': [ ]				*!		*
'am': [1]	*!		*			*

Derbyshire

Figure 13 shows that the same constraints reranked for Derbyshire *(am, art, is, are, are)* preserve all singular person contrasts and level the expression of all plural contrasts. The relatively high rank of *PERS, EXPRESS(SG), and EXPRESS(PL) leads to a result for PL inputs that is identical to that of the Yorkshire grammar, namely a form specified for number but unspecified for person. However, the higher rank of the fusional constraint EXPRESS(PERSVALUE,SG) means that when a SG input is involved, the grammar will always select a distinctive lexical form that uniquely marks both person and singular number.

Figure 13. Tableaux of a Derbyshire Grammar

input: [1SG]	EXP(PERSVALUE,SG)	*PERS	EXP(SG)	EXP(PL)	*NUM	EXP(PERSVALUE,PL)
☞ 'am': [1SG]		*			*	
'is': [SG]	*!				*	
'are': [PL]	*!			*	*	
'are': [1PL]	*!	*		*	*	
'be':	*!		*			
'am': [1]	*!	*	*			
'art': [2SG]	*!	*			*	

input: [2SG]	EXP(PERSVALUE,SG)	*PERS	EXP(SG)	EXP(PL)	*NUM	EXP(PERSVALUE,PL)
'am': [1SG]	*!	*			*	
'is': [SG]	*!				*	
'are': [PL]	*!			*	*	
'are': [1PL]	*!	*		*	*	
'be':	*!		*			
'am': [1]	*!	*	*			
☞ 'art': [2SG]		*			*	

input: [1PL]	EXP(PERSVALUE,SG)	*PERS	EXP(SG)	EXP(PL)	*NUM	EXP(PERSVALUE,PL)
'am': [1SG]		*!		*	*	*
'is': [SG]			*!		*	*
☞ 'are': [PL]					*	*
'are': [1PL]		*!			*	
'be':				*!		*
'am': [1]		*!		*		*
'art': [2SG]		*!		*	*	*

Suffolk

Finally, the Suffolk system *(am, are, is, are, are)* is the Standard English system, which is similar to the Derbyshire system but avoids a distinct form for second person. The low rank of the fusional constraint EXPRESS(2,SG) and the higher rank of the markedness constraints *PERS and *NUM leads to the selection of a completely underspecified form *are* [ ]. This constraint is frequently low-ranked, reflecting the avoidance of too direct reference to the second person, a recurrent cross-linguistic phenomenon, with pragmatic and/or sociolinguistic motivations [Brown and Levinson, 1987] which may become formally crystallized in grammars.

Figure 14. Tableaux of a Suffolk (Standard English) Grammar

input: [1SG]	$\text{EXP}(1,\text{SG})$	$\text{EXP}(3,\text{SG})$	*PERS	*NUM	$\text{EXP}(\text{SG})$	$\text{EXP}(\text{PL})$	$\text{EXP}(2,\text{SG})$	$\text{EXP}(\text{PERSVALUE,PL})$
☞ 'am': [1SG]			*	*				
'is': [SG]	*!			*				
'are': [PL]	*!			*	*			
'are': [ ]	*!				*			
'am': [1]	*!		*		*			
'art': [2SG]	*!		*	*				
'art': [2]	*!		*		*			

input: [2SG]	$\text{EXP}(1,\text{SG})$	$\text{EXP}(3,\text{SG})$	*PERS	*NUM	$\text{EXP}(\text{SG})$	$\text{EXP}(\text{PL})$	$\text{EXP}(2,\text{SG})$	$\text{EXP}(\text{PERSVALUE,PL})$
'am': [1SG]			*!	*			*	
'is': [SG]				*!			*	
'are': [PL]				*!	*		*	
☞ 'are': [ ]						*	*	
'am': [1]			*!		*		*	
'art': [2SG]			*!	*				
'art': [2]			*!		*			

input: [1PL]	$\text{EXP}(1,\text{SG})$	$\text{EXP}(3,\text{SG})$	*PERS	*NUM	$\text{EXP}(\text{SG})$	$\text{EXP}(\text{PL})$	$\text{EXP}(2,\text{SG})$	$\text{EXP}(\text{PERSVALUE,PL})$
'am': [1SG]			*!	*		*		*
'is': [SG]				*!		*		*
'are': [PL]				*!				*
☞ 'are': [ ]						*		*
'am': [1]			*!			*		*
'art': [2SG]			*!	*		*		*
'art': [2]			*!			*		*

3.3 Analysis for Observation 2: No leveling in pronominal subjects

Verbal agreement may differ with pronominal and nonpronominal subjects in some varieties [Ihalainen, 1991, pp107–8] by the so-called 'Northern rule' (n. 11); see [Börjars and Chapman, 1998] for a formal syntactic analysis. The present study is limited to agreement in simple declarative affirmative and negative sentences with pronominal subjects.

Observation 2 noted that within the context of clauses with pronominal subjects there appears to be no leveling of pronoun forms competing with leveling of *be* forms. In other words, the expression of person is more faithful in the class of pronouns than in verbs. The present data show numerous instances of leveling of person distinctions in *be*; however, no dialect grammar levels pronominal forms along the lines proposed in the second column of (9).

(9)

Yorkshire:	Nonoccurring equivalents:
I is	she am
thee/thou is	she art
she is	she is

We propose that this asymmetry is a result of faithfulness constraints being relative to word classes. The architecture of Optimality Theory does not itself rule out pronominal unfaithfulness to person, as it permits both verbal and pronominal unfaithfulness, indicated earlier in Figure 11. Different expressions in the lexical string may be variably faithful in terms of feature specifications; for instance, a first person subject pronoun may cooccur with a verb form specified for [1SG] in one dialect but [SG] in another. In general, faithfulness to the referentially classificatory feature of person is much stricter for pronominal expressions than for verbal expressions.

This point is illustrated by the fact that in Figure 11 earlier, the first two candidates *I am* and *I is* are both possible expressions of the input with its first person singular argument, while the third candidate *She am* is always suboptimal. (Note that *She am* is an optimal expression of a *third* person subject in some English varieties; we suggest that it is suboptimal only as an expression of a *first* person subject.) This generalization can be captured by the following subhierarchy:

(10) $\text{EXPRESS}_{pron}(\text{PERS}) \gg \text{EXPRESS}_{verb}(\text{PERS})$.

These two positional faithfulness constraints are indexed respectively to the morphosyntactic domains of pronominal and verbal expressions. The verbal and pronominal positional faithfulness constraints are separately rankable, but the subhierarchy ensures that the subject pronoun cannot be less faithful to the input person of the subject argument than the verb is.[17]

Further support for the claim that faithfulness constraints are generally indexed to word classes comes from within verbal word classes, namely the greater faithfulness to expression of person in some verb classes as against others. The table in (11) shows that agreement with subject person in Standard English is most differentiated with *be*, slightly less so with lexical verbs, and least so with modal verbs, resulting again in a class-based ranking of faithfulness:

$$\text{EXPRESS}_{be}(\text{PERS}) \gg \text{EXPRESS}_{verb}(\text{PERS}) \gg \text{EXPRESS}_{modal}(\text{PERS}).$$

(11)

	be:		(main) verbs:		modal verbs:	
	SG	PL	SG	PL	SG	PL
1	am	are	hit	hit	will	will
2	are	are	hit	hit	will	will
3	is	are	hits	hit	will	will

As this paper focuses on forms of *be*, Observation 2 is less central to our analysis than Observation 1, but this short discussion demonstrates the need for faithfulness constraints to be specifically indexed to particular word classes.

3.4 Analysis for Observation 3: Leveling in negation

Observation 3 noted that if leveling occurs, it occurs to an equal or greater degree in the negative paradigms of *be*. As with plural leveling, this parallels the typologically attested markedness of the negative [Greenberg, 1966, p50; Givón, 1978, p70; König, 1988, p161; Croft, 2003, p202].

Again, as with leveling in the affirmative, the leveling seen in negation cannot all be attributed to purely phonological simplification: for instance, {*be*, *is*} ⇒ *baint*. We therefore treat variation in negation also as an instance of changes in the inventory of content.

In our analysis of this phenomenon, we draw a crucial distinction between synthetic and analytic negation. We treat synthetic negation as any single verb form that contains both the verbal content of *be* and the negation feature value. This primarily involves forms bearing the contracted negative *-n't*. Payne

---

[17] It is noteworthy that unlike person, number and gender are categories in which pronominal expressions may be less faithful than verbal expressions. In Golin, a Papuan language of New Guinea, both bound and free pronouns are undifferentiated for number contrasts but there is a verbal suffix specialized for first person singular subjects [Foley, 1986, p70]. In Jersey French, the pronoun for both singular and plural first person subjects is *je* but the verb maintains distinct forms [Jones, 2001, p115]. Similarly, in many Indo-Aryan languages, e.g. Hindi, third person pronouns are undifferentiated for gender, but subject gender is marked on the verb.

[1985, p226] distinguishes between negative auxiliaries and negated auxiliaries, the former having inherent negative meaning and the latter simply involving an added inflectional marker to a non-negative morpheme. Kortmann [1999, p10] suggests that although English synthetic negation forms such as *isn't* clearly start out as negated auxiliaries, their patterns of leveling and phonological reduction make them comparable to negative auxiliaries. Zwicky and Pullum [1983] similarly argue that these forms have properties more typical of bound morphemes than of clitics, such as allomorphic variation (*will vs. won't, do vs. don't*).

This paper is primarily concerned with synthetic negation forms rather than analytic negation constructions, as we argue here that person/number leveling is a process predicted to apply specifically in synthetic (contracted) negative morphology (e.g. *ain't*) due to the increase in the 'load' of semantic values borne by a single morphological item. Naturally, if the semantic values of *be* and NEG are carried by different morphological forms, as in an analytic construction such as *am not*, this over-burdening does not occur.

Based on this reasoning, leveling of *be* in analytic negation, as in (12), is not predicted to occur.

(12) I am not ↘
 ↛ *[I ai not, She ai not]
 She is not ↗

 I am ↘
 ↛ *[I are not, They are not]
 They are ↗

If leveling of *be* does occur in negation, it will occur in the synthetic negative paradigm first. This leveling may occur alongside continued differentiation of forms in the paradigm of analytic negation, as in (13).

(13) I am → I am not, I ain't

Our hypothesis is supported by the fact that we found no instances of leveling in analytic but not in synthetic negation in the *SED*, whereas dozens of cases of leveling in synthetic but not analytic negation were found. The more detailed grammar for speaker K5 given in (14), showing both synthetic and analytic negation, illustrates restricted leveling in the synthetic negation paradigm only.

(14)

(I) am	(we) are	(I) 'm not, aint	
(you) are			
(she) is	(they) are	(she) aint	(they) aint

In the discussion that follows, we restrict our focus to leveling in synthetic negation. Further constraints, not included in the analysis here, would regulate the choice of analytic or synthetic expressions of negation [Bresnan, 2002].

The constraint set

Two contextual markedness constraints, given in (15), formalize the intuition discussed above. The high ranking of *[NEG+NUM] would lead to leveling of number distinctions in negative forms of the verb (e.g. *I ain't, we ain't*), while the high ranking of *[NEG+PERS] would lead to leveling of person distinctions in negative forms of the verb (e.g. *we ain't, you ain't, they ain't*).

(15) Avoid overloaded morphology: *[NEG+PERS], *[NEG+NUM]

These two constraints interact with the faithfulness constraints already discussed to yield the typological structure shown in (16).

(16)   *PERS, *[NEG+PERS] ≫ EXPRESS (PERS...)

                EXPRESS (PERS...) ≫ *PERS, *[NEG+PERS]

                *[NEG+PERS] ≫ EXPRESS (PERS...) ≫ *PERS

The first ranking in (16) levels person contrasts, regardless of whether the clause is affirmative or negative. The second ranking expresses person contrasts, regardless of whether the clause is affirmative or negative. The final ranking, crucial to our discussion here, levels person contrasts only in the context of negative morphology. Equally crucial is the observation that no ranking of these constraints will level person contrasts only in affirmative contexts, as there is no markedness constraint to impose restrictions on the unmarked affirmative context.[18]

Constraint ranking and variable outputs

The interaction of the negation constraints with the constraints already introduced generates a typological space that permits a range of possible contrasts

---

[18] We also never find leveling of the affirmative-negative distinction in order to retain person contrasts in synthetic negative verb forms. We might argue that in situations of morphological overload within a verbal domain, faithful expression of verbal features is universally preferable to the expression of nominal features; this asymmetry would resemble the preferred faithfulness to person features in the domain of pronouns as opposed to verbs, discussed earlier in (10). However, negation also has special properties that can be argued to require expression even where other verbal agreement features may not. Affirmative and negative propositions are fundamentally opposed semantically—they cannot be true in the same world—so an output without formal negation marking cannot be considered to be under-specified for affirmative or negative sense (unlike underspecification of person or number). From a functionalist perspective, the expression of negation is fundamental to the clause and may be considered inviolate.

and neutralizations in affirmative and negative paradigms. Below we extend the grammars described for the three sample cases earlier—Yorkshire, Derbyshire, and Suffolk—to include negation constraints. These expanded grammars instantiate the typological possibilities predicted by the rankings in (16). We also present a grammar for Cornwall, as it represents a subtler interaction of negation constraints with person and number constraints.

Yorkshire

As witnessed earlier, Yorkshire has leveling across person, retaining only the number distinction of singular and plural. This division is maintained in the negative paradigms of these speakers as well. As we saw in Figure 12, the constraint ranking for Yorkshire *(is, is, is, are, are)* levels the expression of all person contrasts, both in the singular and in the plural; the same constraints determine the choice of candidate for negative inputs. The constraints on overloaded morphology in synthetic negation do not play a part in the evaluation and are low ranked (Figure 15).

Figure 15. Yorkshire Grammar including Negation Constraints

input: [1 SG NEG]	*PERS	EXP(SG)	EXP(PL)	EXP(PERSVALUE,SG)	*NUM	EXP(PERSVALUE,PL)	*[NEG+PERS]	*[NEG+NUM]
'amn't': [1SG NEG]	*!				*		*	*
☞ 'isn't': [SG NEG]				*	*			*
'aren't': [PL NEG]		*!		*	*			*
'aren't': [1PL NEG]	*!	*		*	*		*	*
'ain't': [NEG]		*!		*				

Derbyshire

In the Derbyshire type of paradigm, a number of contrasts are made in the affirmative paradigm. Although this affirmative paradigm is very different from that of Yorkshire, as there is no leveling in the singular, there is a similarity between Derbyshire and Yorkshire in the context of negation, as the amount of leveling in negation mirrors the amount of leveling in the affirmative in both dialects. In terms of constraint ranking for Derbyshire, this again translates into a low ranking for the two negation constraints (Figure 16).

Although Devon, Wiltshire, Northumberland, Hampshire, Berkshire, and Sussex all have different amounts of leveling in their affirmative paradigms,

Figure 16. Derbyshire Grammar including Negation Constraints

input: [1SG NEG]	Exp(PersValue,SG)	*PERS	Exp(SG)	Exp(PL)	*NUM	Exp(PersValue,PL)	*[NEG+PERS]	*[NEG+NUM]
☞ 'amn't': [1SG NEG]		*			*		*	*
'isn't': [SG NEG]	*!				*			*
'aren't': [PL NEG]	*!	*			*			*
'aren't': [1PL NEG]	*!	*	*		*		*	*
'ain't': [NEG]	*!	*						

their negative system are all accounted for in the same way; the synthetic negation constraints are low ranked and the amount of leveling in affirmative and negative paradigms is identical in all of these systems.

Suffolk

Several distinctions are made in the affirmative *be* paradigm of Suffolk, but this group diverges from the previously discussed in exhibiting complete leveling in negation. The ranking of person and number constraints was seen earlier in Figure 14; when a synthetic negative input is involved, the high rank of *[NEG+PERS] and *[NEG+NUM] becomes apparent, as a general form is always selected (Figure 17).

Figure 17. Suffolk Grammar including Negation Constraints

input: [1SG NEG]	*[NEG+PERS]	*[NEG+NUM]	Exp(1,SG)	Exp(3,SG)	*PERS	*NUM	Exp(SG)	Exp(PL)	Exp(2,SG)	Exp(PersValue,PL)
'amn't': [1SG NEG]	*!	*			*	*				
'isn't': [SG NEG]		*!	*			*				
'aren't': [PL NEG]		*!	*			*	*			
'aren't': [1PL NEG]	*!	*	*		*	*	*			
☞ 'ain't': [NEG]			*			*				

Cornwall

Finally, the affirmative pattern of the Cornwall group is identical to that of Derbyshire, but it differs in its negation pattern. The Cornwall system exhibits more leveling in negation than in the affirmative, but this leveling is not absolute as in the case of *ain't* in Suffolk. This type of partial leveling in negation also occurs in the negative paradigm of Norfolk.

The one distinction that is maintained in the negative paradigm of Cornwall is the third singular form. In this case, it is necessary to posit that the Cornwall system prioritizes a single constraint out of the family of EXPRESS(PERSVALUE,SG) constraints, namely EXPRESS(3,SG), above the negation constraints. With the exception of this very high-ranked constraint, the constraints on morphological overloading in synthetic negation outrank other person and number faithfulness constraints, forcing the selection of a general form in all other cases (Figure 18). This ensures that in the affirmative all singular person distinctions are maintained—due to the relatively high rank of EXPRESS(PERSVALUE,SG)—but in negation only a distinct form for 3SG inputs is maintained.

Figure 18. Cornwall Grammar including Negation Constraints

input: [1SG NEG]		$E_{XP}(3,SG)$	*[NEG+PERS]	*[NEG+NUM]	$E_{XP}(PERSVALUE,SG)$	*PERS	$E_{XP}(SG)$	$E_{XP}(PL)$	*NUM	$E_{XP}(PERSVALUE,PL)$
'amn't':	1SG NEG		* !	*		*			*	
'isn't':	3SG NEG		* !	*	*	*			*	
'aren't':	PL NEG			* !	*			*	*	
'aren't':	1PL NEG		* !	*	*	*		*	*	
☞ 'aren't':	[NEG]				*		*	*		

input: [3SG NEG]		$E_{XP}(3,SG)$	*[NEG+PERS]	*[NEG+NUM]	$E_{XP}(PERSVALUE,SG)$	*PERS	$E_{XP}(SG)$	$E_{XP}(PL)$	*NUM	$E_{XP}(PERSVALUE,PL)$
'amn't':	1SG NEG	* !	*	*	*	*			*	
☞ 'isn't':	3SG NEG		*	*		*			*	
'aren't':	PL NEG	* !		*	*			*	*	
'aren't':	1PL NEG	* !	*	*	*	*		*	*	
'aren't':	[NEG]	* !			*		*	*		

This analysis of negation predicts that there may be variable systems in which the general form *ain't* is alternating with, and is in the process of replacing, a specific form such as *amn't*. We do indeed frequently find this type of variability in the *SED*. These systems are directly accounted for by the current analysis, but as these alternations were very idiosyncratic, with no single type of alternation occurring for more than one speaker, they did not satisfy our criterion for including only stable systems attested in more than one individual and so we do not list all of them here.

Interim summary
The extraction of all invariant (categorical) paradigms for the verb *be* in the *SED* has yielded two significant patterns in the data which confirm previous studies of leveling in English: there is more leveling of person/number contrasts in the plural than in the singular and more leveling in synthetic negatives than in affirmatives.

We have constructed an OT model of person leveling and negation leveling in present-tense English *be* which allows for degrees of leveling in these domains, but which precludes the occurrence of more leveling in the singular (than in plural), or more leveling in the affirmative (than in negative). Even though it is far from complete, we have adopted the minimal constraint set needed to account for our present data and to exclude grammars that appear to be unattested.

The OT analysis so far addresses WLH's Constraints Problem, linking inter-speaker variation and crosslinguistic markedness patterns; the architecture of OT lends itself particularly well to such unified treatments of dialectal and typological variation [Kusters, 2000; Deo and Sharma, 2006]. In the sections that follow, we move to WLH's Transition and Embedding Problems in light of variability within individual grammars.

4 Intra-speaker variation in affirmative and negative declaratives

In the remaining sections we focus on speakers that WLH term 'transitional', 'bidialectal', or having 'heterogeneous systems characterized by orderly differentiation' [p184]. All individual *be* paradigms in the *SED* which were found to contain internal variation, and which were also instantiated in more than one speaker and had complete data sets for affirmative and synthetic negation paradigms, are presented below. As before, the paradigm tables present affirmative and synthetic negative paradigms, with all individuals who exhibit the pattern listed at the top of the table, and slight differences in lexical form for a speaker given in parentheses following the speaker index.

We treat Figure 22, the plural *am* paradigms, as distinct from the others. We cannot characterize the plural *am* varieties purely in terms of person/number information, as plural *am* is always a variant and never occurs as the sole plural form in any person in any of the grammars here. In over half of the paradigms

Figure 19. Variable second person singular

Variable Yorkshire: St3,Y21,Y29,La6

(I) am	(we) are	(I) amnt	
(thee) art/are			
(she) is	(they) are	(she) isnt	(they) arent

Variable Somerset: So7,Do5(thee art/you be)

(I) be	(we) be	(I) baint	
(thee) be/art			
(her) is	(they) be	(her) isnt	(they) baint

Figure 20. Variable first person singular

Variable Monmouthshire: M1,Gl7(she aint)

(I) am/be	(we) be	(I) baint	
(thee) beest			
(her) is	(they) be	(her) aint	(they) baint

Variable Bedfordshire: Bd1,Bd2,Bd3,K3(aint)

(I) am/are	(we) are	(I) aint/ent	
(you) are			
(she) is	(they) are	(she) aint/ent	(they) aint/ent

Figure 21. Variable third person singular

Variable Oxfordshire: O3,Bk3(her aint/ent, her is/she be)

(I) be	(us/we) be	(I) beaint	
(you) be			
(she) is/be	(they) be	(she) aint	(they) beaint

Variable Gloucestershire: Gl5,Gl6,Ha1

(I) be	(us/we) be	(I) baint	
(thee) beest			
(her) be/is	(they) be	(her) aint	(they) baint

≈ *Variable Dorset:* Do2,Do4(her is/she be)

(I) be	(us/we) be	(I) baint	
(thee) art			
(she) is/be	(they) be	(she) isnt	(they) baint

Figure 22. Plural 'am' varieties

Surrey: Sr2,Sr4

(I) are/am	(we) are/am	(I) aint	
(you) are			
(she) is	(they) are/am	(she) aint	(they) aint

Cornwall: Co3,Co4(she); So8('m only pl),Co2('m only pl)

(I) be/'m	(we) be/'m	(I) baint	
(thee) art			
(her) is	(they) be/'m	(her) isnt	(they) baint

Devon/Wiltshire: D1,D3(us),W9(bist)

(I) be	(we) be	(I) baint	
(thee) art			
(her) is	(they) be/'m	(her) isnt	(they) baint

Devon/Hampshire: D5,Ha3(she,we,isnt)

(I) be	(us) be/'m	(I) baint	
(thee) art			
v (her) is	(they) be	(her) aint	(they) baint

with plural *am*, its distribution is precisely coextensive with another form (*be* or *are*), so person and number features are not sufficient to distinguish its distribution and some other factors must be involved. Ihalainen, [1991, pp107–8] observes that in the generalized *am* dialects in East Somerset, *am* is used as an unstressed allomorph of *be*, and so its occurrence appears to be dependent on phonological constraints. We therefore set aside the plural *am* systems in Figure 22 from our analysis.

For the remaining variable paradigms, we can see that Observation 1 (plural leveling), Observation 2 (no pronoun leveling), and Observation 3 (negative leveling) from the previous section still hold. In addition, we can make three further observations:

Observation 4:
Choice of variant forms of *be* and of pronominal forms are often at least partially independent.

We do not discuss this observation further save to note that it forms part of a more general finding here that grammatical variables in the present data do not appear to alternate as systematically as a competing grammars view [Kroch, 2000] would anticipate. Although instances of covariation do occur in the data, e.g. *thee art, you be* in the speech of Do5, a single pronoun frequently occurs with variant verb forms. Some examples are give in (17).

(17) *thee art, thee are* (Variable Yorkshire)
thee be, thee art (Variable Somerset)
I am, I be (variable Monmouthshire)
I am, I are (variable Bedfordshire)
she is, she be (variable Oxfordshire, variable Dorset)
her is, her be (variable Gloucestershire)

Mixing of variant pronominal forms with variant verbal forms has also been illustrated in extracts from taped Somerset speech in [Ihalainen, 1991, pp109–116], repeated in (18).[19]

(18) i. *You taught theeself, didn't ee?*
ii. *I'm not under no obligation about this, be I?*
iii. *They're not ready, be 'em?*
iv. B.I. *What be you, Herb? Seventy-two?*
H.T. *Gone seventy-five.*
B.I. *Seventy-five! Thee!*
W.B. *Thee! Thee! I didn't know you were gone seventy-five.*

Observation 5:

i. The variable patterns can be decomposed into combinations of the invariant patterns already seen.

ii. The general verb form is often in free variation with more specific forms.

Two detailed examples of Observation 5 are given in Figure 23. Each variable inventory can be represented as a partial intersection of two invariant systems. This is not to say that these systems are direct sources of the variable system in geographical space or historical time, but rather that each alternant in the variable system gives rise to one of two grammars very close in terms of

---

[19] The third extract in (18) is used by Ihalainen to illustrate the fact that *thee* is used more frequently in stressed positions than in unstressed ones.

pure typological space. All of the variable systems listed in Figures 19–22 can be described in this way.

Summary of decomposition of all variable inventories:

Variable Bedfordshire = invariant Kent + invariant Suffolk
Variable Yorkshire = invariant Derbyshire + invariant Suffolk
Variable Somerset = invariant Hampshire + invariant Devon
Variable Monmouthshire = invariant Cornwall + invariant Wiltshire
(abstractly: 'art' ≈ 'beest', 'are' ≈ 'be')
Variable Oxfordshire = invariant Hampshire + invariant Sussex
Variable Gloucestershire = invariant Wiltshire + invariant Berkshire
Variable Dorset = invariant Devon + invariant Berkshire
(abstractly: 'art' ≈ 'beest')

Figure 23. Decomposition of variable systems

Variable Bedfordshire = Suffolk + Kent

	sg	pl
1	am, are	are
2	are	
3	is	are

	sg	pl
1	am	are
2	are	
3	is	are

	SG	PL
1	are	are
2	are	
3	is	are

Variable Yorkshire = Suffolk + Derbyshire

	sg	pl
1	am	are
2	art, are	
3	is	are

	sg	pl
1	am	are
2	are	
3	is	are

	sg	pl
1	am	are
2	art	
3	is	are

Observation 6:

i. Most of the variable inventories are *not* comprised of two geographically adjacent dialects.

ii. Every case of variability but one appears to involve variation of a vernacular form with a standard (Suffolk-type) form, even if the second system as a whole resembles some other non-Suffolk dialect.

Reference to Figure 1 confirms the generalization that the decomposition of variable inventories does *not* result in two geographically adjacent inventories. Rather, almost all cases of variability involve variation of a vernacular form with a standard (Suffolk-type) form. The one exception is the variable Somerset inventory, in which a variant from a neighboring dialect (Devon) infiltrates the system.

Thus social prestige of the standard variety and geographical continuity of vernacular varieties appear to be the two forces placing constraints on the types of inventories that arise. The former appears to be a far stronger factor in the *SED* data. A natural sociolinguistic explanation of this situation is that the learning data or environment is comprised of the local vernacular system and the global standardized system.

However, as noted already, the data do not show global covariation of forms, but rather very local alternations in parts of the *be* paradigms. The decomposition of variable inventories showed that the intrusion of an isolated standard form into an otherwise nonstandard inventory does not lead to a completely standard paradigm. Instead, the second system of contrasts that arises from the inclusion of a single standard form almost always resembles another nonstandard system. For instance, the intrusion of the standard form *am* into M1's Wiltshire-like grammar leads to the resulting paradigm resembling the inventory of Cornwall in terms of abstract contrasts, despite the lack of any significant contact with that variety.

The present analysis predicts that in theory any combination from the typological space of possible grammars may occur for a single variable speaker, and the two forces of social prestige and geographical proximity are simply external constraints restricting expression of the full typological range of possible inventories.

If this interpretation is correct, it suggests a model of variation in which the standard grammar is perturbing the vernacular grammar but not necessarily replacing it. The perturbed grammar appears to vary between the vernacular and a second grammatical system that is very close to it in the space of possible grammars, if not in geographical space. The second system usually does not have the overall structure of the standard grammar, but rather merely one additional resemblance to it.

Stochastic evaluation of constraints with stochastic learning as in the Gradual Learning Algorithm [Boersma, 1998; Boersma and Hayes, 2001; Jäger, 2007; Keller and Asudeh, 2002] provides a way of formally modelling this kind of variation. The section that follows offers an account linking Observation 5 and Observation 6 as consequences of the stochastic nature of individual grammars.

5 A stochastic OT model of individual variation

5.1 The Framework: Generalizing from the Categorical to the Quantitative

In this final section, we present a formal model to account for localized individual variability in grammars as witnessed in the *SED* data. As mentioned at the outset, the full power of the Stochastic OT apparatus is not needed in the present analysis as we do not have frequency distributions for each variable system. However, we believe that this approach is useful conceptually and theoretically even in the absence of frequency data, as it allows us to formalize what is meant by individual variation and to offer an account of localized variation, as opposed to the systematic covariation predicted by competing grammars.

Optimality Theory with stochastic evaluation was originally developed by Paul Boersma as part of a theory of functional phonology that addresses the learning of categories, variation, optionality, and probability [Boersma, 1997, 1998, 2000; Boersma and Hayes, 2001]. It is one of a family of generalized OT frameworks that address variation (see [Anttila, 2002; Boersma, 1999b; Hibiya, 2000; Boersma and Hayes, 2001] for reviews). Stochastic OT is distinguished by a particularly well-developed underlying theory, including an associated Gradual Learning Algorithm (GLA), and an implementation within the freely available cross-platform Praat computer program [Boersma, 1999a; Boersma and Weenink, 2000].[20] Stochastic OT differs from standard OT in two essential ways:

i. **ranking on a continuous scale:** Constraints are not simply ranked on a discrete ordinal scale; rather, they have a value on the continuous scale of real numbers. Thus constraints not only dominate other constraints, but are specific distances apart, and these distances are relevant to what the theory predicts.

ii. **stochastic evaluation**: At each evaluation the real value of each constraint is perturbed by temporarily adding to its ranking value a random value drawn from a normal distribution. For example, a constraint with the mean rank of 99 could be evaluated at 98.12 or 100.3. It is the constraint ranking that results from these new disharmonic values that is used in evaluation. The rank a constraint has in the grammar is the mean of a normal distribution or 'bell curve' of these variant values that it has when applied in evaluations; this is illustrated in Figure 24.[21]

---

[20]The GLA is also implemented in OTSoft, also freely available [Hayes *et al.*, 2000].
[21]The diagrams in Figures 24–27 are adapted from [Boersma and Hayes, 2001].

Figure 24. Constraint ranking on a continuous scale with stochastic evaluation

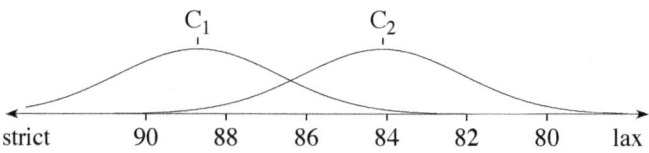

As explained by Boersma and Hayes [2001], an OT grammar with stochastic evaluation can generate both categorical and variable outputs. Categorical outputs arise when crucially ranked constraints are spread far apart on the continuous scale, so that the stochastic variation in ranking values has no discernable effect. In Figure 25, for example, $C_1 \gg C_2$ and the two constraints are spread far enough apart that the bulk of their ranges of variation (illustrated in a simplified way by the ovals) do not overlap. As the distance between constraints increases, interactions become vanishingly rare, reaching a point where variant outputs lie beneath any given error threshhold, or beyond the life expectancy of the speaker. (A distance of five standard deviations ensures an error rate of less than 0.02% [Boersma and Hayes, 2001, p50].)[22]

Figure 25. Categorical constraint ranking with ranges of variation:

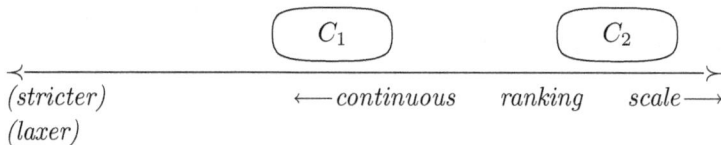

Variable outputs arise when crucially ranked constraints are close enough together for the variation in their ranking values to interact with some observable frequency. This possibility is illustrated in Figure 26, where the bulk of the ranges of variation of two constraints overlaps. Here again $C_1 \gg C_2$, but

---

[22] Units of measurement are arbitrary. With standard deviation = 2.0, a ranking distance of 10 units between constraints is taken to be effectively categorical.

with some discernable frequency during stochastic evaluation C_1 will be ranked at a point in its lower range, call it c_1, while C_2 is simultaneously ranked at a point c_2 in its higher range. As shown in Figure 27, C_2 will then temporarily dominate C_1 in selecting the optimal output, possibly producing a different output.

The frequency of this reversal depends on the ranking distance between constraints and the standard deviation in ranking variance during evaluations (which is assumed to be the same across constraints). If we take the standard deviation to be zero, the constraints are always evaluated in the same strict domination sequence, and we have ordinal OT [Prince and Smolensky, 2004]. Stochastic OT is thus a generalization of ordinal OT. Its associated Gradual Learning Algorithm (GLA) can learn grammars robustly from variable data [Boersma, 1997, 1998, 2000; Boersma and Hayes, 2001].

Figure 26. Free constraint ranking with ranges of variation:

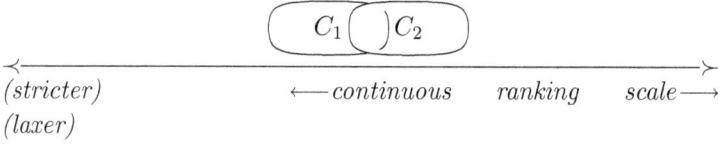

Figure 27. Reversal of constraint dominance:

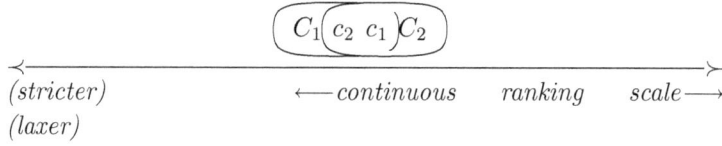

5.2 Stochastic Grammars and the Gradual Learning Algorithm

Boersma's stochastic grammars are based on the optimization function of ordinal Optimality Theory [Prince and Smolensky, 2004].[23] The effective ranking ('selectionPoint') of a constraint C_i is given by the equation [Boersma, 2000, p483]:

---

[23]Other optimization functions have also been explored. See [Goldwater and Johnson, 2003; Jäger, 2007; Jäger and Rosenbach, 2006].

$$selectionPoint_i = rankingValue_i + noise$$

The *noise* variable represents unknown factors that are independent of the linguistic theory embodied in the constraint set. We assume that there is in fact a deterministic function from the total context plus the input to the output, but many aspects of the context are too complex to know in detail. The random noise variable simply models our ignorance of the total context which includes non-linguistic factors that determine the probability of an output (for example by affecting the speaker's sensitivity to aspects of the current context).

The Gradual Learning Algorithm (GLA), implemented in the Praat system [Boersma and Weenink, 2000], models stochastic grammars given particular constraints and exposure to learning data. Starting from an initial state grammar in which all constraints have the same ranking values (arbitrarily set to be 100.0), the GLA is presented with learning data; this may, for instance, consist of input-output pairs having the statistical distribution of (in the present case) a sample of spoken English.

For each learning datum (a given input-output pair), the GLA compares the output of its own grammar for the same input; if its own output differs from the given output, it adjusts its grammar by moving all the constraints that differentially disfavor its own output upward on the continuous ranking scale by a small increment, and moving all constraints that differentially disfavor the given output downward along the scale by a small decrement. The increment/decrement value is called the 'plasticity' and may be assumed to vary stochastically and to change with age [Boersma, 2000]. In the case of constraint subhierarchies, the adjustment process applies recursively in order to preserve their local ordering relations.

Figure 28. Sample stochastic grammar

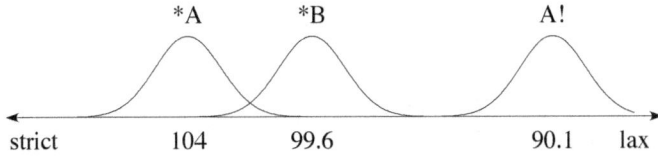

Figure 28 and the tableaux in (19) and (20) illustrate this process. In Figure 28, the markedness constraints *A and *B are ranked fairly close together and the faithfulness constraint A! is ranked lower. If the 'selectionPoint' of *A is higher than that of *B in a given evaluation, then the representative tableau is (19). If the 'selectionPoint' of *A is lower than that of *B in a given evaluation, then the representative tableau is (20).

(19)

	*A	*B	A!
☞ cand$_1$		*	
cand$_2$	*!		

(20)

	*B	*A	A!
cand$_1$	*!		
☞ cand$_2$		*	

Given exposure to data in the environment, the grammar can compare its own output to the output of the learning data for the same input and gradually adjust its own ranking to match external evidence.

If cand$_1$ is always correct in the learning data, i.e. if the surrounding grammars all have the ranking in (19), then each time cand$_2$ is produced by the grammar, the countervailing evidence from the categorical learning data will progressively repel constraints A* and B* further apart, fixing their ranking in that order. If cand$_2$ is always correct in the learning data, then when cand$_1$ is produced by the grammar, the countervailing evidence from the categorical learning data will cause *A and B* to gradually rerank and then continue spreading apart, fixing this reverse order over time.

If both cand$_1$ and cand$_2$ are encountered in the learning data as correct outputs for the same input, i.e. if there is variation in the environment, then the variable data will cause the constraints *A and *B to attract and repel, as in (21), eventually attaining a holding pattern that matches the frequency of variation in the data to which the individual is exposed.

(21)

	*A⇒	⇐*B	A!
☞ cand$_1$		*	
cand$_2$	*!		

	*B⇒	⇐*A	A!
cand$_1$	*!		
☞ cand$_2$		*	

Crucially this means that the stochastic OT model analyzes the acquisition of categorical and variable systems in exactly the same way, and variation is latent in every grammar.

5.3 Analysis for Observations 5 and 6: Localized variation

The present data were subjected to this learning process using idealized categorical and variable frequencies. The noise parameter is arbitrarily set at 2.0 which, as mentioned earlier, models our ignorance of the complete set of factors that may probabilistically influence selection of an output.

A total of 3,200,000 input-output pairs for each British dialect grammar was used to train the Gradual Learning Algorithm [Boersma, 1997, 1999a; Boersma and Hayes, 2001], starting from an initial state grammar in which all constraints have the same ranking values (arbitrarily set to be 100.0). The learning data for categorical dialect systems consisted of 3,200,000 input-output pairs with the same output for a given input 100% of the time. For instance, the categorical system of Standard English consisted of learning data in which 100% of the outputs for [1SG] were the fully faithful feature structure [1SG] abbreviated by the tag 'am'; 100% of the outputs for [2SG] were the general feature structure [ ] abbreviated by the tag 'are', and so on.

The output distributions of the earlier and later grammars for Standard English, shown in Figure 29, were learned by the GLA in this way.[24] The earlier grammar was learned from only 8,000 input-output pairs, while the later grammar was learned by additional exposure to 3,200,000 quantities of categorical data, given the earlier grammar as the initial grammar. The figure shows that the choice of outputs begins to converge towards categoricality.

For the same grammar, Figure 30 shows that the ranking of constraints also becomes more strict with increased exposure to categorical data. The constraint ranking values are shown on the vertical axis; constraint names are horizontally spread out merely for readability. Greater vertical distance between constraints represents decreasing likelihood of ranking reversal. The earlier and later grammars have the same crucial ordinal constraint rankings, but these constraints are spread out differently on the scale. Greater exposure to categorical data incrementally shifts these rankings further apart.

By contrast, exposure to variable data would cause constraints to become closer, as long as there is still plasticity in the system.[25] In the case of variable paradigms, we lacked frequency information for the *SED* inventories and so we simply assumed that each variant form was used 50% of the time. In the case of Variable Monmouthshire, for example, we provided the GLA with data in which the output form *am* was selected 50% of the time with a [1SG] input and the output form *be* was selected for the other 50% of [1SG] inputs, as shown in (22).

---

[24]The output forms 'am', 'are', etc. are mnemonic tags for the abstract feature structure; see n. 16. Only a sample of candidate outputs is included for each input.

[25]Boersma and Hayes [2001] demonstrate how the GLA approximates variable distributions in the environment for a number of test cases.

Figure 29. Output Distributions of Earlier and Later Grammars for Standard English

Output Distributions (Outputs > 1%)				
input	output	% in learning data	% (stochastic)	
			Earlier	Later
[1SG]	am[1SG]	100	69.7	99.9
	are[ ]	0	30.2	
[2SG]	art[2SG]	0	21.8	
	is[SG]	0	10.0	
	are[ ]	100	68.1	99.9
[3SG]	is[3SG]	100	74.2	99.9
	are[ ]	0	25.7	
[1PL]	are[ ]	100	95.8	
	are[PL]	0	4.2	
[3PL]	are[ ]	100	95.7	99.9
	are[PL]	0	4.3	

(22) /1SG/ → be[ ]   50
      /1SG/ → am [1SG]   50
      /2SG/ → beest [2SG] 100
      . . .

Recall Observation 5 that the variable grammars in the data can be decomposed into two invariant grammars, for instance: Variable Monmouthshire (am/be,beest,is) = Wiltshire (be,beest,is) + Cornwall (am,art,is). Figure 31 represents the GLA acquisition of this variable grammar and the two component invariant grammars. Again the constraint ranking values for the three varieties of English are shown on the vertical axis, while the horizontal spread within each variety is simply for readability. The learned distribution of constraints exemplifies Observation 5, as the reranking of two constraints results in two different categorical grammars—not necessarily geographically adjacent—and variation between the two rankings gives rise to an individually variable grammar. These three grammars need not arise through direct contact: all three are simply typologically predicted systems whose attestation in the actual inventory of British dialects may be conditioned by social and historical

Figure 30. Reduction of Variation under Exposure to Categorical Data during 'First-Language' Stochastic Learning by GLA

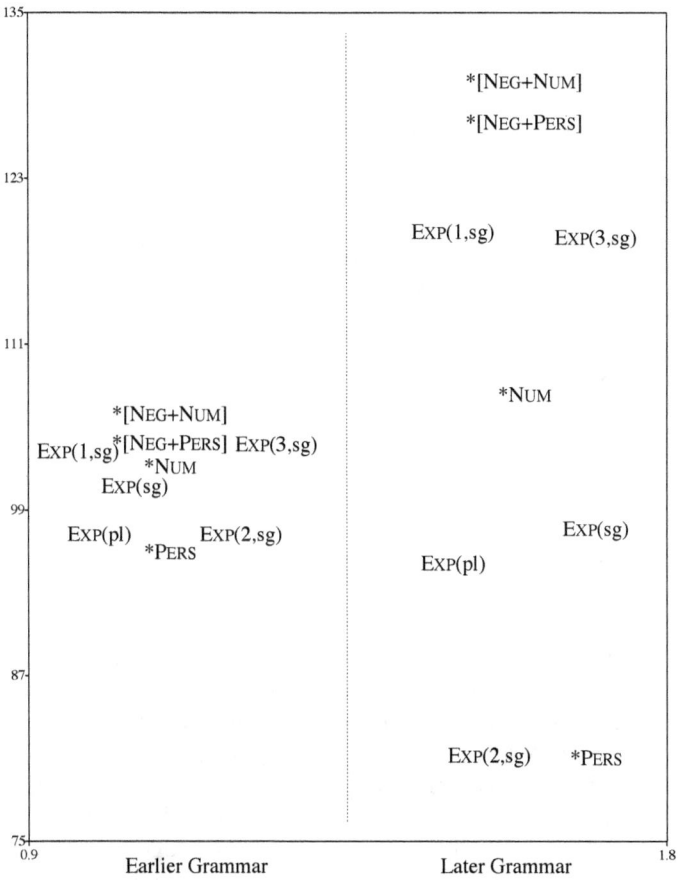

factors.

Figure 31. Decomposition of a Variable Grammar

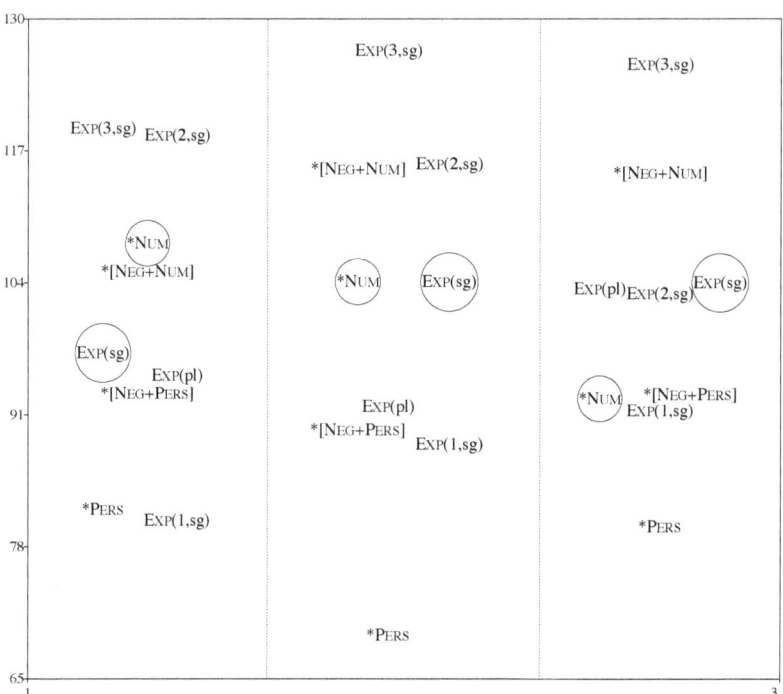

Furthermore, the different rankings of constraints frequently select between candidates that are either more or less specified for certain input features, i.e. they may frequently choose between specific forms and general forms, which was the second aspect of Observation 5. An important correlate of this observation is that reranking of constraints can lead to feature deletion and feature change in the lexical inventory, as a form can come to be partially or wholly underspecified if it comes to always be selected for a range of different inputs, as in Yorkshire. Both of these processes lead to remorphologization, as the lexical entries gain or lose featural specifications.

This highly variable range of systems is not naturally explained by a model using blocking of general forms by more specific forms, nor by an ordinal ranking of violable constraints (ordinal OT) or by a systematically covarying competing grammars scenario.

Finally, as we saw in Observation 6, when a standard form of *be* is variably included in a vernacular grammar, the resulting grammar usually has neither the overall structure of the standard grammar nor that of geographically adjacent grammars. The account given here shows that the two component systems are simply close to one another in the typological space of possible rankings, and the intervention of a standard form leads to an alternation between these two similar rankings.

The point of interest here is that with stochastic evaluation of constraints rankings and hence grammars are inherently variable. There is a region of variant grammars closely surrounding every grammar. The variant grammars belong to the factorial typology of OT constraints. Stochastic evaluation is, in effect, always sampling the typological space of grammars.

Adopting WLH's insight, in their discussion of the Transition Problem, that transitional speakers are of the greatest interest to the study of language change, we have shown that these variable speakers need not be treated as qualitatively different from categorical speakers by a theory of grammar. Furthermore, stochastic evaluation integrates both Embedding (social contact) and Constraints (typology) directly into a theory of constrained and mutable grammars.

5.4 Stochastic plasticity in language change

An alternative treatment of variation in OT is partial ordering of constraints [Anttila, 1997b; Anttila and Fong, 2004], under which variable frequencies of outputs are generated by the total set of possible discrete rankings in a partially ordered set of constraints. We do not assess the respective merits of partial ordering and continuous ranking approaches here, nor the potential for a model of language to incorporate both mechanisms (see [Boersma, 2001] for further discussion). We only furnish some additional sociolinguistic examples of variable phenomena that suggest minimally that some component of contact-sensitive plasticity must be part of every grammar, and that pure grammar-generated frequencies cannot account for all variation.

Recent work has found that sociophonetic variation is acquired at a very early age. Children aged 2-4 frequently reflect the phonetic variation found in their primary caregivers' dialect more closely than that found among other members of the community [Foulkes *et al.*, 1999; Smith *et al.*, 2007]. This finding suggests that the use of at least some variables is determined primarily by children's exposure to whichever dialect ranking their carer has.

Analogous phenomena are found to persist inter-generationally in contact varieties of English. Many contact situations have historically undergone extended periods of bilingualism before language shift occurs. The varieties of English that arise out of bilingualism frequently retain grammatical quirks that descend from the earlier period of bilingualism. Crucially, in some cases, the bilingualism itself no longer exists, yet the disruption to the second language (English) constraint ranking by the first language in earlier bilingual speakers continues to be mirrored in the English acquired by subsequent English-monolingual descendants. As with child acquisition of sociophonetic variation, this phenomenon suggest that learners are highly tuned to outputs in the environment, whatever the original source of those outputs may be, rather than exclusively generating variable rates grammar-internally.

Studies have shown this type of persistence of substrate features in subsequent generations for a number of English varieties: copula omission in African American Vernacular English [Rickford, 1998]; topicalization constructions in Hiberno-English [Filppula, 1991]; phonological variants in ethnically distinct communities in Boston [Laferriere, 1979]; topicalization and left-dislocation in Yiddish English [Prince, 1998]; aspectual marking in Singaporean English [Bao, 2005].[26]

In all of these cases, Speaker A has an L1 and an L2, and the ranking of the L1 can affect that of the L2. Speaker B, who is Speaker A's child, may have become a native speaker of the erstwhile L2 (e.g. nativization of English in Singapore) and may have lost all competence in the erstwhile L1, but may *still* retain transfer features through the direct acquisition of Speaker A's L2 ranking. Furthermore, there is evidence that Speaker B's rate of use of such transfer features will be sensitive to the *extent* of regular interaction with the previous generation. Such frequency effects based on social networks and interaction have been shown to hold widely in the diffusion and adoption of any new linguistic forms (e.g. [Milroy, 1980; Nichols, 1983]).

As with the *SED* data we have examined in the present paper, these situations encompass two broad dimensions of variation: linguistic and social. Copula omission in many creoles and varieties of African-American English, for instance, can vary along both dimensions: First, it shows a predicate effect of the following type: PROG > ADJ > LOC > NP (i.e., all contexts may be variable, but progressive (and *gonna* future) predicates will have higher rates of omission than adjectival and locative predicates, which will have higher rates of omission than nominal predicates). Second, the *degree* to which this variable system is instantiated in a speaker is itself found to be systematically variable. In the table in (23) we offer a simplified example of these two factors in copula omission (see [Rickford, 1998] for a detailed summary of such findings).

---

[26]This list is specific to English varieties that have undergone some degree of shift, so that the original bilingual source of a given grammatical features is opaque to many speakers; direct transfer from one language to another in active bilingualism is much more extensively documented.

(23)

	PROG	ADJ	LOC	NP
Speaker 1	100%	80%	60%	40%
Speaker 2	80%	60%	40%	20%
Speaker 3	60%	40%	20%	5%

In (23), the horizontal dimension reflects a linguistic (internal) factor and the vertical dimension reflects a social (external) factor. In WLH's terms, these are 'constraints' and 'embedding' effects respectively, reflected in 'transitional' individuals.

While both discrete and continuous models—one generating strict frequency predictions and the other subject to markedness and probabilistic effects—could offer an account of linguistic factors, continuous models integrate social factors as well, namely variation in a grammar based on the locus of an individual in the community. The explicit theories of learning and plasticity contained in stochastic OT and its associated family of continuous ranking models seamlessly accommodate variable synchronic and diachronic diffusion effects described in the sociolinguistic literature.

6 Conclusions

This analysis of inter- and intra-speaker paradigms has covered all systems present in the *SED*, excluding only those ruled out by our two initial criteria—the requirements that a full set of affirmative and synthetic negative *be* forms be recorded and that at least two speakers be attested per system.

Invariant inter-speaker (dialectal) systems were found to include exceptionless patterns of leveling in the plural and in the negative, mirroring cross-linguistic typology. This parallel was accounted for in our analysis by the typological space generated by universal constraint subhierarchies in OT.

Intra-speaker (individual) variation was found to frequently involve alternation of isolated forms rather than systematic alternations of two complete dialect grammars. The standard does not therefore appear to be replacing the vernacular in a robust competing grammars scenario; rather, variation is idiosyncratic and inherent in individual grammars.

There are many potential sociolinguistic reasons for the adoption of new individual forms, including salience of forms [Trudgill, 1986], access to the standard, and conscious selectivity on the part of the speaker [LePage and Tabouret-Keller, 1985]. The reasons for adopting a particular form may thus be entirely external to its particular linguistic features, although those features cause the form to be fit into its appropriate place in the speaker's grammatical system, and the constraints of the grammar to be reranked appropriately to allow this fit. If a form is frequently used by an individual, either due to frequent use in the environment or due to its particular social value, it will become a permanent fixture of the speaker's inventory, through gradual movement of the active constraints in the ranking space.

Stochastic OT, together with an appropriate output-oriented system for syntactic representation such as optimality-theoretic LFG (OT-LFG), is a model that allows for such partial intrusion/perturbation by the standard variety. Stochastic OT treats individual grammars as highly plastic cognitive systems sensitively tuned to frequencies in the linguistic environment. One consequence is that it can model how an individually variable grammar (WLH's Transition) samples the typological space of possible grammars (WLH's Constraints), while being constrained by geographical and particularly social contact and exposure (WLH's Embedding). The structure and acquisition of categorical and variable grammars are formally identical under this analysis, simply differing in their degree of variability, which is treated as an inherent property of all grammars.

More systematic covariation can also be captured within the Stochastic OT framework. Such variation may reflect substantive constraint dependencies, seen in phenomena such as the "constant rate effect" in historical syntactic change in English [Clark, 2004]. Systematic covariation may also reflect style sensitivity parameters which boost or depress the ranking values of groups of constraints [Boersma and Hayes, 2001, pp83–84] as in the morphosyntax of case ellipsis in Korean and Japanese [Lee, 2002, 2003, 2006]. In an extreme case, such parameters could define quantal jumps in ranking that would create entirely distinct grammars, modeling diglossia.

The detailed paths of historical change producing the English systems studied here remain a topic for further research, as are the implications for the learnability of morphology. Important work in language development has adopted the central assumptions that there is only one correct form for each slot in a paradigm and that overregularizations are corrected by exposure to the correct form [Pinker, 1984]. Yet, as we have seen, the Gradual Learning Algorithm of the stochastic OT model allows for robust learning from variable outputs of the same input.

We should note in closing that questionnaire responses, like other data collected through elicitation of linguistic intuitions, may inaccurately reflect the use of these forms in actual speech and should be treated with caution [Ihalainen, 1991, p110; Schilling-Estes and Wolfram, 1994, p297; Cornips, 2006]. Our primary interest in these data has been to map the typological diversity in British dialects. The Stochastic OT model of individual dialectal variation that has been presented here should ultimately be tested against genuine frequencies of use as attested in robust sociolinguistic data.

Acknowledgements We wish to thank Lieselotte Anderwald, Brady Clark, Richard Coates, Andrew Garrett, Jane Grimshaw, Bruce Hayes, Ruth Kempson, Paul Kiparsky, Wouter Kusters, Hanjung Lee, Roger Levy, Chris Manning, and Elizabeth Traugott, as well as audiences at the OT Symposium of the English Linguistic Society of Japan (Kobe, November 2000), the Bay Area Typology Workshop (University of California at Berkeley, March 2001), the 2003 Nijmegen Lectures (Max-Planck Institute, Nijmegen, December 2003), the University of Sussex (February 2005) and ICLCE1 (Edinburgh, June 2005) for many comments which have improved earlier versions of this work. We remain solely responsible for all errors of fact and interpretation. This work is based in part on work supported by the National Science Foundation under Grant No. BCS-9818077.

Appendix A: Questions from the *SED* used to create database of forms of the verb *be*

VIII.2.8 HOW ARE YOU?
  [affirmative wh-question]
  North: 2-91. West: 2193-2268. South: 4488-4580. East: 6832-6916.

VIII.9.5 We drink water when WE ARE/ I AM./ SHE IS./ THEY ARE thirsty.
  [affirmative declarative, adjectival predicate]
  North:92-389. West: 2269-2602. South: 4581-4881. East: 6917-7253.

IX.7.1 To find out whether you are right, you ask quite simply AM I right?
  [affirmative y/n question, adjectival predicate]
  North: 390-464. West: 2603-2676. South: 4882-4956. East: 7254-7338.

IX.7.2 ARE YOU MARRIED? IS SHE. ARE THEY.
  [affirmative y/n question, adjectival predicate]
  North: 465-679. West: 2677-2893. South: 4957-5187. East: 7339-7589.

IX.7.3 But AREN'T YOU/ ISN'T SHE/ AREN'T THEY married?
  [negative y/n question, adjectival predicate]
  North: 680-898. West: 2894-3110. South: 5188-5411. East: 7590-7843.

IX.7.4 And if it was you, you'd say to yourself AREN'T I lucky?
  [negative y/n question, adjectival predicate]
  North: 899-972. West: 3111-3183. South: 5412-5484. East: 7844-7926.

IX.7.5 He's alright there ISN'T HE?/ AREN'T I/ AREN'T YOU/ AREN'T THEY?
  [negative tag question]
  North: 973-1258. West: 3184-3479. South: 5485-5781. East: 7927-8252.

IX.7.7 Which of you is English here? you could answer I AM/ YOU ARE/ SHE IS/ THEY ARE.

[affirmative declarative, predicate ellipsis]
North: 1259-1526. West: 3480-3767. South: 5782-6082. East: 8253-8587.

IX.7.9 Oh yes WE ARE/ I AM/ YOU ARE/ SHE IS (English)
[affirmative declarative, predicate ellipsis]
North: 1527-1794. West: 3768-4055. South: 6083-6378. East: 8588-8909.

IX.7.10 Oh no I'M NOT/ SHE ISN'T/ THEY AREN'T (drunk).
[negative declarative, predicate ellipsis]
North: 1795-1988. West: 4056-4271. South: 6379-6605. East: 8910-9160.

IX.7.11 Get away, I'm NOT drunk.
[negative declarative, adjectival predicate]
North: 1989-2063. West: 4272-4347. South: 6606-6680. East: 9161-9245.

IX.9.2 You see a dog chasing your sheep, and you know it's not yours, so you wonder WHOSE IT IS.
[affirmative wh declarative]
North: 2064-2140. West: 4348-4417. South: 6681-6750. East: 9246-9330.

IX.9.4 WHO ARE YOUR PARENTS?
[affirmative wh-question]
North: 2141-2193. West: 4418-4487. South: 6751-6831. East: 9331-9417.

Appendix B: Abbreviations for Region Names

Bd = Bedfordshire; Bk = Buckinghamshire; Brk = Berkshire; C = Cambridgeshire; Ch = Cheshire; Co = Cornwall; Cu = Cumberland; D = Devon; Db = Derbyshire; Do = Dorset; Du = Durham; Ess = Essex; Ha = Hampshire; He = Herefordshire; Hrt = Hertfordshire; Hu = Huntingdonshire; Gl = Gloucestershire; K = Kent; L = Lincolnshire; La = Lancashire; Lei = Leicestershire; M = Monmouthshire; Man = Isle of Man; MxL = Middlesex and London; Nb = Northumberland; Nf = Norfolk; Nt = Nottighamshire; Nth = Northamptonshire; O = Oxfordshire; R = Rutland; Sa = Shropshire; Sf = Suffolk; So = Somerset; Sr = Surrey; St = Staffordshire; Sx = Sussex; W = Wiltshire; Wa = Warwickshire; We = Westmoreland; Wo - Worcestershire; Y = Yorkshire.

BIBLIOGRAPHY

[Aissen, 1999] Judith Aissen. Markedness and subject choice in Optimality Theory. *Natural Language and Linguistic Theory*, 17:673–711, 1999.

[Anderwald and Kortmann, 2002] Lieselotte Anderwald and Bernd Kortmann. Typology and Dialectology: A Programmatic Sketch. In J. van Marle and J. Berns, editors, *Present Day Dialectology, Vol. I: Problems and Discussions*, pages 159–171. Mouton de Gruyter, Berlin, 2002.

[Anderwald, 2001] Lieselotte Anderwald. Was/Were-variation in non-standard British English today. *English World-Wide*, 22, 2001.

[Anderwald, 2002] Lieselotte Anderwald. *Negation in Non-Standard British English: Gaps, Regularizations and Asymmetrics*. Routledge, 2002.

[Anderwald, 2003] Lieselotte Anderwald. Non-standard English and typological principles: The case of negation. In G. Rohdenburg and B. Mondorf, editors, *Determinants of Grammatical Variation in English*, pages 507–529. Mouton de Gruyter, Berlin, 2003.

[Anttila and Fong, 2004] Arto Anttila and Vivienne Fong. Variation, ambiguity and noun classes in English. *Lingua*, 114(9–10):1253–1290, 2004. Special issue on Variation in Form versus Variation in Meaning.

[Anttila, 1997a] Arto Anttila. *Variation in Finnish Phonology and Morphology*. PhD thesis, Stanford University, Stanford, California, 1997a.

[Anttila, 1997b] Arto Anttila. Deriving variation from grammar. In Frans Hinskens, Roeland van Hout, and Leo Wetzels, editors, *Variation, Change and Phonological Theory*, pages 35–68. John Benjamins, Amsterdam, 1997b.

[Anttila, 2002] Arto Anttila. Variation and phonological theory. *The Handbook of Language Variation and Change*, pages 206–243, 2002.

[Bao, 2005] Zhiming Bao. The aspectual system of Singapore English and the systemic substratist explanation. *Journal of Linguistics*, 41:237–267, 2005.

[Bell, 1984] Allan Bell. Language style as audience design. *Language in Society*, 13:145–204, 1984.

[Benua, 1995] Laura Benua. Identity effects in morphological truncation. In J. Beckman, L. Dickey, and S. Urbanczyk, editors, *Papers in Optimality Theory*, University of Massachusetts Occasional Papers 18, pages 77–136. University of Massachusetts, Amherst, 1995.

[Boersma and Hayes, 2001] Paul Boersma and Bruce Hayes. Empirical Tests of the Gradual Learning Algorithm. *Linguistic Inquiry*, 32:45–86, 2001.

[Boersma and Weenink, 2000] Paul Boersma and David Weenink. Praat computer program, 2000. Available On-line, Institute of Phonetic Sciences, University of Amsterdam: http:\\www.fon.hum.uva.nl\praat\.

[Boersma, 1997] Paul Boersma. How we learn variation, optionality, and probability. In B. Caron, editor, *Proceedings of the Institute of Phonetic Sciences 21*, pages 43–58, Paris, 1997. Available on-line (Rutgers Optimality Archive): http:\\ruccs.rutgers.edu\roa.html.

[Boersma, 1998] Paul Boersma. *Functional Phonology: Formalizing the Interaction between Articulatory and Perceptual Drives*. Holland Academic Graphics, The Hague, 1998. Doctoral thesis, University of Amsterdam.

[Boersma, 1999a] Paul Boersma. Optimality-theoretic learning in the praat program. *IFA Proceedings*, 23:17–35, 1999.

[Boersma, 1999b] Paul Boersma. Review of Arto Anttila: *Variation in Finnish phonology and morphology*. *GLOT International*, 5(1):33–40, 1999.

[Boersma, 2000] Paul Boersma. Learning a grammar in Functional Phonology. In Joost Dekkers, Frank van der Leeuw, and Jeroen van de Weijer, editors, *Optimality Theory: Phonology, syntax and acquisition*, pages 465–523. Oxford University Press, New York, 2000.

[Boersma, 2001] Paul Boersma. Review of Arto Anttila (1997): Variation in Finnish Phonology and Morphology. *Glot International*, 5:33–40, 2001.

[Bonet, 1995] Eulalia Bonet. Feature structure of Romance clitics. *Natural Language & Linguistic Theory*, 13(4):607–647, 1995.

[Börjars and Chapman, 1998] Kersti Börjars and Carol Chapman. Agreement and pro-drop in some dialects of English. *Linguistics*, 36:71–98, 1998.

[Bresnan and Deo, 2001] Joan Bresnan and Ashwini Deo. Grammatical constraints on variation: 'Be' in the *Survey of English Dialects* and (Stochastic) Optimality Theory. Stanford University. http:\\www.stanford.edu\~bresnan\download.html, 2001.

[Bresnan, 2000] Joan Bresnan. Explaining morphosyntactic competition. *The Handbook of Contemporary Syntactic Theory*, pages 11–44, 2000.

[Bresnan, 2001a] Joan Bresnan. *Lexical-functional syntax*. Blackwell, Oxford, 2001.

[Bresnan, 2001b] Joan Bresnan. Optimal Syntax. In J. Dekkers, F. van der Leeuw, and J. van de Weijer, editors, *Optimality Theory: Phonology, Syntax and Acquisition*, pages 334–385. Oxford University Press, Oxford, 2001.

[Bresnan, 2001c] Joan Bresnan. The emergence of the unmarked pronoun. In Geraldine Legendre, Jane Grimshaw, and Sten Vikner, editors, *Optimality-Theoretic Syntax*, pages 113–142. MIT Press, Cambridge, MA, 2001.

[Bresnan, 2002] Joan Bresnan. The Lexicon in Optimality Theory. In S. Stevenson and P. Merlo, editors, *The Lexical Basis of Sentence Processing: Formal, Computational, and Experimental Issues*, pages 39–58. John Benjamins, Amsterdam, 2002.

[Britain, 2002] David Britain. Diffusion, levelling, simplification and reallocation in past tense BE in the English Fens. *Journal of Sociolinguistics*, 6(1):16–43, 2002.

[Brown and Levinson, 1987] Penelope Brown and Stephen Levinson. *Politeness: Some Universals in Language Usage*. Cambridge University Press, Cambridge, 2nd edition, 1987.

[Carstairs-McCarthy, 1987] Andrew Carstairs-McCarthy. *Allomorphy in Inflexion*. Croom Helm, London, 1987.

[Cheshire et al., 1993] J. Cheshire, V. Edwards, and P. Whittle. Non-standard English and dialect levelling. In J. Milroy and L. Milroy, editors, *Real English: The Grammar of English in the British Isles*, pages 53–96. Longman, London, 1993.

[Cheshire, 1991] Jenny Cheshire. Variation in the use of 'ain't' in an urban British English dialect. In P. Trudgill and J. Chambers, editors, *Dialects of English: Studies in Grammatical Variation*, pages 54–73. Longman, London, 1991.

[Cheshire, 1996] Jenny Cheshire. Syntactic variation and the concept of prominence. In *Speech Past and Present: Essays in English Dialectology in Memory of Ossi Ihalainen*, pages 1–17. Peter Lang, Frankfurt, 1996.

[Clark, 2004] Brady Clark. *A Stochastic Optimality Theory Approach to Syntactic Change*. PhD thesis, Stanford University, Stanford, California, 2004.

[Cornips, 2006] Leonie Cornips. Intermediate syntactic variants in a dialect—standard speech repertoire and relative acceptability. In Gisbert Fanselow, Caroline Féry, Matthias Schlesewsky, and Ralf Vogel, editors, *Gradedness*. Oxford University Press, Oxford, 2006.

[Coupland, 1984] Nikolas Coupland. Accommodation at work. *International Journal of the Sociology of Language*, 46:49–70, 1984.

[Coupland, 1988] Nikolas Coupland. *Dialect in Use: Sociolinguistic Variation in Cardiff English*. University of Wales Press, Cardiff, 1988.

[Croft, 2003] William Croft. *Typology and Universals*. Cambridge University Press, Cambridge, 2nd edition, 2003.

[de Lacy, 2002] Paul de Lacy. *The Formal Expression of Markedness*. PhD thesis, University of Massachusetts at Amherst, 2002.

[Deo and Sharma, 2006] Ashwini Deo and Devyani Sharma. Typological variation in the ergative marking of Indo-Aryan languages. *Linguistic Typology*, 10:369–419, 2006.

[Filppula, 1991] Markku Filppula. Urban and rural varieties of Hiberno-English. In Jenny Cheshire, editor, *English Around the World*, pages 37–50. Cambridge University Press, Cambridge, 1991.

[Foley, 1986] William Foley. *The Papuan languages of New Guinea*. Cambridge University Press, Cambridge, 1986.

[Foulkes et al., 1999] Paul Foulkes, Gerry Docherty, and Dominic Watt. Tracking the emergence of sociophonetic variation. In B. Caron, editor, *Proceedings of the 14th International Congress of Phonetic Sciences*, pages 1625–1628, University of California, Berkeley, 1999.

[Giles and Powesland, 1985] Howard Giles and Peter F. Powesland. *Speech Styles and Social Evaluation*. Academic Press, London, 1985.

[Givón, 1978] Talmy Givón. Negation in language: Pragmatics, function, ontology. In Peter Cole, editor, *Syntax and Semantics 9: Pragmatics*, pages 69–112. Academic Press, 1978.

[Goldwater and Johnson, 2003] Sharon Goldwater and Mark Johnson. Learning OT constraint rankings using a maximum entropy model. In Jennifer Spenader, Anders Eriksson, and Östen Dahl, editors, *Proceedings of the Stockholm Workshop on Variation within Optimality Theory*, pages 111–120. Stockholm University, 2003.

[Greenberg, 1966] Joseph Greenberg. *Language Universals, with Special Reference to Feature Hierarchies*, volume 59 of *Janua Linguarum, Series Minor*. Mouton de Gruyter, The Hague, 1966.

[Grimshaw, 1997a] Jane Grimshaw. Projection, heads, and optimality. *Linguistic Inquiry*, 28(3):373–422, 1997.

[Grimshaw, 1997b] Jane Grimshaw. The best clitic: Constraint conflict in morphosyntax. In Liliane Haegeman, editor, *Elements of Grammar*, pages 169–196. Kluwer Academic Publishers, Dordrecht, 1997.

[Grimshaw, 2001] Jane Grimshaw. Optimal clitic positions and the lexicon in Romance clitic systems. In Geraldine Legendre, Jane Grimshaw, and Sten Vikner, editors, *Optimality-Theoretic Syntax*, pages 113–142. MIT Press, Cambridge, MA, 2001.

[Hayes et al., 2000] Bruce Hayes, Bruce Tesar, and Kie Zuraw. OTSoft 2.1 software package, 2000. On-line, UCLA: http:\\www.linguistics.ucla.edu\people\hayes\otsoft\.

[Hibiya, 2000] Junko Hibiya. Variation studies and linguistic theory. Paper presentedat the Eighteenth National Conference of the English Linguistic Society of Japan, November 18–19, 2000, Konan University, Kobe, Japan, 2000.

[Hughes and Trudgill, 1987] Arthur Hughes and Peter Trudgill. *English Accents and Dialects: An Introduction to Social and Regional Varieties of British English.* Arnold, London, 2nd edition, 1987.

[Ihalainen, 1991] Ossi Ihalainen. On grammatical diffusion in Somerset folk speech. In P. Trudgill and J. Chambers, editors, *Dialects of English: Studies in Grammatical Variation*, pages 104–19. Longman, London, 1991.

[Jäger and Rosenbach, 2006] Gerhard Jäger and Anette Rosenbach. The winner takes it all—almost. Cumulativity in grammatical variation. *Linguistics*, 44(5): 937–971, 2006.

[Jäger, 2007] Gerhard Jäger. Maximum entropy models and stochastic Optimality Theory. In Annie Zaenen, Jane Simpson, Tracy Holloway King, Jane Grimshaw, Joan Maling, Christopher Manning, and, editors, *Architectures, Rules, and Preferences: Variations on Themes by Joan W. Bresnan*. CSLI, Stanford, 2007.

[Johnson, 1988] Mark Johnson. *Attribute-value logic and the theory of grammar*. CSLI, Stanford, California, 1988.

[Jones, 2001] Mari Jones. *Jersey Norman French: A Linguistic Study of an Obsolescent Dialect*. Blackwell, Oxford, 2001.

[Kager, 1999] Rene Kager. *Optimality Theory*. Cambridge University Press, Cambridge, 1999.

[Keller and Asudeh, 2002] Frank Keller, and Ash Asudeh Probabilistic Learning Algorithms and Optimality Theory. *Linguistic Inquiry*, 33(2):225–244, 2002.

[Kerswill, 2002] Paul Kerswill. Models of linguistic change and diffusion: new evidence from dialect levelling in British English. In *Reading Working Papers in Lingusitics 6*, University of Reading, 2002.

[König, 1988] Ekkehard König. Concessive connectives and concessive sentences: Cross linguistic regularities and pragmatic principles. In J. Hawkins, editor, *Explaining language universals*, pages 145–185. Basil Blackwell, Oxford, 1988.

[Kortmann, 1999] Bernd Kortmann. Typology and dialectology. In B. Caron, editor, *Proceedings of the 16th International Congress of Linguists, Paris 1997*, Amsterdam, 1999. Elsevier Science. CD-ROM.

[Kroch, 2000] Anthony Kroch. Syntactic change. In Mark Baltin and Chris Collins, editors, *The Handbook of Contemporary Syntactic Theory*, pages 699–729. Blackwell, Oxford, 2000.

[Kuhn, 1999] Jonas Kuhn. Towards a simple architecture for the structure-function mapping. *The Proceedings of the LFG '99 Conference, University of Manchester*, 1999. http:\\csli-publications.stanford.edu\LFG\4\lfg99.html.

[Kuhn, 2000] Jonas Kuhn. Faithfulness violations and bidirectional optimization. *The Proceedings of the LFG 2000 Conference, Berkeley*, pages 161–181, 2000. Available online http:\\csli-publications.stanford.edu\LFG\5\lfg00.html.
[Kuhn, 2001] Jonas Kuhn. Generation and parsing in Optimality Theoretic syntax. In Peter Sells, editor, *Formal and Empirical Issues in Optimality-Theoretic Syntax*. CSLI Publications, Stanford, California, 2001.
[Kuhn, 2002] Jonas Kuhn. OT syntax—decidability of generation-based optimization. In *Proceedings of the 40th Annual Meeting of the Association for Computational Linguistics (ACL02)*, pages 48–55, Philadelphia, 2002.
[Kuhn, 2003] Jonas Kuhn. *Optimality-Theoretic Syntax—A Declarative Approach*. CSLI Publications, Stanford, California, 2003.
[Kusters, 2000] Wouter Kusters. Morphological simplification: More than erosion? In D.G. Gilbers, J. Nerbonne, and J. Schaeken, editors, *Languages in Contact. Studies in Slavic and General Linguistics*, volume 28, pages 225–230. Rodopi, Amsterdam, 2000.
[Kusters, 2003] Wouter Kusters. *Linguistic Complexity: The Influence of Social Change on Verbal Inflection*. LOT, Utrecht, 2003.
[Labov, 2001] William Labov. *Principles of Linguistic Change*, volume 1. Blackwell, Oxford, 2001.
[Laferriere, 1979] Martha Laferriere. Ethnicity in phonological variation in change. *Language*, 55:603–617, 1979.
[Lee, 2002] Hanjung Lee. Referential accessibility and stylistic variation in OT: A corpus study. In Mary Andronis, Erin Debenport, Anne Pycha, and Keiko Yoshimura, editors, *CLS 38-1: The Main Session*, pages 361–378. Chicago Linguistic Society, 2002.
[Lee, 2003] Hanjung Lee. Parallel optimization in case systems. In Miriam Butt and Tracy Holloway King, editors, *Nominals: Inside and Out*, pages 15–58. CSLI Publications, Stanford, 2003.
[Lee, 2006] Hanjung Lee. Parallel optimization in case systems: Evidence from case ellipsis in Korean. *Journal of East Asian Languages*, 15(1):69–96, 2006.
[Legendre et al., 1993] Géraldine Legendre, Walter Raymond, and Paul Smolensky. An Optimality-Theoretic typology of case and grammatical voice systems. In *Proceedings of the Nineteenth Annual Meeting of the Berkeley Linguistics Society*, pages 464–478, Berkeley, California, 1993.
[LePage and Tabouret-Keller, 1985] Robert LePage and Andrée Tabouret-Keller. *Acts of Identity: Creole-based Approaches to Language and Ethnicity*. Cambridge University Press, Cambridge, 1985.
[Milroy, 1980] Lesley Milroy. *Language and Social Networks*. Basil Blackwell, New York, 1980.
[Nagy and Heap, 1998] Naomi Nagy and David Heap. Francoprovencal null subject and constraint interaction. *Chicago Linguistic Society 34: The Panels*, pages 151–66, 1998.
[Nichols, 1983] Patricia Nichols. Linguistic options and choices for black women in the rural south. In Barrrie Thorne, Cheris Kramarae, and Nancy Henley, editors, *Language, Gender, and Society*, pages 54–68. Newbury House, Rowley, MA, 1983.
[Nordlinger, 1998] Rachel Nordlinger. *Constructive Case: Evidence from Australian Languages*. CSLI, Stanford, California, 1998.
[Orton et al., 1962–71] Harold Orton, E. Dieth, et al. *Survey of English Dialects*. University of Leeds, Leeds, 1962-71. published for the University of Leeds by E.J. Arnold.
[Payne, 1985] John R. Payne. Negation. In Timothy Shopen, editor, *Language Typology and Syntactic Description. Volume I: Clause Structure*, pages 197–242. Cambridge University Press, 1985.
[Pinker, 1984] Steven Pinker. *Language Learnability and Language Development*. Harvard University Press, Cambridge, Massachusetts, 1984.
[Prince and Smolensky, 2004] Alan Prince and Paul Smolensky. *Optimality Theory: Constraint Interaction in Generative Grammar*. Blackwell, Oxford, 2004.

[Prince, 1998] Ellen Prince. On the limits of syntax, with reference to topicalization and left- dislocation. In P. Culicover and L. McNally, editors, *The Limits of Syntax*, volume 29 of *Syntax and Semantics*. Academic Press, New York, 1998.

[Rickford, 1998] John Rickford. The creole origins of African-American Vernacular English: Evidence from copula absence. In Salikoko S. Mufwene, John R. Rickford, Guy Bailey, and John Baugh, editors, *African-American English: Structure, History and Use*, pages 154–200. Routledge, New York, 1998.

[Schilling-Estes and Wolfram, 1994] Natalie Schilling-Estes and Walt Wolfram. Convergent explanation and alternative regularization patterns: 'were/n't' leveling in a vernacular variety. *Language Variation and Change*, 6:273–302, 1994.

[Smith et al., 2007] Jennifer Smith, Mercedes Durham, and Liane Fortune. "Mam, my trousers is fa'in doon!": Community, caregiver, and child in the acquisition of variation in a Scottish dialect. *Language Variation and Change*, 19:63–99, 2007.

[Trudgill and Chambers, 1991] P. Trudgill and J. Chambers. Verb systems in English dialects. In P. Trudgill and J. Chambers, editors, *Dialects of English: Studies in Grammatical Variation*, pages 49–53. Longman, London, 1991.

[Trudgill, 1983] Peter Trudgill. *On Dialect: Social and Geographical Perspectives*. Blackwell, Oxford, 1983.

[Trudgill, 1986] Peter Trudgill. *Dialects in Contact*. Blackwell, Oxford, 1986.

[Trudgill, 1999] Peter Trudgill. *The Dialects of England*. Blackwell, Oxford, 2nd edition, 1999.

[Trudgill, 2004] Peter Trudgill. *New Dialect Formation: The Inevitability of Colonial Englishes*. Edinburgh University Press, Edinburgh, 2004.

[Urbanczyk, 1995] Suzanne Urbanczyk. Double reduplications in parallel. In Jill Beckman, Laura Walsh Dickey, and Suzanne Urbanczyk, editors, *Papers in Optimality Theory*, volume 18 of *University of Massachusetts Occasional Papers in Linguistics*, pages 499–531. GLSA, UMASS, Amherst, 1995.

[van Oostendorp, 1997] Marc van Oostendorp. Style levels in conflict resolution. In Frans Hinskens, Roeland van Hout, and W. Leo Wetzels, editors, *Variation, Change and Phonological Theory*, pages 207–29. John Benjamins, Amsterdam, 1997.

[Weinreich et al., 1968] Uriel Weinreich, William Labov, and Marvin Herzog. Empirical foundations for a theory of language change. In Winfred P. Lehmann and Yakov Malkiel, editors, *Directions for Historical Linguistics: A Symposium*, pages 97–195. University of Texas Press, Austin, 1968.

[Wolfram, 2000] Walt Wolfram. Issues in reconstructing earlier African-American English. *World Englishes*, 19(1):39–58, 2000.

[Zwicky and Pullum, 1983] Arnold Zwicky and Geoff Pullum. Cliticization versus inflection: English 'nt'. *Language*, 59:502–513, 1983.

Devyani Sharma
Queen Mary University of London, London, United Kingdom.
d.sharma@qmul.ac.uk

Joan Bresnan
Stanford University, California, United States.
bresnan@stanford.edu

Ashwini Deo
Yale University, Connecticut, United States.
ashwini.deo@yale.edu

INDEX

Aarts, Bas, 170
accommodation, 2, 8, 117, 132, 135–137, 139, 144, 266
Adams, J. N., 201–203, 252
adaptation, 6, 7, 45, 48–51, 81–83, 85, 87, 89, 91–97, 99–104, 110, 135
adaptiveness; adaptive advantage; adaptive systems, *see* adaptation
Adger, David, 184, 217
agents
  behaviour of, 2, 43, 87–89, 128
  infant, 46
agreement, 185, 213
  subject-verb, 185, 249, 267, 278, 281, 284
agreement, subject-verb, 185
Aissen, Judith, 284
alignment, 2, 6, 9, 31–35, 144–146, 170, 171, 230
Allwood, Jens, 132
Álvarez Blanco, Rosario, 228
Anagnostopoulou, Elena, 184
analogue, 125
Andersen, Henning, 87, 144, 151
Anderson, Anne H., 15, 17, 21, 22, 24, 35, 122, 125, 126, 139
Anderson, Stephen R., 185, 213
Anderwald, Lieselotte, 267, 268
Anttila, Arto, 266, 302, 311
appearance of design, 82, 87, 100, 104, 105
appropriateness, 121, 129–130, 135
Archer, Dawn, 147, 148

Arias Álvarez, Beatriz, 240, 242
Armijo Canto, Carmen E., 246
artificial life, 7
Asudeh, Ash, 301
Aunger, Robert, 100
Axtell, Robert, 43

Bakhtin, Mikhail M., 145
Ball, Catherine N., 155, 156, 168
Bannon, Liam, 15
Bao, Zhiming, 312
Barry, A. K., 229, 232
Bartlett, Frederic Charles, 13, 100
Batali, John, 71, 87, 89
Bayes' law, 96
Bell, Allan, 266
Belpaeme, Tony, 122, 128, 133, 137
Benua, Laura, 282
Bergman, Jörg R., 15
Bergs, Alexander, 143, 144
Bezuidenhout, Anne L., 129
Bickerton, Derek, 91, 99
biological evolution, *see* evolution, biological
Bisang, Walter, 148
Blackburn, Patrick, 191, 193
blending inheritance, 71–79
Bloom, Paul, 13, 54, 83, 84
de Boer, Bart, 87
Boersma, Paul, 266, 277, 301–305, 307, 311, 314
Bonelli, Elena Tognini, 154, 155, 162
Bonet, Eulalia, 214, 281
bottleneck, 7, 89–97, 103, 104

generational, 46
Bouzouita, Miriam, 6, 8, 9, 181, 188, 200, 202, 204–206, 217, 218, 221, 223, 224, 226, 232, 237, 239, 242, 246, 249, 251–253
Boyd, Robert, 86
Brennan, Susan E., 15, 16, 24, 122, 123, 138
Bresnan, Joan, 277, 279, 282, 283, 292
Brighton, Henry, 82, 87, 89
Brinton, Laurel, 145, 147, 148
Briscoe, Ted, 82, 122
Britain, David, 275
Brown, Penelope, 288
Buffum, Mary E., 246
Bybee, Joan, 150, 171
Börjars, Kersti, 289

calcification, 4, 8, 180, 252, 253, 256, 257
Cangelosi, Angelo, 42, 43, 95
Cann, Ronnie, 6, 8, 180, 188, 190, 196, 198, 199, 204, 217, 221, 239, 248, 252
Cardinaletti, Anna, 184
Carstairs-McCarthy, Andrew, 275
case, 191, 196, 248
  constructive, 188
Castillo Lluch, Mónica, 223, 225, 228, 230, 236, 246–248
Chambers, J. K., 267
Chapman, Carol, 289
Chenery, Winthrop H., 246, 247
Cheshire, Jenny, 267, 268, 273, 275
Chomsky, Noam, 1, 82–84, 90, 109, 144
Chouinard, Michelle M., 16
Christiansen, Morten H., 89
clarification/clarification request, 3, 5, 7, 16, 17, 28, 41, 51, 132

Clark, Brady, 277, 314
Clark, Eve V., 16, 121, 125, 132, 133
Clark, Herbert H., 14, 15, 24, 41, 121, 122, 132, 144
cleft
  ALL-, 152–169, 171
  IT-, 152, 155, 164, 168, 169
  pseudo-, 8, 143, 152–156, 160, 168
  reverse, 153, 155, 157, 164, 166
  specificational, 152, 155–165, 168, 170, 171
  WH-, 152–156, 163–169, 171
clitic, 4, 8, 180–185, 221–259, 281
  cluster, 179–181, 183–185, 188, 198, 204–206, 209–212, 214–216
  enclisis, 221–239, 241–243, 245, 246, 249–253, 255–258
  placement, 221–247, 249, 251, 253, 257–259
    postverbal, *see* clitic, enclisis
    preverbal, *see* clitic, proclisis
  proclisis, 221–225, 227–232, 234–243, 245–247, 249–258
  pronoun, 179, 180, 186, 203
    1st/2nd person, 183, 207, 208, 212–217
    accusative, 182, 184, 186, 205, 211–213, 253
    dative, 182–184, 186, 199, 205–209, 211–217
    emergence, 205–209
    ethical dative, 183, 184, 207, 208, 212, 215, 216
    null, 193
    reflexive, 183, 184, 192, 205, 212, 214

strong, 202, 203, 206, 213
Cojocariu, Corina, 146
Collins, Peter C., 152
common ground, 122, 144, 147
communication
    graphical (*see also* Music Drawing Task), 6, 14
    linguistic (*see also* Maze Task), 6, 14
    protocol, 44–45
communicative success, 14, 46
Company Company, Concepción, 247
competing grammars, 299, 310
compositionality, 7, 91–95, 104, 122
Comrie, Bernard, 90, 91
concept, 3, 111, 125
    creation, 4, 137
constraint
    case, 186, 199
    cognitive, 8, 179, 180, 188, 252
    faithfulness, 282
    feature geometry, 184
    markedness, 282
    parsing, 185, 189, 200
    partial ordering, 311
    Person Case, 8, 179, 180, 212–218
    processing, 89, 90, 200–203, 258
    subhierarchy, 284, 289
    syntactic, 187
construction grammar, 143, 148–152, 170
constructionalization, 148, 160
content, 127
context, 127, 191
    contextual cues, 135, 136
    contextual interpretation, 131
    dialogic, 143–148, 154, 155, 158, 161, 163, 166–168, 171
    dialogual, 143–148, 155, 168, 171

convergence, 13, 14, 17, 25, 41, 49, 99
conversation
    interactive, 147, 153, 171
    topic of, 43, 44
Cooper, Robin, 6–8, 117, 138
coordination, 2, 3, 6–8, 14–16, 19, 24, 30–36, 117–118, 132, 133, 138, 146
    equilibria, 34
    informational, 132, 137
    interactive, 128
    language, 132, 137
    semantic, 19, 122, 126, 127, 132–137, 139
copula omission, 312
copying fidelity, 62, 67, 79
Cornips, Leonie, 314
Cornish, Hannah, 86, 100, 102, 104
correction, 134
Coupland, Nikolas, 266, 275
covariance, 61, 62, 64, 67, 70, 75, 314
coverage
    meaning, 46, 47
    word, 46, 47
Croft, William, 54, 89, 144, 149, 280, 281, 290
Cruse, D. Alan, 149
Cuervo, María Cristina, 184
Culpeper, Jonathan, 147
cultural evolution, *see* evolution, cultural
cultural transmission model, 42
Cuyckens, Hubert, 149

Darwin/Darwinism, 53, 54, 56, 57, 62, 72
Dasher, Richard B., 147
Davidse, Kristin, 152
Dawkins, Richard, 54
De Smet, Hendrik, 149

Deacon, Terrence W., 89
deception, 43–45
Delin, Judy L., 152
Den Dikken, Marcel, 153, 155, 169
Denison, David, 171
Dennett, Daniel C., 54
Deo, Ashwini, 283, 296
description
    abstract, 22
    figurative, 21
Detges, Ulrich, 145, 147
Devine, Andrew M., 204, 252
diachronic change, 180, 210, 217, 221, 236, 245–248, 255, 257, 258, 265
dialect, 267, 268, 273, 285, 313
dialogicity, 145, 146, 155, 161, 162, 166, 167
dialogue
    game, *see* language games
    gameboard, 135
    move, 132, 145
    system, 112, 138
Diewald, Gabriele, 143, 159
diffusion chain, 100, 101
disfluency, 16
disposition, *see* usage pattern
Doherty, Gwyneth, 14, 25, 34, 35
domain, 4, 5, 115, 116, 125
drawing, 14, 18–20, 25, 27, 28, 31, 32, 34, 35
    abstract, 19, 20, 30
    figurative, 19, 20, 30
Ducrot, Oswald, 145
Dynamic Syntax, 8, 180, 189–203, 221, 248–257
dynamics
    concept-level, 137, 138
    domain, 66
    evolutionary, 68
    exemplar, 71–78
    lexicon, 41, 44, 46–48
    population, 49, 50, 65, 78
    of registers, 126, 127
    replication-mutation, 65
    of selection, 60
    of the system, 61

Eberenz, Rolf, 224, 240, 246, 247, 256
Elvira, Javier, 224, 225
English, *see* languages, English
Epstein, Joshua M., 43
evidence
    negative, 130, 133
    positive, 130
evolution
    biological, 55, 78, 82, 83, 86, 104, 105
    cultural, 54, 55, 81, 82, 85–87, 89, 94–96, 98, 100, 104, 105
    of language, *see* language, evolution
evolutionary game theory, 53, 55
exemplar theory, 7, 118

Fadden, Lorna, 153
Fay, Nicholas, 13, 99
feature
    checking, 279
    subject number, 267, 283
    subject person, 267, 284
feedback, 5, 8, 126, 132–133, 139
    corrective, 132
    negative, 133, 134
    positive, 133
Ferreira, Victor S., 200
Filppula, Markku, 312
finite state machine, 89
first-order logic, 127
Fischer, Olga, 170
Fisher, Ronald A., 55

fitness, 59–65, 67, 69, 74
  of an agent, 43, 44
Fodor, Jerry A., 15
Foley, William, 290
Fong, Vivienne, 311
Fontana, Josep, 226
foraging
  environment, 43
  model, 42, 46
Ford, Cecilia E., 144, 145
formal semantics, 41, 109, 122, 126, 137
Foulkes, Paul, 311
Francis, Roger, 152
Francis, Winthrop Nelson, 94
Frank, Steven A., 56, 66
Fried, Mirjam, 149, 150, 157
Fussell, Susan R., 15

Gärdenfors, Peter, 138
Gahl, Susanne, 71
Gaines, Brian R., 15
Galantucci, Bruno, 13, 99
Garrod, Simon, 8, 9, 13, 14, 17, 21, 22, 24, 25, 33–35, 122, 125, 126, 139, 222, 253
van Gelderen, Elly, 148
generalization, 128
generation, *see* production
generative grammar, 1, 53, 109, 144
genotype, 78
geographical factors, 299, 301, 308
Gerken, LouAnn, 100
Gessner, E, 224, 225, 234
Giles, Howard, 266
Ginzburg, Jonathan, 6–8, 16, 41–44, 48
Givón, Talmy, 148, 179, 290
Goldberg, Adele, 149, 150
Goldwater, Sharon, 304
Gradual Learning Algorithm, 302, 304–306

Grammatical Framework (GF), 110–115, 117
grammaticalization, 4, 143, 148–152, 160, 165, 170, 179
Granberg, Robert A., 183, 204–206, 208, 213, 223, 224, 228–231, 252
Greenberg, Joseph, 280, 281, 290
Gregoromichelaki, Eleni, 250, 253
Gries, Stefan Th., 171
Griffiths, Thomas L., 96
Grimshaw, Jane, 185, 277, 279, 281, 283
Groenendijk, Jeroen, 127
Gumperz, John J., 15
Gómez, Rebecca L., 100

Haiman, John, 146
Halliday, M. A. K., 125, 130
Harbour, Daniel, 184, 217
Harnad, Steven, 42, 43
Harper, Robert, 112
Haspelmath, Martin, 148
Hauser, Marc D., 54
Hawkins, John A., 81, 90, 100, 180
Hayes, Bruce, 266, 301–304, 307, 314
Healey, Patrick G. T., 6, 8, 13, 15, 17–21, 23–25, 30–32, 34, 99, 117, 125, 126, 139
Heap, David, 184, 266
Hedberg, Nancy, 153
Heine, Bernd, 86, 148, 159
Hibiya, Junko, 302
Hilpert, Martin, 171
Himmelmann, Nikolaus P., 148, 160
van Hoecke, Willy, 182, 216
Hoekstra, Teun, 82
Holquist, Michael, 145
Hopper, Paul J., 144, 148, 153–155, 168, 171
Horn, Laurence R., 154

Horner, Victoria, 100
Hornstein, Norbert, 192
Huber, M., 147, 155
Huddleston, Rodney D., 152
Hughes, Arthur, 275
Hurford, James R., 82, 86, 87, 92

Ihalainen, Ossi, 267, 271, 289, 298, 299, 314
imperative, 147, 222, 224, 229, 232–237, 239, 241–243, 246, 256
inappropriateness, 129–130, 135
incrementality, *see* parsing, incremental
information structure, 144, 152, 153, 167
innateness, 82–86, 90, 96–98, 104, 105
innovation, 2–7, 111, 115, 117, 121, 143–144, 146, 150, 171
input, 277, 305
interaction, 127
    adult-child, 132
    history, 24, 25, 30, 35, 36
interpolation, 222, 223, 246–248, 256, 257
invisible hand, 99, 104
iterated learning, 68, 71, 86–88, 91–97, 100, 101

Jäger, Gerhard, 6, 7, 301, 304
Janda, Richard D., 151
Janse, Mark, 252
Jefferson, Gail, 15
Jensen, Britta, 234
Jespersen, Otto, 146
Johnson, Mark, 277, 304
Jones, Mari, 290
de Jong, Edwin D., 42
Jullien, Stéphane, 154
juxtaposition, 13, 17, 32, 34, 35

König, Ekkehard, 147, 290
Kager, Rene, 284
Kalish, Michael L., 96, 100
Kaplan, David, 126
Karmiloff-Smith, Annette, 13
Kay, Paul, 154
Keenan, Edward L., 90, 91
Keller, Frank, 301
Keller, Rudi, 99, 144
van Kemenade, Ans, 156
Kempson, Ruth, 6, 8, 180, 187, 188, 190, 192, 201, 202, 204, 206, 221, 239, 248, 249, 252
Keniston, Hayward, 242, 246, 247
Kerswill, Paul, 266
Kiaer, Jieun, 180, 187, 188, 201
Kim, Kyu-hyun, 153, 155, 165, 168
King, Robert, 1
Kiparsky, Paul, 144, 170
Kirby, Simon, 6, 7, 13, 42, 54, 84, 86, 87, 89–94, 96, 97, 100
Koizumi, Masatoshi, 187
Komarova, Natalia L., 68
Kooij, Jan G., 82
Kortmann, Bernd, 267, 291
Krauss, Robert M., 15
Kroch, Anthony, 299
Kryk-Kastovsky, Barbara, 147
Kuhn, Jonas, 277, 279
Kusters, Wouter, 275, 282, 296
Kuteva, Tania, 86
Kytö, Merja, 147

Labov, William, 266
de Lacy, Paul, 284
Laferriere, Martha, 312
Lambrecht, Knud, 152
Langacker, Ronald, 149–151
language
    acquisition, 1, 7, 9, 16, 55, 81, 82, 84, 86, 90, 97, 100, 101,

116–118, 304, 305, 308
change, 1, 2, 5, 6, 8, 9, 13, 14, 111, 118, 144, 265
ecological effect, 42
ecologically functional, 42
evolution, 1, 6, 7, 9, 54, 55, 66, 71, 79, 97, 118
games, 24, 25, 30, 35, 112, 115, 122, 125, 132, 133, 137
increasingly complex, 51
micro-, 5–7, 13–15, 17, 19–36, 116, 117, 121, 124, 125, 130
proto-, 91–93
use, 126, 130
languages
Bantu, 213
English, 8, 9, 115, 151
Early Modern, 147, 155, 163–165
Middle, 151, 156
Modern, 151
Old, 151, 155
Present Day, 151, 156, 162, 165
German, 114, 115
Latin, 8, 179–218, 223, 248, 252, 258
romance, 4, 154, 182, 186
Spanish
Medieval, 8, 179–218, 221–239, 245, 246, 248–254, 257, 258
Modern, 8, 221, 222, 243–246, 248, 256–258
Renaissance, 221, 222, 239–243, 245–248, 254–256, 258
Larsson, Staffan, 6, 8, 117, 122, 144, 255
Lazar, Moshe, 226, 260
leísta, 184, 253

learning, *see* language acquisition *and* iterated learning
Lee, Hanjung, 314
left-
dislocation, 153, 164, 187, 312
peripheral constituents, 204, 216, 222, 224, 227–229, 234–237, 249, 251, 252, 255, 256
Legendre, Géraldine, 185, 279
Lehmann, Christian, 148
LePage, Robert, 313
Lepore, Ernest, 15
Lesman St. Clair, Ann, 246
leveling, 267, 275, 277–296
Levinson, Stephen, 288
Lewis, David K., 34
lexical
accuracy, 46
actions, 190, 193, 195, 209–211
lexical actions, 249, 250
lexicon
dynamics, *see* dynamics, lexicon
optimization, 281
stabilization, 47
Lightfoot, David, 1, 170
Lightfoot, Douglas J., 170
Lindström, Jan, 147
linguistic
change, *see* language change
community, 24, 41, 81, 128, 139, 150, 171, 311
convention, 34, 99, 122
interaction system, 41
linguistics
corpus, 9, 111
formal, 5
historical, 1, 6, 86
psycho-, 6, 9, 14
socio-, 6, 117, 266, 275, 301, 308, 311, 313

LINKed structures, 198–201, 208, 215–217, 255–257
local language, *see* language, micro-
location description, 15, 17, 21, 27, 28, 32, 35
long distance dependency, *see* unfixed node
Luckmann, Thomas, 15

Müller, Gabriele M., 154
Macura, Zoran, 6–8, 41–44, 48
MAGIC whiteboard, 18, 25, 27, 31, 34
Mann, William C., 144, 145
Map Task corpus, 15, 16, 123
markedness, 267, 280, 282, 290, 313
Marten, Lutz, 213
Martin-Löf, Per, 111
Martins, Ana Maria, 180, 228, 229
Maynard Smith, John, 55
Maze Task, 15, 17, 21–25, 27, 28, 30, 32–33
MCI, 3, 7, 41–51
    -non-realized population, *see* population, introspective
    -realized population, *see* population, MCI-realized
McIntyre, Angus, 14
McMahon, A., 151, 152
meaning
    activity-specific, 126
    coverage, *see* coverage, meaning
    dynamic, 126
    spaces, 49
    utterance-token, 127, 129, 134
    utterance-type, 126, 129
meaning potential, 126–131, 139
    structured, 130, 131
Meillet, Antoine, 170
meme, 54, 55

Mesoudi, Alex, 86, 100
metacommunicative interaction, *see* MCI
Meyer-Lübke, Wilhelm, 247
Meyer-Viol, Wilfried, 191, 193
micro-language / microsocial speech, *see* language, micro-
Miller, Jim, 152, 155
Mills, Greg J., 17, 32
Milroy, James, 144
Milroy, Lesley, 171, 312
minimum description length, 89
misalignment, 13–17, 24, 34–36
miscommunication, *see* misunderstanding
misunderstanding, 4–7, 132
Mitchell, Tom M., 138
Monachesi, Paola, 185, 213
Montague, Richard, 5, 109
mood, 221, 222, 224, 243, 246, 256–258
Moore, Colette, 158
Music Drawing Task, 17–20, 23–25, 27, 28, 30–32

Nagy, Naomi, 266
nativism, *see* innateness
natural selection (*see also* Darwin), 56, 82–86, 104
negation, 224, 267, 271, 290–296
negotiation, 8, 35, 121, 132, 138, 139
neural network, 89, 127, 133, 134
Nevalainen, Terttu, 145
Nevins, Andrew, 214
Newmeyer, Frederick J., 151
Nichols, Patricia, 312
Nieuwenhuijsen, Dorine, 224, 225, 239, 240, 247
Noël, Dirk, 149
Nordlinger, Rachel, 188, 279
Nowak, Martin A., 54, 68, 97

Nølke, Henning, 145

Oberlander, Jon, 152
ontology, 4, 5, 35, 114, 130
van Oostendorp, Marc, 266
Optimality Theory, 9, 170, 185, 266, 277–296
    LFG, 277, 314
    Stochastic, 266, 271, 302–314
Ormazabal, Javier, 185, 214
Orton, Harold, 267, 268
Otsuka, Masayuki, 189
Oudeyer, Pierre-Yves, 87, 95
output, 277, 305
output filter, *see* case

Pérez-Guerra, Javier, 164
Parisi, Domenico, 42, 43
Parodi, Claudia, 246
parsing, 8, 90, 113, 189, 192, 279
    incremental, 189, 196, 198
Partee, Barbara H., 122
partial tree, *see* tree growth
Patten, Amanda, 152, 168, 169
Paul, Hermann, 1
Payne, John R., 290
Perera, Nadine, 112, 114
perspective, 125, 145–147
phenotype, 78
Pickering, Martin, 8, 9, 13, 14, 33, 34, 122, 222, 253
Pierrehumbert, Janet, 71
Pinker, Steven, 13, 54, 83, 84, 314
plasticity (*see also* semantic plasticity), 305, 311
polysemy, 103
population
    introspective, 41, 46, 48, 51
    MCI-realized, 41, 46, 48, 51
population settings
    mono-generational, 41
    multi-generational, 41

Portner, Paul, 122
Powesland, Peter F., 266
presupposition, 135
Price equation, 56, 60–62, 64–66, 68, 70, 74–76, 78
Price, George, 55–67
priming, 2, 33, 34, 55
Prince, Alan, 277, 284, 304
Prince, Ellen F., 152, 312
Prisoner's Dilemma, 65
probabilistic effects, 313
problem of linkage, 84, 85, 90, 96
processing economy, 253, 257
production, 8, 113, 180, 189, 200, 204–205, 279
pronoun (*see also* clitic pronoun), 289, 298
proof theory, 112
protolanguage, *see* language, proto-

Pullum, Geoff, 291
Purver, Matthew, 34, 189, 255
Pustejovsky, James, 138

question, 146, 153, 163, 167, 168, 171
Quirk, Randolph, 152

Ramsden, Herbert, 227, 229
Ranta, Aarne, 6–8, 112–114
Recanati, Francois, 127
referring expressions, 124
register, 5, 125, 126, 130, 139
    ad-hoc, 125, 126
    resource, 125, 126
reinforcement, 130
relative clause, 90, 91, 198
relevance, 199, 201, 203
repair, 15, 16, 34, 35
replication, 7, 53–55, 63, 64, 67, 68, 79
    vertical, 55

replicator, 54, 55, 67, 71, 79
requirement
    case, 191, 194, 195
    structural, 189–191, 193, 194, 198, 199
resource, 7, 109–111, 115, 117, 125
    grammar, 5, 113, 114, 116, 118
revision, 130
Richerson, Peter J., 86
Rickford, John, 312
Rini, Joel, 247
Ritt, Nikolaus, 54
Rivero, María Luisa, 181, 184, 213, 214, 251
Roberts, Ian G., 148
Robinson, Mike , 15
romance languages, *see* languages, romance
Romero, Juan, 185, 214
Rosenbach, Anette, 304
Rossari, Corinne, 146
Roulet, Eddy, 145
Roussou, Anna, 148
routinization, 9, 180, 253, 255–258
Rubio Perea, Engracia, 246

Sánchez Lancis, Carlos, 223, 247
Sacks, Harvey, 14, 15, 144
Sag, Ivan, 192
Saxton, Matthew, 16, 35
Schegloff, Emanuel A., 15, 41
schema, 13, 33, 149–151
Schilling-Estes, Natalie, 267, 268, 314
Schmidt, Kjeld, 15
Schober, Michael F., 15, 16
Schwartz, James, 56
Schwenter, Scott A., 145, 146
scrambling, 180, 185–188, 192–201, 209–212, 218
    local, 186, 188, 193, 196, 206, 211
    long-distance, 187, 188, 193, 196
    multiple long-distance, 187, 188
selection, 55–67, 69, 78
Selten, Reinhard, 99, 104
semantic
    change, 6, 8, 121
    negotiation, 122, 132–135
    plasticity, 122, 127, 128, 133
    potential, 128
    representation, 127, 130
    system, 125
    update, 132, 133
semantic system, 112
semanticization, 161–163, 166, 167
Sharma, Devyani, 6, 9, 117, 170, 296
Shaw, Mildred L. G., 15
simplification, 4
simulation, 86, 87, 89, 91–94, 99, 105
simulation studies; multi-agent, 41
situated
    interpretation, 129, 133, 134, 136
    meaning, *see* meaning, utterance-token
situation, 128
    source-, 128
    -type, 130, 131
Smith, Adam, 99
Smith, Andrew D. M., 87, 94
Smith, Jennifer, 311
Smith, Kenny, 86, 87
Smolensky, Paul, 277, 284, 304
Spanish, *see* languages, Spanish
Sperber, Dan, 89, 203, 252
spoof, 32, 33
Staaff, E., 227
standard, 301, 313
stationary distribution, 97

Steels, Luc, 14, 54, 87, 94, 95, 122, 128, 133, 137
Stefanowitsch, Anatol, 171
Stephens, Laurence D., 204
Stokhof, Martin, 127
Strotmann, Andreas, 113
sublanguage, *see* language, microsyncretic, *see* underspecification

Taavitsainen, Irma, 145
Tabor, Whitney, 148
Tabouret-Keller, Andrée, 313
Takano, Yuji, 187
Taylor, Charles E., 87
Teal, Tracy K., 87
Thompson, Sandra A., 144, 145
Tizón-Couto, David, 164
Tonkes, Bradley, 87
topical object, 132, 134
Traugott, Elizabeth Closs, 6, 8, 9, 143–145, 147, 148, 150, 151, 156, 170
Traum, David, 122
tree growth, 189–191, 193, 197, 211, 216, 217, 253
trials
    courtroom (as data source), 147, 148, 155, 167
Trousdale, Graeme, 143, 150, 151, 156
Trudgill, Peter, 266, 267, 272, 273, 275, 313
turn-taking, 15, 17, 144–147, 153, 162, 163, 167, 168, 171
Tversky, Amos, 13
type theory, 111
    with records, 117
typology, 267, 290, 308, 313

underspecification, 7, 8, 138, 186, 209, 210, 214–217, 281
    content, 191
    structural, 189, 192–195, 214
unfixed node, 186, 187, 192–197, 199–201, 203, 206, 209, 212–217, 248–253, 255, 256
universals, 81–84, 86, 89–91, 96–99, 104, 109, 266
Urbanczyk, Suzanne, 282
usage pattern, 128–129, 131, 133–135
    complex, 131, 136
    component, 131
        activated, 131
    structured, 139
    update, 130
usage set, 128–129
use
    conservative, 130
    creative, 130

variation, 5, 6, 9, 105, 302–313
    inter-speaker, 272–276, 313
    intra-speaker, 296–301, 313
    syntactic, 8, 182, 222, 245, 246, 255, 257, 258
verb-centered, 245–246
verbal adjacency, 247, 256
vernacular, 301, 313
vertical replication, *see* replication, vertical
Visser, F. T., 156
vocabulary
    ad-hoc, 121
    problem, 138
Vogt, Paul, 87, 89, 94

de Waal, Frans, 44
Waltereit, Richard, 145, 147
Wanner, Dieter, 246, 248
Warglien, Massimo, 99, 104
weak pronoun, *see* clitic pronoun
Wedel, Andrew, 54, 71, 72
Weenik, David, 302, 305

Weinreich, Uriel, 144, 265–267, 296, 311, 313, 314
wh-expression, 181, 216
Wide, Camilla, 147
Wierzbicka, Anna, 171
Wilkes-Gibb, Deanna, 24, 122
Wilson, Dierdre, 203, 252
Wittgenstein, Ludwig, 112, 128
Wolfram, Walt, 267, 268, 272, 314
word coverage, *see* coverage, word
word order variation, *see* scrambling
Wray, Alison, 91
Wu, Yicheng, 199

Yu, Alan C. L., 71

Zuidema, Willem, 87
Zwicky, Arnold, 291

www.ingramcontent.com/pod-product-compliance
Lightning Source LLC
Chambersburg PA
CBHW050836230426
43667CB00012B/2019